The Neurocognition of Da

Dance has always been an important aspect of all human cultures, and the study of human movement and action has become a topic of increasing relevance over the last decade, bringing dance into the focus of the cognitive sciences. Since the first edition of *The Neurocognition of Dance* was published, research into the cognitive science of dance has expanded extensively, with the number of scientific studies focusing on dance and dance-related topics in cognitive psychology growing significantly.

Featuring three new chapters addressing topics that have become highly relevant to the field in recent years – neuroaesthetics, entrainment and choreographic cognition – as well as progress in teaching based on novel methods, this comprehensively revised and updated edition of *The Neurocognition of Dance* is full of cutting-edge insights from scientists, researchers, and professionals from the world of dance.

Also now including online material such as links to video clips, colour images and hands-on material for practical application, this book is an essential companion for students and professionals from a variety of fields including dance, cognitive psychology, sport psychology and sport science, movement science, and cognitive robotics.

Bettina Bläsing is a Responsible Investigator at the Center of Excellence Cognitive Interaction Technology (CITEC) at Bielefeld University, Germany. She studied Biology at Bielefeld University and Animal Behaviour at the University of Edinburgh, Scotland. Bettina worked as a science journalist and editor, as scientific coordinator at the University of Leipzig and as a postdoctoral researcher at the Max Planck Institute for Evolutionary Anthropology before joining the Neurocognition and Action Research Group at Bielefeld University in 2006. Her main research interests are mental representations of movement, body and space, the control and learning of complex full body movements and manual actions, and expertise in sports and dance.

Martin Puttke was formerly a dancer, headmaster and artistic director of the State Ballet School Berlin. He was also the ballet director of the State Opera Ballet Company Berlin and of the Aalto Ballett Theater Essen. He is a renowned ballet pedagogue. In 1988 he became a Professor at the Hochschule für Schauspielkunst 'Ernst Busch' Berlin. His main interest is the renewal of the school of classical dance by his new system DANAMOS.

Thomas Schack is Professor and Head of the Neurocognition and Action Research Group at Bielefeld University. He is Principal Investigator at the Center of Excellence Cognitive Interaction Technology (CITEC) and member of the Research Institute for Cognition and Robotics (CoR-Lab). His main research interests concern mental movement representation, mental training, cognitive robotics and the neurocognitive basis of complex movement.

The Neurocognition of Dance

Mind, Movement and Motor Skills

Second Edition

**Edited by Bettina Bläsing,
Martin Puttke and
Thomas Schack**

Routledge
Taylor & Francis Group

LONDON AND NEW YORK

Second edition published 2019
by Routledge
2 Park Square, Milton Park, Abingdon, Oxon, OX14 4RN

and by Routledge
711 Third Avenue, New York, NY 10017

Routledge is an imprint of the Taylor & Francis Group, an informa business

First edition published by Psychology Press 2010

British Library Cataloguing-in-Publication Data
A catalogue record for this book is available from the British Library

Library of Congress Cataloging-in-Publication Data
A catalog record has been requested for this book

ISBN: 978-1-138-84785-9 (hbk)
ISBN: 978-1-138-84786-6 (pbk)
ISBN: 978-1-315-72641-0 (ebk)

Typeset in Times New Roman
by Keystroke, Neville Lodge, Tettenhall, Wolverhampton
Printed and bound by CPI Group (UK) Ltd, Croydon, CR0 4YY

eResources are available for this title at:
www.routledge.com/9781138847866

Contents

PART II

The science perspective

PART III

Neurocognitive studies of dance

Notes on contributors

Philip Barnard is a retired cognitive psychologist whose research programme focused on theorizing about how memory, attention, language, body states and emotion all work together. He collaborates with Company Wayne McGregor and Scott deLahunta to develop productive and applicable synergies between choreographic processes and our knowledge of cognitive neuroscience.

Galeet BenZion published numerous articles related to kinesthetic learning in the context of teaching basic concepts of mathematics and overcoming dyslexia. In recent years, she has refined a systematic approach that dramatically increases the reading level and comprehension of recent immigrant teenagers who arrive in the United States with limited literacy skills.

Bettina Bläsing is a Responsible Investigator at the Center of Excellence Cognitive Interaction Technology at Bielefeld University (Germany). She studied biology at Bielefeld and Edinburgh (UK) and undertook postdoctoral research at the Max Planck Institute for Evolutionary Anthropology, Leipzig (Germany). Her research interests include the control and learning of complex motor actions, embodied memory and expertise in sports and dance.

Beatriz Calvo-Merino is a cognitive neuroscientist trained at University College London (UK) and Universidad Complutense de Madrid (Spain). Her research topics at the Institute of Cognitive Neuroscience, London, include visual and motor mechanisms of body perception and the sensorimotor neural and cognitive underpinnings of aesthetic perception of performing arts.

Emily S. Cross studied psychology, dance and theatre in California (US), and subsequently completed MSc and PhD degrees in cognitive neuroscience. As Professor of Social Robotics at the University of Glasgow (UK), she leads a team that uses training procedures, functional neuroimaging, and dance, acrobatics and robots, to explore experience-dependent plasticity in the human brain.

Holk Cruse studied biology, physics and mathematics at the University of Freiburg (Germany). From 1981 until 2008 he was Professor for Biological Cybernetics/ Theoretical Biology at the University of Bielefeld (Germany). His research focuses on insect locomotion, including behavioural studies as well as software and hardware simulation on both the reactive and the cognitive level.

Scott deLahunta works as a writer, researcher and organiser on international projects that bring dance into conjunction with other disciplines and practices. He is Professor of Dance, Centre for Dance Research, at Coventry University (UK) and Senior Research Fellow, Deakin Motion Lab, at Deakin University (Australia). He is co-Director of Motion Bank at the Hochschule Mainz University of Applied Sciences (Germany).

Corinne Jola is a cognitive neuroscientist (PhD, University of Zurich, Switzerland) and a dancer/choreographer (MA, Laban/IWANSON Munich, Germany), who lectures in psychology at Abertay University Dundee (UK). She has published extensively in peer-reviewed journals and book chapters on the cognitive and neuronal underpinnings of dance. Her artistic work has been staged throughout Europe.

Guido Orgs is a cognitive neuroscientist and dancer, who conducts research on the neuroaesthetics of performing dance. He is a lecturer in the Psychology Department at Goldsmiths, London (UK) and Director of the MSC in Psychology of the Arts, Neuroaesthetics and Creativity.

Martin Puttke studied classical ballet at the State Academy Berlin (Germany), and ballet pedagogy as a student of Nikolai I. Tarassow at the University of Theatre Arts Moscow (Russia), where he received his diploma in 1975. He worked as a pedagogue, Director and Artistic Director of the State Academy Berlin and was appointed professorship in 1988. He was also Ballet Director at the State Opera House Berlin and Director of the Aalto Ballett Theater Essen. He was awarded the German Dance Prize 2016.

David A. Rosenbaum (PhD, Stanford 1977) has worked at Bell Laboratories, Hampshire College, University of Massachusetts, Pennsylvania State University and University of California (US). He was Editor of the journal *Experimental Psychology: Human perception and performance* (2000–2005), and received a Guggenheim Foundation Fellowship (2012).

Thomas Schack has studied sports science, philosophy and psychology, before completing a PhD in psychology at the Chemnitz University of Technology (Germany) and a post-doctoral habilitation at the German Sport University Cologne. At Bielefeld University (Germany), he is Head of the Neurocognition and Action Research Group, and the graduate school at the Center of Excellence Cognitive Interaction Technology. His research focuses on the cognitive architecture of human motion; cognitive and biomechanical elements in motion control of humans and robots; and related psychological training for rehabilitation and competitive sports.

Malte Schilling is a Responsible Investigator at the Center of Excellence Cognitive Interaction Technology at Bielefeld University (Germany). He undertook postdoctoral research at the International Computer Science Institute (ICSI) in Berkeley, California (US), and at the Sony Computer Science Laboratory in Paris (France). His research focuses on internal models, their grounding in behaviour, and their application in higher-level cognitive function like planning ahead or communication.

Elizabeth Waterhouse was a dancer in The Forsythe Company and is now a doctoral student at the Graduate School of the Arts, Universität Bern/ Hochschule der Künste Bern (Germany). Together with Bettina Bläsing, she directs the Volkswagen Stiftung project 'Motion Together', bringing artists together with scientists to explore the topic of entrainment.

Gregor Zöllig is Artistic Director and a choreographer at the dance theater Staatstheater Braunschweig (Germany). He studied dance at the Folkwang University of the Arts at Essen and the John Cranko School, Stuttgart (Germany). After 6 years as a dancer, he founded his own company. He has been Director and choreographer of dance theater companies in Osnabrück and in Bielefeld (Germany), where he initiated the 'Zeitsprung' and 'Tanzwärts' community dance projects.

Foreword to the second edition

At its publication in 2010, *The Neurocognition of Dance: Mind, movement and motor skills* was recognized as unique in its scope and depth of interdisciplinary engagement. Catalyzed by the initial 2007 interdisciplinary symposium 'Intelligence and Action – Dance in the focus of cognitive science' at Bielefeld University, the volume gathered the research of participants – cognitive scientists, neuroscientists, choreographers and ballet pedagogues, some with experience in both fields and others collaborating across the science/art disciplinary divide – and extended it to a worldwide community of researchers and students interested in dance in specific and action more generally. The resulting volume has served as a touchstone within a wide range of research fields, including performance studies, studies of disability and aging, animal studies, physical therapy, education, philosophy and conflict resolution.

The dance–sciences research community first fostered in Bielefeld has grown and extended its interests over the ensuing years, with participation in the working group more than doubling over the two following 'Intelligence and Action' symposia (2009 and 2015). Bielefeld's Centre for Interdisciplinary Research (ZiF – Zentrum für Interdisziplinäre Forschung) offered an inspiring, productive environment within which to present, discuss, debate, and – yes – dance, together. Also in this period, the Dance Engaging Science workgroup, a research initiative supported by the Motion Bank project and the Volkswagen Stiftung, brought scientific and dance(ing) researchers together in Frankfurt am Main for three meetings in 2011–12 (see http://motionbank.org/en/content/dance-engaging-science). New research partnerships formed in both Frankfurt and Bielefeld have been highly fruitful, advancing the study of dance from inter-methodological perspectives through enhanced collaboration between the expanded cohort of empirical scientists and dance practitioner–researchers.

Scientific and performance research are both quickly moving fields. Interdisciplinary research, however, demands additional measures of time, teaching, respect and care in order for its enhanced benefits to be tapped. This volume responds to a need for the current state of the (inter)discipline to be represented by offering updates or extensions to many of its previously published studies, along with three new inclusions. Scott deLahunta and Philip Barnard describe their research team's development of three analytic lenses through which to study creative thought and development processes, predicated on their long-term research on and with choreographer Wayne McGregor and his ensemble. Framing dance as inherently communicative movement, Guido Orgs, Beatriz Calvo-Merino and Emily S. Cross offer a wide-ranging review of approaches to understanding dance aesthetics and the roles played by vision, embodied experience, and social and conceptual dynamics in dance appreciation. Finally, Elizabeth Waterhouse provides an interdisciplinary review of concepts of entrainment and a perfomer's perspective on William Forsythe's work *Duo*.

This second edition will hopefully continue to excite and inspire a growing research community, as its predecessor volume has done.

Freya Vass-Rhee
Research Associate, Intelligence in Action and Dance Engaging Science
Lecturer in Drama and Theatre
University of Kent, Canterbury, United Kingdom
January 2018

Foreword to the first edition

A joint interest of dance and embodied cognitive science is to understand movement and action. Dancers have to learn highly complex movement sequences; they need to understand why and how they move, to cognitively grasp the structure of movement, in order to maximize their performance. A dancer's skill thus includes not only physical abilities but also a wide range of cognitive skills pertaining to controlling a body in a physical environment. How movement and action emerge, how they are perceived, mentally represented and planned, are also focal research questions in biomechanics, sports and the cognitive sciences in general. These questions regard the human mind and the many ways it relates to the body, for instance, how the brain's sensory-motor system is involved in perceiving and conceptualizing movement. A more profound understanding of such issues may also come to bear in dance instruction.

Emanating from an intense workshop convention at Bielefeld University's Centre for Interdisciplinary Research (ZiF – Zentrum für Interdisziplinäre Forschung) in late October 2007, this book presents a collection of studies and perspectives related to the cognitive science of dance. Bringing together dance professionals and leading scientists from the cognitive and movement sciences, this convention was at the same time inspiring and unusual, as here disciplines encountered each other, which at first sight did not seem to have much in common. But soon it became apparent that there were a lot of things to be exchanged.

The atmosphere of departure that marks the work presented in the present book derives to a great extent from the impressions shared by the contributors that problems and approaches are brought together which may give rise to a fruitful new line of research. Dance, coming to the focus of the cognitive sciences only recently, turns out to be a fascinating area of study. For practitioners, the scientific examination of their area of practice may contribute to supporting and extending their experience, both in performance and in instruction.

It is hoped that this book will become a pioneering contribution and a lasting reference in an exciting new field of scientific endeavour. As managing director of the ZiF I would be glad if the atmosphere of our institute has been inspiring in this embarkment.

Ipke Wachsmuth
Artificial Intelligence Group, Technical Faculty &
Center of Excellence Cognitive Interaction Technology (CITEC),
University of Bielefeld, Bielefeld, Germany
January 2009

Acknowledgements

Eight years have passed since the first edition of *The Neurocognition of Dance: Mind, movement and motor skills* has been published, and since then, the number of those who have joined the community and contributed to the progress in this exciting new field has grown extensively. They are too many to be named individually, yet they all deserve our sincere thanks! Specifically, we thank all members of Dance Engaging Science | Motionbank, as well as all participants of the 'Intelligence and Action' meetings at the ZiF Bielefeld in 2007, 2009 and 2015 for sparkling ideas and fruitful discussions, in addition to the hard work and patience they have put into multidisciplinary collaboration projects that helped to advance the field in recent years.

We thank the Volkswagen Foundation, Tanzplan Essen 2010 (Tanzplan Deutschland, Kulturstiftung des Bundes) and the Center of Excellence Cognitive Interaction Technology 'CITEC' (EXC 277, funded by the German Research Foundation, DFG) at Bielefeld University for supporting our research and collaborations and giving us the great opportunity to continue our quest in neurocognitive dance science. We also thank the ZiF Bielefeld and its fabulous team for hosting the three 'Intelligence and Action' meetings in a professional, relaxing and inspiring atmosphere that made us all want to come back.

We are grateful to Michael Arbib, Juliane Honisch, Andrea Kiesel, Eva Monsma, Frank Pollick and our other excellent reviewers for their approval and helpful comments that have contributed to improving the quality of this book, and for guiding us in planning and preparing the second edition. We thank Jonathan Harrow, Jeremy Leslie-Spinks and Travis Dorsch for translating two chapters from the German, and for English language revision.

Finally, we wish to thank the editorial team at Psychology Press, in particular Sharla Plant, Tara Stebnicky and Becci Edmondson (first edition) and Ceri McLardy, Alex Howard, Louise Hake and Kelly Winter (second edition) whose friendly and professional support and patience guided us through the different stages of writing and editing this book.

Bettina Bläsing, Martin Puttke and Thomas Schack
March 2018

Introduction

Moving towards a multidisciplinary neurocognitive science of dance

Bettina Bläsing, Martin Puttke and Thomas Schack

What happens in our brains when we observe someone performing a simple movement task, or a complex dance sequence? What does it mean to 'understand' an action, or a movement, as such, and how does this relate to language? Why do we have the ability to imitate the actions of others, and how does this help us to learn? How do we understand what our interlocutor might feel by watching his facial expression, gesture and body movement? And how do we apply this mutual understanding in a social context in real time to interact successfully with each other, to join into others' actions, to compete or collaborate, and to communicate?

When we think about learning and performing complex movements, probably in interaction with others, sooner or later, dance comes to mind. Dance has always been an important aspect of human cultures, and bringing dance into the focus of the cognitive sciences can broaden our understanding of the nature of human minds and brains.

Dancers' specific expertise includes not only exceptional physical abilities but also a wide range of cognitive skills. Dancers have to learn highly complex 'designed' movement sequences combined in choreographies that might last for hours. They have to be able to perform their part not only perfectly, reproducing the movements without variation under varying conditions, but also with adequate expressive quality, no matter how nervous, tired or exhausted they are, seemingly independent of their own emotional state. While dancing, they constantly have to keep track of their surroundings, space and objects, partners, dynamical qualities of the music, and their audience. While learning movement sequences during training or rehearsals, they have to be able to immediately transfer steps from one side of the body to the other side and from the forward to the backward direction, as well as from one direction in space to another, without losing orientation. In contemporary dance and ballet, dancers often work with movement tasks they have to solve in rehearsals or even during live performance, applying their own ideas and experiences to create novel movement material through improvisation, individually or together with partners. Choreographers rely on these skills and apply them to create and develop the pictures and scenes they have in their minds, to convey the message, intention and the stories they want to tell, and to arouse mental and emotional reactions in the audience.

This broad spectrum of tasks and skills involved in dance suggests that many of the concepts and ideas that are now in the focus of the cognitive sciences have been on the minds of dancers and choreographers for a long time, yet, most commonly, without scientific reflection or application. Indeed, the interest the dance world takes in the (neuro-)scientific side of their art is equally young as the interest cognitive and brain scientists take in dance, or more broadly, in concepts of embodiment, the situatedness of the human mind in the physical world and related questions of human motor action. Yet, a mutual fascination has grown during recent years, and the body of literature is constantly growing. Recently, several comprehensive books have been published that reflect current developments in the field representing and integrating different perspectives (e.g., Karkou, Oliver and Lycouris, 2017; Hansen and Bläsing, 2017).

Since the cognitive sciences have discovered the importance of embodiment, the concept of minds being grounded in the physical environment in which they have evolved and with which they constantly interact (Wilson, 2002; Glenberg, 2010), movement of the human body in real-world scenarios has become a topic of increasing relevance. Questions of how human motor action is controlled and how complex movements are learned concern not only scientists interested in muscle physiology and biomechanics, but also those trying to understand how cognitive processes like thinking, reasoning and learning are generated in the brain. Experimental psychology has investigated a broad range of interrelations of the control of body postures and movements with perception, mental processing and action planning (e.g., Prinz, 1997; Hommel et al., 2001; Koch, Keller and Prinz, 2004); for example, in paradigms like the Simon effect (Simon and Rudell, 1967), the end-state comfort effect (Rosenbaum et al., 1990), or mental rotation (e.g., Parsons, 1987; see Zacks, 2008 for review). Central topics in these complementary lines of research are the coupling of action and perception, common neural structures involved in action execution, observation and simulation (Jeannerod, 2001; 2004), and basic principles of motor control and motor learning (Rosenbaum, 2009; Schack et al., 2014).

More than two decades ago, scientists in Parma, Italy, discovered the so-called mirror neurons in the monkey brain – neurons that fire during the execution of a specific action as well as during the observation of the equivalent action performed by others (Gallese et al., 1996; Rizzolatti and Sinigaglia, 2010). This discovery and the subsequent arising interest in the principles of a neurocognitive 'mirror system', or *action observation network* (Calvo-Merino et al., 2006), in the human brain have initiated an extensive shift within the neurosciences towards the coupling of neural correlates for action observation and action execution (see Arbib, 2002; Gallese et al., 2011, for different perspectives). Complementary research in cognitive psychology investigates general principles of the interplay between perception, cognition and action in humans (Schütz-Bosbach and Prinz, 2007a; 2007b), offering new approaches to understanding processes underlying (motor) learning, communication and social interaction. This scientific research has a high potential to substantially inform and enrich contemporary dance didactics as well as the work of ballet masters and choreographers.

In recent years, cognitive psychologists and neuroscientists have started to work with dancers to find out if and how their highly specialized expert training may have enhanced or modified their cognitive abilities; how their brains integrate all the necessary information while they perform highly sophisticated physical tasks, lined up in hour-long choreographies that have to be flawlessly remembered, at the same time as producing expressions of deep emotional quality that have the power to captivate the audience (for reviews, see Bläsing et al., 2012; Karpati et al., 2015; Sevdalis and Keller, 2011). Some of these scientists have also followed a career in dance or choreography themselves, reflecting Corinne Jola's claim for an embodied neuroscience that includes the physical engagement of scientists with their topic of research (see Chapter 13). Dance professionals, on the other hand, have developed an increasing interest in participating in research projects and, furthermore, in shaping these projects towards their own questions and perspectives as well as targeted output formats, including choreographic ideas, stage performances and teaching methods.

Questions and ideas that derive from the interconnection of complex movements and related cognitive processes are not only of interest to professional dancers and choreographers. Preschool and primary school teachers apply movement(-based) learning tasks as tools and vehicles for learning in general, including the learning of rather abstract principles in mathematics or grammar. Pedagogues have come to the conclusion that children who are allowed to run, jump and dance become more motivated, better learners, and that physical movement can sometimes teach children more about geometry and dynamics than can pictures and words. Learning to move in different ways, pace and qualities, to express feelings with the body, to interact with space, rhythm, sound and each other, allows children and adults to grow more self-confident and courageous. Learning to dance on a professional level, and learning to teach others how to dance, can be a great challenge and gratification for body and mind. A professional career in dance, however, can also become a thorny path if the teaching methods applied diverge too far from the basic physical, neural and cognitive principles of human motor learning. Therefore, one of the aims of this book is to share scientific perspectives on the *neurocognition of dance,* and to give an impetus to integrate scientific knowledge and principles into the ways of teaching dance, as well as to integrate body knowledge acquired via (dance) movement into teaching in general.

In October 2007, our first 'Intelligence and Action' symposium took place at the Centre for Interdisciplinary Research (ZiF) at Bielefeld, Germany, entitled 'Dance in the Focus of Cognitive Science'. This meeting brought together dancers, choreographers, dance teachers, pedagogues and scientists from the fields of neuroscience, psychology, cognitive and movement science, providing a platform for mutual introductions into others' disciplines and, in particular, ideas and approaches to thinking, learning and movement. Many of the attendees reported that this meeting was one of the most inspiring and mind-opening events they had ever encountered, raising the impression that the combination of talks, dance performances, choreographic workshops and lecture demonstrations had been jigsaw pieces that fitted together beautifully, revealing promising parts of an impressive whole picture. One of the outcomes of this symposium was the first edition of *The Neurocognition of Dance: Mind, movement and motor skills*.

Two years later, the second 'Intelligence and Action' symposium followed, entitled 'New Perspectives in Dance and Cognitive Science'. Most of the participants from 2007 came back, and many more joined us for this meeting that resulted in the consensus that the time had come for conducting multidisciplinary projects on questions of mutual interest rather than presenting individual works and results to each other. In the following years, several network groups worked in this direction, including, for example, Watching Dance: Kinesthetic Empathy (www.watchingdance.org/index.php) and Dance Engaging Science | Motionbank (http://motionbank.org/de/content/dance-engaging-science). In 2015, the third 'Intelligence and Action' symposium took place at the ZiF, focusing on the outcomes of projects that had been conducted within the Dance Engaging Science network, and was therefore entitled 'Dance Engaging Science: Expanding on the cognitive perspective'. Since then, collaborations between partners from these networking groups have developed further, and new projects are on the way. This book presents a range of such projects along with complementary lines of scientific, artistic and pedagogical work, all of them focusing on different aspects of dance.

What is new in the second edition of *The Neurocognition of Dance*? First, all chapters have been updated, to different degrees. The extent to which individual chapters have been modified varies, depending on the authors' ideas and preferences. All authors have included their most recent publications, and several have added new topics from their current work, and developments of projects they had already sketched in the first edition. The number of scientific studies focusing on dance and dance-related topics in cognitive psychology has grown extensively since the first edition of this book was published, and a representative, yet not exhaustive, number of these studies is described in Chapters 9 to 13. Progress in teaching based on novel methods is documented in Chapter 1 by Martin Puttke, who presents his DANAMOS (Dance Native Motion System), and in Chapter 2 by Galeet BenZion, who shares her recent teaching experience using KTM (Kinematics Teaching Methodology), an approach that she has already presented in the first edition.

Second, we have added three new chapters addressing topics that have been highly relevant to the field in recent years: neuroaesthetics (e.g., Christensen and Calvo-Merino, 2013; Cross and Ticini, 2012), (neuro-)entrainment (e.g., Phillips-Silver, Aktipis and Bryant, 2010), and choreographic cognition (e.g., Grove, Stevens and McKechnie, 2005). Chapter 12 presents research into the neuroaesthetics of dance – a topic to which all three authors have contributed substantially. Chapter 3 provides a multidisciplinary perspective on (studying) entrainment in dance and its particular role in William Forsythe's choreography. Chapter 5 introduces concepts and methods of choreographic thinking and provides access to tools developed in collaboration with Wayne McGregor and his company Random Dance.

By adding these three new chapters and up-to-date content throughout, the book has not only gained a broader spectrum of topics and perspectives, but the divisions between the different fields have also become less significant, pointing towards an increasing number of integrated approaches taken by the authors. Indeed, several authors (including Bläsing, Puttke and Waterhouse) argue strongly in favor of multi- or cross-disciplinary approaches that involve experts from the arts and science as well as from applied fields. A strong position in this regard is adopted by Corinne Jola in Chapter 13, who recommends new projects that encompass the demands of dance as both an art form and scientific research, without one or the other taking the lead and thereby shaping the outcome.

Third, we have been given the opportunity to add online material to the printed copy of this book, incorporating multimedia in addition to text and images. Dance, as a movement-based art form, gains a lot from this extension to additional formats of contributions and complementary material, such as links to video clips, colour images, hands-on material for practical application, and direct access to extended literature from different fields. We feel that the value of this book has been largely increased by these add-ons that can be accessed by our readers and give the authors the opportunity to share their thoughts and ideas, experiences and works not only through the written word, but also through audiovisuals, which is particularly relevant with regards to dance.

This book is addressed to a diverse audience, to those readers who are used to analyzing scientific theory as well as to those who create, perform or teach movement. We know that the aim to make this book equally informative and enjoyable for all of them is a challenge. We have therefore structured the content of our book in such a way that chapters written from similar perspectives are grouped together, in order to provide our readers with a line of orientation. First, professionals from the world of dance illustrate how their artistic, pedagogical and scholarly work relates to the cognitive processes of action planning, motor control and learning. Second, scientists introduce corresponding theories and methods representing different approaches to studying complex movements and show how these can be applied to dance. Finally, researchers with strong personal links to the dance world present interdisciplinary research projects that integrate cognitive neuroscience and dance and propose ideas for future collaborations.

In the first part of the book (The dance perspective), professionals from the dance world report practical work and share their experiences of how dance relates to cognition in dance education, pedagogy and choreography. Martin Puttke introduces his novel teaching concept DANAMOS in Chapter 1. By giving examples from his rich experience of developing world-class dancers, Puttke shows how teachers can improve dancers' physical and artistic qualities by substantiating the training process with cognitive methods. Galeet BenZion in Chapter 2 introduces her pedagogical concept, the Kinematics Teaching Method, which she has developed to help children with learning difficulties, especially related to dyslexia, to acquire their own ways of learning by creating meaningful movements. Processes underlying dancers' abilities to coordinate and synchronize their movements, to switch flawlessly between unison and counterpoint, or to take turns in improvisation are studied in Chapter 3. As a former dancer of The Forsythe Company, Elizabeth Waterhouse provides an insider's view on William Forsythe's choreography, in which entrainment is the basis for the dancers' sophisticated interaction and improvisation. In Chapter 4, choreographer Gregor Zöllig describes the process of finding novel movements while creating choreography. Zöllig, who portrays himself as a traveller in that 'other land of dance', prefers a working style that integrates the ideas and improvisations of his company into the creative process of dance making. Scott deLahunta and Philip Barnard, in Chapter 5, share insights into the processes of developing choreography encountered during their work with Wayne McGregor and Random Dance. The formalized model derived from these experiences is not only relevant for dancers and choreographers, but also provides a framework for monitoring creative processes in many fields, including (but not restricted to) the arts and science.

In the second part (The science perspective), the authors present basic approaches to motor control, providing different perspectives on the way movements are initiated, adapted and stored in memory. The contents of these chapters range from theoretical foundations to experimental studies and computer-simulation models. In Chapter 6, Thomas Schack introduces his cognitive architecture model that is based on the concept of mental representations of movement in long-term memory. By illustrating how his model can be applied to the study of complex movements in sports and dance, Schack raises implications for psychological training methods. The concept of goal postures and their vital role in motor planning is outlined in Chapter 7, where David Rosenbaum shows how continuous movements, from everyday grasping actions to dance, are anticipated and stored in memory via the mental representation of goal postures. In Chapter 8, Holk Cruse and Malte Schilling demonstrate how a biomimetic computer simulation of an insect's walking behaviour can be augmented to develop internal world models and, progressively, become 'cognitive'. A computational approach is taken, based on artificial neuronal networks used to explain phenomena ranging from motor control to subjective experience and even illusions. Finally, Bettina Bläsing in Chapter 9 presents different approaches to studying dancers' particular expertise in motor learning and movement-related memory processes.

In the third part (Neurocognitive studies of dance), scientists present studies that bridge the gap between neurocognitive research and dance, aiming to enlighten our understanding of the ways in which the human brain processes different aspects of movement. Beatriz Calvo-Merino, in Chapter 10, demonstrates how the discovery of 'mirror neurons' in the brain has influenced the way cognitive neuroscientists think about movement, and presents her studies on action observation, dance expertise and aesthetic evaluation involved in watching dance. Evidence of the essential role of the action observation network in the human brain for learning complex movement sequences is provided in Chapter 11, where Emily S. Cross reports how she and her colleagues have investigated how activity in dancers' brains changes over the course of learning a new choreography, and how this differs depending on the learners' experience and the characteristics of the model. Chapter 12 introduces concepts of dance aesthetics and related communicative processes, and illustrates how these are implemented in the human brain. Guido Orgs, Beatriz Calvo-Merino and Emily S. Cross present studies that investigate the neuroaesthetics of movement, and ask why dance spectators like or dislike what they see and how their own experience might shape their preferences. In Chapter 13, the book concludes with a comprehensive outline of the current situation and a proposition for future directions of joint research in dance and cognitive neuroscience. By taking into account not only artistic and scientific concerns but also operational issues (e.g., output formats and funding), Corinne Jola provides a strong, well-balanced yet ambitious synopsis that has the potential to guide and inform future developments in the field.

With this book, we want to share our ideas and insights with a broader audience; with scientists and dance practitioners, with teachers, trainers, therapists, and with everyone interested in dance and cognition. We hope to initiate and inspire processes of mutual exchange and stimulation between dancers and cognitive scientists, psychologists and choreographers, and ballet teachers and neurobiologists, aiming at a deeper understanding of dance as movement of the human body and mind. We would like to recommend this book to students and professionals from the fields of psychology, neuropsychology, cognitive psychology, sport psychology, sport science, movement science, motor control, motor development, kinesiology, dance, choreography, dance education, dance therapy; to teachers who use or want to use (dance) movement as a means of teaching, or who want to teach dance to students of any age, as well as to everyone interested in and fascinated by the skillful movement of mind and body. We hope that our enthusiasm will be shared by many of our readers, and we are looking forward to learning about their ideas and projects in the near future.

References

Arbib, M. A. (2002). The mirror system, imitation, and the evolution of language. In: K. Dautenhahn & C. Nehaniv (Eds.), *Imitation in Animals and Artifacts*. Cambridge, MA: MIT Press.

Bläsing, B., Calvo-Merino, B., Cross, E. S., Jola, C., Honisch, J., & Stevens, C. J. (2012). Neurocognitive control in dance perception and performance. *Acta psychologica*, 139(2), 300–308.

Calvo-Merino, B., Grèzes, J., Glaser, D. E., Passingham, R. E., & Haggard, P. (2006). Seeing or doing? Influence of visual and motor familiarity in action observation. *Current biology*, 16(19), 1905–1910.

Christensen, J. F. & Calvo-Merino, B. (2013). Dance as a subject for empirical aesthetics. *Psychology of aesthetics, creativity, and the arts*, 7(1), 76.

Cross, E. S. & Ticini, L. F. (2012). Neuroaesthetics and beyond: New horizons in applying the science of the brain to the art of dance. *Phenomenology and the cognitive sciences*, 11(1), 5–16.

Gallese, V., Fadiga, L., Fogassi, L., & Rizzolatti, G. (1996). Action recognition in the premotor cortex. *Brain*, 119(2), 593–609.

Gallese, V., Gernsbacher, M. A., Heyes, C., Hickok, G., & Iacoboni, M. (2011). Mirror neuron forum. *Perspectives on psychological science*, 6(4), 369–407.

Glenberg, A. M. (2010). Embodiment as a unifying perspective for psychology. *Wiley interdisciplinary reviews: Cognitive science*, 1(4), 586–596.

Grove, R., Stevens, C., & McKechnie, S. (2005). *Thinking in Four Dimensions: Creativity and cognition in contemporary dance.* Carlton, VIC: Melbourne University Press.

Hansen, P. & Bläsing, B. (2017). *Performing the Remembered Present: The cognition of memory in dance, theatre and music.* New York: Bloomsbury Methuen Drama.

Hommel, B., Müsseler, J., Aschersleben, G., & Prinz, W. (2001). The Theory of Event Coding (TEC): A framework for perception and action planning. *Behavioral and brain sciences*, 24, 845–937.

Jeannerod, M. (2001). Neural simulation of action: A unifying mechanism for motor cognition. *Neuroimage*, 14(1), S103–S109.

Jeannerod, M. (2004). Actions from within. *International journal of sport and exercise psychology*, 2(4), 376–402.

Karkou, V., Oliver, S., & Lycouris, S. (Eds.). (2017). *The Oxford Handbook of Dance and Wellbeing.* Oxford: Oxford University Press.

Karpati, F. J., Giacosa, C., Foster, N. E., Penhune, V. B., & Hyde, K. L. (2015). Dance and the brain: A review. *Annals of the New York Academy of Sciences*, 1337(1), 140–146.

Koch, I., Keller, P., & Prinz, W. (2004). The ideomotor approach to action control: Implications for skilled performance. *International journal of sport and exercise psychology*, 2(4), 362–375.

Parsons, L. M. (1987). Imagined spatial transformations of one's hands and feet. *Cognitive psychology*, 19, 178–241.

Phillips-Silver J., Aktipis C. A., Bryant G. A. (2010). The ecology of entrainment: Foundations of coordinated rhythmic movement. *Music perception*, 28, 3–14.

Prinz, W. (1997). Perception and action planning. *European journal of cognitive psychology*, 9(2), 129–154.

Rizzolatti, G. & Sinigaglia, C. (2010). The functional role of the parieto-frontal mirror circuit: Interpretations and misinterpretations. *Nature reviews. Neuroscience*, 11(4), 264.

Rosenbaum, D. A. (2009). *Human Motor Control.* London: Academic Press.

Rosenbaum, D. A., Marchak, F., Barnes, H. J., Vaughan, J., Slotta, J. D., & Jorgensen, M. J. (1990). Constraints for action selection: Overhand versus underhand grip. In: M. Jeannerod (Ed.), *Attention and Performance XIII* (pp. 321–342). Hillsdale, NJ: Lawrence Erlbaum.

Schack, T., Bläsing, B., Hughes, C., Flash, T., & Schilling, M. (2014). Elements and construction of motor control. In: *Routledge Companion to Sport and Exercise Psychology: Global perspectives and fundamental concepts* (pp. 308–323). London: Routledge.

Schütz-Bosbach, S. & Prinz, W. (2007a). Perceptual resonance: Action-induced modulation of perception. *Trends in cognitive sciences*, 11(8), 349–355.

Schütz-Bosbach, S. & Prinz, W. (2007b). Prospective coding in event representation. *Cognitive processing*, 8(2), 93–102.

Sevdalis, V. & Keller, P. E. (2011). Captured by motion: Dance, action understanding, and social cognition. *Brain and cognition*, 77, 231–236.

Simon, J. R. & Rudell, A. P. (1967). Auditory SR compatibility: The effect of an irrelevant cue on information processing. *Journal of applied psychology*, 51(3), 300.

Wilson, M. (2002). Six views of embodied cognition. *Psychonomic bulletin and review*, 9(4), 625–636.

Zacks, J. M. (2008). Neuroimaging studies of mental rotation: A meta-analysis and review. *Journal of cognitive neuroscience*, 20(1), 1–19.

Part I
The dance perspective

1 Learning to dance means learning to think!

Martin Puttke
(Translation by Jeremy Leslie-Spinks)

It all began 30 years ago, in 1978, with an accident. I had a student, a 16-year-old boy, artistically one of the most talented youngsters in the school, although the results of his physical assessment at the entrance audition had put him in the lowest class. During a break between classes, this boy and some of the others were playing about in the studio, enjoying the height of the jumps which, as dancers, they were able to achieve with the help of a springboard, never thinking that after a soaring flight through the air, a safe landing is extremely important. He landed wrongly, breaking his landing leg diagonally right across the shin, with extreme lateral dislocation of the fractured lower leg. There followed months of medical treatments and procedures, then weeks in plaster and finally the verdict of the doctors, which was the end of his dream of becoming a professional dancer.

At the time of the accident I was at the beginning of my teaching career, and had been away for several weeks. Faced with a problem of this type, I found myself at the limit of what I had been taught, even though I was every bit as motivated as these young ballet students. I had just returned home, bursting with knowledge from my studies at the Theatre Academy in Moscow. I remember visiting him in hospital, and asking him what he thought he would do in the future, to which I received the tearful answer: 'The only thing I can do and want to do in my life is to dance! Nothing more or less. To dance!'. My reply was as carefree and inexperienced as his jump from the springboard had been. I said to him: 'Then you will!'

During the next 4 to 5 years, he had to undergo two further operations; however at the end of this period he had also taken gold medals in two of the most significant international ballet competitions, Helsinki (1984) and Jackson, Mississippi (1986). In sporting terms, he would be described as a world champion twice over. He became an internationally celebrated star, one of the very few German dancers able to point to a worldwide career. He continued to dance until his 44th year; a very advanced age for a male dancer. How was this possible for a dancer, obviously hampered over long periods by serious physical limitation, and almost to the point where he could have been in a handicapped category, to achieve in the Olympics of dance?

It had already occurred to me during normal classes at the beginning of my teaching activity that a high percentage of dancers' mistakes are not due to lack of ability or preparedness, but rather to a completely erroneous notion of the character and sequence of a movement which they are required to learn. One example is when the teacher demonstrates a movement with a 30-, 40- or 50-year-old body, after which the student attempts to repeat and reproduce this movement with the body of a 10-, 12-, 14- or 16-year-old. No attention is paid to the different starting points in terms of the physical, intellectual, characteristic and emotional development of this child or teenager. The child's perception and understanding of a movement proceeds in ways that are completely different from those imagined and intended by the teacher. A child, in other words, is not a miniature version of an adult.

I have always been fascinated to watch divers jump from the 10 metre board, carrying out the most complicated twists and turns without ever having had the opportunity to learn these actions under real conditions because of the extremely high risk of injury. The question arises: How is this possible? I discovered that the athletes undergo an intensive regime of mental training in advance, working over and over again with film sequences until the movement is perfect in their heads, both in point of technique and as regards the given time limit. Thus it was that I began to work with the injured dancer on cogitation (analysis, or mental control) and the concrete pictorial objectification (mental image, or mental representation) of a movement or a movement sequence in an incredibly time-consuming process of tackling the movement mentally, until a specific quality had been achieved. Only at this point did I allow him to reproduce and execute the movement (sensorimotor representation). (The terms 'mental control', 'mental representation' and 'sensorimotor representation' can be referred to in the cognitive architecture of dance movement model: see Chapter 6.) As a rule, the dancer was made to start the process of working on a dance sequence by lying on the floor, to eliminate the sensation of body weight (I subsequently discovered this to be the decisive moment from the point of view of the neurologist). He had to close his eyes for a given period of time, then give me the verbal feedback on his picture of the movement until the required quality had been achieved. We then worked on the movement in a standing position. With verbal corrections from me, and the corresponding verbal feedback from the dancer, the sequence acquired yet more quality. For anyone familiar with the daily working routine in a ballet studio, this was an apparently unnatural procedure. The speed of the movement sequence was then increased, until it could be executed within the time limits required by the music, after which I allowed the dancer to mark the sequence with maximum economy of movement, at the same time picking up and correcting any potential mistakes of impulse or the preparation of steps. There followed a short warm-up phase, then finally I allowed the dancer to execute the movement under real condi-tions, i.e., with music, dealing with approximate real spatial requirements and the corresponding investment of strength and attack.

The quality of movement execution was convincing, and in many respects improved. The process of learning the most complicated movement sequences, normally requiring weeks, months or sometimes even longer, had been carried by this technique of 'doing nothing' (which is to say, not dancing) to a whole new level. This 'ideokinetic training' bore no relationship to the usual excessive physi-cal training of ballet dancers. One could undertake conditioning, relative to the physical shape of the dancer, in a relaxed and well balanced manner, as the dancer always knew precisely what he had to do. This was my first confrontation with the interrelation between dance and thought; the mental representation of a movement sequence in the brain, and its physical reproduction. It seemed to me essential in this process that the dancer should not start the movement-learning process from the standpoint of his own coenaesthesis, but should instead work consciously to influence the movement through step-by-step mental correction, gradually developing the quality. The actual development of the physical execution of the step starts at a much higher level, which is to say that the concept of the movement is already clear in the head, before the dancer has even taken a step. It then needs to be conditioned and repeated often enough for it to become automatic (see also Chapter 6). The principle of 'learning by doing' in dance has acquired an entirely new meaning. If I prepare the movement mentally in advance, the body finds it much easier to respond with the appropriate technical and aesthetic form, or to satisfy the relevant artistic and interpretive demands. If we eliminate this process, the body is faced with an exhausting, and normally (depending on talent) a very long process of searching and feeling. Not infrequently, this path might lead to a dead end.

Dance is in the first place an artistic, rather than a sporting, activity. This is, however, dependent on optimal mastery of the technical challenge, the artistic and interpretive requirements, and the demands made on the body as an instrument of artistic expression. The less the dancer is subject to physical and technical difficulties or insufficiencies, the greater is his artistic freedom in the performance and interpretation of dance. The dancer can only work freely with his body in artistic performance when he no longer fears the danger (particularly in some of the unbelievably difficult contemporary choreographies) of landing any moment on his nose or on his behind. The unbelievable quality of his long-term memory capacity for movement sequences (see also Chapter 9) becomes clear, when we realise what actually happens onstage under performance conditions. Not only must his body function at optimum efficiency, but he also has to manage the tempo changes emanating from a live orchestra, which can throw his carefully memorised program completely out of kilter. The careful work of many weeks, precisely defining movement in space and time, can be rendered meaningless in a fraction of a second. Contact with the partner or with other dancers brings further unpredictability to the performance, as they too react in their own way and without warning to unrehearsed occurrences onstage during the dance. Often enough, the presence of hundreds of spectators and the awareness of their expectations can force the dancers into a condition of psychological stress which can only be described as borderline. All of this happens under the strict condition that a creative or interpretive event of absolute emotional conviction has to be projected 'over the footlights'. Any ostensibly technical demonstration or visible correction would destroy the artistic expression. This places emotional, mental and physical loads of the highest intensity on the dancer, loads that as a rule are found only at the limits within which we function.

There is a need for independent scientific research into the psychology and physiology of the dancer, because education for professional classical and modern dancers (especially for dance in the theatre) takes place during the most compli-cated phase of human life. It starts in childhood. It continues into puberty, the most difficult phase of human physical and mental and emotional development. The body, simultaneously at the mercy of all these influences, is being instrumentalised. It ends with the first stages of adulthood, usually at 18 years old: self-discovery and a whole new set of rules at the same moment! The body is trained to become an instrument, which in the interpretation of a rôle can also be seen as an object. A very complicated interrelationship arises between the person of the artist (subject) and the body as the instrument of artistic expression (object). This very particular subject–object relationship creates a particular interface between dance and cogni-tive science that would require an interdisciplinary collaboration of psychology, neuroscience, biology and philosophy, among other disciplines, to be understood. Anyone who recalls the errors and confusions of their own puberty will certainly understand how hard it must be in this profession to satisfy the simultaneous demands of normal academic school, training for a career, and one's own sudden coming of age, and to bring it all into proportion. There is no other profession, or at any rate none that I can think of after long consideration, which demands such a complex interaction of body and mind at such a high level. A profession which, however, compared with other artistic professions or indeed professions in general, receives so little public recognition.

Let us look briefly at the school of classical dance, in which somehow or other the finished product must be produced. It has passed through many stages in the course of its history. The significant beginning took place in the course of the last century in St. Petersburg and later in Leningrad, when the legendary Agrippina Vaganova filtered out from among the prodigious quantity of existing steps from Italian, French and Russian styles and techniques, the decisive material for the training of professional dancers and combined it into a system. Her revolutionary achievement lay in the reduction and simplification of the overwhelming mass of material to its essentials. This system is still working today, and can form the basis for dance training in our time. The resulting canon of movements rests basically on an understanding of the body as an instrument of artistic expression, which has freed itself from certain norms and restrictions of normal human move-ment ranges. In other words: Normally we move forwards; to move backwards can sometimes leave us looking at least clumsy, if not indeed handicapped. Our anatomy only allows free movement, and a significantly larger volume of move-ment, in forward direction, while in retrograde movement the hip joint somewhat restricts movement. The British cyberneticist Kevin Warwick described the prob-lem almost wistfully, when he referred to the human body as 'extremely limited in its capabilities', and wished to be able to 'rebuild myself.'

In dance the physical structure of the body and sometimes even the normal rules of physics appear not infrequently to have been dissolved. The body is equipped by means of the particular training of classical dance, and the spectrum of its movement, and thereby also its expressive possibilities are significantly expanded. Particularly in contemporary choreography, the body is frequently expected to display a facility for self-transformation which carries every organic sequence of movement to absurd extremes. Part of the basis for this results from classical dance training, in the course of which, for example, the body is trained to execute a specific movement sequence either forwards or backwards, with one leg and then with the other, without the slightest alteration to the sequence structure. One example of this would be the element *battement tendu*, which starts forwards or backwards, with the right and the left leg: four variations on the one same tiny piece of choreography. Parity is thus inculcated for both legs, as is the ability to execute steps in different spatial directions, an indispensable prerequisite for the dance of any choreographer. When one considers the difficulty experienced by nondancers simply in walking backwards, one can measure what an unbelievable challenge is being posed here to the motor-control system – a challenge for cognitive science and the understanding of movement in dance. Or in the words of a great musician and composer, Friedrich Liszt, who observed with eloquent simplicity that one does not play the piano with two entities (by which he meant two hands, the right and the left) but with one two-handed entity or with ten equally important fingers.

For every human being, the predisposition towards right or left is a matter of natural fact. The execution of a dance movement becomes in this context a matter of course, regulated by processes of self-activation. The motor system functions as a cybernetic system. The problem when learning a dance technique, especially the practically objective classical technique, is that in general these regulations are negated or at least insufficiently observed. Individual movement experiences, stored in the movement memory bank, and natural reflexes play a subsidiary role. Their integration into the methodological process means an a priori acceptance on the part of the individual, as opposed to their negation in favour of an alien system of movement. For artistic practice in general and for artistic education and training in particular, this creates a paradigm change. There has been no lack of argument in the past over this problem, the relationship between the individual and the technique of dance, and this applies even to the most different modern dance styles and techniques, each giving priority to either one side or the other. Dance research has concentrated principally on the perspective of anthroposophic science, sociocultural context, and the ethnological or artistic and historic roots. Observations based on natural science have so far been relatively marginal, and where they exist at all, have been neither correspondingly recognised nor further developed, in the way that, for example, Martha Graham, Agrippina Vaganova or Rudolf Laban most appropriately did as they developed their systems and analyses during the twentieth century. The training or re-training of the movement apparatus and its psychomotor control almost exclusively by way of the physical sensations of the student produces in my experience a real labour of Sisyphus, where many things are left to chance, and failure is every bit as likely as success. This has been, however, in principle, the only method of teaching ballet for several centuries, on the basis of 'learning by doing'.

To work, to repeat, to sweat, again and again – this has brought classical dance into disrepute as an inartistic, exclusively technically oriented school of movement.

Modern dance, on the other hand, is based on a natural, organic feeling for move-ment. Individual movement patterns become the starting point for the training of the body and for artistic expression, and are seen as the source of artistic renewal for dance in the twentieth century. So the techniques of classical ballet and modern dance remain, as ever, in opposition, and their shared elements remain marginalised both in training techniques and in education. The revolutionary inte-gration of dance steps into a unified system by the brilliant Agrippina Vaganova during the first half of the twentieth century is even today not properly studied for its inner content and context, but instead is taught and learnt as an aesthetic and technical norm or standard. The canonising of classical dance becomes stand-ardisation. The natural and organic roots from which classical dance developed over 200 years recede into the background. They are unrecognisable, unimagin-able, irreproducible in the technical structure of the movement sequences, and in this sense undetectable. The contradiction between classical and modern dance seems even today to remain obstinately real, although the will and the readiness of many to eliminate this antagonism has long been in existence. Creating awareness of the function of our movement apparatus, the mental analysis and imagery of single movements or sequences as described above, renders the holistic, equal and organic qualities of an artificial dance movement comprehensible. I can discern here enormous possibilities for the amelioration of the learning process, because the traditional methods of imitation and endless repetition can also easily inculcate false structures in the movement memory (see Chapters 6 and 9). To learn com-pletely new sequences and experiences of movement, the student is able by means of ideokinetic training to 'override' his coenaesthesis. My basic assumption must be that my coenaesthesis mirrors that of a normal untrained body, capable of a limited range of unilateral movement, considerations which the dancer (or the pianist) must indubitably overcome in order to work professionally.

In the famous essay 'On the Marionette Theatre' (1987/1810) by Heinrich von Kleist, we find the following interesting proposition relative to the problem of mental imagery. The author addresses the central question of whether human action is governed by feeling or by rationality. The narrator recounts his conversation with a dancer, much admired for his grace, whom he has seen several times visiting the Marionette Theatre. The dancer explains how he admires the natural graces of the puppets, and how much he himself is able to learn from them to what extent a natural harmony of movement can exist, independent of conscious thought (see also Chapter 8). Beside the jointed puppets of the Marionette Theatre, the narrator mentions the example of a graceful young boy who becomes aware of his grace and perfect harmony of movement, in which he resembles the famous statue of the *Boy With Thorn*. Realising that he is being observed, the boy tries under conscious control to repeat the movement in its original beauty, and fails in the attempt. During the conversation, the thesis arises that either completely unselfconscious movement (as in the string puppets of the Marionette Theatre) or at the opposite extreme, complete intellectual control of every action (as in the case of a perfect actor) both produce the desired 'natural' grace. Complete grace and 'naturalness' are thus the property of someone who either functions in a childlike state of complete naiveté and unselfconsciousness or who regulates his behaviour through total rational control;

> so grace itself returns when knowledge has as it were gone through an infinity. Grace appears most purely in that human form which either has no consciousness or an infinite consciousness. That is, in the puppet or in the god.
> (von Kleist, 1987/1810: translated from the German by Idris Parry)

With reference to the dance profession: the expression of the highest professionalism in dance is precisely complete grace and naturalness of a very high order, achieved by a completely intellectual control and mastery of the mechanical skills. The ability of a pianist to employ left and right hands as a holistic movement system is undoubtedly a prerequisite for good piano playing. It is, however, many times surpassed by the psychomotor performance of a dancer, who must use the entire body as a whole, of which the individual components must function both completely independently and at the same time in the closest interrelation with each other. In addition to the equivalence of left and right, in dance there is also the equivalence of arm and leg, of forwards and backwards. There is no question that some talented individuals certainly exist who possess this capability and who even, despite bad teachers or ballet masters, achieve better than average artistic performance levels. These talented individuals, however, are seldom seen. These parities, which manifest themselves in a highly developed canon of movement, are taught in the training of classical dance. With the help of a system of body coordination and various arm or leg positions, the steps of classical dance are strictly regulated. All movement must run through these positions. These are so fundamental that they are also used in other styles of modern dance. They depend entirely on the value system, the parities and the equivalences previously alluded to, and they produce on the basis of their aesthetic significance the spatial and biomechanical integration inherent in the context.

The cognitive architecture of dance movement, and in particular of the transitional movements, must be learnt, understood and absorbed by the dancer. He must know, prior to the beginning of the movement, why the movement is executed, otherwise it may easily be meaningless. This clearly demonstrates the interrelation between cognition and biomechanics. Analysis of hierarchically structured movement sequences (in classical dance, the clear separation between principal elements and assisting or preparatory movements; examples are given in Chapter 9), mental comprehension of the so-called node points, and their physical reproduction exercise a defining influence on the memory structure of the movement (Chapters 6 and 9 elaborate on these topics from a perspective of cognitive movement science). Their verbalisation, very unaccustomed and therefore deeply disliked by students and dancers, creates the opportunity even prior to physical reproduction, to monitor and improve quality of movement. The canon of classical dance consists of about 450 separate movements and elements of movement, which are taught in every academic ballet school in the world in the course of an education lasting around 8 years. This is intended with the help of the coordination system, the positions of the arms and legs and the canon of movement, to develop the body into an artistic instrument. Every movement is first demonstrated separately by the teacher, then repeated hundreds or even thousands of times by the student, until it has established itself in the memory and can be physically executed. The body will be, so to speak, constructed as an artistic instrument from these separate elements, as the individual building blocks may then be combined into complicated movement according to form or need. Even today, prevalent notions of teaching unfortunately look as mechanical as this process sounds. The separate parts of the body are put together like some sort of human jigsaw puzzle, on the basis that, the better the individual elements are trained, the better will be the dancing at the end of the process. This is a fatal confusion. For the whole is not equal to the sum of its parts. Even worse, however, is the fact that a mechanistic model has established itself in the mindset and understanding of classical dance which deprives all classical interpretation of its vital nourishment. One could also say that the dance has lost its soul! Or, to quote Heinrich von Kleist again:

> 'Does that mean,' I said in some bewilderment, 'that we must eat again of the tree of knowledge in order to return to the state of innocence?'
>
> (von Kleist, 1987/1810: translated from the German by Idris Parry)

This inefficient mechanistic method of working and teaching is quite often abandoned by ballet teachers who, unconsciously, through ignorance of the exact technical structure, teach movement from the starting point of their own understanding of dynamics and semiotics. From the point of view of artistic and dance requirements they often achieve better and more convincing results; but nevertheless, this approach is hardly suitable as a methodological or didactic policy, whether for the training of dancers or of ballet teachers. Subjectivity and a high level of empirical experience are of little value for the generalisation and development of a carefully thought out and objective teaching basis and method. Generations of dancers, teachers and choreographers have taken the proposition of innocence to heart, and have advocated a new doctrine; the omnipotence of the artistic, with no consideration for the psychological–physical features of the dancer's body. Existential orientation and feeling were established as supreme in artistic interpretation. Where once the 'soul' was considered lost, it was now seen to predominate. This ideal was created by great and superbly gifted dancers above all in the area of modern dance; however, without solving the basic problem. On the contrary, it has led among other things to an artistic development among choreographers and dancers loosely although not inaccurately described as 'navel gazing'.

The possibilities, methods and propositions of neurocognition and biomechanics can, I believe, help us to find a way out of this vicious circle. As far as I am aware, there is in the present school of classical dance no method which has sought scientific support so ambitiously that it has consistently modified its teaching concept and didactics. In principle we are still teaching along the same lines as our predecessors 50 or 100 years ago. We impart feelings and belief to the students as the basic premise of action, instead of giving them methods to recognise the movement, to implement it correctly by awareness of its inner context and structure. The antagonism towards science, so frequently observed in dance, corresponds to the dogma of exclusive artistic sensibility, which is thoroughly disproved by other schools of independent thought. Curiosity over the new, as opposed to the old, reliable, protracted way of proceeding, seems to have been carefully suppressed. In my practical teaching work so far, I had only been able to proceed from a basis of empirical observation and experience. My attempts prior to the fall of the Berlin Wall to accede the excellent scientific research results in psychology, biomechanics, sports medicine and the first-rate sporting prowess of the German Democratic Republic (GDR) were hopeless. This entire area was a carefully guarded state secret. By all estimations of art and culture in the GDR, it seemed that dance was not then considered quite such a matter of national priority. Even today I continue to experiment in teaching with various approaches to communicating, memorising and reproducing dance movement, both in training and in the theatre, and I am increasingly fascinated by the possibility, parallel to artistic parameters, of a completely new ballet methodology based on neurocognitive and biomechanical parameters.

One of my students, artistically and physically very gifted and highly motivated, seemed to promise a future as a good dancer. He had only one problem; he could not turn, which, not only for classical dancers, was a catastrophe, as pirouettes are part of the basic equipment of all types of dancer. Every correction and countless attempts were all in vain, and brought us both to the brink of despair. The body simply refused to turn balanced on one leg. Following the experience with ideokinetic training detailed at the beginning of this chapter, it occurred to me to stop all our practical training. I asked him to lie down on the floor (as in the previous example, it was very important to achieve the static removal of the feeling of his body weight) and to close his eyes. He then had to imagine a picture of the complete sequence of movement in his head. When he thought he had this picture clear, I asked him to describe it to me. Everything ran smoothly until he came to the decisive moment of the push-off, a highly complex movement procedure. He stammered and said: 'I can't see anything'. I asked him to create the picture again. The results were identical, and as he exclaimed, 'I have a blackout!', I answered dryly, 'Thank God, because exactly there is your crucial mistake.' He had thought that the more precisely he executed the preparation (the movement sequence leading up to the actual push-off), the better would be the ensuing pirouette. This preparation, however, is a completely formal procedure, which has nothing to do with the actual turn. The generation of the turning impulse is the crucial moment. After I had spent several minutes going through the complex generation of this impulse mentally, and he had provided me with verbal descriptions of the activity to prove, so to speak, the quality of the images running through his head, and after we had gone through the various stages from lying to sitting to standing, from slow to fast, I decided: 'Now you may turn.' He took his position, executed the preparation, pushed off and turned for the first time in his life three complete, slow, clean pirouettes. Some dancers work on this all their lives and never understand it, and we had achieved it by 'doing nothing', apart from a very specific type of concentration. Subsequently this delightful experience came in useful when I made the ironic comment to dancers who were working 'unthinkingly', that dance must really be for lazy people, if they were first to think and only afterwards to move.

This type of mental training proved successful for this student for other movement sequences, particularly when I was getting him ready to compete in the great international Junior Competition in Lausanne. Since I was not usually able to travel with him, he had to go alone. When he experienced serious problems during the competition with the execution of a particular series of jumps, he telephoned me to ask for my advice. I made him describe everything, gave him the corresponding corrections, he repeated them over the telephone, danced his round on the following day, and came away with first prize in the Prix de Lausanne.

However, I was soon to learn how careful one must be with generalisations of this kind of mental preparation. For several years I have been teaching courses for ballet and dance teachers. In the course 'Creating Combinations', I showed a dance teacher a brief combination of jumps. These are sequences created by the ballet master or teacher for the class, and they must be constructed according to specific methodological, artistic, pedagogic and musical principles in order to produce optimal results. I asked him to repeat the sequence. He got his legs into such a tangle that he had to stop. We repeated the same procedure: I show, he repeats, then breaks off in the middle. With the not inconsiderable side effect that the teacher had made himself look foolish in front of the other seminar participants, he had become completely blocked, and no longer wanted to do the exercise. The situation needed resolving, and so I said to him: 'No problem, I'll show you this exercise again, but first I'll tell you beforehand how you should try to remember it. Because perhaps your problem wasn't that you don't know the steps which you may have thought too complicated.' I should add that he was a well-trained dancer, and in purely technical terms his body was certainly in condition to execute these little jumps and movements correctly. I explained to him: 'So just look at the spatial and dynamic sequence of the movement. Don't try to remember the individual movement details.' Absolute silence reigned in the studio, and everyone waited for the outcome of this experiment, which as a parallel to the 'doing nothing' method ought to lead to success by way of 'remembering nothing'. After I had demonstrated the combination to him once again, and reminded him not to try to recall the details, he stood up and executed the combination faultlessly. The other participants in the seminar applauded, the situation was saved, and I was the richer by a new experience. I then asked him to repeat the sequence much faster. Again he succeeded, and I remembered a remark by the famous Russian piano teacher Neuhaus, who in his laconic fashion pointed out the link between the thinking process and the manual virtuosity of a pianist: To play fast means to think fast (. . . and to dance fast!). The conscious attempt by the seminar participant to reproduce the technical and spatial structure of each *single* movement proved not only to be unhelpful, but to disturb his rendition of the whole sequence to the point where he was obliged to break off. If in the first example (the student pirouette), concentration on the minutest detail was important, here the concept of the sequence was in the foreground. The latter has great significance, particularly in dance training, as dance here reaches back unconsciously into areas of previous movement experience and reproduces them under new, different spatial, dynamic, technical and therefore artistic conditions. Experienced dancers have already mastered this principle, and thus considerably facilitate the acquisition of new choreography. In this manner, the aesthetic, content and musical ideas of the choreographer remain at the beginning of the staging of a new ballet or dance, at the level of a certain immaturity of movement, always the only goal worth striving for (see Chapter 4). Technical claims can no longer dominate interpretive obligations, and the dancer remains an artist, and never, in the worst case scenario, an athlete.

As has been scientifically established, listening to the same music aids the process of movement recall. Listening to music also activates areas in the brain that are responsible for movement. In the same way as a feeling for the weight of one's own body can, in my experience, interrupt thought processes in the ideokinetic method of work, a maximal exertion of strength can also hinder the learning and contextual understanding of new movement. It is essential to take this into account in the learning or correction of movement sequences. The reminder of one's own body might impede the thought process. Maximal use of strength might lead to a similar problem in the initial stages of learning movement and impede precisely the comprehension of the cognitive structure of dance movement. Its repeatability, its free, spontaneous or goal-oriented application for artistic interpretation is rendered considerably more difficult, as the body gives priority to its 'feeling oriented' function. It should definitely be noted that this process is relevant to learning or correction of movement sequences. On the other hand, experienced and very well trained dancers rely quite rightly on the application of their technical resources and on their subconscious feelings to summon up established and rehearsed sequences of movement, which are already stored in their movement memory banks (or movement repertoire; see Chapter 10). This is why I very often get my students or dancers to 'mark' the movement with a maximum of 50% of energy, simply so that I can see the movement impulses, which already provide me with a complete evaluation of the truth. At this point, an interesting reaction takes place in the dancer. The vehement exertion of energy, the 'learning by doing' method, often leading to inexact and unclean execution, disappears, and the dancer has to regulate movement by means of a *conscious* thought process. Some students have hated me for this method, as it is a natural human tendency sometimes to try to solve problems, not by ratiocination, but by striking out.

In the course of attempting to optimise learning, memorisation and reproduction with the help of ideomotoric or ideokinetic working methods, I have found myself, mainly on the basis of movement analysis which I was necessarily obliged to complete, more and more frequently thrust into the area of biomechanics, the architecture of movement and its internal integration, and I arrived at the realisation: The clearer the movement structure, the easier it was to perceive its internal architecture, and the easier became its cognitive acquisition. This brought a completely new principle of learning to my method of teaching classical dance. The approximately 450 steps or elements of the complete canon of classical dance represent a treasure of enormous value, but on the other hand there is the great danger of the standardisation of artistic movement. From this variety of classical steps, I have filtered out the principles of movement which form the basis for the execution of single steps or sequences of movement, and achieved a further simplification and reduction to, in total, seven elements that now form the core of the DANAMOS concept I have developed during 30 years of teaching practice. However, to avoid any possible misunderstandings: a precise knowledge of the canon of classical dance is in any case the *conditio sine qua non*! These seven basic elements only serve to make possible a greater clarity and simplicity in teaching, development and correction, and this not only in classical dance. This is because the working out of the canon of classical dance has as its goal, not the mechanical learning of the external form of these steps, but instead the disclosure and both cognitive and physical acquisition of the context of all movements. These elementary movement principles are of so basic a nature that they are of essential significance to every dance style and technique.

As the model for the semantic and functional context of these basic elements, I chose an analogy to the subsystem grammar of linguistics: the section morphology. In linguistics, all languages can be analysed by means of morphology, both regarding grammar and in relation to single words and their constituent elements, the morphemes. Morphemes are the smallest, indivisible units of a word which can still retain sense, e.g., the words 'chair' or 'child'. This term 'morpheme' and its function in grammar is used here as an analogy, to simplify the presentation of the system of natural human movement in its basic elements; in other words, to denote the smallest, indivisible kinetic unit which can still be of functional significance. These smallest units of movement, drawn from the motor system of the human body, are to be understood as morphemes of human motor action, as an analytic and pedagogic tool.

These seven elements, or morphemes, that refer to classical dance elements are taught separately at the beginning of ballet teaching in any professional ballet school. Later, they reappear as constitute elements in all 450 more complex movements of the classical canon. When practicing very complex movements, one or more of these seven morphemes might no longer be perceived as fundamental by performers, educators or ballet masters, because their focus of attention tends to shift to external aspects, technically challenging moments and artistic design. The DANAMOS system serves to make the crucial functional movement concepts underlying the complex classic canon explicit and transparent, in order to help dancers, dance learners and teachers understand not only *what* to do, but *how*, and *why*.

The seven morphemes of DANAMOS

1   *The body centre of mass (COM):* its translation and rotation on the ground and in the air, e.g., all poses on one or two legs, all kinds of *pas degagé*, pirouette, turn and jump.
2   *The body axis:* its different use and coordination with the COM (1st morpheme) while the body is anchored on the ground or in the air, moving in translation

(locomotion) or rotation (turning). Importantly, the upper body and head are inclined 2–3° forward. (Note that this is in stark contrast to everyday ballet practice and the corresponding drawings in ballet textbooks, where usually the upper body is kept absolutely vertical or even slightly inclined backwards, which can cause severe problems in locomotion and turning for many dancers.)

3   *Lifting and lowering the whole leg:* all kinds of *battements*; movement mainly in the upper leg, actuating the hip joints, while the knee is stretched or slightly angled, like in attitude. The relevance of this morpheme to arm movements is explained below.

4   *Bending and stretching the leg:* all forms of *pliément*; lower leg and thigh are active, actuating feet (ankle joint), hips and knee joints. Both leg segments articulating at the knee are in active and simultaneous motion, while the hip, ankle joint and feet are participating passively. The relevance of this morpheme to arm movements is explained below.

5   *Flexing and extending the lower leg:* all movements of the free leg, e.g., in *battement tendu* into *demi plié* or *battement fondu, rond de jambe en l'air* or *battement developé* in the classical canon. Only the lower leg is moving actively, while the upper leg participates passively until cessation of movement. This morpheme is strongly linked with the 3rd morpheme (lifting and lowering the whole leg). The relevance of this morpheme to arm movements is explained below.

6   *Rotation of the leg in the hip joint:* all kinds of *rond de jambe* on ground and in the air *en dehors* and *en dedans*.

7   *Turning of the torso while legs stay anchored (pivoté):* both legs maintain their anchoring position on the ground or in the air while the torso and the hips carry a turn 90° or 180°, strongly linked with the 1st morpheme. The 7th morpheme refers to the '*pivoté*' rotation in the classical ballet canon, or pivot turn in jazz dance. (Note that in ballet classes this turn is often incorrectly described as '*fouetté*'. However, '*fouetter*' means 'to whip', here whipping with the whole or the lower leg, as in *battement fouetté, pirouette fouetté* or *grand pirouette fouetté* which includes the 7th morpheme as a constitute element.)

To illustrate the morphemes (see Figure 1.1), I have chosen elements from the classical dance canon and, for comparison, movements from an everyday or sports context that are grounded in the same kinematic principles, in order to render the interrelationship between artistic and natural movement comprehensible and to offer novices a glimpse into the movement canon of classical ballet.

Movements and postures of the upper body, head and arms: In contrast to the active character of the lower body with reference to the seven morphemes of DANAMOS, the movements and postures of the upper body and head fulfil a reactive function that will not be described here (because of its relevance and complexity, it would need an extra chapter). The 3rd, 4th and 5th morphemes can also be applied to the functionality of the arm movements (*port de bras*),

Figure 1.1a The 1st morpheme of the DANAMOS system: the body centre of mass. (Graphics by Marek Hertel, Berlin 2017; © Martin Puttke.)

Figure 1.1b The 2nd morpheme of the DANAMOS system: the body axis. (Graphics by Marek Hertel, Berlin 2017; © Martin Puttke.)

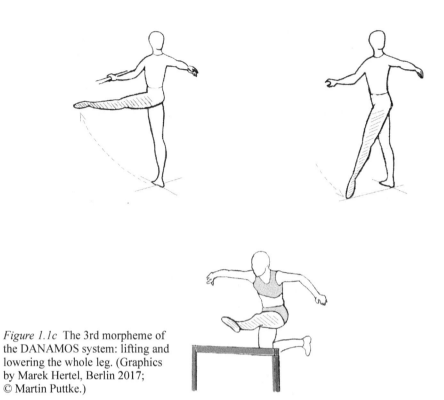

Figure 1.1c The 3rd morpheme of the DANAMOS system: lifting and lowering the whole leg. (Graphics by Marek Hertel, Berlin 2017; © Martin Puttke.)

Figure 1.1d The 4th morpheme of the DANAMOS system: bending and stretching the leg. (Graphics by Marek Hertel, Berlin 2017; © Martin Puttke.)

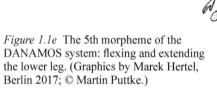

Figure 1.1e The 5th morpheme of the DANAMOS system: flexing and extending the lower leg. (Graphics by Marek Hertel, Berlin 2017; © Martin Puttke.)

Figure 1.1f The 6th morpheme of the DANAMOS system: rotation of the leg in the hip joint. (Graphics by Marek Hertel, Berlin 2017; © Martin Puttke.)

Figure 1.1g The 7th morpheme of the DANAMOS system: turning of the torso while legs
stay anchored. (Graphics by Marek Hertel, Berlin 2017; © Martin Puttke.)

with analogous use of the upper arm and lower arm compared to the legs. In ballet
practice, the standard terms 'arm' or 'leg' are often used, and so the different
functions of the upper and lower arm or leg are less recognisable. Yet the distinction between the 4th and 5th morphemes in both legs and arms constitutes one
of the most significant preconditions for virtuosity in any dance technique, not
only in pirouettes, turns, on the ground or in the air. To deconstruct movements of
arms and legs means that instead of *four* extremities dancers have to distinguish,
control and coordinate, there are *eight* segments performing different actions
that might even contrast each other in time and space. When the basic elements
of the classical canon are taught, this functional difference must be acquired
and fixed in movement memory, to be available later for the flawless execution of
more complex movements and movement sequences. At a later stage of practice,
the tendency to regard arms and legs as whole entities and use them in an undiffe-
rentiated manner often represents the biggest obstacle for the development of an
'unencumbered' virtuosity.

Dance meets physics: Lessons from the biomechanics lab

It is the most outstanding skill of a good teacher to be able to give feedback that enables the student to improve his performance directly and immediately, with or without understanding straightaway where that improvement comes from (even though understanding the underlying mechanisms may later lead to a meaningful 'aha' effect). Immediate improvement is only possible if the teacher's feedback focuses on the main functional movement problem (see Hossner, Schiebl and Göhner, 2015) in a way that is implicitly or explicitly understandable for the student. If, in contrast, the teacher's feedback addresses a variety of aspects that contribute more or less to the movement problem, this might lead to confusion and frustration on the side of the student. In classical ballet, the range of superficial, non-functional aspects that can be addressed by teachers is vast, and it is therefore even more important to provide teachers and students with tools that help them to efficiently target the core of the movement problem (see Wulf, 2007). In order to substantiate the functional aspects of meaningful teacher's feedback, we investigated the kinematic data of 11 dancers executing *pirouettes en dehors* before and after instructions that were based on DANAMOS. We indeed discovered significant differences in the dancers' performance before and after these instructions were given. Movements were recorded using a 3D motion-capture system with 12 infra-red cameras tracking 42 passive retro-reflective markers fixed on relevant positions of the dancer's body.[1] The technical analysis of the movement structure, timing and coordination of body parts enables scientists and practitioners to gain an enhanced understanding of the quality of pirouettes, in addition to their visual perception and experience-based evaluation.

Well-composed movements, in which the relative positions of certain body parts hold for a time along the main trajectories, can be ascertained from the analysis of relative kinematics of markers placed on the dancer's body (Land et al., 2013; Volchenkov and Bläsing, 2013; Volchenkov, Bläsing and Schack, 2014). In order to track changes in the body shape of a dancer during the performance of pirouettes, we used the Procrustes analysis (Gower and Dijksterhuis, 2004), which is customary in shape-matching and shape-recognition, since it allows consequent subtraction of all translations, scaling and rotations while preserving the relative spatial configuration of markers. This was important because our aim was to analyse the inherent movements of the body *per se*, relative to its axis and COM, and not the rotation (which is naturally the predominant movement component in a pirouette) or translational movement components such as the shifting of the whole body into any spatial direction. We moved the origin of the frame of reference to the instantaneous geometrical center of the dancer's trunk calculated with respect to the trunk markers at each time frame. After the consequent transformations removing the translational, scaling and the mean rotational components of the movement, the remaining kinematic signal (the shape velocity vector) represented instantaneous changes in the dancer's body shape registered for every marker. The results of the Procrustes analysis of the kinematic data as tracked from the *pirouette en dehors* executed by a professional dancer is shown in Figure 1.2.

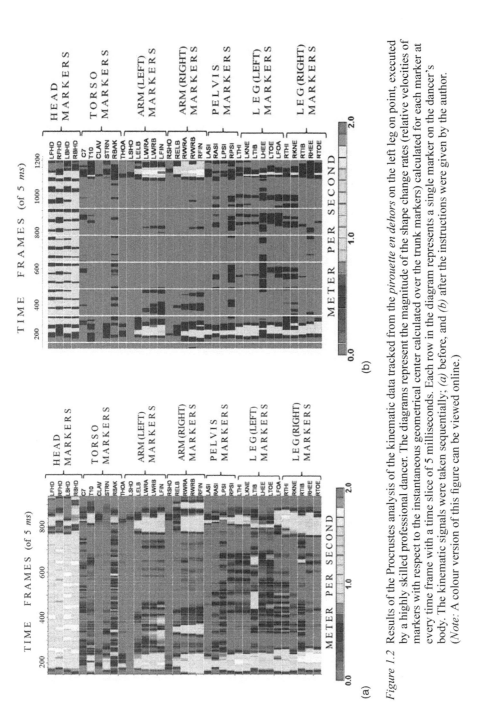

Figure 1.2 Results of the Procrustes analysis of the kinematic data tracked from the *pirouette en dehors* on the left leg on point, executed by a highly skilled professional dancer. The diagrams represent the magnitude of the shape change rates (relative velocities of markers with respect to the instantaneous geometrical center calculated over the trunk markers) calculated for each marker at every time frame with a time slice of 5 milliseconds. Each row in the diagram represents a single marker on the dancer's body. The kinematic signals were taken sequentially; *(a)* before, and *(b)* after the instructions were given by the author. (*Note:* A colour version of this figure can be viewed online.)

The kinematic signal representing the shape changes in the *pirouette en dehors* has the form of two vertical bands exhibiting the onset and terminal phases of the movement, separated by an 'inertial phase', during which the relative positions of most markers, except the head markers (represented in the four upper lines of the diagrams), remain almost unchanged in the chosen frame of reference. The synchronous shape changes clearly reflect the blocks of markers matching the natural division of the body. The strong periodic signal from the four head markers spanning the whole inertial phase arises due to rapid rotations of the head while spotting. Adaptations applied after the instruction was received clearly regard the closing of the arms at the instance of the turn and the relative movement onset of legs and upper body.

The highly skilled dancer performs the *pirouette en dehors* on the left leg on point (turning right). The right leg (future non-supporting leg; the legs adopt a slightly opened and bended position, a *demi plié*) pushes with the foot against the floor in turning direction (5th morpheme), transferring the turning impulse to the body COM. Both COM and turning impulse must simultaneously be transferred to the stretching left leg (4th morpheme). The pirouettes displayed were performed before (*left*) and after (*right*) key correction was given. Significant differences in the temporal structure and distribution of energy in the whole body become visible at first sight.

In the first condition (as shown in Figure 1.2a), before instruction was given, the dancer opens the right arm with high amplitude and speed in order to increase the rotational momentum. Following this impulse, the upper body shifts to the turning direction towards the opening arm. As a consequence, the upper body moves slightly away from the axis, which is actively compensated by this highly gifted and experienced dancer by pulling back towards the axis during the turn. This stabilising activity becomes visible in the diagram as increased activity in the 'RBAK' marker sitting on the right shoulder blade, as well as the pelvis and leg markers. Despite the impressive number of 13 turns executed, the overall impression is one of internal restlessness: the technical challenge is fulfilled, but the inner balance as the basis for artistic presentation is lost.

The following correction is then applied, with reference to the 5th morpheme. When opening the right arm to gain momentum, the upper arm should open only minimally to support the upper body, and the lower arm should be closed again in opposition to the turning direction into the first position (with both arms meeting in a rounded posture in front of the body). After the correction is applied (as shown in Figure 1.2b), the overall image of the turn becomes much cleaner, with much less correction movements in the upper back (marker 'RBAK') and the lower body, while the number of turns is immediately increased up to 18 (after which the dancer, somewhat surprised, abruptly finishes the pirouette in a pose when I call 'Thanks, you can stop now!').

This impressive example shows that the dancer's errors, which prevent the perfect execution of a pirouette, do not need to be explained in detail, but instead can be eliminated via a simple correction of the morphological core. The example illustrated in Figure 1.2 demonstrates clearly how, in the highly complex technique of classical dance, even the smallest inaccuracies can cause severe shortcomings in the course of the movement, and therefore how crucial it is for dance pedagogues and ballet masters to differentiate basic errors from their consequences.

In a complementary study, we used a force plate[2] to examine jumps, including the *petit pas assemble*, performed by students of the Dance Department of Gymnasium Essen-Werden. *Assemblé* is one of the most difficult of all ballet steps in the sense of analysing, explaining the kinematic process, and teaching. The dancer launches into an *assemblé* jump from an upright standing position, and makes a preliminary downward movement by flexing at the feet, knees and hips *(demi plié)*. The jump starts on two feet, with the working leg performing a *battement glissé/dégagé*, brushing out and lifting vertically off the ground. At the same time, the dancer vigorously, but not hastily, extends the feet, knees and hips, with the second foot then meeting the first foot before landing. The two legs can be joined already in the air into a fifth position (both legs are closed in a stretched position, one leg in front of the other) or later when they return to the fifth position on the floor (one foot in front of the other). The finishing phase is thus controversially taught: the instruction given here intentionally makes no reference to these different definitions. The purpose of the instruction ('When you jump, bring the floor with you!') was simply intended to produce an organic and strong jump (see Puttke and Volchenkov, 2018).

The twist and mechanical energy time curves that were recorded during jumps *assemblé* performed by three students before and after the instruction ('When you jump, bring the floor with you!') are shown in Figure 1.3 (note that these students were never taught before by the author). These time curves help to carefully trace out the differences in evolution of jumps while identifying the key times and phases. The magnitude of the turning force *(torque,* feet joint) and the corresponding amounts of energy applied by the students to the force platform before the instruction was given (dashed curves) is systematically less than after the instruction was given (solid curves) – the dancers obviously tried to 'pick up the floor' while taking off, which resulted in increased take-off velocity and clearance (jump height).

The metaphorical instruction 'bring the floor with you' elicits a significantly better result than the technical description of the entire jumping process. The interplay of simultaneously performed fine-tuned activities, particularly in classical ballet, is so complex that it is hard to grasp and to describe. A deconstruction into individual technical components is likely to lead the dancer astray, as he does not think of details while executing the complex movements. Instead, this 'intellectual' approach will rather destroy the flow and 'spirit' of a movement. Thus, it is often more beneficial to focus attention away from internal and towards external processes (see Wulf, 2007), in order to work more efficiently in physical as well as cognitive terms. To achieve this, a suitable metaphor for efficient movement performance is crucial. As Gaby Wulf (2007: p. 120) states:

> To understand how an external focus would produce a more economical movement pattern, keep in mind that our body is an energy-efficient system

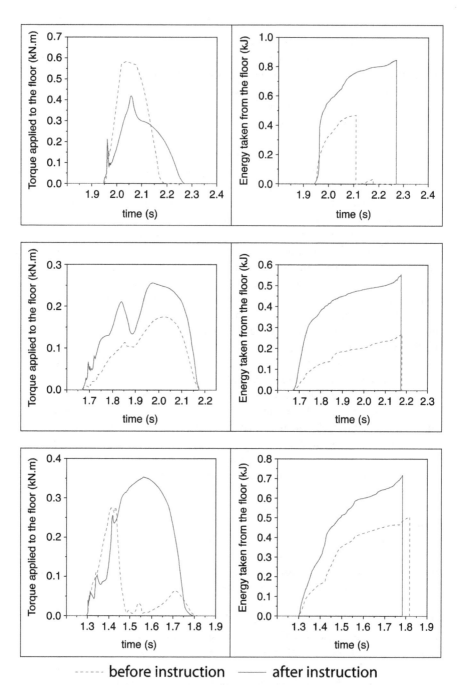

----- before instruction ——— after instruction

Figure 1.3 Twist (torque) time curve (*left column*) and kinematic energy time curve (*right column*) recorded during a *petit pas assemblé* (a small jump from one foot to both feet) performed by three students before (dashed line) and after (solid line) the instruction ('When you jump, bring the floor with you!') was given by the author.

that tries to conserve energy. If attention is directed to the effect, or outcome, of an action – as it is when an external focus is adopted – there should be a greater coherence between the outcome and the sensory consequences of that action. This increased sensory–motor coherence allows the motor system to adjust more adaptively to task demands. As a result, only the minimally necessary number of motor units required to produce the desired outcome would be recruited.

The DANAMOS concept provides a platform for physics and neurocognition to describe and complement the aesthetics of ballet from different angles, and thereby to constructively contribute to the technology of classical dance. The term 'classical' no longer only applies to the aesthetic of such 'classics' as *Swan Lake* or *Giselle*, but, by means of a revelation of internal structure, to every form of dance. Classical dancers trained this way are able to develop a great affinity with modern dance (which is confirmed by several concrete examples in the course of my teaching activity). The enrichment of classical dance by interdisciplinary cooperation and research in the areas of neuroscience, psychology, biomechanics and philosophy could bring a completely new quality to the teaching of classical dance, and I am convinced that it would bring to an end the ever present antagonism between classical and modern dance. Dancers and teachers need in their actions and movements to take the following premise much more to heart than they have hitherto done: *Learning to dance means learning to think!*

Notes

1 To track ballet movements, we used a MTS (Vicon Motion Systems, Inc.) based on 12 high-resolution cameras outfitted with IR optical filters and rings of LED strobe lights streaming data at 200 fps (frames per second); the cameras detected the 3-dimensional spatial positions of passive retro-reflective spherical body markers with millimeter accuracy. Markers were attached to key anatomical locations according to the standard Vicon full-body marker placement protocol (Plug-in Gait).
2 A force plate is a rectangular metal plate, about 0.8 m × 1.0 m, with piezoelectric or strain gauge transducers attached at each corner to give an electrical output that is proportional to the force on the plate. Force platforms have a broad range of applications, including clinical gait analysis and sports technique analysis. A platform measures the force exerted on it by the subject, and according to Newton's third law of motion, this also gives the force exerted by the platform on the subject (the ground reaction force - GRF), as well as a *twist* given to the platform by the subject (torque, or moment of force). The corresponding mechanical energy (work) curves are obtained by integrating numerically the GRF vector along the path travelled by the force.

References

Gower, J. C. & Dijksterhuis, G. B. (2004). *Procrustes Problems*. Oxford: Oxford University Press.
Hossner, E.-J., Schiebl, F., & Göhner, U. (2015). A functional approach to movement analysis and error identifikation in sports and physical education. *Frontiers in Psychology*, 6, 1339.

Land, W., Volchenkov, D., Bläsing, B., & Schack, T. (2013). From action representation to action execution: Exploring the links between cognitive and biomechanical levels of motor control. *Frontiers in Computational Neuroscience, 7*(127), 1–14.

Puttke, M. & Volchenkov, D. (in publication: 2018). Motion analysis as pedagogic tool in dance: Learning to dance means learning to think. In: B. Müller & S. Wolf (Eds.), *Handbook of Human Motion*. New York: Springer.

Volchenkov, D. & Bläsing, B. (2013). Spatio-temporal analysis of kinematic signals in classical ballet. *Journal of Computational Science, 4*(4), 285–292.

Volchenkov, D., Bläsing, B., & Schack, T. (2014). Spatio-temporal kinematic decomposition of movements. *Engineering, 6*(08), 385–398.

von Kleist, H. (1987/1810). Über das Marionettentheater [On the Marionette Theatre]. In: H. Sembdner & H. von Kleist (Eds.), *Sämtliche Werke und Briefe [Complete Works and Letters]*, Bd 2, pp. 338–345. Munich: Verlag. (Originally published in Berliner Abendblätter, 1, 1810.)

Wulf, G. (2007). *Attention and Motor Skill Learning*. Champaign, IL: Human Kinetics.

2 The Kinematics Teaching Methodology

Marrying kinesthetic stimuli with reading instruction

Galeet BenZion

Introduction

'Having too many degrees is a waste of energy and effort' my 15-year-old daughter declared one day as we were having dinner. 'You have no idea how wrong you are' I thought to myself, but stopped short from responding because, as my grandmother used to say, 'there is a time and a place to have meaningful conversations with teenagers and the dinner table is not one of those places'. So I thought to myself how it was due to each degree that I have earned, that I was able to obtain new insights about the process of teaching and learning and become the effective teacher that I am. The first edition of this book presented the Kinematics Teaching Methodology (KTM) which was developed based on my doctoral research study. In this second edition, I am revisiting KTM: discussing its implementation steps and giving examples of concrete application in the classroom with two groups of students (8- and 9-year-old students, and 13- and 14-year-old students).

The origins of KTM

About 20 years ago, while taking full time Ph.D. level courses in English (my native language was very different), working two jobs, and functioning as a wife, I hit a mental block. I was not able to recall anything academic related. I attempted to implement many memory-enhancing techniques unsuccessfully,[1] so much so that I sought the help of a counselor who asked a simple question: 'What is your best way of remembering things?'. Spontaneously I replied 'I can remember choreography like no other.' 'What do you mean?' she inquired. 'Well, I can just remember how movements connect to each other, how they flow, it just makes sense to me,' I explained. 'Well, is there a way that you can use that to remember the content of your academic courses?' While I had no answer for that at the time, I left her office thinking that I should find an answer to this, and if I did, I could possibly overcome the mental block I was experiencing.

I remember reading my psychology notes and beginning to translate them to movements. I had to keep asking myself the following questions: What does that mean? In what situation would this be relevant? How would that affect me or society? The next step was creating series of movements that represented the answers which were essentially connections I created to make sense of the new concepts and vocabulary I needed to memorize. I rehearsed the movements as I was spelling them and saying the terms aloud. I was soon able to dance these sequences while having flashes of the meaning spark in my head. I then realized that I no longer needed to dance the movements; I could just think of the topic, which sparked a visual of the movements, concepts and terms they represented. I was fascinated. I never knew that such a learning process existed or was possible. I wondered if there were children who, like me, were movement inclined and who could possibly benefit from this type of learning. Encouraged by my math professor who claimed that there were many students who experienced difficulty with math, I set out to find a group of students and attempted to use dance moves and choreography to teach them math concepts which they had not mastered in the traditional classroom.[2]

I put together a small qualitative study that attempted to identify how the use of dance can be made effective in the teaching of geometrical concepts. My conclusions were published in *The Neurocognition of Dance: Mind, movement, and motor skills* (BenZion in Blasing, Puttke and Schack, 2010). I called this process the Kinematics Teaching Methodology (KTM).

The application process of KTM

KTM spelled out a nine-step process that resulted in higher academic achievement in math.

Step I: Verbal and visual introduction

Introducing the topic, explaining the purpose of a lesson, and using visual(s) to support the visual learners. I use both a Smartboard and a document camera in order to elicit students' interest by projecting the day's topic, the purpose of lesson, its goals, and a visual or short movie clip. For example, in order to introduce the concept of similes, I have projected sets of two pictures, one after the other, and asked students to think of how these pictures are related.

Step II: Creating an individualized shape bank

Students discuss the material they need to master, and attempt to make meaningful connections to their lives. The logic here is that abstract concepts are better remembered if they are connected to a meaningful personal experience which has left a memorable impression on the learner. An essential question that should be asked as part of this process is: What does this remind you of? Follow-up questions could be:

- How is your situation and the one we are learning about different or similar?
- What lesson is there to learn from your experience?

- What guiding principles should you take away for life given this new information?
- What are the implications (on you, your family, your immediate community, your country, or the world) of this information?
- How do you feel (i.e., are you hopeful, confident, confused, or discouraged) about this information? Explain why?
- What key words should you remember about this topic?
- How will you remember the spelling of this vocabulary?

Once students have shared personal connections to the material, they develop a shape bank, the purpose of which is to help establish a high level of confidence using one's body as a means for remembering abstract concepts. The shape bank should include large, small, tall, wide, on-one-foot, or while-sitting shapes. These shapes should be documented on paper by students by drawing stick figures, so that there is a record of the shapes for later use.

To encourage the process of creating a shape bank, I play instrumental music and instruct students to dance freely in space. I explain that when the music stops, they are to 'freeze' in space. The parameters of the shape should be explained at this point. For example: 'Your next frozen shape needs to be low and close to the floor.'[3] The freeze concept is a still moment in time that requires learners to hold their position in space without any motion; that is, to create a shape. Adhering to the freeze is essential in order to develop students' attention and concentration, and their abilities to adhere to their own intuitive movement choices, to tune in to their movements as they occur, to stop the movement process in any given moment without losing concentration, and to control their bodies (such as avoiding a fall). I repeat the dance/freeze process several times. After each freeze I ask students to document their shapes on paper with a stickman sketch (as in Figure 2.1). Having worked with teenagers, I have learned that many are self-conscious, which prevents them initially from being able to focus on this process. However, incorporating this process frequently in the classroom results in students becoming less concerned about how they look, and more focused on their own movements, and the meaning of their kinesthetic expressions.

One additional important implementation strategy (which helps learners to avoid barriers to their success) is for the teacher to model how he/she is able to commit to creating movement sequences to music. Prior to the demonstration, the teacher explains the purpose of this demonstration: 'The purpose of this demonstration is to show you how I am able to commit to my own authentic movements while not worrying about how I look, what you think, or any judgement on your part. I would appreciate your help in just focusing on my face as I dance. Ask yourself, is she totally committed to her own movements? Or is she worried about us watching her? If I am showing in any way that I am not concentrated on my own movements, I failed this exercise.' After this instruction is given, the teacher asks a responsible student to get the music started, and then to stop the music after about 15 to 20 seconds. At the end of this process, the students make their comments, then they take center stage and the teacher manages the process.

Step III: Creating an individualized transition bank

The purpose of developing a transition bank is: (a) to increase the students' ability to dance through space, (b) to expand their expressiveness while dancing, and (c) to draw on a larger range of transition options in order to make meaningful connections to abstract academic concepts that they need to master at school. Specifically, transitions are any assortment of movements that are characterized by a clear path in space, or style. Paths in space can be characterized as circles, arcs, or lines in any direction and from or to any height. Style refers to moving in staccato, legato and marcato.[4]

An approach to developing a transition bank is to instruct students to dance while expressing qualities, such as robotic movements which would correspond to creating transitions performed in staccato. The teacher could also instruct students to dance while expressing a mood or tone – depressed or tired movements would correspond to a legato style; and anger to marcato. Learners begin to dance as the music plays and freeze when the music stops. I repeat rehearsing the transition bank several times. Regardless of how the transition bank is taught, transitions, just like shapes, are always documented on paper (by students) so that they are able to use them later when making connections to academic content. Each transition is noted as a shape with a symbol immediately above it.[5] Table 2.1 lists transition symbols.

For example, Figure 2.1 demonstrates that a shape which began hovering to the left will transition via an erect body to hovering to the right. The transition will be executed in a staccato style. There will be a shift of weight from a bent left leg, to a bent right leg, and the left arm will arch in space from the left side, to end reaching over the head on the right side.

In order to implement KTM successfully, Steps II and III (creating individualized shape and transition banks) should precede any instruction that aims at incorporating movement into the teaching of academic curriculum and abstract concepts. This is because understanding shapes and transitions are essential building blocks for using kinesthetic movement for building conceptual knowledge.

Table 2.1 Transition annotation symbols

Transition style	Annotated symbol
Staccato	
Legato	
Marcato	
Elevation in height	
Decrease in height	

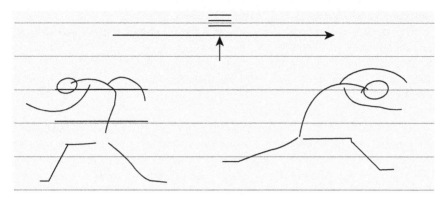

Figure 2.1 A transition documented by a student on paper.

Step IV: Introduction of curricular content

The teacher revisits the concept or focus of the lesson and tasks students with figuring out a kinesthetic representation (i.e., a dance phrase) that they will be able to perform and explain to themselves and their peers. This step is very quick as it is essentially a bridge to Steps V and VI, which will fill the majority of the instructional time.

Step V: Individual and group exploration

At this step, students are creating or putting together kinesthetic representations for academic curriculum. They begin by working alone (usually 15 minutes, which is set on a timer but often ends up being longer as students find themselves immersed in the work and thus they ask for additional time). Next, they explore and refine their work by inviting a trusted friend to provide substantive comments.

At the beginning of Step V, students have quite a lot of material in front of them to use as reference: class notes taken about the topic, vocabulary words discussed and explored, their own annotation regarding connections that they made with the text, and their own shape and transition banks. Some students have difficulties beginning the work, and so I use the following scaffolding strategy.

Teacher question: 'What is your goal for right now?'
Sometimes a student's response is 'I don't know', accompanied with an indifferent shrug.
Teacher reminds the student that a classroom involves thinking and figuring things out.
Teacher takes a seat and indicates that he/she is not moving until a substantive answer is received.
(I am yet to have this strategy fail with any of my teenagers, especially those with limited schooling or compliance issues.)

Teacher question: 'Where should you write your goal down?'

Student points to notebook and begins to write.

Teacher question: 'Is five minutes enough for you to figure this out and write the answer down?'[6]

Student answers.

Teacher final comment: 'I am setting the timer for 5 minutes and will be back to check on you'.

When I revisit the student, in order to assess progress, I check to see if the student's answer includes both previously developed material and newly created material. In many cases, the process of putting together kinesthetic representations involves self-talk (see also Chapter 6). Self-talk is an affirmation strategy for evolving knowledge and understanding, and should be encouraged by teachers. Upon noticing self-talk, a teacher should listen and attempt to identify misconceptions which can be addressed immediately. Teachers should be prepared for self-talk to generate a low level of voices coming from different ends of the room, and this might seem to be a distraction – but students are actually working independently and making progress.

Since much of the instructional time is dedicated to this step, a teacher should observe students as they are working, and approach to check-in with students when it seems that a student is 'stuck', needs assistance, or just to make sure that students are using their time efficiently. One strategy I like to use is advance warning: in an agreed-upon longer amount of time (such as 15 or 20 minutes), give 5 minutes, then 3 minutes and finally 1 minute warnings prior to the timer going off. This gives students an opportunity to request additional time (which I usually need to negotiate given the overall time allotted within the lesson). My philosophy about learning guides my decision in this matter. That is, if I see that students are working efficiently I tend to allow them the additional time requested. If students are not using their time efficiently, I see no reason for the time extension. Similarly, in the event that one student is interrupting or wasting time, I speak with them outside of the room to check for issues and problems, and to reorient them. I find that with teenagers, who are highly irritable and sensitive, speaking privately can yield tremendous results.

Step VI: Rehearsing group work

The teacher instructs learners to rehearse their kinesthetic presentation and be prepared to explain it verbally to the entire class. During students' work, the teacher rotates among the groups, making him or herself available to answer questions or provide clarification. Listening to students' discussions and reasoning is key in helping to keep students on task and able to make kinesthetic connections to abstract material. Using positive comments with students is a strategy that builds a strong sense of trust between the teacher and students. 'I'm impressed that you are listening respectfully to each other's comments; this helps both of you to stay focused', or 'Your comment to your friend was specific, which will help her to refine her presentation further' are some comments which I often repeat.

Step VII: Final review and rehearsal

The teacher calls for everyone's attention and instructs each individual or group to rehearse their presentation one last time. This step takes but a couple of minutes.

Step VIII: Class presentations

Each group demonstrates its work (kinesthetic, written, and oral explanation) to the entire class. At the end of each demonstration the group explains their work process. The teacher facilitates a discussion between the presenting group and the 'audience' with the purpose of clarifying and answering questions. This step could take up to 20 minutes, depending on how many students or groups are presenting.

Step IX: Final performance and summary

The teacher instructs all groups to perform their kinesthetic representations one last time in unison. To make this happen, classroom furniture is shifted to accommodate the performing students. The teacher then concludes the session by calling on students to summarize key concepts and vocabulary essential for this unit. I have worked in classrooms which were too small, or with large teenagers, making it necessary to divide the number of performers into several smaller groups. Yet combining groups to perform together is beneficial: first, because it is a good way to have students' sharing a space while still focusing on their own presentations; and second, because it allows the 'audience' to choose whether to look at the overall impression of all the dances, or whether to focus on one student or group – either way, it advances the viewer's point of view and helps them to appreciate the movements as they are performed live.

Application of KTM in a Title I American public school

Introduction

For the past 8 years I have been working as a teacher of English for Students of Other Languages (ESOL) in Fairfax County Public Schools (FCPS), one of the largest and most prestigious school systems in the United States. As an ESOL teacher, I have been fortunate to be asked to work with relatively small groups of students whose other teachers indicated that the general classroom instruction did not yield the progress expected in reading. Thus, I have been given the freedom to design instruction such that the county's curriculum is taught on one hand, while simultaneously implementing instruction that yielded the most results. Specifically, I have worked with elementary and middle school students (8–15 years old) providing reading, writing and comprehension instruction.[7]

Students' background

An ESOL teacher in FCPS is responsible for providing language services to immigrant students who received the bulk of their schooling in countries outside of the United States, and/or students whose parents indicated that the primary language spoken at home is one other than English. The majority of the students I have been working with represent a segment of the population which only recently immigrated to the United States, has limited literacy skills in their own language, and who have minimal financial stability.

Teaching children[8] for 9 months of the year, 5 days a week, about an hour on average every day, allowed me to assess very closely their readiness to be successful in school. Whether it is young children (7 to 10 years old), or teenagers (12 to 15 years old), they all bring both challenges and advantages to the teaching–learning process. Common to both groups of students is that they all begin the year thinking that dance and movement have nothing to do with learning abstract concepts in the classroom, and are initially hesitant to use movement as part of their learning. They all have some background or understanding of social dance, with the minority having significant experience dancing in their communities (dances such as break-dance, hip hop or salsa) or taking dance classes in a local dance studio. All have less than basic English skills which requires an extensive use of pictures and sentence frames[9] in order to begin communicating the most basic daily needs.

Both groups of students had other common traits. The first was that they all had difficulty following multi-step instructions (with the exception of a few young girls in the elementary level[10]), which therefore required my repeated cueing[11] in order to teach them to become self-reliant on reference material (class notes, dictionaries and thesauruses to name a few), all of which were made available during instruction. The second trait was that almost all students, regardless of their age, were not proficient writers. To be specific, their rate of producing the stick figures was very slow, as was their rate of reading, and their comfort level when reading their own writing or the anchor charts posted in the classroom. For the older students, this could have been explained by both interrupted schooling and by previous schooling that did not emphasize reading and writing. Finally, everyone (regardless of age) had limited basic communication skills. In order to understand each other, we used a variety of strategies: students helping each other to translate from their home language into English; use of picture and student dictionaries including online dictionaries; and use of thesauruses (hardcopy as well as online) to find words that best expressed our thoughts. Once the exact words were found, I modeled numerous times what students meant to say to create a language rich environment[12] which I supported with visuals and vocabulary word walls.[13]

There were also differences between the two groups of students. My elementary school boys seemed to be fascinated with movements and were eager to dance whenever the opportunity presented itself. The great level of energy the boys demonstrated, however, led to the need to explain how to use the space safely so that no one hurt themselves. The girls, on the other hand, were more cautious when using movements: their kinesthetic representations seemed less vigorous and much more calculated than those of the boys. My middle school students, on the other hand, were extremely conscious about what their classmates were going to say about them. They also had minimal patience listening to the teacher or addressing their own needs. Many tended to be dismissive of adults and classwork and thus they took significantly longer before they were able to focus on kinesthetic representations and getting their work accomplished. A great deal of preparation and practice was needed in order to establish behavioral parameters, which were essential in an effective classroom environment. These behavioral parameters included: (a) observing someone's dance performance patiently and quietly without making any comments or using distracting body language; (b) making respectful comments by phrasing them as questions with the goal on understanding the performer's intent rather than providing general impressions; and (c) offering suggestions only upon the performer's request.

The middle school students needed a great deal of practice before they were able to feel comfortable with their own movements. A few strategies were used to increase their level of comfort using KTM. First, KTM's Steps II and III were used as warm-ups prior to doing anything else. Second, application of Steps II and III was undertaken when breaks were needed. Third, implementation of Steps II and III began with a time limit of just a few minutes and then gradually increased over time as students' stamina increased. Fourth, I spent time explaining the value of being able to state clearly one's thoughts. Specifically, the most rewarding use of KTM was when students were able to coherently explain how the movements they performed were related to or reflected the abstract concept in discussion. Since none of the students had much experience interpreting movement, the performer needed to enact their kinesthetic sequence clearly, and explain it coherently so that the observers were convinced that the kinesthetic representation did actually reflect what was intended.[14] Fifth, allowing ESOL students to explain themselves in their native language, before finding the words to describe the same in English, helped to build confidence. The logic behind this strategy was based on the students' obvious frustration when they would attempt to say something in English, but could not find the words to express themselves, so would throw their hands in the air and make angry remarks in Spanish. They proceeded to tell me that they knew how to express themselves in Spanish, and so I encouraged them to answer in Spanish. My next step was to coach the students to work together to translate the thought into English. It was remarkable to see how a group of teenagers worked together to help one member find the words to express him/herself. Once I understood what they meant to say, I rephrased the statements into grammatically correct sentences. This process showed students that reaching a coherent thought could be done in any language, including English.

Regardless of the age group, I found that my ESOL students needed specific instruction in three curricular areas, all of which are related to reading. The first is sight words, the second is homophones, and the last is identifying and using adjectives. The following section provides examples of teaching sight words and homophones by implementing KTM.

Sight words instruction

Understanding the term 'sight words', and mastering the group of words that are a part of this vocabulary pool, i.e., their meaning and spelling, helps to create a strong foundation in English as a written and spoken language. In American schools, sight words instruction is included in every kindergarten through to fourth grade. ESOL students who possess limited literacy even in their own mother tongue, and who have no background in English, need to receive this instruction regardless of their age. The following section explains the concept of sight words, and provides an example of a classroom lesson using KTM.

What are sight words?

Sight words are common English words that are found in every text no matter its difficulty.[15] Words such as 'I', 'am', 'you', 'here', 'her', etc. are so prevalent that it is critical that young children learn them quickly to support their reading. The problem with these words is that most do not follow common phonemic rules, and this hinders spelling accuracy and the ability to remember meaning. In addition, English is not a phonetic language – meaning that many English words' spelling does not represent their pronunciation. For example, the word 'four' includes a silent *u* which is an exception to the sound the vowel *u* would make in words such as 'us', 'upon' and 'under'.

Moreover, English has numerous homophones, such as the words 'for' and 'four', which have completely different meanings although they sound exactly the same. Another example of homophones is 'to', 'too' and 'two'. All three sound exactly the same, but their spelling is different. The sound the letter *o* makes in the word 'to', does not follow the pattern of the sound it makes in words such as 'orange', 'oil' or 'olive'. Why is the word 'too' spelled with a double letter *o*, rather than the letter *u*? What is the phonetic logic for the spelling of the letter 'two'? These questions represent the complexity of the issues of homophones and sight words, both of which ESOL students need to master. Below is a lesson designed to teach this curriculum by implementing KTM.

Lesson 1: Introduce the spelling of sight words and homophones 'to', 'two' and 'too'

Objective: students will be able to distinguish the kinesthetic difference between the spellings of these homophones, and remember the meaning of these words from recalling the context in which they are used.

Step 1: Verbal and visual introduction

Introduction: 'Good morning friends. Today we'll learn words that don't spell the way they sound. Before we begin we'll figure out if we know the spelling of the words I'm going to teach you. After you write the words down, we'll have a fun activity that will help us remember the spelling of these words. If you're not sure about the spelling of these words now, don't worry about it because you'll be an expert by the end of class.' Implement a pretest: Distribute preprinted index cards with students' names; the teacher dictates the words to students who write them down; then the cards are collected. Results are analyzed later.

Steps II and III: Creating individualized shape and transition banks

Since KTM has been previously introduced, practiced and annotated in my classroom, I am referring to this material and asking students to go back and look at their notes, then to dance these shapes and transitions to music.[16]

Step IV: Introduction of curricular content

I explain: 'Many words in English are not spelled the way they sound. Many words sound the same but are spelled differently, which means they all have different meaning. We need to learn the correct spelling of these words so that when we write them down we write what we mean. Let's take a look at the words "to", "too" and "two".'

I ask students if they know the different meanings of these words and write each word on my lined easel paper. Next, we explore together a context for each of these words. I model three sentences that put these words in context (see Figure 2.2), and then invite students to share their own sentences.

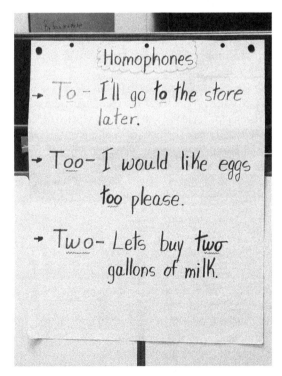

Figure 2.2 Putting homophones into sentences to explore context.

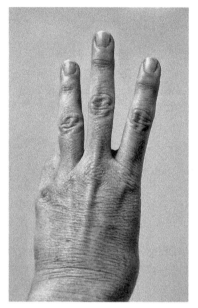 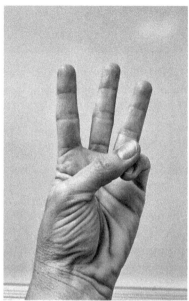

Figure 2.3 Using your fingers to represent the letter *W*.

We continue by creating a short movement phrase for each word (based on our previously created shapes and transitions). The phrase represents the spelling of the word in context. I begin with a demonstration:

'In order to remember that the word "two" includes the letters *W* and *O* in order, I'm going to flash three fingers to represent the letter *W*.' (see Figure 2.3).

Immediately afterwards I'm going to create the letter *O*. I explain to students that the order of my movements needs to mirror the correct spelling of the word and that I am also going to move in space in the same direction I would write the word (i.e., from left to right). In this case, I will execute the letter *T* prior to *W* followed by the *O*. I choose a sentence that will place the word two in context: 'I have two legs.' I proceed with modeling how I am going to dance the spelling of the word 'two' (see Figure 2.4).

Steps V to IX: Involving exploration, rehearsal and presentations

The bulk of the kinesthetic work, and the ability to use dance as a means for advancing cognitive processes is created in these steps. Implementing these steps successfully would require allowing the following to take place.

Students are given time to 'dive into' their own work. While elementary grade students may begin working immediately, teenagers are more concerned with how they look and what their peers think of them. I use portable easels in my classroom as dividers to help my teenagers focus on their kinesthetic representations and thus accomplish the required work.

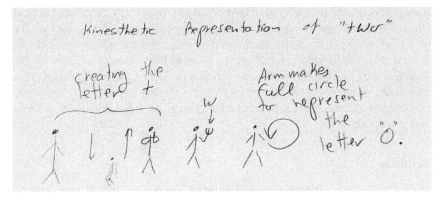

Figure 2.4 Kinesthetic representation of 'two'.

I video the students throughout this process and certainly during the presentation, then proceed to share the recording with them.[17] I find that during the first few recording and sharing sessions, teenagers are more focused on their overall appearance. With time and experience they are much more able to focus on the quality of the dancing and its representation. Comments that teenagers share during the first few viewings of the video often include; 'This is so embarrassing', 'I hate how I look', 'I don't want to look at myself' and 'I don't want anyone to see me dance'. However, comments that were shared once the students gained experience using movement and looking at movement in terms of what it represented were quite different: 'I was really focusing on my dancing . . . it felt good', 'My dancing really showed the sentence I was thinking about', 'I like this way of learning; I can move any way I want' and 'I like that the teacher lets me make my own sentences'. Perhaps the most powerful comment has been: 'I feel I have a voice and I remember things better this way'. The comments at the beginning of the process demonstrate that the students did not intuitively or easily connect with kinesthetic represent-ations because they brought their insecurities and inhibitions to the process. Most of that changed the more we practiced using KTM and discussing the negative effects of giving mean and unappreciative comments to each other.

I am very involved with my students during these steps. While it is true that I allow my students to set the path of their learning, I do touch base with them frequently to make sure that they are staying on task. At the end of this repeated touching-base process, I have a strong idea which students have grasped both the spelling and meaning of the words taught, and which still struggle. During Step VIII (which is when students present their dances, discuss their narratives and explain how their dances reflect their sentences), I take notes on each student's or group's presentation (see Appendix V – online – for a rubric I commonly use). After this step, we review what we have learned and how to remember each word. I ask the students: What makes remembering spelling easy? What makes it hard? Why do you think it is hard? This is an opportunity to explain that remembering new abstract information rests on both how well we understand it and on how strong the connections are between the new and the previously established inform-ation. If students want to remember the spelling of particular words, they need to help themselves see the words over and over again and attempt to remember the context which facilitated the spelling. In order to help students retain what they have learned, I assign homework, which is a review of the material learned as well as an upcoming quiz (the date of which I do not share with students as I would like them to internalize the information for general use rather than for a particular date and time).

Reflection

My personal goal working with this specific student population is to help the students improve their reading level, which historically has been numerous years below grade level. Specific areas identified as critical for improvement were: (a) increase of their active[18] and passive[19] vocabulary, (b) expand their background knowledge of many topics, and (c) enable them to discuss intelligently both fiction and non-fiction texts. For this to take place the students would need to have sufficient topic-specific vocabulary and a basic understanding of sentence structure.

Two sets of data were recorded with the elementary and middle school grade levels. The first examined sight words spelling at the beginning of the year (BOY) vs. the end of the year (EOY), and the second recorded students' reading level at the BOY, and at the EOY. Overall, 92% of the students increased their perfor-mance by more than 14%, with 47% of the students increasing their achievement by 35% from an average of 65% to a perfect score. Also, 53% of the students increased their academic achievement by 12%, from an average of 55% accuracy to 77% accuracy.

The reading achievement data demonstrated that 90% of the students increased their reading level by at least two grade levels within one academic year. Of the students who were tested with the entrance level testing kit (The Bench Mark Assessment),[20] 100% increased their reading level by an average of five (letter) levels. One student did not make any improvement in reading fluency, but this student was suspected to have a reading disability. Interestingly, he did pass all of the 8th grade language arts standards.

Numerous strategies played a role in this academic achievement. The first factor was understanding students' life circumstances and responding to their crises in real time. Specifically, my students brought minimal schooling experience from their home country, on top of which they had to deal with an unstable home-life: an only-parent father who had a car accident and could not provide for his daughter; and a mother who had just lost her unborn baby having no husband, but her 13- and 10-year-old daughters to support her. My students would come to class looking depressed, would put their head down on the desk with eyes closed, and would not participate or make eye contact with anyone. After the initial touching-base and giving basic instructions to the class, I would speak to them individually outside the classroom. I had to listen, show compassion, and find a way to help them refocus on what they could do and how to be successful with the learning at hand. Only then, could I turn to focusing on KTM.

The second strategy implemented consistently was KTM, which gave us all an opportunity to set personal goals on top of lesson goals. Students reached these goals by being given the trust and freedom to work on their own, or with a partner if needed, and to be accountable for their own work. KTM offered an alternative to what could have been a regimented classroom experience[21] by incorporating a variety of stimuli, activities and opportunities to learn via various modalities.

Thirdly, I incorporated a great deal of discussion as a way to establish comprehension. Melissa Hare Landa believes that writing begins with conversation (2005). To expand her definition, I believe that writing begins with a specific awareness of an idea expressed via words. Thus, daily instruction included a discussion[22] to help the students place the target words within a relevant context. The goal was to encourage students to share what they knew of a topic, and to allow them to ask questions and make statements. If there was a need to build background knowledge, I would use my computer and a variety of databases and internet sources to source visuals, videos, interviews or anything that could advance students' interest in the topic. Our conversation helped students learn how to frame their thoughts and ideas into grammatically correct sentences arranged in an order which stated the topic and included examples and discussion.

The fourth strategy for academic achievement was tactile stimuli, i.e., writing. I used writing as a medium for students to express their thoughts and define their intentions. Their notebooks included words taught, additional words that they were interested in, illustrations to support the meaning of these words as well as stick figures representing sight words in phrases, and sentences they created that helped them remember the content taught. The students treasured these notebooks because they functioned as an authentic source of reference for them.

I also included musical–rhythmic stimuli. Whenever possible, I attempted to integrate a rhythm to the context taught so that it could be remembered with greater ease. Students who were musically and performance inclined seemed to 'inhale' these rhythms as if they were air. My bias towards rhythm and music aside (which was a good enough reason for me to incorporate music and rhythm in the classroom),[23] I noticed that my students were glued to their telephones where they watched and listened to music videos virtually nonstop. While not all students loved singing the jingles which I made up, it seems that their memory was awakened as soon as I hummed the rhythm or melody. Just hearing the melody allowed the abstract concepts to surface, i.e., they were able to demonstrate what they had learned. This phenomenon was observed with all students regardless of age, gender or country of origin.

Guided reading was my sixth strategy: a method for differentiated reading[24] with small groups of students while others were working independently. Guided reading allows a teacher to meet with several small groups on a rotating basis each lesson. My teenage students may have looked like young adults, but emotionally, they were craving the chance to work with an adult in a small group situation where they could ask questions that they would not like to ask in front of the entire class. We met at the 'Guided Reading Corner' in my classroom. The area was set up so that they were facing me and our books, while I was facing the classroom. This gave them the feeling that whatever was in discussion was discrete. Each group read a text according to their reading level, and thus made progress in reading fluency and comprehension.

The last strategy that helped my students was a shift from tests to unannounced quizzes. I did this because I believe that what is taught at school is information useful for life and therefore it needs to be retained long term. My students took some time before they got accustomed to this notion as they were used to studying the night before a test only to forget the information as soon as the test was over.

Implementing KTM: Dos and don'ts

If you have been a classroom teacher for a while, you will be familiar with the often-repeated 'I'm finished' declarations that students produce as soon as they think they have finished a task. In my experience, and especially in recent years, many students confuse quality with speed and thus making this declaration seems more important to them than the process of learning itself. Obviously, some students are both meticulous and quick to produce high quality work, but for many, the 'I'm finished' statement is really an expression of 'I'm not sure what else I should be working on' or 'I'm tired and am in need of a break'. To take advantage of the 'I'm finished' statement, I check-in with the student, and ask a series of questions including:

- What have you been working on?
- What concepts have you incorporated?
- Show me your annotations! Are you able to read them? What stood out for you?
- What, of all the material we have covered, can I expect to see in your kinesthetic demonstration?
- Have you practiced your dance? Is it flawless? Are you able to explain to the audience each part of it?

Then I ask the student to demonstrate his/her kinesthetic phrase. If a student seems to be anxious, tired or lacks focus, I state that now is a perfect time for a 3 minute break. I instruct the students to get some water, use the restroom, or take a minute and close their eyes. When we reconvene, we pick up where we left off. I ask the student to break down his or her kinesthetic representation into segments and explain each one. At this point, I provide feedback and ask questions to make sure that the student understands the purpose of each shape and transition in their kinesthetic representation. I listen to specific vocabulary related to our lesson that would demonstrate understanding of the material taught.

With respect to implementing KTM within a block schedule,[25] I organize my block as follows: quickly touching base with the students (1 minute), an introduction to the concept to be taught (1 minute), a kinesthetic warm-up (5 minutes), a mini lesson which explores the concept even further[26] (20 minutes), time for students to develop KTM representation of the concept (30 minutes),[27] performance (20 minutes), reflection/discussion (7 minutes), connection to tomorrow's lesson (1 minutes), and clean-up (3 minutes). Additional tactile, visual and auditory activities are found in Appendix VI (online).

In thinking about the implementation of KTM with children as opposed to teenagers, it seems that while both groups become happy to move in space, the teenagers are so self-conscious that some time needs to be allotted to teaching them how to use movement effectively, and explaining to them the cognitive benefits of using kinesthetic stimuli for their own advancement. This type of explanation is not necessary with young children as they are eager to dance and are intuitively able to make the connections you hope they will make. Teenagers may resist and mock your attempts to use movement in the classroom, but they definitely appreciate when a teacher sticks to her guns and finds a way to get them to fully commit to the learning process. One student has even stated: 'We wanted to see if we could break you'. In other words, some teenagers will deliberately misbehave in order to test their teacher because they view authority as a power challenge.

Summary

At the beginning of my career as an educator, I have spent a significant amount of time studying instructional theory and brain function as related to teaching and learning. Up until 2010, I was able to develop KTM under close-to-perfect conditions, i.e., I had sufficient time, and complete freedom to make instructional decisions based solely on children's needs. As a practitioner working in public schools, these conditions changed. I have received a great deal of guidance as to what to teach, when to teach, how often to teach, and who to teach. That said, due to my placement as an ESOL teacher, I was asked (based on supporting data) to work with students who clearly needed to be taught in a small class environment, being offered a non-traditional teaching approach. I have been able to maintain the freedom to decide how to teach which has allowed me to first build meaningful and trusting relationship with my students, and second, has led my students to see substantial improvements in their own reading. One of my students commented at the end of last year: 'I never thought I would like learning, but I do now after you made me use this KTM stuff'.

Using many of my instructional strategies has enabled me to flawlessly manage my classroom, and KTM has proven an essential fertilizer for differentiated instruction. Yet my work is still not complete, as there are still some unanswered questions. Will students be able to retain over time the spelling which they learned via KTM? Will this retention be maintained when students return to spend their entire day in the regular (large size) classroom where KTM is not used? And perhaps most importantly, have students internalized KTM so that they could use it on their own in the future when needed? These are all questions which a longitudinal researcher might want to study one day.

A thank you note

Eternal thanks to Terry Phillips, Karim Daugherty and Yusef Azimi; my principals for the past 8 years, who have given me the opportunity to implement KTM, along with my other instructional strategies, in order to expand the learning opportunities of our second-language learners.

Notes

1 Memory-enhancing techniques included mnemonics, rhythm and songs, index cards, indexing, bulleting, and the use of color and highlighting, among others.
2 For the sake of this discussion, 'traditional classroom' is one that does not include any substantive dance approach for the purpose of teaching academic content. This was verified after a conversation with these students' classroom teacher.
3 See Appendix I (online) for specific shape parameters.
4 The term 'style' is loaned from music: *staccato* meaning movements that occur and seize repeatedly; *legato* meaning movements that are performed in a smooth and connected manner (with no stops); and *marcato* meaning movements performed with emphasis.
5 This process mirrors the annotation process which is taught in the English classes in American middle schools. In essence, students are required to respond to text by using symbols that represent connections they made to the text while reading. See Appendix II (online) for a complete chart of text annotations.
6 Five minutes is a negotiable amount of time which, given student input, can be changed.
7 Instruction included building basic and intermediate level vocabulary, sight words, development in various subjects, and improving reading fluency and stamina as well as writing expression.
8 I use the word 'children' to mean students from 6 to 15 years old.
9 Sentence frames are common sentences which are used every day. They are written on sentence strips and posted in the classroom so that students are able to use them when needed. Sentence frames include a missing word so that students can adapt the sentence to a particular situation. See Appendix III (online) for sentence frame examples.
10 These girls showed a tremendous amount of care and willingness to please, which resulted in them being able to use the posted instructions on their own.
11 Cueing was always framed as a question. For example, 'What are you supposed to do next?', 'Where is that posted in the classroom?' and 'In your own words, what will you get accomplished next?'
12 A 'language rich environment' is a commonly used term in the field of education, meaning a setting created by the teacher where students are able to hear spoken English in different situations and practice speaking it in a supportive environment.
13 'Visuals' and 'word walls' are concepts in creating a language rich environment in the elementary grades. Visuals are (highly engaging) pictures, both printed as well as projected directly from a computer onto the board, and word walls are large vertical spaces in the classroom where words taught to students are posted for reference and later use.
14 The performance aspect included in KTM served as a great motivator for students because they wanted to produce a demonstration that was flawless. Knowing that they needed to feel confident during their presentation helped them to practice their kinesthetic representations over and over again.
15 See Appendix IV (online) for sight words taught in each American grade.
16 These steps take about 3 minutes. Of course, depending on the instructional time used, teachers could use a longer time segment here in order to develop a larger shape and transition bank.

17   Make sure you ask permission to video tape students. You may also need to check with your school office to see if parental permission for video was granted. I first share the video with the individual student, and only upon their consent do I then share the video with other students.
18   Active vocabulary is the vocabulary that students know and are using voluntarily.
19   Passive vocabulary is the vocabulary that students know but are not using voluntarily.
20   The Bench Mark Assessment is a product of Fountas and Pinnell, which Fairfax County Public School uses to assess beginning reading levels; see: www.fountasandpinnell. com/bas/.
21   A regimented classroom experience is one where the teacher gives a lecture, lasting most of the instructional time, followed by time to complete worksheets.
22   To clarify: a discussion is different to a lecture. My discussion included a question posed, followed by a conversation about the question through which a variety of vocabulary words and concepts were developed, clarified and learned.
23   This bias was established because music and rhythm have helped me to memorize sets of information which I could not otherwise recall.
24   Differentiated reading allows a teacher to group students according to their reading level, to select appropriate texts for each group, and therefore to dedicate each reading session to the group's comprehension or fluency needs.
25   The school's block schedule allots 88 minutes (rather than 44 minutes) for each subject.
26   My mini lessons open with an explanation of the concept to be studied. I then project examples on the board which feature various difficulty levels, to be analyzed and written down by the students. Next there is an opportunity for students to create and share their own examples. Finally, the concept becomes more abstract, so that students get to practice thinking critically by eliminating examples based on a given rule.
27   This element takes the longest because it incorporates thinking in the abstract, writing, reasoning out loud and kinesthetic practice.

References

BenZion, G. (2010). Overcoming the dyslexia barrier: The role of kinesthetic stimuli in the teaching of spelling. In: B. Blasing, M. Puttke & T. Schack (Eds.), *The Neurocognition of Dance: Mind, movement and motor skills* (pp. 123–150). New York: Psychology Press.
Landa, H. M. (2005). *Listening to Young Writers: Developing writing competency through conversation, engagement and assessment.* Gainesville, FL: Maupin House.

Further reading

Crowther, D. S. (2003). *Key Choral Concepts: Teaching techniques and tools to help your choir sound great.* Springville, UT: Horizon Publishers.
Evan Moor Educational Publishers. (2007). *Word Family Stories and Activities.* Monterey, CA: Evan Moor.
Evan Moor Educational Publishers. (2008). *High Frequency Words: Stories and activities (level B).* Monterey, CA: Evan Moor.
Evan Moor Educational Publishers. (2008). *Phonics Games: Centers for up to 6 players (Grades K-1).* Monterey, CA: Evan Moor.
Evan Moor Educational Publishers. (2008). *Phonics Games: Centers for up to 6 players (Grades K-2).* Monterey, CA: Evan Moor.
Fountas, I. C. & Pinnell, G. S. (2001). *Guiding Readers and Writers: Teaching comprehension, genre, and content literacy.* Portsmouth, NH: Heinemann.

Frank Schaffer Publications. (2007). *Phonics (grade 2).* Greeensboro, NC: Frank Schaffer Publications.

Hajdusiewicz, B. B. (1997). *More! Phonics Through Poetry: Teaching phonemic awareness using poetry.* Culver City, CA: Good Year Books.

Lynch, J. (2005). *Making Word Walls Work: A complete, systematic guide with routines, grade-perfect word lists, and reproducible word cards to help all children master high-frequency words.* New York: Scholastic Inc.

Miller, D. (2007). *Making the Most of Small Groups: Differentiation for all.* Portland, ME: Stenhouse Publishers. Northeast Foundation for Children. (2007). *Responsive Classroom: Level 1 resource book.* Turners Falls, MA: Northeast Foundation for Children, Inc.

Onish, L. B. (2004). *Reading Skills Card Games Sight Words.* New York: Scholastic Inc.

Scholastic Inc. (2002). *100 Write-and-Learn Sight Words Practice Pages (Grades K-2).* New York: Scholastic, Inc.

Scholastic Inc. (2003). *Write-and-Learn Word Family Practice Pages (Grades K-2).* New York: Scholastic Inc.

3 In-Sync

Entrainment in dance

Elizabeth Waterhouse

This is a chapter about the phenomenon of *entrainment*, a discussion that I would like to motivate by a short case study from the field of contemporary dance. Entrainment names the process through which entities become synchronized and/or rhythmically coordinated. In the scientific literature about animals entraining their movement to a beat, or conversation partners entraining their speech patterns and gestures; the term 'dance' is sometimes used as a metaphor to describe this quality of rhythmical relation (Ancona and Waller, 2007; Hall, 1984; Schmidt et al., 2014). Here, approaching the discussion of entrainment from my perspective as dancer and dance scholar, I discuss the potential and challenges that entrainment can bring as a concept for analyzing interaction between dancers. In this chapter I chart a path beginning and ending with the practice of choreographer William Forsythe: from the motivating artistic example of William Forsythe's choreography *Duo* (1996–2016), through the scientific literature, and then returning with a refrain to entrainment in ballet history and the examples of William Forsythe's contemporary pieces *Artifact* (1984) and *Eidos:Telos* (1995). Through this I intend to show the value of introducing a more nuanced notion of entrainment, to describe the processes already active in the field. Not just in-sync with the music, entrainment is a confluence of motoric, communicative and social competencies.

Introduction: The case study of William Forsythe's *Duo* (1996–2016)

People are dancing together – someway, somehow. What do you envision? Perhaps ballet dancers moving in formations upon a stage? Or a Ghanaian gathering involving a rich texture of sound with drummers, singers and dancers? Or a small club, filled with couples weaving and bobbing with similar, but not identical, rhythms? In my case, I am reflecting upon a duet from my own dance lineage—a choreography called *Duo* by William Forsythe (see Box 3.1).

The duet premiered on 20 January 1996 at the Ballett Frankfurt. After a blackout, fluorescent lights turn on to reveal two women at the front of an empty stage, standing before a black velvet curtain. Their black leotards are nearly but not *precisely* identical – a fact that eluded me until the performers pointed it out in interviews over 20 years later.[1] The dancers wait, focusing straight ahead. Since they face the same oblique angle and are separated by more than half the width of the stage, they cannot see each other's faces. The dance begins with movement synchronization: entrainment. The first motion of unison takes place without an overt visual or musical cue to precipitate it. The dancers do not exchange eye contact, nor is there music at the beginning of the piece. The dancers begin with breathing together, giving subtle amplitude and airy consistency to their motion, and helping them to bind their time. When the dancers hear that the audience is hushed, feel that they have adjusted to the light and intuit that they are both ready, they commence a delicate curved motion – unwinding their right arm and stepping backwards to a pose (*tendu*), inhaling and exhaling.

Since 1996, *Duo* has been performed in Ballett Frankfurt/The Forsythe Company by only a small number of two female or two male dancers (primarily Regina van Berkel, Jill Johnson (see Figure 3.1) and Allison Brown; and since 2013 a version for men performed by Brigel Gjoka and Riley Watts). Regina van Berkel and Riley Watts both confirmed that the beginning of the piece is very difficult for the dancers; the neon lights are harsh and at times one's heart is fluttering in anticipation of performance. One is also very far away from one's partner, a separation at odds with the intimacy of the piece. Riley Watts described that when he first learned to dance *Duo,* he would sometimes imagine himself physically connected to his partner, via an extra arm touching his partner's shoulder, so that they would initiate the first movement with one impulse, synchronously.[2] Furthermore, dancer Jill Johnson observed that the first movement of unison was not the start of entrainment, but actually part of a larger process:

> The entire trajectory of the piece stems from the intimacy and entrainment between the dancers from preparations prior to the piece, to the moment we would walk on stage in the dark, dance the piece together and even beyond the bows and finishing the piece.[3]

Over the course of *Duo*'s history from 1996 to 2016, the choreography, as well as the music for piano and acoustics composed by Thom Willems, have been revised. Despite these changes, the dancers affirm that the essence of *Duo* has stayed the same. With many differences of degree and kind, *Duo* is a dance involving the interplay of synchrony – what dancer Allison Brown has described as:

> [. . .] meeting, arising and coming to each other and being in unison and being out of unison, in aligning and disaligning, but staying together; and this seeing each other with other senses and other body parts than the eyes.[4]

Dancer Riley Watts has described *Duo* as pertaining to the art of elastic temporal integrity. Dancer Brigel Gjoka recounted that *Duo* is something that you live, rather than do.[5]

I have begun this chapter on entrainment, or the process whereby entities become synchronized and/or rhythmically coordinated, with this in-depth account of *Duo,* to suggest the details of the case study that have motivated my investigation of this

Figure 3.1 Regina van Berkel (*left*) and Jill Johnson (*right*) performing William
   Forsythe's choreography *Duo* (1996). (Photo by Dominik Mentzos.)

concept. The choreography *Duo* by William Forsythe is one in which the dancers'
ability to synchronize is important – both to the performers' descriptions of their
experiences and to spectators' accounts of the reception of the work. This quality
of partnership was shaped by the rehearsal process and context. First, William
Forsythe invented sequences, or phrases of steps. These were then memorized by

---

Box 3.1*   William Forsythe's choreography *Duo

Duo is a work choreographed by William Forsythe with music composed by Thom Willems. The piece is performed by two dancers and is approximately 10–20 minutes in duration. *Duo* premiered on 20 January 1996 on the Ballett Frankfurt program *Six Counter Points.* Female dancers Jill Johnson and Regina van Berkel danced these initial performances of *Duo* with Willems' music for live piano and electronics. After the premier, *Duo* was performed internationally by the Ballett Frankfurt (1996–2004) by different pairs of two female dancers. In 2012–2013, William Forsythe rehearsed *Duo* with new dancers in The Forsythe Company, and male dancers Brigel Gjoka and Riley Watts performed the piece in galas in the German cities of Darmstadt and Weimar. In 2015, Brigel Gjoka and Riley Watts toured a revised version of *Duo,* retitled *DUO2015,* internationally on the *Life in Progress* world tour of Sylvie Guillem; and this version featured a new score by Thom Willems. The 'original' version of *Duo* was licensed to The Curve Foundation in Edinburgh and has entered the repertoire of Ballet de Lyon, Netherlands Dans Theater, CCN – Ballet de Lorraine, Gaulthier Dance and Batsheva Dance Company.

William Forsythe (born 1949) is an American choreographer. He has been active in the field of choreography for over 45 years, most notably as the director of Ballett Frankfurt (1984–2004) and The Forsythe Company (2005–2015). Forsythe's choreographic works and approach to teamwork are acknowledged for reorienting the practice of ballet from its identification with classical repertoire to a dynamic 21st century art form. Asking, 'What else can dance look like?' Forsythe's deep interest in the fundamental principles of organization has led him to produce a wide range of projects including installations, films and web-based knowledge creation. Forsythe is currently Professor of Dance and Artistic Advisor for the Choreographic Institute at the University of Southern California Glorya Kaufman School of Dance.

See: www.williamforsythe.com and http://synchronousobjects.osu.edu

---

the two dancers (Jill Johnson and Regina van Berkel), who learned them while working alone in the choreographer's office, through detailed review of their notes and a video tape. In interviews, both dancers expressed that working so intimately, in a small space that was not a typical rehearsal space, shaped their approach. Regina van Berkel comments that after this:

> We always did the phrases together! It was not that one did that phrase and practiced that phrase alone. No. We went always together. [. . .] We felt, harmonized![6]

Affirming this, the choreographer decided to work with the chemistry that they had acquired. In the archival video of the third rehearsal, Forsythe is heard speaking off camera to Jill Johnson and Regina van Berkel. In one sentence, that accelerates in tempo while diminishing in intensity, Forsythe says: 'I definitely want to do unison [*pause*], and then break it up because not many people can do unison and you two can – so let's do it'.[7]

As a dance scholar, one of my interests is to understand how dancers achieve the expertise of being able to dance together, such as in the example of *Duo*. Another focus is how to produce knowledge about this practice, from the position of a scholar outside of the event. In this short account, I have indicated that the dancers' testimonies show the complicated manner that the skill or skills of entrainment relate to the framing of shared goals within an artistic ensemble, the history of rehearsing and touring a piece, and to the specific spaces and contexts of dancing. What is also important, as dancer Riley Watts has emphasized to me, is how 'personal' and 'nuanced' entrainment can be. In what follows, I focus less on the methodology to research entrainment and more on the existing literature, outlining how the concept of entrainment has migrated from the natural to the biological sciences into studies of music, communication and dance. In so doing I highlight the aspects that I believe are most important for a nuanced treatment of entrainment in the domain of dance research.

Research overview of entrainment

Today, in contemporary French, the word *entrainment* means 'to train oneself', such as the movements that one might perform in a gym. Outside of this colloquial meaning, entrainment has come to name a field of science, in the natural and biological sciences, examining synchronization, or more broadly, rhythmical coordination. Etymologically, the verb *entrain* comes from the French *entraîner* (16th century) – meaning 'to drag away from oneself', or 'to draw as an accompaniment or consequence'. In the late 19th century, the word was used colloquially to describe entering a railway train. Entrainment is also a term for the chemical process of evaporation used in sugar refinement.[8]

In physics, entrainment names the phenomenon whereby rhythmical oscillators interact and stabilize (Rosenblum and Pikovsky, 2003). The first recorded observation of this special synchronization was by Dutch physicist Christiaan Huygens (1629–1695). Huygens, supposedly while lying ill in bed, realized that the two self-made pendulum-clocks he had hung on a wooden beam would, over time, shift from being asynchronous to swaying together in opposite directions (i.e., out of phase). He described this in a letter to the Royal Society of London (1665) as 'an odd kind of sympathy' (Czolczynski et al., 2011). Odd, because Huygens could not see nor mathematically prove the process producing the relation. Huygens first assumed the cause was air currents. After testing this, he eventually deduced there must be micro-movement of the beam between the clocks, movement invisible to the human eye. Physicists later confirmed that this is precisely the case – solving non-linear equations describing how the initial energy of the two clock oscillators was redistributed or shared between the pendulums over time, through the real coupling of the beam.

The physics of oscillation is a broad field, of which entrainment is only one small part. Oscillation refers to a dynamic movement that can be understood as the rhythm or pattern of back and forth motion that can be modeled as waves. The physics of entrainment describes only self-sustaining, coupled independent harmonic oscillators, which over time come in-sync or into a consistent rhythmical relation. This definition is specific. *Self-sustaining* means that the movement of the oscillator is powered internally, without help from an external source (Rosenblum and Pikovsky, 2003; Jenkins, 2013). Resonance is not an example of entrainment, because it is induced by an external energy (i.e., a violin string vibrates in resonance to another violin string that has been plucked). Importantly, entrainment is not a synonym for the phenomenon of self-sustaining oscillation. Rather, two or more independent, self-sustaining oscillators must *couple* or influence each other, so that their rhythms undergo a process of change, leading to stabilization – a dynamic system is produced. This coupling may be material, like Huygen's beam, or achieved through bringing the oscillators close to one another. Once mathematics is involved, it becomes clear to a physicist which types of systems can be categorized as entrainment and which cannot (i.e., specific problems in non-linear system dynamics). For this reason, the physics of entrainment has not been used to model swarm activity.

Since Huygen's time, the development of non-linear mathematics by French mathematician Henri Poincaré (1854–1912) and the recent advent of computational modeling have allowed theorists to understand increasingly complex, even chaotic systems, including examples of entrainment. The study of entrainment has also expanded from inorganic to organic systems – to encompass research of rhythmic interaction in the fields of animal and human biology, human psychology, the social sciences, and in the last decade, ethnomusicology and music perception. Below I highlight several areas of entrainment research in different domains for the purpose of framing the specific concern here – that of entrainment in dance. A more thorough review, undertaken for the neighboring field of music, can be found in Clayton, Sager and Will (2005).

Biological literature adopting the concept of entrainment gained momentum in 1960 with the 10-day symposium 'Biological Clocks' at Cold Spring Harbor Laboratory in New York. This meeting brought 150 international scientists together, including Jürgen Aschoff and Victor Bruce, to discuss timing mechanisms in humans and animals (Bünning, 1960). With daily or circadian rhythms, such as the alignment of human sleep cycles to the light cycle of day and night, it was possible to model the frequencies of these rhythms as oscillators – to consider their interaction and phases of alignment. Biological entrainment was defined as when organisms' internal, or *endogenous*, oscillatory rhythms or motion would synchronize to an external signal or *zeitgeber*, translated as 'time-keeper' (Bruce, 1960). This zeitgeber would provide an external pacing or signal in any mode – such as through light, an auditory rhythm or sound, or a dominant motion. Organisms were hypothesized to have something like internal clocks or circuits regulating their timing propensities, thus keeping with the self-oscillation principle of entrainment. In the last two decades, scientists have analyzed: the synchronous blinking of fireflies; circadian entrainment of human sleep cycles to light cycles; people tapping their fingers to a beat or jogging to music; dancers performing the Samba and the Charleston in the lab; and jazz trios playing in London clubs. Turning to the rhythms of brain dynamics and activation, research of entrainment has also examined neural entrainment to a stimulus of a musical beat and meter with EEG measurements (Nozaradan et al., 2011).

The concept of entrainment has also been incorporated within the social sciences, especially within organizational theory, and in sociology. In the former, scholars have asked how pacing agents shape the organization of teams' activity – analyzing how it is revealed empirically through the employees' negotiation of deadlines, changes in working tempo, or via other cues and signals. In this domain, entrainment has been defined as the adjustment of pace or cycle of an activity to match or synchronize with that of another activity (Ancona and Chong, 1996). Such studies make use of quantitative methods in the social sciences for marking events in time and analyzing coincidences and rhythms within these data architectures, extracted from testimony and fieldwork (Ancona and Waller, 2007). These methods, different from phase analysis, show the methodological split in empirical research of entrainment; meaning, studies may consider time-based data as phase-based, or rhythms marked by discrete events over time, or both of these (Iqbal and Riek, 2016).

In addition to organizational science, sociological theory has also been impacted by the concept of entrainment. Collins (2013) has described that, 'when persons are physically nearby, recognize that each other is attending to the same thing, and share a similar emotion, a process is set off that builds rhythmical entrainment.' Collins (2004) links this tendency to the sociological concept of *effervescence* by Émile Durkheim. The association of entrainment and emotion is not specific to sociological literature. In their study of musical activity and parent–child interactions, Phillips-Silver and Keller (2012) have named two interlinked and vital components of entrainment: the rhythmicity of the body or bodies in time and an affective synchrony, of sharing a state with another person. Methodology for researching these affective aspects is still preliminary, valuing musician testimony or even the authors' musical expertise (as in Keil, 2010; Leman, 2016). Studies of musical entrainment have generally focused on the positive affects of entrainment (Phillips-Silver and Keller, 2012), rather than asking to what extent musical entrainment is a pleasing phenomenon, and how much this depends on cultural or aesthetic experience (see Clayton, Sager and Will, 2005). Collins' (2013) critical sociological study of entrainment in examples of violence is exceptional in this regard.

At large, the study of entrainment in ethnomusicology has led to a surge of research in the last decade, providing literature that addresses both Western and non-Western forms. A review conducted by Clayton, Sager and Will (2005) promotes how music scholars might research entrainment with regard to the specific experience of music listeners and players, and the structures of composed music. As is in the case here, Clayton and colleagues (2005) advocate for a 'nuanced' understanding of entrainment. Additionally, musicologists have promoted focusing upon the social and embodied aspects of musical entrainment, serving an embodied turn to counter the Western ideal of *absolute music* (Leman, 2016) and also to address non-Western contexts where dance and music are less strictly divided as they are in Western culture (Lewis, 2013; Armstrong, 2016; Plancke, 2014).

The concept of entrainment in music is broad enough to extend to cases of dance. Spanning synchronization and rhythmical coordination, musicians' entrainment is generally understood as 'coordinated rhythmic movement', foregrounding the feedback loop of auditory perception, and involving musical movement and a shared social context (Phillips-Silver, Aktipis and Bryant, 2010). The empirical literature on musical entrainment ranges from single to complex inquiries, such as: tapping one's finger to a beat (Repp, 2005); violinist dyads playing short exercises in the laboratory (Thompson et al., 2015); and a flamenco ensemble consisting of dancers and musicians (Maduell and Wing, 2007). Club situations have been of particular interest, as will be described further in the following section. These studies have examined the variables of tempo and pulse, as well as the interplay of motion with sound production. Despite the help of an overarching definition of entrainment (as coordinated rhythmical motion), analysis of what precisely is understood to be coordinated and rhythmical is warranted (see Waterhouse, Watts and Bläsing, 2014, for further breakdown of the terms 'rhythmical' and 'coordination'). Also in question is whether musical entrainment can also occur at other levels, and to other aspects, such as pitch and timbre (Kouwenhoven, 2005).

Posing overarching themes, Phillips-Silver and Keller (2012) have described common features of entrainment in music. This includes the human abilities of 'turn-taking' or alternating turns, such as in musical call and response structures; 'chorusing' or making unison sounds as in a choir; and 'complementary action', meaning performing different sounds at the same time or rhythmically related music. Phillips-Silver and Keller have also reviewed terminology for the cognitive skills that enable musicians to coordinate their sound: naming the abilities of 'adaptive timing' and 'integrative attending' to different aspects of the overall dyad or group sound, and 'anticipatory imagery' based on shared knowledge of the musical score. In addition to the explicit cues for musicians to begin all together or to follow a conductor, Phillips-Silver and Keller have also described the role of 'coordination smoothers' such as swaying, gesturing, inhaling and giving implicit cues. The extent to which such parameters are also valid in contemporary dance, and in particular the example of William Forsythe's *Duo,* is discussed in detail by Waterhouse, Watts and Bläsing (2014).

Music scholars have also concerned themselves with the range of entrainment, from spontaneous to practiced. At times, entrainment is inadvert, even unintended, as observed in passages played in a North Indian Classical Rage performance, where tanpura rhythms that should be independent demonstrated influence on one another (Clayton, 2007). With regard to the culture of Western music, Leman (2012) has underscored that practice or rehearsal that aims at 'getting synchronization *right*' is required. He points out that, 'in order to musically entrain spontaneously, one has to practice hard'. This emphasizes entrainment as a sensorimotor skill, based on learning and knowledge.

Yet this still does not imply that musicians are able to explain exactly *how* they accomplish entrainment. Concerned with the distinction between knowing-that and knowing-how, jazz and blues musician and music scholar Charles Keil (2010) has proposed that his 'native' terms for entrainment in blues and jazz – 'swing', 'groove', 'in the zone' and 'flow'– are for him synonymous with entrainment. He comments that entrainment is a 'technical term from physics favored by some ethnomusicologists who may be uncomfortable using African–American slang'. He finds common ground in Steven Feld's definition 'in sync but slightly out of phase', which he agrees might be a 'more precise technical definition of entrainment as groove'. Keil's insight is gradually gaining support from empirical studies of time-data of jazz musicians, such as Doffman's (2008) studies of the importance of elastic playing, a bit before and after the beat, for groove in jazz trios. Further study of degrees of entrainment, in the form of elasticities, resistances or synergies, and their link to social factors such as leadership dynamics and cultural preference, are also underway (Alborno et al., 2015).

To conclude this overview of the entrainment literature relevant to studies of entrainment in dance, I would like to turn last to studies in the domain of communication. In contrast to pulse-based entrainment in music or dance, human communication is not necessarily pulse based: rather, it is characterized by prosody and the rhythm of turn-taking among interlocuters (Phillips-Silver, Aktipis and Bryant, 2010). Levinson and Holler (2014) underline that human communication is not purely an acoustic or semantic phenomenon, but rather a multimodal one, involving different senses and modes, including vocal and visual signals, made by the hands, face and body, and often movements of the spine and trunk. Garrod and Pickering (2004) have shown how alignment between partners in dialogue is reached in an interactive way via entrainment on different levels, including the convergence of gesture and body posture, and also the 'interactive alignment' of representations at different linguistic levels. Additionally, communication has been shown to be partner-specific, even involving the formation of 'conceptual pacts', or shared conceptualizations for an object (such as agreeing with me that the first motion in *Duo* is called 'showerhead'; see Brennan and Clark, 1996). Entrainment may also require subjective dimensions that do not become visible to an observer but are experienced by and crucial for the entrained agents (Leman, 2012; Clayton, 2012). Thus, entrainment is likely to be achieved differently by those with and without background knowledge, or histories, or common cultural references. Unresolved questions in entrainment science at large include the limits of entrainment (for example the range of tempi, or the minimal amount of movement required), the manner in which it is learned and the extent to which it is innate, and how broad and codified the affective components are, across cultures and contexts.

Studies of entrainment in dance

In the broad literature cited in the previous section, there are some common metaphoric references to entrainment as a 'dance', even when dance is not the phenomenon of study (Ancona and Waller, 2007; Hall, 1984; Schmidt et al., 2014). From the perspective of dance studies, it is very interesting to consider what characteristics make a phenomenon interpreted as dance-like to people who are not experienced dancers or scholars of dance. In these examples, the perception of corresponding movement and music seems to be a key, as has been noted in other cases of audience preference (Holland, 2004, cf. Lepecki, 2006). Another marker is that the 'dance' produces complexity of organization – as in Ancona and Waller's (2007) interpretation of a software team 'simultaneously creating multiple rhythms and choreographing their actions to mesh with different pacers at different times'. Other literature defines dance specifically as auditory–motor entrainment, or 'the capacity to entrain, or move in time with an auditory pulse' (Schachner, 2013). This equates dance as the ability to align movement to a musical beat. Western choreographers, however, have developed many instances of dance that attest this approach (on Merce Cunningham, see Copeland, 2004; on William Forsythe, see Vass-Rhee, 2010). With more subtle language, one can easily describe this problem. First, that auditory–motor entrainment is a feature common to many dances across cultures, but not without exception. Second, it is a hypothesis that entrainment features broadly in people's understanding of what dance is, and that this entrainment usually focuses on the auditory–motor features, as opposed to other aspects.

The current literature on entrainment in dance is a small but growing field of study – focusing on both novices and expert dancers, in a great range of dance genres. In the field of psychology and empirical musicology, these studies are motivated by the wish to understand the influence of music upon dancers and focus on the skills that dancers use to rhythmically attune to each other and to music. The investment to measure entrainment in dance appears to serve the paradigm turn of analyzing music as an embodied phenomenon, i.e., cognitive representations of music and the role of having a body and moving one's body therein (Clayton, Sager and Will, 2005; Leman, 2016).

Empirical studies of entrainment in dance have considered live examples of dancing in and outside the laboratory, as well as video and motion capture recordings. Many different dance forms have been examined: the Samba (Naveda and Leman, 2010), standard ballroom (Xarez, 2013), partner dances of Cape Verde (Xarez, 2011), expert and novice Greek folk dances (Sofianidis, Hatzitaki and McKinley, 2012), and professional Australian dancers performing a contemporary dance trio live in front of an audience (Ferguson, Schubert and Stevens, 2014). Researchers have analyzed entrainment of European dance students moving their arms in an eight count *port de bras* to study the influence of mirror usage and spatial orientation on entrainment (Brown and Meulenbroek, 2016); and how novices learning dance sequences fared with and without music, noting how complex music could hinder learning (Betteridge, Stevens and Bailes, 2014). Scientists have examined how dancers (compared to non-dancers) perform on certain activities of entrainment, such as tapping one's finger to a beat (Miura et al., 2016) and synchronizing with a partner, while performing movements in different dance styles (Washburn et al., 2014). In general, these studies validated the hypotheses that compared to non-dancers, dancers are more precise and more consistent at synchronizing full body or fine motor gestures to music, a metronome and each other. Preliminary results show that music, a dance partner, or tools such as a mirror, do have an effect on a dancers' tempi and synchronicity, but there are not yet consistent findings about how. They also suggest that the way dancers move to music entails a spatiotemporal engagement, that itself is highly complex, and may be a foundation of musicality rather than a result (Leman, 2012).

In addition, club dancing has been a particular focus. Researchers have considered club dancing in context at London's Carwash disco (Ellamil et al., 2016), as well as simulated club environments in the laboratory, for example to determine the effects of bass drum music on dancing (Van Dyck et al., 2013). Experiments have even examined silent discos and the effect of the same or different music on memory of co-dancers faces – finding that dancers who had listened to the same music had better recall of each other's faces (Woolhouse, Tidhar and Cross, 2016). Lastly, researchers have examined dancing with technology, such as the 'Dance the Music' interface (Maes, Amelynck and Leman, 2012), and the interaction of toddlers with a humanoid robot QUIDO (Takana et al., 2005). However, such work is future-oriented, in expectation of future contexts of dancing with machines for recreational and learning purposes.

Predominantly, the research cited thus far has been of an empirical nature, conducted outside of the field of dance studies in the humanities. Within the field of cultural studies, research of entrainment in dance has reflected upon non-Western forms such as BaYaka Pygmies' dances (Lewis, 2013), Congolese Song-Dance performance (Plancke, 2014), and the Ghanaian dance *Gahu* performed by dancers, singers and drummers (Armstrong, 2016). These interpretations lay emphasis on the social aspects of entrainment, and the manner in which it leads to communal identity and wellbeing. Entrainment has also been studied in pedagogical situations of Japanese *Nihon buyo* dance transmission, from an ethnographic perspective and methodology (Hahn and Jordan, 2014). This study in particular draws upon concepts from social psychology to show how cognitive structures of learning might relate to entrainment, as anticipation along different timescales. As a final example, a recent study considered Lindy Hop dancers performing in the Jack and Jill competition, taking an approach of ethnomethodology in the paradigm of Conversation Analysis. Video footage was analyzed, frame by frame, to decode the movement rhythm of footfalls and gestures, the gaze and facial expressions of the dancers, as well as the reactions of the audience. This was then used to analyze the rhythmic attunement of dancers and the audience, and to consider how improvisation featured in a choreographic setting of expectations, based on expert understanding and practice of a dance form (Albert, 2015). Aside from the aforementioned study of a dance trio (Ferguson, Schubert and

Stevens, 2014), the only example of studying entrainment in the field of European contemporary dance is our prior work on entrainment in *Duo* (Waterhouse, Watts and Bläsing, 2014).

Diversity of the phenomenon of entrainment

In order to cohere this overview of the literature on entrainment and to make the nuances of the concept more precise, I now describe the criteria proposed to theorize the diversity of entrainment and thereby to enable the comparison of entrainment across domains. First, the provisional definition I have used for entrainment should be taken as a guide, rather than as a rigid definition: *entrainment is the phenomenon recognizable when entities coordinate rhythmically and/or synchronize over time.* Most loosely speaking, it is becoming in-sync. Yet, Clayton and colleagues (2005) have pointed out that not all entrainment culminates in perfectly coinciding rhythm or synchrony – indeed 'rhythmical process may adjust towards the frequency or phase of another rhythmic process without attaining absolute synchronization'. What is important in entrainment is how oscillators adjust towards a 'consistent relationship' or discernable pattern, even if that relationship is complex (Bluedorn, 2002).

What is the range of these consistent relationships? Clayton (2012) and Phillips-Silver and colleagues (2010) categorize different levels of entrainment, from one body to many bodies: self-entrainment within a particular human being as the coordination of body parts (intra-individual); mutual entrainment between two persons (inter-individual); and social entrainment within groups (intra-group) and between groups (inter-group). Secondly, Hahn and Jordan (2014) describe multi-scales of mutual entrainment, relating to different scales of time. These span the immediate timescale of movement anticipation, the relationship with one's partner, the episodic structure of dance lessons (or performances) focused upon learning a dance sequence, annual events related to dancing, and most broadly the historical–cultural timescale of tradition. Entrainment is recognized to be multi-modal, involving multiple sensory modalities, in particular visual, auditory and haptic feedback. Lastly, entrainment often occurs in more complicated contexts than with an isochronous pulse, to a wide range of tempi, and may produce in-phase or out-of-phase relations, as well as hierarchal rhythms.

A framework for a unified study of entrainment across domains has been proposed by Phillips-Silver and colleagues (2010), who give an operational definition of entrainment as 'spatiotemporal coordination resulting from rhythmic responsiveness to a perceived rhythmic signal'. This point of view underscores that entrainment is predicated on the abilities to perceive and produce rhythmic information and real-time integration between sensory and motor systems, or feedback-loops: this view is strongly supported by the embodied cognition perspective (Varela, Thompson and Rosch, 1991; Noë, 2004). Specifically, the extent to which attention, perception and expectation are rhythmical processes, drawing upon entrainment, and why humans have a propensity for entraining to simple rhythms is still being determined within cognitive psychology (Jones and Boltz, 1989). Hahn and Jordan (2014) have defined entrainment as:

> [. . .] the idea that as two people interact, they continuously and reciprocally influence each other's planning states; that is, they become contingently coupled, prospectively, at the levels of action, perception, and thought simultaneously.

This nuanced understanding of entrainment is one that I would support, based on my experience as a dancer in the context of The Forsythe Company.

Entrainment in ballet history: William Forsythe's *Artifact* (1984) and *Eidos:Telos* (1995)

Exiting my review of the literature base for the study of entrainment in dance, I now return to the field of practice and my *Heimat* of the genre of William Forsythe. In this section, I present the manner in which entrainment is part of the history and everyday practice of learning to dance in classical ballet. I then turn to the contemporary ballets of William Forsythe, to show how these pieces draw upon ballet dancers' skills to entrain and spectators' expectations about entrainment. Writing with brevity and speed, I hope to set in motion the potential of this concept, and to prompt further, *closer* readings of case studies of entrainment in dance.

In European and American contexts of ballet, many dancers use the term 'unison' to describe synchronizing. Ballet dancers understand unison as the intentional act of performing the same movements at the same time. Unison is achieved through practice and is supported by listening to music. The term has migrated into dance from the field of music, with origins in the Middle French *unisson* (16th century) or Medieval Latin *unisonus*, meaning 'of the same sound as something else'.[9] The phenomenon of dancing in unison in ballet has a long history, linked to the social and political history of the technique. The spatial patterns of dancers in ballet, making harmonious movements and symmetric formations, are derived from European court dances. These were named the *corps de ballet*, literally the 'body of the ballet', like the *corps d'armée* (16th century). Dancing ballet was a highly cultivated skill. To rectify the poor performance of courtiers in ballets, in 1662 King Louis XIV established the Academie Royale de Danse – a move that dance studies scholar Mark Franko (1993) describes as precisely the moment when ballet was established as a 'discipline'. Unison has lingered both in choreographies and in the daily technique of ballet training, where exercises are perfected all together in groups.

Entrainment in ballet can be understood on many levels. First on the level of one body, within the coordination of shoulders, arms and head in classical ballet called *épaulement*. *Épaulement* is a technique dear to Forsythe, described as a 'perceptually gratifying state [that] synthesizes discrete parts of the body with multiple layers of torqued sensation that leads to the specific sense of a unified but counter-rotated whole' (Foster, 2016). Mutual entrainment also occurs between partners in ballet, especially male–female partners performing *pas de deux* or duets.

Entrainment also plays a role at the level of group formations, or within the corps de ballet, who dance both synchronized and rhythmically related motion. Choreographer William Forsythe describes the interplay of these different levels of rhythm as *counterpoint*: 'a field of action in which the intermittent and irregular coincidence of attributes between organizational elements produces an ordered interplay'.[10] While Forsythe has his own aesthetic of counterpoint, and process of choreographing it, he observes that counterpoint is evident not only in his, but also in other choreographers' works, including those of George Balanchine, Anne Teresa De Keersmaeker and Trisha Brown.

Another broad term commonly used by dancers to describe moving together is 'partnering', which usually involves touch (Vidrin, in press). A leader and follower are designated across many duets. In classical ballet, as well as in social dances such as the Waltz, Samba and Lindy Hop, traditionally the man leads the woman. In contemporary dance performance and improvisation, including Contact Improvisation, these roles may not be gender-bound, pre-determined or fixed for the duration of the dance. Dance studies has described how negotiation of the roles of leading and following, even in forms of dance that name the learning and performance of these roles, reflects social values and subtle power negotiations (see Novack, 1990; Taylor, 1998). These studies show that, as Clayton (2012) aspires for music, dance is a 'particularly good forum for investigating the interdependence between timing coordination and social power relationships'.

During my time in Ballett Frankfurt/The Forsythe Company (2004–2012), William Forsythe used the term 'entrainment' infrequently in the studio. Prior to this, in an interview in 1998, Forsythe named entrainment as one of four factors important to his work (these were: counterpoint, proprioception, entrainment and authenticity). Referencing *The Dance of Life* (1984) by Edward Hall, Forsythe described entrainment as 'the process that occurs when two or more people become engaged in each other's rhythms' (Spier, 1998). Scholar Steven Spier elaborates further; that for Hall entrainment is 'innate and metaphysical; at a quotidian level, it is a phenomena that allows conversations to happen – the pauses, sounds, nods, and body language'. In my view, Forsythe understands entrainment as a confluence of musical, motor, social and communicative competencies – again, it involves much more than being in-sync or aligned with the music.

As a dance studies scholar, I am interested in the factors that explicitly sustain and produce entrainment between dancers; I am also concerned with how entrainment becomes organized within a choreographic piece. Not only does unison occur in many of Forsythe's choreographies – the group patterns of marching in *Artifact* (1984), the waltz scene opening the second act of *Eidos:Telos* (1995), and the initial rush of tables being dragged forward by the dancers in *One Flat Thing, reproduced* (2000) – but Forsythe also creates complicated instances of entrainment, involving counterpoint of light, sound, text and movement. To explore the relevance of entrainment as a lens for examining these choreographies, I would briefly like to cite two examples.

First, consider the first act of the ballet *Artifact*, where Forsythe's staging of entrainment creates a spellbinding affect, echoing the beauty of ensemble work in classical ballet. Female dancers clad in dark tights perform synchronous motions in dim lighting. They open and close their arms – stepping up to point, like a flock of birds. The lighting shows their limbs, and veils their faces in shadows. Their movements softly slice the air, accompanied by a brooding music for solo piano (composed by Eva Crossman-Hecht) with a clear musical pulse. Puncturing this sound layer, the dancers' unison clapping choruses as one sound, breaking the fourth wall of the audience. Short text fragments add another layer to the visual–acoustic counterpoint, spoken by a female dancer in historical costume and a male performer with a megaphone. *Artifact* shows that unlike in classical ballets, where dancers try to silently mask movements that require much effort (hushing breath and silencing steps), Forsythe chooses to compose motion and sound production: clapping, stepping and speaking. To emphasize the importance of the dancers' sound in Forsythe's choreographic pieces, Vass-Rhee (2010) has called them 'vocal choreographies'.

While my description of entrainment in the scenes described above foregrounds harmonious aspects, in *Artifact* there are rhythmical features that are asynchronous, perplexing and even violent – such as the repeated crashing of the curtain during the *pas de deux* in the second act. In my next example, the end of *Eidos:Telos*, I will emphasize the chaotic side of entrainment. During the final scene of *Eidos:Telos* dancers work in groups, yelling cues and counts that are droned out by deafening music and sudden blackouts. The stage becomes an affective field with frightening, martial tenor. Order and chaos vacillate. Unison emerges fleetingly – duets and groups of dancers move in parallel to others running, falling down, and collectively striking a wire that stretches across the entire length of the stage. The wire turns the stage into a musical instrument whose reverberations are both seen and heard. In this complex activity, each dancer's urgency is not masked by decorum, as is typical in classical ballet. Individualities do not blend into the background, or into one another; rather, people emerge in a complex field of dynamics. Each individual heaves, runs and contributes, with an effort that seems to grow in parallel to the sonic amplification of live trombones.

With these two examples, I wish to underline Forsythe's mastery in staging the range of entrainment dynamics. Forsythe's choreographies place dancers at the brink of order and disorder, and at the limits of their perceptual capability (Vass-Rhee, 2011). Working with harmony and causing chaos, Forsythe has been accused of ruining or critiquing the norms of classical ballet; including that pleasing harmony or synchrony is beautiful and good, and should thus be visible, whereas chaos and irregularity are vulgar, and should be hidden. Through this aesthetic challenge, Forsythe interferes with how spectators of a contemporary ballet might anticipate being lulled by pleasing entrainment of movement to music – the idea of ballet as the 'joy of the evident'.[11] Simply put, the staging of entrainment in Forsythe's ballets contradicts the normative idea of dance, as dancers entraining to a musical pulse, and instead explores the range of entrainment across modes, scales and affects.

The diversity of entrainment observed by scientists is choreographic range for Forsythe: the playing field. Forsythe's pieces span the categories of entrainment cited in the biological literature. Forsythe's choreographic modes of entrainment vary from rehearsed unison to structured collective improvisation. Entrainment is across the senses or multimodal. This often includes dancers using their voices, producing noise with their bodies, and making conversational sounds, in words or with breath. Forsythe creates entrainment both with and without an external musical pulse and to a diverse range of tempi. Levels of entrainment vary from the coordination of one person's body parts, as *épaulement*, to mutual entrainment between two persons, and social entrainment within or between groups. Entrainment modes vary from simple unison, to turn-taking, and complex rhythmical relations. In summary, entrainment science provides concepts for thinking degrees or phases of togetherness, categories that, in the case of William Forsythe, are actually an insightful means to analyze the broad nature of rhythmical attunement in his choreographic work.

Conclusion

I would like to finish my discussion by addressing four difficulties I find within the entrainment discourse. Firstly, within the diverse literature on entrainment across domains, there is inconsistency in the manner that scholars in the sciences and the humanities define and use the term, including: emphasizing pace, discussing self-sustaining coupled oscillation, and synchronizing movement to a beat. Also, dancers have astutely asked me: Are there skills fundamental to entrainment and if so, what are these? To avoid the tautology of saying entrainment is based on entrainment, or reducing entrainment to one definition that fails to find the nuances of what is really at stake, I advocate that entrainment be viewed as a *process* through which entities become rhythmically coordinated and/or synchronized. This is in accordance with the view of entrainment as happening on many levels, modes and timescales simultaneously.

Secondly, key aspects of the definition of entrainment in physics and mathematics might not be applicable in the wide-ranging examples in nature. Logically, classical objects, displaying *self-sustaining* rhythmic oscillation such as interacting pendulums, clocks or metronomes, are very different to animal or human bodies – even though these bodies contain oscillators they depend upon, such as those in the brain. Also, the second important aspect of the definition of entrainment is that the system's parts must be *coupled* – as in the material coupling Huygens' clocks by the beam. For humans and animals, the connection is often immaterial: relating to culture and communication. In my opinion, both of these considerations call to scholars, including those in the humanities, to further understand entrainment: to contribute understanding of bodies, transmission and connection that are difficult to theorize from the perspective of the physics of entrainment.

Thirdly, while rhythmic action to music features prominently in non-dancers' expectations of dance, many choreographic approaches challenge the definition of entrainment in dance, as movement coordinated to an external musical pulse. Contemporary dance is a heterogeneous phenomenon involving diverse musical environments, at times featuring interaction between dance and music, or dancers and musicians. Even in the case of dancers performing rehearsed moves to recorded music with a beat, I take the position that the specific installation of the music in space (loudspeaker directions, volume, etc.), interaction with this via movement and the sound of one's own and others' bodies, all influence how entrainment takes place. Thus I agree with Leman (2012) that entrainment in dance is of spatiotemporal, not purely temporal, nature, and that it should be considered in its ecological context. In my view, studies of entrainment of dance must break with the narrow definition of dance in the music literature, and further explore the understanding of entrainment as a musical, social and communicative phenomenon.

Fourthly, affective aspects of entrainment are challenging to study. The entrainment literature has drawn considerable attention to the emotional and empowering aspects of entrainment to music, linked to wellbeing and pleasure. Conversely, in sociology, Collins (2013) has written of the role of entrainment in violent interactions, showing that entrainment not only produces positive affects. Diverse affects appear as well in Forsythe's ballets, often veering between beauty and terror. Further research is needed to describe how entrainment can be both a conduit of compassion, dialogue and collaboration, and also a means of competition and violence. Methodological development to research affective aspects, drawing from micro-analysis of video and ethnographic methodology (as in Collins) is a promising route to this. Another is dialogue with dancers, who know their phenomenon *by heart*.

To conclude, I would like to suggest that one promising avenue for the future methodology of entrainment research in dance is mixed methodology: research involving both qualitative and quantitative approaches, either used in phases or hybridized, without placing more or less value on any paradigm. The philosophy of mixed methodology is that different modes of inquiry regarding the same focus or phenomenon produce a system to triangulate findings (Johnson, Onwuegbuzie and Turner, 2007). This addresses explicitly that when studying a human phenomenon, informants' stories may or may not confirm the numbers (and vice versa), and that this affords the opportunity to research *why* this is the case. Similarly, background literature on the same phenomenon in various disciplines might foreground different aspects or follow distinct motivations. Examining the conjuncts and disjuncts between observations and discourses itself is a part of mixed methodology, providing gaps to analyze what is at issue in any case, and to reconsider how broadly findings can be generalized for a community, culture or humans at large (see Ancona and Waller, 2007). In the future studies of entrainment in dance, I hope for a pact between the sciences and the humanities and greater attention to mixed methodology. This should aid connecting dancers' intimate stories and expertise with analysis of live and mediated dance, to produce evidence for a phenomenon that is always in-between and in-process.

Notes

1 The citations and remarks are based upon interviews and fieldwork conducted between 2014 and 2017 with *Duo* dancers Allison Brown, Regina van Berkel, Jill Johnson, Brigel Gjoka and Riley Watts. This understanding of *Duo* would not exist without their generous contributions.

2 Interview with Regina van Berkel on 22 April 2017; and discussion with Riley Watts and Bettina Bläsing in January 2014.
3 Email written by Jill Johnson on 28 June 2017.
4 Interview with Allison Brown on 23 September 2016.
5 Citation from Riley Watts, published in Waterhouse, Watts and Bläsing (2014: p.8); and interview with Brigel Gjoka on 6 March 2016.
6 Interview with Regina van Berkel on 22 April 2017.
7 Archival video of the third rehearsal of *Duo* from January 1996.
8 *The Oxford English Dictionary of English Etymology*, p. 317 and *The Second Edition of the Oxford English Dictionary*, Volume V, p. 303.
9 *The Second Edition of the Oxford English Dictionary*, Volume XIX, p. 75.
10 Definition taken from: https://synchronousobjects.osu.edu/content.html (accessed May 2018).
11 Citation from William Forsythe taken from a documentary film from 1994: Figgis, M. (1997/2007). *Just Dancing Around (2007)*, Kultur Video, DVD, 10:00–10:59.

References

Albert, S. (2015). Rhythmical coordination of performers and audience in partner dance. Delineating improvised and choreographed interaction. *Etnografia E Ricerca Qualitativa*, 8(3), 399–428.

Alborno, P., Volpe, G., Camurri, A., Clayton, M., & Keller, P. (2015). Automated video analysis of interpersonal entrainment in Indian music performance. *Intelligent Technologies for Interactive Entertainment (INTETAIN), 2015 7th International Conference*. 15(4), 57–63.

Ancona, D. & Chong, C. L. (1996). Entrainment: Pace, cycle, and rhythm in organizational behavior. In: B. Straw & T. Cummings (Eds.), *Research in Organisational Behavior* (Vol. 18, pp. 251–284). Greenwich, CN: JAI Press.

Ancona, D. & Waller, M. J. (2007). The dance of entrainment: Temporally navigating across multiple pacers. In: B. A. Rubin (Ed.), *Workplace Temporalities* (pp. 115–146). Bingley, UK: Emerald Group Publishing.

Armstrong, K. (2016). The ecology of *Gahu*: Participatory music and health benefits of ewe performance in a Canadian drum and dance ensemble. *Legon Journal of the Humanities*, 17–35.

Betteridge, G. L., Stevens, C. J., & Bailes, F. A. (2014). Beat it! Music overloads novice dancers. *Applied Cognitive Psychology*, 28(5), 765–771.

Bluedorn, A. C. (2002). *The Human Organization of Time. Temporal realities and experiences.* Stanford, CA: Stanford University Press.

Brennan, S. E. & Clark, H. H. (1996). Conceptual pacts and lexical choice in conversation. *Journal of Experimental Psychology: Learning, memory, and cognition*, 22(6), 1482.

Brown, D. D. & Meulenbroek, R. G. J. (2016). Effects of a fragmented view of one's partner on interpersonal coordination in dance. *Frontiers in Psychology*, 7, 614.

Bruce, V. G. (1960). Environmental entrainment of circadian rhythms. *Cold Spring Harbor Symposia on Quantitative Biology*. 25, 29 –48.

Bünning, E. (1960). Opening address: Biological clocks. *Cold Spring Harbor Symposia on Quantitative Biology*. 25, 1–9.

Clayton, M. R. (2007). Observing entrainment in music performance: Video-based observational analysis of Indian musicians' tanpura playing and beat marking. *Musicae Scientiae*, 11(1), 27–59.

Clayton, M. (2012). What is entrainment? Definition and applications in musical research. *Empirical Musicology Review,* 7(1–2), 49–56.

Clayton, M., Sager, R., & Will, U. (2005). In time with the music: The concept of entrainment and its significance for ethnomusicology. *European Meetings in Ethnomusicology,* 11, 3–142.

Collins, R. (2004). *Interaction Ritual Chains.* Princeton, NJ: Princeton University Press.

Collins, R. (2013). Entering and leaving the tunnel of violence: Micro-sociological dynamics of emotional entrainment in violent interactions. *Current Sociology,* 61(2), 132–151.

Copeland, R. (2004). Merce Cunningham: The modernizing of modern dance. New York: Routledge.

Czolczynski, K., Perlikowski, P., Stefanski, A., & Kapitaniak, T. (2011). Huygens' odd sympathy experiment revisited. *International Journal of Bifurcation and Chaos,* 21, 2047–2056.

Doffman, M. R. (2008). *Feeling the groove: Shared time and its meanings for three jazz trios.* Ph.D. Dissertation, Music Department, Open University.

Ellamil M., Berson J., Wong J., Buckley L., & Margulies, D. S. (2016). One in the dance: Musical correlates of group synchrony in a real-world club environment. *PLOS ONE,* 11(10): e0164783.

Ferguson, S., Schubert, E., & Stevens, C. J. (2014). Dynamic dance warping: Using dynamic time warping to compare dance movement performed under different conditions. *Proceedings of the 2014 International Workshop on Movement and Computing.* ACM, 94/99.

Foster, S. L. (2016). Why is there always energy for dancing? *Dance Research Journal,* 48(3), 11–26.

Franko, M. (1993). *Dance as Text: Ideologies of the baroque body.* Cambridge: Cambridge University Press.

Garrod, S. & Pickering, M. J. (2004). Why is conversation so easy? *Trends in Cognitive Sciences,* 8(1), 8–11.

Hahn, T. & Jordan, J. S. (2014). Anticipation and embodied knowledge: Observations of enculturating bodies. *Journal of Cognitive Education and Psychology,* 13(2), 272–284.

Hall, E. T. (1984). *The Dance of Life: The other dimension of time.* New York: Anchor Press.

Holland, K. (2004). Action against dance festival fails. *Irish Times,* 34. (Cited in A. Lepecki (2006), *Exhausting Dance: Performance and the politics of movement.* London: Routledge.)

Iqbal, T. & Riek, L. D. (2016). A method for automatic detection of psychomotor entrainment. *IEEE Transactions on Affective Computing,* 7(1), 3–16.

Jenkins, A. (2013). Self-oscillation. *Physics Reports,* 525(2), 167–222.

Johnson, R. B., Onwuegbuzie, A. J., & Turner, L. A. (2007). Toward a definition of mixed methods research. *Journal of Mixed Methods Research,* 1(2), 112–133.

Jones, M. R. & Boltz, M. (1989). Dynamic attending and responses to time. *Psychological Review,* 96(3), 459–491.

Keil, C. (2010). Defining "groove." Schriftenreihe herausgegeben vom Forschungszentrum Populäre Musik der Humboldt-Universität zu Berlin. In: *PopScriptum.* www2.rz.hu-berlin.de/fpm/popscrip/themen/pst11/pst11_keil02.pdf (accessed March 2018).

Kouwenhoven, F. (2005). Some remarks on music as reorganized time. In: M. Clayton, R. Sager, and U. Will, In time with the music: The concept of entrainment and its significance for ethnomusicology. *ESEM CounterPoint 1,* 11, 88–92.

Leman, M. (2012). Musical entrainment subsumes bodily gestures – Its definition needs a spatiotemporal dimension. *Empirical Musicology Review,* 7(1–2), 63–67.

Leman, M. (2016). *The Expressive Moment: How interaction (with music) shapes human empowerment.* Cambridge, MA: MIT Press.

Levinson, S. C. & Holler, J. (2014). The origin of human multi-modal communication. *Philosophical Transactions of the Royal Society B: Biological sciences,* 369(1651), 20130302.

Lewis, J. (2013). A cross-cultural perspective on the significance of music and dance to culture and society insight from BaYaka pygmies. In: M. A. Arbib (Ed.), *Language, Music and the Brain* (pp. 45–65). Cambridge, MA: MIT Press.

Maduell, M. & Wing, A. M. (2007). The dynamics of ensemble: The case for flamenco. *Psychology of Music,* 35(4), 591–627.

Maes, P. J., Amelynck, D., & Leman, M. (2012). Dance-the-music: An educational platform for the modeling, recognition and audiovisual monitoring of dance steps using spatiotemporal motion templates. *EURASIP Journal on Advances in Signal Processing,* 2012(1), 1–16.

Miura, A., Fujii, S., Okano, M., Kudo, K., & Nakazawa, K. (2016). Finger-to-beat coordination skill of non-dancers, street dancers, and the world champion of a street-dance competition. *Frontiers in Psychology,* 7, 542.

Naveda, L. A. & Leman, M. (2010). The spatiotemporal representation of dance and music gestures using topological gesture analysis (TGA). *Music Perception,* 28(11), 93–111.

Noë, A. (2004). *Action in Perception.* Cambridge, MA: MIT Press.

Novack, C. J. (1990). *Sharing the Dance: Contact improvisation and American culture.* Madison, WI: University of Wisconsin Press.

Nozaradan, S., Peretz, I., Missal, M., & Mouraux, A. (2011). Tagging the neuronal entrainment to beat and meter. *Journal of Neuroscience,* 31(28), 10234–10240.

Phillips-Silver, J., Aktipis, C. A., & Bryant, G. A. (2010). The ecology of entrainment: Foundations of coordinated rhythmic movement. *Music Perception,* 28(1), 3–14.

Phillips-Silver, J. & Keller, P. E. (2012). Searching for roots of entrainment and joint action in early musical interactions. *Frontiers in Human Neuroscience,* 6, 26.

Plancke, C. (2014). Affect, creativity, and community-making in a Congolese song-dance performance: Or how to follow the movement of the social. *Journal of the Royal Anthropological Institute,* 20(4), 653–669.

Repp, B. H. (2005). Sensorimotor synchronization: A review of the tapping literature. *Psychonomic Bulletin and Review,* 12(6), 969–992.

Rosenblum, M. & Pikovsky, A. (2003). Synchronization: From pendulum clocks to chaotic lasers and chemical oscillators. *Contemporary Physics,* 44(5), 401–416.

Schachner, A. (2013). The origins of human and avian auditory-motor entrainment. *Nova Acta Leopoldina NF,* 111(380), 243–253.

Schmidt R. C., Nie L., Franco A., & Richardson M. J. (2014). Bodily synchronization underlying joke telling. *Frontiers in Human Neuroscience,* 8, 633.

Sofianidis, G., Hatzitaki, V., & McKinley, P. (2012). Effects of expertise and auditory guidance on traditional dance performance. *Journal of Dance Medicine and Science,* 16(2), 57–64.

Spier, S. (1998). Engendering and composing movement: William Forsythe and the Ballett Frankfurt. *The Journal of Architecture,* 3(2), 135–146.

Tanaka, F., Fortenberry, B., Aisaka, K., & Movellan, J. R. (2005). Developing dance interaction between QRIO and toddlers in a classroom environment: Plans for the first steps. *Proceedings of the 2005 IEEE International Workshop on Robot and Human Interactive Communication.* 223–228.

Taylor, J. M. (1998). *Paper Tangos.* Durham, NC: Duke University Press.

Thompson, M., Diapoulis, G., Johnson, S., Kwan, P., & Himberg, T. (2015). Effect of tempo and vision on interpersonal coordination of timing in dyadic performance. In: M. Aramaki, R. Kronland-Martinet, & S. Ystad (Eds.), *Proceedings of the 11th International Symposium on CMMR, Plymouth, UK* (June 16–19, pp. 16–23). Marseille, France: Laboratory of Mechanics and Acoustics.

Van Dyck, E., Moelants, D., Demey, M., Deweppe, A., Coussement, P., & Leman, M. (2013). The impact of the bass drum on music-induced movement. *Music Perception: An interdisciplinary journal,* 30(4), 349–359.

Varela, F. J., Thompson, E. T., & Rosch, E. (1991). *The Embodied Mind: Cognitive science and human experience.* Cambridge, MA: MIT Press.

Vass-Rhee, F. (2010). Auditory turn: William Forsythe's vocal choreography. *Dance Chronicle,* 33, 388–413.

Vass-Rhee, F. (2011). *Audio-visual stress: Cognitive approaches to the perceptual performativity of William Forsythe and ensemble.* Ph.D. Dissertation, Dance Department, University of California Riverside.

Vidrin, I. (in press). Partnering as rhetoric. In: H. Blades, C. Waelde, & S. Ellis (Eds.), *A World of Muscle, Bone & Organs: Research and scholarship in dance.* Coventry, UK: Centre for Dance Research at Coventry University.

Washburn, A., DeMarco, M., de Vries, S., Ariyabuddhiphongs, K., Schmidt, R. C., Richardson, M. J., & Riley, M. A. (2014). Dancers entrain more effectively than non-dancers to another actor's movements. *Frontiers in Human Neuroscience,* 8, 800.

Waterhouse, E., Watts, R., & Bläsing, B. (2014). Doing duo – A case study of entrainment in William Forsythe's choreography 'Duo'. *Frontiers in Human Neuroscience,* 8, 812.

Woolhouse, M. H., Tidhar, D., & Cross, I. (2016). Effects on inter-personal memory of dancing in time with others. *Frontiers in Psychology,* 7, 167.

Xarez, L. (2011). Dances of Cape Verde: Tempo, preferences, and entrainment. *International Symposium on Performance Science.* 209–214.

Xarez, L. (2013). Entrainment in ballroom dances: The influence of the pair in the synchronization with the music. *International Symposium on Performance Science.* 119–214.

4 Searching for that 'other land of dance'

The phases in developing a choreography

Gregor Zöllig
(Translation by Jonathan Harrow)

What makes and what moves dance? How is it possible for a choreographer and dance ensemble to join together in capturing and developing those sensations and images in movement and dance that will actually move an audience? How is it possible for a choreography to come together; for all those involved to be totally present; and for a performance to be so magical?

As a contemporary choreographer, I shall try to describe how I develop dance pieces together with my ensemble, what my personal contribution is, and what the dancers and other members of my team also contribute to creating a dance performance. Nonetheless, right before I start, something makes me rather apprehensive: the most important thing – the coming together of a work as a whole, the merging of inspirations, and finally, the moment in which everything comes to life and is completely present – is something that cannot be put into words. Yet I shall try to do my best, and report on the background, the hand and body tools, the materials, the ideas, but, above all, the processes that contribute to the birth of a dance performance. This all focuses on what constitutes the art of choreography, and what Hans Züllig, who headed the Folkwang Universität in Essen for many years, defined as follows:

> All of us feel something, but it is finding precisely that form of movement that makes something resonate in another person; that is the great secret.
>
> (Cébron, 1990: translated from the German)

As a contemporary choreographer, my main concern throughout most of the phases of developing a dance piece is the one aspect: finding and inventing movement. On the one hand, I am searching for where a movement comes from, for the reason why I do something on the stage. On the other hand, alongside this intensive interest in the origin of a movement, I want something to be addressed on the stage. My dance pieces have to be about something. However, as in so many other art forms, this is often something that cannot simply be put into words without something quite essential becoming lost. With this as my background, I explore the topic of a piece in search of a statement, a focus. Then I work together with my ensemble to develop and define a credible expression of this statement in movement. I seek movements and scenes that the dance ensemble will realise in different formations. During the choreographic process, these movements and scenes are explored, tested and examined in detail. The final product is what could be called a shaped perception. If it is to succeed at the moment of presentation, there will no longer be anything random about this perception generated by bodies moving through space. Its expression will be an honest truth emerging simultaneously in the choreographer, the dancers and the audience.

Working with the team

A choreography emerges through the interaction of many persons. The dance piece, the performance, is the outcome of an intensive creative process in which all my colleagues have introduced their ideas on movement sequences and scenes. My role as the choreographer is to initiate, to test and to decide. Everything essential for shaping and developing my dance pieces lies in my hands. This makes me the author of a work to which many people have contributed. Together with my chosen team of dancers, the rehearsal director, the choreographic assistant, the dramatist, the set and costume designer, and the conductor or composer, I have found my own way of producing choreographies and I have created an environment in which this is possible. Over the last 18 years, I have built up three contemporary dance ensembles by realising my ideas on what I call a 'choreographic forum'. My goal has always been, and continues to be, to create a place, a laboratory, a haven that permits creativity, the search for movement, and the exploration of movement – a haven that inspires one to move, makes movement possible, and develops it further.

The phases in the process of developing a piece

In the following sections, I will discuss in more detail how this creative space emerges and how we work in it. I shall start with a brief overview of the individual phases in developing a dance piece, followed by a description of the range of materials and elements that contribute to each successive phase in this process.

The *first phase* in developing a dance piece is to seek and develop ideas on the chosen topic. The aim is to discover a way to find an access to the topic that opens it up for dance and for body language; to accentuate existential aspects of the given topic through the body; to study these; and to define a personal approach. I explore these ideas together with my team (the dramatist, set and costume designer, and conductor), and we develop a statement that will serve as the basis for the second phase. In this *second phase*, we create a conceptual framework for the further development of the piece. This framework creates the space for what we do in the *third phase,* which develops the essence of the choreography – namely, the appropriate movements and scenes for the dance piece: improvising with the dancers. The *fourth phase* is dedicated to working out and rehearsing the movements, scenes and ideas. This is the precision work on the sequences and structures of the piece. In the *fifth phase*, we arrange the sequence of the piece for the stage. The set, lights and music are all coordinated. The final phase is the *dance performance itself*, the outcome of an enormous number of steps and decisions. If it is a success, it is a complete gestalt that is far more than the individual elements that have gone into making it.

First work phase: Inspiration, focus and access

When creating my first choreography, I never even considered that it might become difficult to find new ideas. I felt that my resources were unlimited. It was only when it came to my fifth choreography that I first suspected the possible risk of repeating myself. By the tenth piece, this feeling had become a certainty: however, every new piece has to be a new beginning – personally selected in order to embark on a new voyage of discovery full of joy and curiosity. Every new dance piece demands a new beginning.

Such a new beginning requires new ideas, new movements. To find these, I have to break with routines, free myself from set ways of thinking and looking. Otherwise, I shall never discover what lies beyond the known. Nothing is as precious and precarious as seeking and communicating ideas. Although the experience and knowledge I have gained during the course of my career as a choreographer form an important and indispensable basis for my work, this can sometimes be an obstacle when searching for hidden ideas. For example, I cannot allow myself to try to be 'realistic' at this stage and start thinking about how to implement an idea as soon as it emerges. If you begin with such pragmatic aspects in mind, you soon get stuck. As soon as you think that something is 'too expensive' or 'too elaborate', then a good idea may well have already died.

Therefore, this new beginning that marks the start of work on a new dance piece initially consists of intensively analysing the topic without taking choreographic considerations into account. Such an analysis is simultaneously both intellectual and intuitive. I read the specialist literature, view films and visit exhibitions and museums. I carry out field research and explore spaces and their impact; for example, a steelworks in Duisburg, the Felix Nussbaum House in Osnabrück, Hamburg harbour, or the Mahrzahn housing estate in East Berlin. I hold discussions with my team: to analyse various aspects, and to reach for and gather everything related to the chosen topic. I search for my own personal access, for the images that correspond to my feelings and my associations. I try to get myself into the mood for which I am searching.

At the same time, I open myself up to the ideas, associations and images that come from my team. That is not always easy, and it takes a lot of energy. I have to explain my idea, and the team has to understand it and work with it. If choreographers cannot describe their idea, and if this literally cannot be put into words, then how can they convey it? If others cannot grasp the idea, does this mean that it is not any good? As a choreographer, I have to invest a great deal of effort in informing my dancers precisely about the motives underlying my idea. I must search for the forms of expression and possibilities of communication that convey what I am thinking. It is the dancers who will convey my ideas. The more clearly they understand what I want, then the more clearly the idea will be communicated to the audience. By this, I not only mean gaining an intellectual understanding, but also thinking with the body. That is what makes the initial dialogue with my dancers so important during the phase when I am starting to develop the dance with them. This dialogue and its outcome form the initial nucleus of the piece. I engage in intensive intellectual discourse with my team about the statement we want to make with our dance performance.

SPEEDLESS, one of my choreographies, provides a good example of how this interpretation of a topic emerges. This choreography looks at the worlds of human work – but from the perspective of the loss of time, the acceleration of productivity, and the pressure imposed by ubiquity. When preparing the piece, we asked ourselves what does it look like today: this balance between work-load, active leisure time, a relaxed, socially functioning family life, and life with friends in an everyday world that is no longer fixed in one place? Working on this question highlighted the tension between achievement and burnout; our task now was to find movements that would express the extremes of this tension in bodily form. Setting this objective led to a piece about the way we all yearn to gain control over time.

Second work phase: Defining and limiting the concept

The outcome of searching for inspiration, of discussing the topic with my team, and finally of focusing on a specific interpretation is a written concept, a type of timetable that sets out how I shall develop the dance piece together with my colleagues. This sets the initial framing conditions. The set designer presents a model for the stage. The costume designer presents sketches of what the dancers should wear. We determine the dramatic structure, the various themes and aspects of the scenes and pictures to be designed, and the improvisation tasks for the dancers. The choice of topic determines which music to use. This shapes the content and the atmosphere of a dance. How music is used is also an important dramatic element. For example, the decision to dance movements in time to or against the music can set important accents and can decisively shape what the dance is saying. The same applies for pauses and silences.

Setting limits to the artistic scope by specifying a concept does not imply limiting or even narrowing artistic creativity. Quite the opposite: the concept provides creative friction and tension. It is a kind of 'scaffold' supporting the development of the dance piece; a constraint that encourages creativity. It is not the concept that dictates which forms are developed but the creative work on it. However, it is the framework provided by the concept that first makes this work possible.

Third work phase: Improvisation – the rehearsal stage as a research lab

When the audience sees the performance, the stage presence of the dancers and the complete ensemble should be something magical. The performance should be an outstanding moment, better than anything they have seen before. This is only possible when all the persons involved in the stage presentation devote their full attention and power to the dance piece and focus their energies on its essence. The more authentically dancers are centred in their internal attitudes, energies and states, the more strongly the audience will also experience the same effect.

In order to achieve this necessary authenticity and vitality, I push my individual dancers to contribute their own genuine feelings and ideas to the development of the piece. I assign them a task and ask them to respond to it personally. This turns them into co-authors of my choreographies, whose own ideas contribute decisively to the design of the dance pieces. They are free to express their ideas and associations by drawing on stage props, voice, language or other dancers. For example, in PULS1, we were interested in the ideal of the perfect body. A dancer dressed only in her underwear deformed her body by tying countless belts round her stomach, hips, shoulders, breast and legs. Tightening all these belts, she squeezed her body as if she was wearing a narrow corset. Then, she covered her naturally blonde hair with a dark brown wig; and, over her mouth, she placed a sheet of paper on which she had painted bigger lips. Manipulating her body in this way left the dancer scarcely able to breathe and greatly restricted her movements. This example shows how much courage and honesty are needed to make a personal contribution to a piece and to portray this on the stage. This is why the most important aspect during the phase of improvising, seeking and finding movement ideas and sequences is for everybody to be able to try them out without feeling shy or inhibited. My dancers have to feel that they are in a protected space.

While we are improvising, rehearsals are not open to the public. The space we work in has to be defined by respect, trust and frankness. During the improvisation phase of developing a dance piece, the physical space becomes a mental space in which creativity can emerge. The senses are addressed on all levels. Dance is in the air! The dance studio becomes a playground, a research lab and a meeting place. Each person involved in the production should, may and needs to be creative. They have to share concepts, introduce ideas and take their own stance; they have to question, be open to inspiration, and inspire. Working with guest choreographers, guest trainers and artists of all kinds also plays an important role: they introduce new ideas and push the team to adopt new perspectives and new ways of working.

There are a lot of surprises when trying things out in the dance studio. We make new discoveries. Many new ideas and impulses emerge intuitively from the dancers' spontaneous acts. For example, one of the dancers in my ensemble – an Italian – improvised on the topic of sex in advertising. He took two mozzarella cheeses and held them to his naked chest, proudly presenting his new breasts. Glancing flirtatiously at the audience, he started to squeeze the soft cheese balls, sensually licking the cheese from between his fingers. Integrating such discoveries and ideas, pursuing them further, building them into the process, but thereby always remaining open to change, are essential aspects of developing a dance piece. Much of my work is intuitive: something directly addressing my inner core does not have to be logically explicable. Anything can influence the rehearsal process negatively: a poor working climate, just as much as a prop that seems to be standing in the way. The rehearsal process is a sensitive framework that needs to be cultivated with care. As the choreographer, I have to understand my dancers and their needs, and always ensure that communication channels remain open.

Spending many hours a day working together with 20 people in a very intensive mental and physical space requires a great deal of self-discipline, social competence, and empathy from me, my dancers, and everybody else involved. Without this, it will not work. Teamwork with all its intensity, sharing a concentrated focus on seeking and exploring ideas on movement that will go on to become part of a dance piece – this teamwork plays a major role in determining the intensity and charisma of a dance ensemble's performance on the stage. My task is to create the space for this type of work and to fill it with life. I have to inspire my artistic team and spur their enthusiasm. They have to live for the topic. Everything that shapes this mental space also influences the dancers' creativity: the working climate, the choice of music, each discussion on the topic, every improvisation we show to each other, and each text. In other words, everything we do and everything we open ourselves up to leaves its traces and influences our exploratory work.

I now shall describe the most important elements of this improvisation work: the potentials of the human body and of movement; the materials that trigger intuitions about movement, objects and fantasies; and finally, the individuality of expression. These are all materials and tools that we use when developing and realising ideas to create a dance piece.

It all starts with the body

The body is a dancer's instrument. Dancers know their bodies in all their parts – in fact they know every fibre very precisely. They have enormous experience in working with their bodies and they can perform the movements they have rehearsed with great awareness and deliberation. The body is an infinitely rich reservoir of different movements. Visual ideas and fantasies about movements emerge physically in and through the body. This is why my work as a choreographer and dancer includes exploring the human body in all its dimensions, and pushing it to its limits.

The *anatomic perspective* portrays the body as a bag of skin holding together a great number of different elements. The task is to analyse these elements – again and again. But how do dancers analyse this anatomic unit? How do they become aware of everything that comes together in a human body? For example, dancers may ask themselves: How many bones do I have? What does it feel like if I initiate movements in which the only thing I move is my bones, and what type of movement is then generated? Or dancers can imagine having a ball inside their bodies that they roll through all their joints. They let the ball rotate, producing movements that all proceed from their joints. Alternatively, dancers may ask themselves: How can I manage to be able to feel my organs? How can my body fluids inspire me? Blood, sweat and tears, but also urine, sperm, mucus and spittle can be the sources for many internal images, and they can also trigger emotions. Hair and nails are further potential sources of inspiration. Loose flowing hair inspires a different motivation for movement than hair that is neatly tied back.

The *physical perspective* leads to a further class of questions when analysing the body: How elastic and flexible is my body? How often can I twist it? How high can I jump? What skills can I practise with my body and what can I do that nobody else can do? Which processes in my body can I gain access to through dance? How much power and stamina does my body have? How much can it achieve? How does my body react to group processes or to my physical surroundings?

The *sensory perception*, instincts and intuitions can be analysed as a further dimension of corporality: Which images, movements and emotions emerge through my senses? For example, touch: hands offer only one possible way of experiencing touch, so it is amazing to discover that the belly or back can also feel. The entire surface of the skin is one great big organ of touch. The senses of smelling, hearing, tasting and seeing take our perceptions on voyages of discovery. If I block my sense of hearing, for example, this will shift the inner balance within my body. My other senses will become more alert. I hear myself more strongly. I hear my heart beat. I return to my self. I go inside my self. I perceive myself more strongly as a person. I am exploring intuitions when I ask: Which places do I seek when I want to be alone? Which distances to persons do I adopt when I want to be seen? When I find a person unsympathetic, how close do I let this person come?

Finally, the *perspective of the interplay between mind and body* (spiritual body techniques) opens up for dance professionals. Far Eastern relaxation techniques such as tai chi or yoga, or different forms of meditation, make it possible to experience how mind and body influence each other. Dervishes use rotating movements in centuries-old dance rituals to enter trance states. Exploring such techniques makes it possible to experience bodily intensities that transcend borders in the truest sense, and provoke further questions: How strongly does my mind, and my thought, influence movement? How strongly, in turn, does movement influence my mind and my thought? Which body postures elicit which mental reactions? For example, how does a stooped walking posture influence my mood, and what do I feel when I stand up straight?

For me, the natural sequences of the human body's movement are a central source of choreographic inspiration. Over and over again, I find new forms and ways of moving the human body that have never been seen before. Strictly speaking, every individual has her or his own body language: it is incredible how many different body languages there are. There are complete universes for us to discover here!

Movement and its logic

Exploring the logic of a movement is very important in order to aid understanding. You can view this logic on different levels: as a physical process within the context of a movement sequence; and as a part of a narrative action. Jean Cebron brings all these levels together in his course materials when drawing on Rudolf von Laban's approach to the essence of movement:

Movement is the outcome of a liberation of energy through a muscular response to an internal or external stimulus. This response generates a visual outcome in time and space.

(Züllig, 1999: translated from the German)

Movement follows the laws of physics. The logic of every movement is subject to the laws of gravity – the force drawing everything towards the centre of the earth. Movement is generated by applying energy to overcome this force: think of the logic of a swinging pendulum. Dance works both against and with gravity. The way a body sinks into itself also follows the laws of gravity.

Body and soul: Intuition in movement

Movement expresses something spiritual. To get to the bottom of a movement, it is important to proceed from the internal impulses with which it begins. A movement may be triggered by a feeling, a thought, a memory, or any other perceivable stirring of the soul. Intuitions can trigger movement sequences that function without the discursive use of reason, and without conscious conclusions. The motivation for having to move can also be described as an internal need or an internal compulsion: following an impulse that I have to move because I cannot do otherwise. The art in finding new movements is to link up with such internal impulses and work out their bodily expression in a precise way. This search is based on hard work and discipline, but creativity is also to be found in continuously trying out a movement in new ways until it is right in every sense. If you want to find and discover new movements, you have to remain open and curious.

A multitude of sources trigger movements intuitively during improvisation work. Movement is everywhere! Life is full of it and impossible without it. Everything moves. Everyday life offers an inestimable wealth of movement inspiration: facial expressions and gestures; human behaviours, rituals, and traditions; human history; the movements of different kinds of animal through the air, on land, and in the water; processes in nature such as a tree moved by the wind or a volcanic eruption; and technical and artificial sequences of movement, such as machines in operation or dense road traffic. To open up intuition as a source of ideas on movement, I work with group tasks that place my dancers in situations that oblige them to act and react immediately without thinking.

Sometimes I create a playful approach to elicit intuitive reactions. For example, I spread ten chairs about in a room. Nine dancers are sitting on the chairs and one dancer is left standing. This dancer is 9 metres away from the empty chair. The rules of the game are simple: The standing dancer has to choose one walking pace that he or she is not allowed to change and then try to sit down on the empty chair. The seated dancers' task is to sit on the empty chair before the standing dancer reaches it. Each dancer who leaves a chair is not allowed to go back and sit on that same chair again. This creates a tension that triggers the players' intuition. At the same time, the dancers have to develop a grasp of the total situation and act without thinking. Another way to awaken intuition is to work with internal images that trigger movement motivation and sensations – for example, the feeling of powerlessness. Which movements and images does this evoke? One possible image for the feeling of powerlessness is 'I simply want to run away and hide in a crack in the floor'. Another is 'It's enough to drive you up the wall!' A third is 'I could smash everything to bits!' This creates impulses for spontaneous movement ideas that we can work with during the phase of improvisation.

One powerful means of awakening movement intuitions is music. A piece of music that reminds me of a feeling has an immediate impact. Improvising with this emotion brings movements into the room in which memory comes alive. A further way of looking for and finding movement intuitions in this way is to imagine spacial situations. For example, I imagine I am standing in a wooden crate and trying to free myself through movement. Also, the movement itself and its physical logic can serve as an impulse for seeking movement ideas: using falling, for example, I can try to attain a continuous fall through constant movement. Another example is being off balance by imagining a boat in heavy seas.

Bodies inspire bodies: Partners in movement

A further important resource for discovering movements is working with a partner. When seeking steps for duets, trios, and so forth, I take very different approaches. The task is to create lifts and simultaneous sequences of movement for two or more dancers that will evoke a specific theme. My experience has shown that one good basis for this is contact improvisation. The main element the dancers have to deal with during the improvisation is complete trust in their partner: leaning on, being carried, rolling with, being caught by the partner, and so forth. (Note that being caught is not only with the partner's hands, but also with other parts of the body, such as the belly.)

A good example for developing movements through partner work is my piece *EIN SOMMERNACHTSTRAUM [A Midsummer Night's Dream]*. Here, I wanted to show how Helena adores and attaches herself to Demetrius by getting her to 'stick' to his feet. He moves quickly through the room while she hangs between his feet, repeatedly throwing herself before him. During rehearsals, we were searching for a sequence to represent this movement idea that would, on one hand, not impede the flow of Demetrius' walk while also, on the other hand, make Helena's movement clearly visible as her attempts to show her love.

To develop the marital row between Titania and Oberon in the same piece, I began by asking each dancer to individually search for 15 ways to touch a chair with different parts of the body. They sat on the chair, stood on it, carried it away, or threw it down. After they had used the chair to try out these ways of touching, I asked my dancers to transfer exactly the same movements to their partner's body. This produced dynamic sequences full of power and unusual touch. First having the opportunity to try out these ways of touching on an object and then transferring these to their partner's body made the dancers less shy about grabbing their partners. Naturally, we had to find a way of performing these movements so that nobody was injured, despite being 'thrown' about the room.

Material movement: Spaces, costumes and objects

When searching for movement, I find that stage spaces, costumes or objects can be strong partners because they confront the dancers with limitations, thereby manipulating and changing their movement. For example, in the piece *VIER TEMPERAMENTE*, my ensemble danced on 10 centimetres of sand. We grappled with this material repeatedly during the rehearsal process, trying out the various possibilities it generated. Sand can be very cold and dusty. At the same time, it is a lot of fun to throw yourself into it with your whole body, to sprinkle your limbs with sand, and to delve into it with your hands and feet. A sandy ground is very unpredictable, because it does not permit a firm stance. It always gives way. Working with the sand provided a good framework for finding new movements and images. At the same time, it confronted me as the choreographer with the challenge of protecting the health of my dancers. In such a situation, you have to adapt training to changed rehearsal conditions. For example, I had to make sure that my dancers received a special type of fitness training to protect those body parts exposed to greater strain by some of these movement sequences.

A costume can be decisive for a choreography: it can enhance movement, to make it possible, or it can limit movement, thereby providing a meaningful frame. A costume can characterise a person. Clothes can be a second skin; they can function as memorabilia, or as a symbol. Dressed in a suit, I am showing that I am preparing myself for an important occasion. By taking off a dress and standing only in my underwear, I expose myself and show my vulnerability. In my choreography *SCHUHSTÜCK*, for example, a female dancer strives to put on high platform shoes. She wants to place herself on a 'pedestal'. We played with this heightening, with walking vulnerably, and walking proudly – as well as with the changes to the lines of the body.

Objects can acquire new meaning in a choreography. For example, a funeral wreath becomes the partner in a sensuous dance solo. We all know that such a wreath is normally used to pay one's last respects to somebody who has died and it serves to decorate a grave. However, in my piece *METHUSALEM*, this wreath becomes the object of a game expressing the idea of facing the end of life joyfully and with aggressive vitality.

Individuality

The members of my ensemble come from various countries, have been brought up in many different ways, and have all kinds of social backgrounds. I have worked with dancers from Germany, Costa Rica, Ecuador, Japan, Portugal, Sweden, Russia, Australia, Italy, and so forth. All these different backgrounds also provide an impulse for creative inspiration that should not be underestimated.

When improvising with movement, I have come to recognise that every human being has his or her own personal style and individual form, dynamic and logic of movement. There is no generally valid expression of sorrow or joy. Each person shows grief in a different way, and has a personal idea of smiling or of being happy.

My 16 dancers will find at least 16 different ways to express boredom, anger or being in love. This uniqueness and individuality in dancers is an inestimable source of ideas that find their way into my work as a choreographer.

Fourth work phase: Choosing and fine tuning

Only roughly 15% of the ideas developed during the improvisation phase actually end up in the dance piece. For each piece, we collect up to 500 ideas. As the choreographer, I have to carefully examine which scenes are so unique that their content will retain its place on the stage. I generally exclude ideas that existed beforehand or have been used elsewhere.

When an improvised scene achieves the essential expression and the dynamic course of the humour and the drama match, then the next stage is to make it repeatable. If we are to recreate appropriate sequences and forms of movement, we have to analyse them precisely, which is why we record all our improvisations on DVD. This allows us to preserve and identify the successful moment so that we can return to it later and work it out precisely. The ideas we have found during improvisation have to be followed up rigorously. The more we persist in working on a movement idea, the more precisely we work it out thoroughly during improvisation, the more intensively the audience will also experience the resulting scene.

Once dancers have mastered a movement, they know exactly what to do. They understand the intention, the form, the dynamic, the timing and the spacial structure of the movement sequence. They begin to play with it and can interpret the smallest nuances of expression. The expression of a movement can be amplified when all dancers learn the same movement. Synchronised movement sequences require a formation in space, a group choreography that I work on developing with my dancers. One of my important tasks as choreographer is to decide which movement sequences are suitable for a group choreography and which are not.

This is the phase in which I specify the sequence of steps and actions for the entire performance. Together with the dramatist, I check the contents and embed them into a complete dramatic context. The choreographic assistant specifies all the dance steps. The movements are improved, the synchrony of the group choreographies rehearsed, and the sequences are specified and coordinated in space.

Fifth work phase: Setting the stage

Roughly 2 weeks before the premiere performance, the stage technicians start work. The actual set is erected for the first time. The course of the dance piece is adjusted to the spacial conditions on the stage. To complete the performance, a lighting concept is developed and applied. This is joined by sound (music and orchestra), costume and make-up, creating an initial impression of how the entire performance will look. Fine adjustments are made during the final rehearsals. Everything must be perfect for the dress rehearsal.

The performance

When actually performed, a successful choreography is a kind of miracle. My subjective 'awareness of form' as a choreographer and the 'expressive awareness' of the dancers reach out and touch the awareness of the audience. Now that the essential movements have been found and the souls of the audience are touched, the piece is finally complete. The whole development of the dance piece is directed towards this moment, when the members of the audience understand what the dancers are expressing, and they understand this with their minds, their bellies and their hearts. This requires a special form of truth and being. If it succeeds, then everybody involved – those on and behind the stage – are completely and really there, and through this presence, they manage to make the piece 'complete': a story told through dance with its own precision that succeeds without language.

Epilogue: My search for that 'other land of dance'

Finding one's own access to a topic is like opening a secret door to a hidden land – that other land of dance! Developing a piece is like taking a journey through this land in which perception and energy can, so to speak, explode into being. Something that starts with a feeling or a thought – perhaps only with a 'premonition' – becomes movement. Sometimes it is pure chance that delivers the idea for a piece: a melancholic feeling when listening to Tom Wait's 'Waltzing Mathilda' that suddenly evoked a memory of my grandfather and his life leading to images that developed into movements. This resulted in the solo *TOM TRAUBERT'S BLUES*.

My dance pieces make it possible to feel everyday life through the story narrated by the personal movements I have discovered and developed together with my dancers. This links together thought, perception, feeling, body and individuality. It is movements – mediated by an idea, a thought, a strong feeling – that create an unbelievably powerful presence on the stage: a presence that is filled with perceptual truth. Dance begins when words fail, when wordlessness expresses itself in the body, when the internal urge tells of existential life.

References

Cébron, J. (1990). Das Wesen der Bewegung. Studienmaterial nach der Theorie von Rudolf von Laban [On the essence of movement. Study material according to the theory of Rudolf von Laban]. In: U. Dietlich (Ed.), *Eine Choreographie entsteht: Das kalte Gloria. Mit einem Beitrag von Jean Cébron. (Folgwang-Texte) [A Choreogrphy Emerges: The cold Gloria. With a contribution by Jean Cébron]* (pp. 73–96). Essen: Die Blaue Eule.

Züllig, H. (1999). Horst Vollmer: Ein Tanzland aus dem Geiste der Tanzausbildung [A country of dance in the spirit of dance education]. In: *Tanzland NRW – extra.* Düsseldorf: Ministerium für Arbeit, Soziales, Stadtentwicklung, Kultur und Sport des Landes Nordrhein-Westfalen.

5   Seeing the 'choreographic mind'

Three analytic lenses developed
to probe and notate creative
thinking in dance

Scott deLahunta and Philip Barnard

Scholars and scientists working in a wide range of disciplines have debated issues associated with creative thinking from numerous perspectives. The products of these debates include many contrasting scientific models and theories (e.g., see Sawyer, 2006; Runco, 2014), as well as edited collections and 'handbooks' of studies of creative thinking (e.g., Kaufman and Sternberg, 2010). Some less technical approaches illustrate creative thinking through the lens of practice, publishing written contributions by, interviews with or accounts of individuals who have made significant creative contributions in their fields (e.g., Baron, Montuori and Baron, 1997; Root-Bernstein and Root-Bernstein, 1999). There are also a vast number of popular books addressed towards a lay 'airport bookshop' audience, and a search of the Amazon catalogue with the term 'creativity' yields some 24,000 hits. While this massive literature covers creative thinking across the arts and sciences, as well as across commerce and day-to-day problem solving, dance and choreography are largely absent from these debates. Why this is the case is not entirely clear, although in Sawyer's *Explaining Creativity* (2006, 129), contemporary dance is considered too 'marginal' an art form apparently to afford study in its own right. Another possibility is that the traditions of visual arts and literature produce fixed objects that can be probed for explanations of the creative thinking that went into creating them. This strongly contrasts with the ephemeral products of contemporary dance, and suggests that finding ways to make creative thinking in dance more explicit in descriptive terms might encourage theorists to expand their work to include this form of creative endeavour.

Against this backdrop, the choreographer Wayne McGregor and his company (see Box 5.1) initiated a series of collaborative interdisciplinary projects researching aspects of creativity in dance. The goals of these projects were particularly aimed at enhancing expert practitioner knowledge of dance through applying insights from cognitive science and, through this, potentially extending their processes or creative capabilities in dance making (deLahunta, Barnard and McGregor, 2009). The projects drew primarily on two forms of cognitive theory; distributed cognition (Kirsh, 2006), and Interacting Cognitive Subsystems (ICS), a model for human information processing (Barnard, 1985). This research produced a variety of output including a collection of published co-authored papers, new processes

---

Box 5.1 **An introduction to the choreography of Wayne McGregor**

Wayne McGregor is a London-based contemporary choreographer whose working methods have drawn inspiration from dance artists such as Merce Cunningham, Trisha Brown and William Forsythe. Like many contemporary choreographers, McGregor collaborates closely with his performers during the creative process, in McGregor's case inviting their contributions to the basic dance material for each new piece. Since founding his dance company Random Dance in 1992, his work quickly became known for its distinctive movement style and the integration of dance with film, visual art and digital media.

He has made collaboration a hallmark of his approach to dance making, consistently seeking out extensive creative and interdisciplinary research partnerships with artists and scientists. One result was a long-term enquiry into 'choreographic and physical thinking', which involved the establishment of a research department inside his dance company called R-Research. With privileged access to the development work of the company, R-Research: facilitated various collaborative research projects focused on creativity in dance; oversaw academic publication and international residencies; and set up new education partnerships. In 2013, the results of over a decade of this original research were celebrated in the exhibition, 'Thinking with the Body', at London's Wellcome Collection. It was both an examination of McGregor's particular choreographic processes, and an exploration of how mind, body and movement interact in each individual person.

Web resources (accessed March 2018):
http://waynemcgregor.com/about/wayne-mcgregor/
https://en.wikipedia.org/wiki/Wayne_McGregor
http://wellcomecollection.org/exhibitions/thinking-body-mind-and-movement-work-wayne-mcgregor-random-dance

---

applied by McGregor in the rehearsal studio, and creative-thinking tools developed for educational contexts.

The authors of this chapter established their collaboration with McGregor during an earlier interdisciplinary research project named 'Choreography and Cognition' (2003–2004).[1] This project included experiments to probe variations in dance artists' understanding of the basic principles of phrasing (deLahunta and Barnard, 2005), as well as developing our comprehension of the potential of collaboration processes using insights from social science (Leach, 2006). The work we will be discussing in this chapter evolved from this initial project into a shared concern with developing a deeper understanding of the 'intelligences' involved in dance making in the frame of 'choreographic thinking'. We were particularly interested in the conceptualisation or 'ideation space' that governs the process of making, and we envisioned a notation system related to this process with which a choreographer could 'write their own formula'. Drawing on insight from ICS, we hypothesised that we could expose parts of the creative process in dance that might be considered latent or 'hidden in' intuition, and to do so it would be necessary to devise means of collecting more information about how creative connections are formed and developed over time (Barnard, deLahunta and McGregor, 2008).

We subsequently proposed and developed three forms of categorisation, or *analytic lenses*, to organise the sharing of important attributes of artistic processes and creative thinking. The first lens we developed was designed to capture the constituent activities of making and their time course. We refer to this as a Process Model. The second lens highlighted the representations and ideational processes that underpin creative design; and we refer to this as a Bridging Model. The third lens was developed as a methodology to enable us to probe deeper into the creative thinking, *in situ*, during development and across the making, in our study of works by one prominent choreographer. We refer to this lens as Process and Concept Tracking (PACT). This chapter will summarise and exemplify the nature, uses and potential value of these lenses in the following sections.

Our aim in developing these lenses was not to 'explain' creative processes, but to enrich our descriptions of them in a way that was firmly based in the practice of an art form. We designed our categorical distinctions to be descriptively adequate, non-judgmental and, rather than relying on practitioners' memories, grounded in real time sequential tracking of how ideas develop over the course of making a specific work. Our focus was initially on deepening the understanding of expert practitioner knowledge in the field of dance and exploring the potential uses of our enriched descriptions to provide support for this practice. As a form of creative endeavour, choreography raises numerous questions about whether creative work with movement is different from other art forms such as music, writing, graphic arts and cinema. While this was not the focus of our research, we discovered that the results could potentially be applied to creative process in other art forms. In particular, we will show how our Bridging Model might come to offer a language to enable both laboratory researchers and practice-based researchers to structure and interrogate relationships within and across artistic disciplines (e.g., in music and sculpture), and to analyse forms of questioning and thinking in sci-art collaboration (Barnard and deLahunta, 2017a).

While this chapter will be tightly focussed on enriching our *descriptions* of specifically choreographic thinking, others working within the frameworks of cognitive science will most likely be concerned with how creative thinking might best be *explained* or *modelled*. Clearly, we cannot even attempt to explain creativity without reference to psychological models of how our minds work and models of how social groups function. It is therefore important to bear in mind throughout the subsequent sections that we are presenting candidate descriptive models, not candidate explanatory ones. However, adequate description is a precursor to explanation. As we have already suggested, the material products of contemporary dance are ephemeral, and this may be one reason to explain why there is less in the scientific literature on creativity in dance.

Process Model: Constituent structure and temporal course of artistic processes

Our first lens, the Process Model, focuses on categorising the constituent processes involved in the making of an artwork, how those constituent processes are organised, their temporal trajectories, and the inter-relationships across different strands of activity. Figure 5.1 shows the specific Process Model that we developed for McGregor's work with his own company in the period between 2005 and 2013. The figure identifies three broad threads of activity that will interlink with our other lenses. They are:

1   aspects of the conceptualisation of the piece,
2   methods used in the course of artistic discovery,
3   production activities: associated, in this case, with choreography to be performed in a traditional theatre.

The temporal organisation of constituent activities from inception to performance is clearly a variant of charts used in project management to identify schedules for activities and their interdependencies (Gantt, 1910). Were we to take different artists who work in fundamentally different ways, the categorisation and temporal sequences might look different, and in some cases defy realisation in this form. However, we contend that attributes and contents of a useful range of artistic processes can be exposed in this type of notation. It is not unlike a musical score, but in this case showing the annotated constituents of overt and latent attributes of temporally extended processes.

Like all notational forms, this one is expressing some attributes while leaving others unspecified. In this particular case the Process Model we developed was, in part, a response to McGregor's vision of creating a computer program that might generate solutions to 'choreographic problems' (deLahunta, 2008; Leach and deLahunta, 2015). While the notation is somewhat intricate, it merits close inspection if only because it acknowledges and directly confronts the problem of how we address the target of our research, namely; how to go about capturing the very richness of these kinds of artistic processes and the thinking underlying them. We were specifically interested in using this notation to specify the full range of physical and mental activities and, within this bigger picture, to identify where empirical studies designed to probe 'choreographic thinking' using experience sampling methods might usefully be focused (e.g., May et al., 2011), and where augmentations to the work of the company might be practicable. In Figure 5.1, the circular arrows reference processes currently used (labelled Ps) that could be open to study, and possible augmentations (labelled As) to the creative work of the company. The 'Choreographic Thinking Tools' was our most extensive case study (deLahunta, Clarke and Barnard, 2011). These were initially developed to inform

Time of Making ——▶

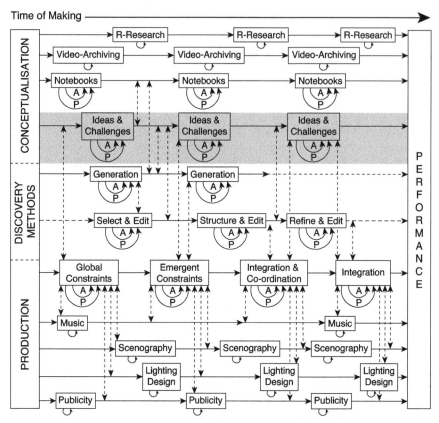

Note: The number of boxes (constituent activities) in any given thread and their temporal extent will vary from production to production. The row of activities labelled 'ideas and challenges' is highlighted not only because these are central, but also because they obviously underpin, and are affected by, outcomes of actions and constraints in all the other rows.

Figure 5.1 A Process Model: an illustrative Gantt-style diagram of the stages in the evolution of a Wayne McGregor | Random Dance production, labelling aspects of conceptualisation, discovery methods and production methods across the time of making.

McGregor's methods of working with his dancers on the creation of movement material for a dance using task-based methods, as detailed in Box 5.2. This particular augmentation applied to the phase of making indicated by the two boxes labelled 'generation' in Figure 5.1. Subsequently, further collaborative research lead to the development of a teaching resource for schools published as *Mind and Movement* (McGregor et al., 2013). The diagram shown in Figure 5.1 also helped us to consider whether any proposed augmentations were, in practice, likely to enhance or disrupt the flow of creation.

The act of drawing up the diagram shown in Figure 5.1 brought into sharp focus two observations. Our first observation was that while we could observe the development of the material over time, we could not as easily observe the evolving ideas driving decisions about movement generation, selection and structuring. The number of individual decisions that occur in the course of creating a work in the company is not only vast, but, as McGregor subsequently acknowl-edged in an interview, the development and shaping of his own conceptualisation underlying those decisions was something he kept to himself (McGregor and Barnard, 2013).

The second observation was how the hidden landscape of McGregor's evolv-ing conceptualisation intersected with all the other evolving threads, as signified in Figure 5.1 by the vertical double-headed arrows. Although we could think of examples of artistic decisions made by McGregor that were affected by these intricate intersections, our knowledge was at best piecemeal. In *AtaXia*, which premiered in 2004, we explored McGregor's interest in movement disorders and their underpinnings in cognitive neuroscience in our initial collaborative research project 'Choreography and Cognition'. Although the final production contained numerous references to movement disorder and brain functions (such as dynamic moving images of the firing of neurons), it was not clear in which strand these particular artistic decisions about movement and graphic imagery were grounded. We needed a better instrument for collecting information about the creative process: but at that time there seemed to be few systematic studies of creative chor-eographic thinking *in situ* that drew on insights from science.[2] We felt that we needed to expand our exploration beyond the specific components of the Process Model. The focus of that expansion was to think about how understandings of the intersections highlighted in the Process Model (Figure 5.1) might be shaped by the bigger picture in which they were embedded.

Bridging Model: Representations and ideational processes underpinning creative design

The nature of creative endeavour, be it in fine art, graphic design, choreography or even science, involves bridging between the sources of inspiration and a cultural context. Sources of inspiration are made up of potentially rich and diverse resources that drive a given form of artistic enquiry, while the cultural context is the social and material environment into which the products of artistic endeavour are deliv-ered. What intermediates between resources and products is a process of artistic design, and the Bridging Model shown in Figure 5.4 summarises the relationships involved in this process. Here we focus specifically on dance making, though this kind of model can in principle be applied to any design practice such as technology design or the development of diagnostic tests and therapeutic interventions for mental illness (Barnard, 1991; 2004). Figure 5.4 is composed of boxes that describe and represent contexts, assumptions, facts, observations and methods while the six arrows index seven specific ideational processes that are called into play when working with designs (analyse, assimilate, evaluate, select, modify, contextualise and synthesise).

Box 5.2 Choreographic task-based methods of working and thinking tools

Sample task instructions:
Imagine an object. You reduce it to a line drawing. You visualise an element or an aspect of that line and you describe what's visible. Then think of another object or go to another aspect of that object and describe that.

Think of a familiar song or piece of music. Focus on the memory or the feeling or sensation that it invokes in you. Translate that memory feeling or sensation into 3-D and draw its meaning or aspects of its meaning.

Figure 5.2 Choreographic thinking tools: A dancer holding in focus a geometric spatial image (dancer: Agnès López Rio).

Our research into the development of choreographic thinking tools focused on the generation part of McGregor's process when he collaborates with his dancers to create the movement vocabulary for a particular dance. He does this partly through asking his dancers to create movement in response to task instructions requiring the use of one or more forms of imagery as stimuli for the dancers (see Figure 5.2). The tasks here are relatively simple, but require a lot of mental work, some obvious and some not so obvious. The first task involves imagining and holding in focus a geometric spatial image that does not actually exist in space, and this has to be internally generated in the mind's eye. The instruction to 'describe or draw it' is a suggestion of the action (with no further directions). The second task invokes an internal aural image of something familiar in the mind's ear and then translates this to a visual three-dimensional image, all internally generated in the mind. These relatively simple tasks still require a number of unusual decisions to be made, and the dancers approach them in the spirit of creative problem solving, with task constraints limiting the decision-making space. McGregor observes the resulting movement solutions, then selects and amplifies sections for potential re-use.

The 'Choreographic Thinking Tools' project concentrated on moving the focus of attention around 'points in mental space' and across the interconnected imagery spectrum. Critical to developing this approach was the concept of the three loops (see Figure 5.3), which is a variant of the model for

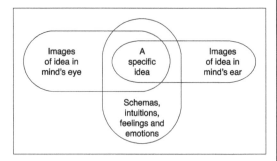

Figure 5.3 Choreographic thinking tools: The three loops supporting mental imagery.

human information processing (ICS; Barnard, 1985).

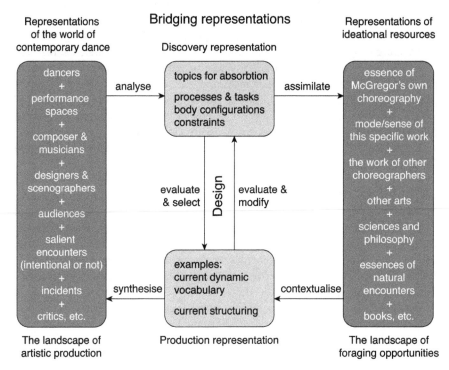

Representations of the world of contemporary dance

Bridging representations

Representations of ideational resources

Discovery representation

| dancers + performance spaces + composer & musicians + designers & scenographers + audiences + salient encounters (intentional or not) + incidents + critics, etc. | topics for absorbtion processes & tasks body configurations constraints | essence of McGregor's own choreography + mode/sense of this specific work + the work of other choreographers + other arts + sciences and philosophy + essences of natural encounters + books, etc. |

analyse   assimilate

evaluate & select   Design   evaluate & modify

examples:
current dynamic
vocabulary

current structuring

synthesise   contextualise

The landscape of artistic production

Production representation

The landscape of foraging opportunities

Figure 5.4 Bridging Model of generic representations and thought processes underpinning creative design.

On the left hand side of Figure 5.4 is a box labelled 'Representations of the world of contemporary dance' – or, more widely, any other landscape of artistic production. We know a great deal about what is out there in the world of contemporary dance, with information and context provided by specific dancers, performance spaces, audiences, DVDs of productions, company archives and so on. We can also usually say something about the 'Representations of ideational resources', shown on the right hand side of Figure 5.4: an artist often reports drawing upon books, poetry, senses of meaning in the essence of their own work and that of others, images or even the meanings that come out of natural encounters with people, places or events (see also Chapter 4). Wayne McGregor, like many other artists, forages voraciously over such sources and is very articulate in explaining how he uses them, which was an advantage for our research, as described in the following section.

In the centre of Figure 5.4 are two further boxes labelled 'Discovery representation' and 'Production representation'. These are called into play at the time of making an artwork, and provide a different perspective on the activities captured in the previous Process Model (see Figure 5.1). In the case of McGregor, he will have a number of topics in mind that he is explicitly using to generate the imagery for the processes and tasks that he will bring into the studio for the dancers to work with in order to generate his movement vocabularies. These processes and tasks are open to categorisation and description as elements of a 'Discovery represent-ation'. In a related collaborative study by cognitive scientist David Kirsh, the mix of methods McGregor uses here has been classified as task-based making, showing and making-on (Kirsh et al., 2009). 'Task-based making' was illustrated in Box 5.2. 'Showing' is the choreographer initially demonstrating some movement material. 'Making-on' is the choreographer instructing the dancer what to do in words, gestures or physical manipulations. The notion of a 'Production representation' in this context refers to those products of discovery that are recognised and eventu-ally selected in the course of creation as likely candidates, i.e., repeatable short dance phrases, to be included in the final performance, which takes place in 'the landscape of artistic production'.

Whereas the temporal trajectory and alignment of different activities was captured in the Process Model, the Bridging Model draws attention to a bigger picture. It can elucidate the substance of a given artistic endeavour, its cultural context and the mental operations associated with an actual artistic enquiry and its resulting artwork. In the main, the products of contemporary dance are ephemeral, as constituted in live performance without lingering or permanent material instant-iation. However, in both the discovery and production representations correspond-ing documentation often exists in recordings and trace formats such as videos, scores, notebooks and diagrams. These can be very useful materials themselves for fostering retrospective inspection of the notational elements of both the Process and Bridging Models (Blackwell et al., 2004). Indeed, in recent years, alongside narrative accounts of processes, dance artists are increasingly making these record-ings and trace formats available to the research community (deLahunta, 2013; Van Imschoot, 2005).

The easier part of exposing design work is usually that of characterising the substance of any representations involved. There is, as already noted, much to work with in terms of emerging materials, artefacts, documents, and interviews with or writings by the artists themselves. The difficult part is characterising the ideational processes indexed by the arrows that interlink the boxes in Figure 5.4, and underlie the creative skills deployed in choreographic thinking. We later illustrate (in the section on Process and Concept Tracking) how an interview methodology can shed at least some light on theses ideational processes (analyse, assimilate, evaluate and select/modify, contextualise and synthesise). Additionally, there are often collective processes involving the input of multiple design 'thinkers' in addition to the chore-ographer (e,g., scenographers, lighting designers, composers and costume design-ers). It is in these ideational processes that the difficult-to-articulate aspects of creativity lie. However, being hard to describe does not mean it cannot be under-stood. While we still lack widely agreed general theories, there does seem to be agreement that successful creative practice involves deep expertise, a large number of small steps and many individual decisions (Sawyer, 2006). These components are clearly open to deeper exploration within the framework of our Bridging Model and, as such, add a qualitatively different set of possibilities for enriching our understanding of the 'intelligences' underlying choreographic thinking than that afforded by the Process Model.

This perspective on design is not intended to reduce creativity to some simple-minded elements, but to provide a rich way of probing and indexing the real intricacies of creativity in action. The labelled boxes and arrows serve this purpose. When we interview an artist or use other texts or sources, we may be able to locate a remark in a particular part of, or relationship in, Figure 5.4. Indeed, the labelled boxes and arrows can even act as a means of framing specific questions to explore choreographic thinking.[3] A recent interview with McGregor focused on how the idea of shape in music, a component in the 'Representations of ideational resources' box in Figure 5.4, contributes to his own choreographies. Trained in music himself, a musical score can provide him with a window on how the composer is thinking, rather than with content to be described or visualised in dance. Among other things, he uses the score as one form of 'Discovery representation' from which aspects of the music can be *assimilated* (one of the seven ideational processes), into his ideational resources and choreographic thinking rather than as a 'production representation', where such a score would be used to support performance. The following quote illustrates that, for McGregor, the score itself can be an important ideational resource:

> So if I were working with a contemporary composer like Steve Reich or Mark-Anthony Turnage, the notations in their score already give you some sense of order and shape and form, things that they were thinking about. So in a Reich score, he will notate where there is a change of thought, by number, so the score is all notated down. Obviously the music is written but then he indicates massive changes of theme with a number like five and then six and seven. So through that score you have got it organised in a particular way that gives you some sense of shape.
>
> (Barnard and deLahunta, 2017b: p. 337)

By locating an idea or an inspiration in a particular category or relationship, we provide a potentially shareable convention in which it becomes possible to examine similarities and differences in the way one production compares with another, or to explore and notate how different artists approach the same or different tasks, questions and issues. Providing this platform for discussion, exploration and potential augmentations of artistic practice can offer practical insights to stimulate the thinking of practitioners. The stimulation occurs by providing ways of seeing more clearly how the elements of creative skills are realised and how they could undergo systematic development in the future. The development of 'Choreographic Thinking Tools', as described earlier, was greatly enhanced by having this platform, which enabled and supported focused enquiry.

In the case of choreography, as with other domains, the Bridging Model casts the activities involved as design processes placed in a context. It highlights how sources of inspiration and the current 'landscape of artistic production' shape the processes of artistic design and decision making. Yet how might we know more about what is going on in these evolving processes of design and decision making for a particular choreographer or artist working on a specific piece? In certain respects we can know something about this from how explanations might be framed in the lead up to and after the event in interviews, program notes or the accounts of experts such as dance scholars. As already mentioned, we can see what might be revealed in documents and artefacts left over from the process. However, key items such as programme notes and interviews leading up to an artistic production may be designed for presenting a particular 'public face' for the production, and dance scholars may be representing and re-casting material viewed for pedagogical purposes. To pursue our own research goal of understanding choreographic thinking *in situ* for the purposes of augmenting the creative capabilities of the artists, we needed to develop a means of recording the drivers of any changes in conceptualisation over time. The reasoning behind changes is most likely to remain inscrutable, without additional information about what brought them about at or around the time when the decisions were actually taken.

PACT: Details of choreographic thinking through Process and Concept Tracking

The Process Model (Figure 5.1) provided an organised description of the activities that occur across the time of making a 'typical' Wayne McGregor | Random Dance production. The Bridging Model (Figure 5.4) introduced a set of four basic representations (landscape of ideas, artistic production, discovery and production representations), each of which can be further elaborated or specified, and seven ideational processes underpinning design and artistic decision making that are also open to deeper elaboration. One key dimension of that elaboration relates to how design concepts progress at the time of the making of a particular production – the very issue that was brought into focus when we initially laid out the Process Model. To explore in greater depth how our seven ideational processes and four categories of representation actually work in the real world of choreographic practice, we developed the Process and Concept Tracking (PACT) methodology for probing choreographic ideas or concepts that underpin a particular artistic outcome, how they originated and changed throughout the course of making, and how these conceptualisations intersected with the artist's use of discovery and production representations.

In framing our empirical protocol we drew upon the literature describing techniques developed for so-called 'knowledge elicitation'. These are a class of techniques widely used in artificial intelligence research, cognitive science and anthropology in which the knowledge of a domain expert is systematically probed to extract underlying content linked to an area of expertise (e.g., Cooke, 1994). We also drew upon some wider thinking about the nature of expertise and the use of latent, or the rather implicit, knowledge signalled earlier (for a recent overview of approaches to expertise, see Campitelli et al., 2015). The PACT protocol is simple: an interviewer has an agenda for charting the 'choreographic ideas' and what is involved in precipitating developments and changes in these ideas over time, as indicated by the 'Ideas and Challenges' conceptualisation thread high-lighted in the Process Model (see Figure 5.1). The aim was to focus on the heart of artistic decision making in the period leading up to and during the time of making, and all the process intersections involved. In designing the categories to probe, we also drew upon key elements of the Bridging Model (see Figure 5.4). We settled upon 15 categories of information that we sought to track and elaborate (see Appendix A). Seven of these categories directly probed properties of the current evolving conceptualisation and the means used to realise them. Another seven cat-egories probed challenges, changes and the reasons for these changes, and the final category probed how the production was given a 'public face'. These 15 categories were organised into a graphic coloured coding sheet that acted to provide the prompts during the interviews and for making brief concurrent notes. It also served as a means of subsequently summarising and indexing the analysis of the resulting printed transcript that constituted the 'data' from each PACT session. The figure in Appendix B illustrates the structure of the coding sheet, along with individual panels identified and cross-indexed by number to the definition list shown in Appendix A. This coding sheet (Appendix B) and the content of Appendix A formed the common ground between choreographer and interviewer.

Using this basic protocol, we conducted four studies. Three of these involved the choreographer Wayne McGregor and tracked the making of the productions for his company of FAR (premiered 2010), UNDANCE (premiered 2011), and ATOMOS (premiered 2013). We carried out a fourth study at the Trinity Laban Conservatoire in which a sample of MA Choreography students was trained in the use of the technique to record the progress of their MA thesis projects. In this latter study, pairs of students worked together, each student acting as interviewer for the other in the role of artist, and then swapping roles.

In the three studies with McGregor, each interview was recorded and trans-cribed. These transcriptions were analysed by the two authors of this chapter; one a specialist in choreography research and the other a cognitive scientist. The pro-cess of analysis involved checking the transcripts and then discussing each of McGregor's responses to the probes. Key points were identified and assigned to the 15 categories to index the content-tracking threads. Where ambiguities of category assignment occurred, the point was generally assigned or noted in more than one category (e.g., indexed in both 'Core ideas' and as 'Key challenges'). In the process of analysis, segments of the interview on a particular topic were identified and discussed. For each segment, a key phrase was extracted to capture the essence of the topic being addressed and/or a point that had been made. This key phrase was entered onto the coding sheet, replacing any rough notes taken during the interview, to index the point and its place in the transcript. The figure in Appendix C shows a sample of key phrases entered into five of the 15 categories for the interview recorded on 8th August 2013 during the making of ATOMOS. In the context of the other 10 categories and as just one of a sequence, the full composite of phrases from all 15 categories can act as a summary of the state of play at that particular time.

By way of illustration, on that date in August, McGregor described one point about his decisions concerning the making of movement 'atoms', which was a key concept for this production, in the following words:

> ... atoms I've just scratched the surface of. I've got interesting movement material, but I want to go further in the idea before I decide about it. Some of the stuff will exist exactly as it is. I want to go back and see whether there are some atoms I should just get rid of totally, just get rid of, burn some and make some more, but still only have these 31, then see how I would organise them.
>
> (Wayne McGregor, PACT interview, 8 August 2013)

This particular segment of text was categorised as concerning 'Means / generation strategies' and summarised in its PACT entry with the key phrase 'Might burn some atoms and make more' (as highlighted in the figure in Appendix C; the fuller text is also shown in Figure 5.5). However, its meaning does not exist in isolation and can only really be grasped in the context of the content of other categories – notably the idea of an atom itself and the relationships it holds to other concepts in the ideations space, such as pixelation, growth and prime numbers.

Grasping a trajectory of choreographic thinking requires examination of a sequence of such summaries and can also benefit from being combined with the Bridging Model discussed earlier. Together they can shed a clear light on the nature of the iterations and transformations that occur when artists (as experts) move from a source of inspiration to the 'landscape of artistic production', and how, along the way, they contextualise ideas into properties within production representations. Figure 5.5 helps to illustrate the bigger trajectory from which conceptual iterations and transformations can be extracted using the PACT process.

Box 5.3 outlines a narrative account of several extractions from the ATOMOS PACT process. It provides an insight into the process' grounding, its connection with the ideation space, the imagery of new properties, and the methods used in studio work and in structuring the products of that work. It illustrates how sources and key ideas give rise to an abstract property that is initially contextualised for making movement material and then is iteratively reformulated in the feedback loop between McGregor's discovery and production representations.

A second narrative account serves to illustrate how intricately interwoven are the distinct threads of reasoning. Box 5.4 focuses on the use of human data technology and how a core idea can undergo transformation in the face of practical constraints and obstacles. This trajectory is dendritic rather than linear. A number of design avenues are explored until a particular resolution is settled upon. Whereas some concepts fall away completely, this particular thread was persistent, leaving open the possibility that one or more of its discarded elements may re-emerge in some future work. Were they to do so, their origins are discoverable as they have been already captured in the PACT process and are 'on the record.'

The PACT analysis process involves three basic steps: transcription, selection of key phrases, and assignment to categories. However, the analysis should not be seen as following strict coding rules with a right and wrong way to complete each

Box 5.3 **An illustration of key ideas in creative thinking across the making process**

A persistent concern of McGregor's is an interest in essence to be found in qualia, which was also a central thread in the conversations leading up to FAR, and it re-emerges first as the key to the possible title of a new work inspired by physics (Quantum). In December, Quantum is replaced by ATOMOS, which brings the specific property of 'indivisibility' into focus – one that also figured years before in the background projections for ATAXIA (2004). By May, the idea of indivisibility is coupled with the notion of something having the property 'uncuttable'. Here, McGregor is contemplating exploring how the idea of 'uncuttability' might work within his practice in the studio. We also see two key ideas combining: 'atoms' with 'growing'. In August, after 2 weeks in the studio, McGregor has most of the 'atoms' he is looking for. Now the questions are about qualities and what is to be kept or discarded. In the final stages, a set of prime numbers (mathematically indivisible) returns to the scaffolding of his decision making and subsequently determines the structuring of the piece.

Box 5.4 **An illustration of interwoven threads in creative thinking**

Early on during pre-studio thinking, another conceptual thread relates to McGregor's interest in using human data technology – in the studio, on stage and perhaps as a means of recording variation across all performances. At this point, McGregor's thoughts focus on the connections between emotion, data and movement, including references to body data, states of arousal and invisibility. In February, the idea appears as a key challenge: How might it be realised practically and artistically? In May, it is being considered again as a core idea, but now as 'body broadcasting'. By the fifth session it is becoming a trickier, intimate question. In the rehearsal studio in early August it returns to the world of methods of making: What might you do with the data in the studio and how? The core idea persists and ultimately becomes a process of recording his dancers' reactions to the film *Blade Runner* – the key resource mapping into all aspects of this production, and including thoughts relating to how you might know whether or not an individual is a 'replicant'. The resultant data is then used to derive and print abstract imagery onto the dancers costumes by Studio XO (2013).

step. Rather the interview transcripts and the coding sheets are best viewed as a resource that can be probed, filtered and represented in many different ways. For example, in the case of the ATOMOS sequence, columnar extractions from the PACT process were presented in 2013 as part of a 6 week exhibition at the Wellcome Collection, London, exposing the public to more than a decade of interdisciplinary

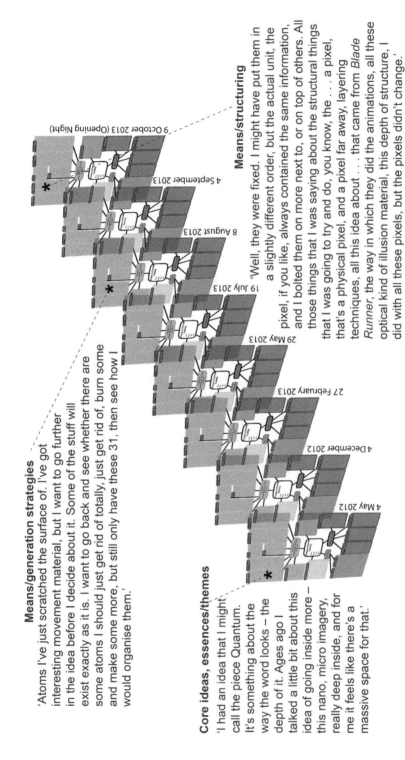

Means/generation strategies

'Atoms I've just scratched the surface of. I've got interesting movement material, but I want to go further in the idea before I decide about it. Some of the stuff will exist exactly as it is. I want to go back and see whether there are some atoms I should just get rid of totally, just get rid of, burn some and make some more, but still only have these 31, then see how I would organise them.'

Core ideas, essences/themes

'I had an idea that I might call the piece Quantum. It's something about the way the word looks – the depth of it. Ages ago I talked a little bit about this idea of going inside more – this nano, micro imagery, really deep inside, and for me it feels like there's a massive space for that.'

Means/structuring

'Well, they were fixed. I might have put them in a slightly different order, but the actual unit, the pixel, if you like, always contained the same information, and I bolted them on more next to, or on top of others. All those things that I was saying about the structural things that I was going to try and do, you know, the . . . a pixel, that's a physical pixel, and a pixel far away, layering techniques, all this idea about . . . that came from *Blade Runner*, the way in which they did the animations, all these optical kind of illusion material, this depth of structure, I did with all these pixels, but the pixels didn't change.'

Figure 5.5 The sequence of eight coding sheets from PACT interviews for the ATOMOS process (2012–2013), with examples of segments of transcript indexed on the coding sheet.

collaborative research embedded in Wayne McGregor | Random Dance (Wellcome Collection, 2013). As we noted earlier, our intention is not to reduce the elements of choreographic thinking, but to empower and enrich our understandings of its many forms. In the discussion to follow we will further illustrate the range of these three analytic lenses.

Extending knowledge of dance/choreography and augmenting practice

We have now provided concrete illustrations of our three interlinked analytic lenses. In summary, the Process Model focussed on the constituent activities of making and their time course; the Bridging Model highlighted the representations and ideational processes that underpin creative design; and the Process and Concept Tracking (PACT) methodology enabled us to probe deeper into the choreographic thinking, *in situ*, during development and across the making of works by one prominent choreographer. We opened this chapter by observing that, within the vast and diverse literature on creative thinking, dance and choreography was sparsely covered. Our aim has not been to 'explain' or theorise about creative processes in dance, but to enrich our descriptions of them. Our use of the three analytic lenses in combination has opened up new pathways for such enrichment. We sought not just to enhance expert practitioner knowledge of dance, but also to consider how that understanding might support the augmentation of expert practice, to enrich artistic research and education and to facilitate interdisciplinary collaboration.

In relation to the enrichment of research and education, we noted that our broader enquiry had, in conjunction with empirical research on imagery, made use of both the Process and Bridging Models to help frame 'Choreographic Thinking Tools' in order to augment and develop the practice of both expert and student dancers (deLahunta, Clarke and Barnard, 2011; McGregor et al., 2013). These were targeted at augmenting the discovery representations (Bridging Model) invoked during movement vocabulary generation stages at the time of making (Process Model). While the PACT process was primarily developed to enrich and deepen our understanding of the nature of, and changes to, artistic ideas, rationales and decisions, an unforeseen outcome of our four studies was that the PACT process itself could act as a tool to augment current practice rather than just remaining a vehicle for research. PACT was designed not only as 'data' collection, but also to offer an artist a unique opportunity to reflectively forage over a terrain of decision making in a way that is non-judgemental or neutral with respect to whether or not something was a good decision. McGregor found the process of exploring this ideational landscape a valuable form of support for his own working practice and has publicly remarked that the methodology enabled him to explore his own ideas in a deeper and richer way than he otherwise would (McGregor and Barnard, 2013). For McGregor, PACT has become a new 'discovery representation'. Initially developed to increase understanding of dance creation so we could explore ways to augment it, PACT has now become a part of the creation process, offering possible augmentations to the 'Ideas and Challenges' thread of the Process Model.

In the course of the three McGregor productions in which PACT was carried out, we also explored use of the same protocol with some of his collaborators. Interestingly, a common thread from their feedback was that the categorical and non-judgemental form of probing provided them with a valuable vehicle through which they could expose what they wanted to say about their artistic processes rather than by responding to a more selective questioning regime. Similarly, the students who used the PACT process at Trinity Laban also noted that the discipline of successively recording their choreographic thinking in explicit category headings not only helped to develop their ideas, but also provided substantial material for use in writing up their MA theses. The non-judgmental way in which PACT questions draw out and differentiate possible influences on process as changes over time is unusual in artistic education, which has a tradition of evaluating creative work on the basis of qualitative judgements reflecting aesthetic preference.

Augmenting wider studies of creative thinking and interdisciplinary understanding

In relation to using the three analytic lenses to enrich understanding of choreographic and other forms of creative thinking, we are encouraged by the preliminary outcomes from the three productions whose developmental course we have tracked with PACT and studied using the Process and Bridging Models. Based on McGregor's work we now have access to a rich resource that is indexed in a way that enables us to pose questions and find evidence about the nature, origins and changes to his creative thinking. This resource systematically draws out new material and the four representations and seven processes (analyse, assimilate, evaluate, select, modify, contextualise and synthesise) of the Bridging Model provide a categorical framework that supports analysis of and discourse about the mechanics of creative design. The original Process Model continues to provide a useful instrument for parsing the organisation of the time of making in the studio. It is important to note that all of these categorical lenses can be applied, adapted and used to notate a wide range of creative endeavours other than dance. With respect to pedagogy, PACT in particular exposes the realities of choreographic decision making in its raw rather than idealised form. This includes blind alleys as well as pragmatic resolutions to difficult conceptual and operational challenges (see Boxes 5.3 and 5.4).

Even though the Process Model, the Bridging Model and PACT were all developed as descriptive tools rather than explanatory ones, they nonetheless could play a significant role in the exploration and analysis of other domains of creative endeavour. So, for example, we invite readers to take the Bridging Model and consider how they might wish to fill out the content of the four boxes for a pure or applied science, such as genetics or medicine, or for other arts practices such as musical composition or photography. We contend that these can all be considered as forms of design activity or creation and are amenable to similar forms of probing. While one cannot attempt to explain creativity without reference to psychological models of how our minds work and models of how social groups function, we can bring them all into focus through the lens of the Bridging Model. Within the very broad reaching field of the cognitive and social neurosciences, there are many theoretical positions on creative thinking that are not necessarily mutually exclusive. More likely than not, any given approach or theory will only be of limited scope. Each approach of theory will be directed at a particular set of phenomena, such as insightful problem solving, divergent thinking or individual differences in uses of imagery or other forms of creative potential.

Both the Bridging Model and our PACT analysis emphasise that creativity is based in deep expertise and knowledge over *all* elements of the Bridging Model. When coupled with the fact that designs of any complexity or interest most likely result from a lot of hard work, design iterations, and collaborations, our work endorses the view that creativity rests on many small decisions of different kinds (e.g., see Sawyer, 2006). To this extent our Bridging Model should be seen as an integrated framework for probing the similarities and differences in the conduct of creative endeavours within and across disciplines. One of the few cases in the literature on creativity that takes contemporary dance into account is Root-Bernstein and Root-Bernstein (1999), who also emphasise the transformation of ideas in creative processes. In reference to such transformations, PACT provides greater enrichment of the substance that needs to be explained in either its specificity or in some more generalised form, while the Bridging Model enables us to contextualise where, when and how particular transformations may be of significance. Neither the Bridging model nor the PACT methodology negates other scholarly resources. Neither are they conventional tools to support data collection. However, the systematic tracking and indexing of data derived from the creative process adds a new dimension to scholarly and practice-based research possibilities.

The Bridging Model has a further property of note on which it seems apposite to conclude: it offers a means of addressing deep-rooted barriers to interdisciplinary collaboration through exposing assumptions that are intrinsic to disciplinary knowledge. Here we have characterised the generation of an artwork in terms of its representations and processes, and used the PACT methodology to elaborate substantive illustrations. As already noted, the Bridging Model has also been used to characterise the paradigms of science and applied science work (e.g., see Barnard, 1991; 2004; Long and Dowell, 1989). The 'methods' sections of a typical scientific paper are clearly 'Discovery representations' that, by convention, must be sufficiently complete and explicit to allow other scientists to replicate that study; while the presentation of a scientific lecture, or an instructional text for building suspension bridges, respectively form pedagogical or engineering 'Production representations' that contextualise knowledge in the science base for a specific purpose. In contrast, the 'Discovery' and 'Production representations' that exist in the arts emphasise individuality and distinctiveness. They are typically unique in their own ways and replication often has negative connotations. However, the Bridging Model can be used to explore and expose fresh insights at the interdisciplinary overlap of the collaborations. For example, the 'Choreographic Thinking Tools' developed within Wayne McGregor | Random Dance (McGregor et al., 2013) are a 'Production representation' for pedagogy that itself resulted from a creative process of design grounded in collaborative research using the methods of scientific discovery (e.g., see May et al., 2011), and drawing on the ideational resource of the theory base of cognitive psychology (e.g., see deLahunta, Clarke and Barnard, 2011). The Bridging Model shows how the individuality and distinctiveness of an arts paradigm is maintained while using science in a particular way. This research into 'Choreographic Thinking Tools' also led eventually to a teaching resource with a character consistent with its artistic parentage and scientific grounding (McGregor et al., 2013). This consistency can be shown by the Bridging Model using the concept of 'audit traces' as a means to question and expose *what* is learned in interdisciplinary collaboration and *how* (Barnard and deLahunta, 2017a).

Conclusion: Suggestions for readers

The three analytic lenses described in this chapter all developed into a fusion of arts research with applied cognitive psychology. In each case the aim was to enrich descriptions of arts practice initially with a view to modest augmentations of the particular practice in question, which subsequently enabled broader fundamental enquiries about the nature and possible evolution of studio practice and education. Our discussion elaborated a number of ways in which the Process Model, Bridging Model and PACT process were actually put to some practical use in the work of a professional dance company, its education department and their associates. The overall enterprise was itself a very particular form of interdisciplinary collaborative research, eventually revealing how such research itself might be better understood.

We invite readers in the arts to stand back from these examples and pose questions for themselves about the potential benefit of applying such tools for thought within their own practice, and to consider how they might be extended, what opportunities they could offer, and what assumptions they might bring to light as well as the limitations. The particular Process Model we developed, for example, assumes that there are generative processes in place that can be locally and optionally augmented. If the specific artistic process being studied resists the concept of generation, the categories can be adapted. The only fixed category in the Process Model is time. The Bridging Model distinguishes between representations of the real world and sources of inspiration. It identifies eight processes that categorise the thinking involved as iterative design activity moves from these sources of inspiration to the artistic productions. The seven processes linking the boxes of the Bridging Model can act as probes by both experts and novices to organise study and analysis of the artistic process, whether in the context of interviews or in conducting classroom discussions and debates. Critical questions should arise regarding the adequacy of the various categories for mapping rich and diverse domains. For example: Are there too few categories and what extra distinctions might be of use? What about ineffability? Where a domain resists decomposition as design, what alternatives might there be to a discourse of sharing that adds to the more conventional art-based forms of narrative that are already extensively debated? How are the processes themselves changed as a result of applying the various lenses? That this happens with the PACT process has already been discussed and exposed as an augmentation of creative thinking, which was the original aim of the research at the outset. One of the advantages of having all three lenses is that they are intended to work this way; for one to help frame thinking about another.

As mentioned earlier, the Bridging Model has been put to use in thinking about the practice of pure and applied sciences (Barnard, 2004; Long and Dowell, 1989). Here we invite readers in the sciences interested in interdisciplinary collaboration to consider how the three lenses, working together in combination, might open up questions and thinking about how their work and knowledge might find non-trivial use in arts practice. In particular they might ask where and how their science base or methods might contribute to the iterative design cycles of the Bridging and Process Models. Having knowledge of scientific domain may be noteworthy and inspirational, but this does no real artistic work within these cycles. Similarly, scientific work pursued at this interdisciplinary juncture may struggle to represent its outcomes as viable standard results from a science perspective. In interdisciplinary collaborative research, compromises may be necessary that break the requirements for reporting work in a high quality scientific journal. Additionally, it is important to recognise that ideas and knowledge in the arts may be realised in materials, objects or behaviours. How might a scientist start thinking about the relationship between their normal forms of communication, which rely in the main on verbal and written forms, and the kinds of ideas brought into focus and communicated in the arts through more tacit means?

In this chapter we have sought to use analytic lenses to help frame the questions and enable conversation amongst science and arts practitioners. By exposing arts-based, science-based and collaboration-based practice within a common framework such as the Bridging Model, possibly supplemented by PACT interviews, we could potentially facilitate reciprocal understandings of the different languages of science and art, and through that generate greater frequency of positive outcomes to interdisciplinary collaborations.

Notes

1 See: www.choreocog.net/ (accessed March 2018).
2 A major exception was the 'Choreographic Cognition' (1999–2008) Australian research project, which explored a wide range of topics including communication between dancers, audience response, and improvisation and memory (Stevens et al., 2003).
3 A recent example involved developing 'cognitive interviews' for choreographic domain experts in the context of an Australian research project entitled 'Thinking Brains and Bodies: Distributed cognition and dynamic memory in Australian dance theatre'. http://tinyurl.com/hhfnv8k (accessed March 2018).

Appendix A: Categories of PACT knowledge probed and elaborated

Describing your process in the categories listed below:

- enables structured reflection and facilitates accessing and sharing information about your process;
- captures what you are thinking about and how things change over time (each PACT inherits the previous one);
- requires making decisions about what is noteworthy;
- acknowledges that categories are not mutually exclusive and that everything is interconnected.

Note on terminology: A property is an attribute of a referent. So, for example, the source of inspiration might be the archaeological site of Jantra Mantra (the referent) and the property in focus might be 'scale' in measurement.

Properties of conceptualisation and the means to realise it:

1 *Core ideas:* can also think in terms of 'essences' and 'themes'. The original ideas or concepts, e.g., Jantra Mantra = measurement, scale, time. May be ideas of a domain, or may be ideas to do with the choreography itself.
2 *Means/generation strategies:* tasks, making-on, showing, and other means of making. Improvisation and games. The structuring ideas are also captured here.
3 *Imagery:* emerging in own mind, e.g., of music, a location, or of even an emotional feeling.
4 *Sources (material sources):* reading particular books, theoretical references, the work of other artists, research questions, etc.
5 *Integration global constraints:* can come from the choreographer's mind or from the interaction of the choreographer's mind with the world. Global constraints will apply throughout, e.g., working with a company of 10 dancers; or a commission to work with Turnage. A range of constraints are normally set from the outset. The premiere date is a global constraint.
6 *Integration local constraints:* practical problems with studios, sick dancers, or the performance space results in having to work differently on certain days. Disruptions to the day-to-day working process.
7 *Any other issues on concepts:* to use for your own categories, or where some idea does not fit elsewhere.

Key challenges, changes and mediators of change:

8 *Key challenges (drivers of change):* problems that have no easy solutions. A global constraint might become a key challenge.

9 *Other changes of note:* to use for your own categories, or where a remark about change does not fit elsewhere: e.g., working in a new way or clarification of selection criteria.

10 *New key properties:* occurrences that change the properties of conceptualisation: e.g., shortening a list of key words used to generate movement vocabulary.

11 *Critical incidents or observations in studio/generation:* specific occurrences that happen while making.

12 *Altered constraints:* global or local constraints, e.g., budget or venue changes.

13 *Critical incidents or observations outside generation context:* discussions with collaborators, e.g., developing a new score or making strategy.

14 *Serendipitous instigators of change:* occurrences or developments that have happened by chance and have invoked an idea that led to a change: e.g., noticing something in the street or on TV.

Ancillary item:

15 *Public face of production:* something you use as an application representation for the purpose of telling others what it is about. It may have an affect on subsequent things, e.g., critics and writers/journalists. An emerging space of discourse that may extend beyond the specific work in focus.

Appendix B: The PACT coding sheet

The PACT coding sheet is used for eliciting and coding properties concerning core ideas, strategies, imagery, sources, constraints and changes that apply at a particular point in time while making. Linked to the category numbers of PACT knowledge (see Appendix A), the properties of ideas are located in the upper part of the figure (1–7), and the changes in the lower part (8–15).

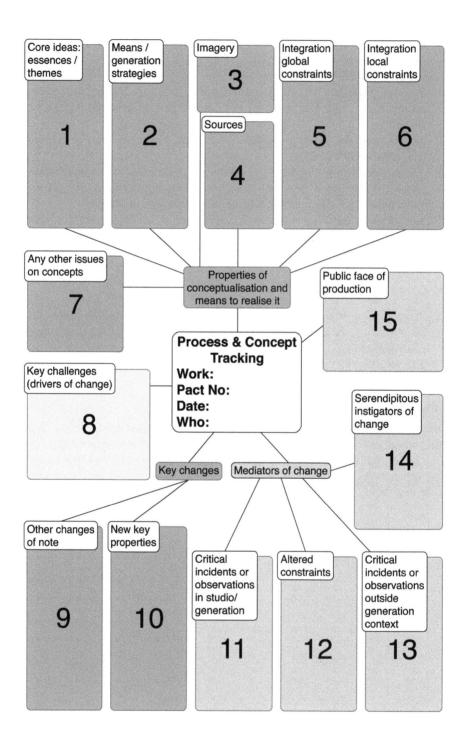

Appendix C: Sample of key phrases from a PACT coding sheet

Key phrases were recorded in an interview with Wayne McGregor on 8th August 2013 during the making of ATMOS. This sample covers five of the 15 categories from the PACT coding sheet.

Core ideas: essences / themes

Atomisation, growth & emotion as themes taken for granted.

Has a sense of musical texture of the whole.

Cutting holes in things that should not be there.

Prime numbers for structuring reaffirmed – if 3-D might use higher primes with projected dancers.

Also 3-D printed object still in mind.

New idea – what is the smallest perceptible movement that can be seen; and how could he structure from these? It's time based p16.

New idea – text-based organisational structure to replace counting (time) p16.

Means / generation strategies

Creating 31 atoms, revisiting only for development / Now up to 27 (some from own references, from structured tasks using different ideas – biometrics, emotions, visualising personal data, cinegraphic text, some from the film, atomising meaning of text & using Becoming).

Material for subsequent cutting holes in, developing, growing and building.

Might burn some atoms and make more.

Some of music in studio from XXX, also other CDs but all music that WM has NOT used before.

Using Roundhouse intervention to explore what it might mean to grow material live (p9/10), up to 16 mins using rules/play/games.

Pixelation & text task – idea to think that they are making not performing. Has more than enough means & methods.

New key properties

Dynamic quality that gets embedded in atom and then does not change.

Richness in floor imagery with black hole in it but decisions still need to be made.

Will have cohesion but also interested in things that don't feel right: cutting holes in things that should not be there: dance not feeling that it goes there / lights that don't feel part of the environment p8.

Length of sequence in growing (critical incident OGC).

Working with multiple structures at the same time p9.

What is the smallest perceptible movement that can be seen?

Key challenges (drivers of change)

Getting material already to hand down to 65 minutes.

Nailing the technical aspects in the very near future / projector stuff / Nancy etc. the 'quandry of the moment' p16.

Getting the real printed floor with a black hole in the middle.

Public face of production

Reaffirms Wellcome, *Evening Standard* & CNN (XXX) publicity happenings.

But still not sure about boundaries – perhaps 'an iconic film'.

WM did not like photos from original photoshoot – too 'dancy' – new ones with more pixelated feel.

Key to abbreviations:
A number following a p – such as p16 – indexes the page number of the full transcript from where the key phrase was extracted; WM references Wayne McGregor; OGC references 'outside generation context'; CD = compact disc; XXX is substituted here for the name of a specific composer; 'Becoming' is the name given to an 'eleventh dancer' taking the form of AI software driving the image of a conceptual dynamic 3-D body used to stimulate the development of movement material in the studio; Nancy refers to the costume designer (Nancy Tilbury).

References

Barnard, P. J. (1985). Interacting cognitive subsystems: A psycholinguistic approach to short term memory. In: J. Ellis (Ed.), *Progress in the Psychology of Language* (Vol. 2, pp. 197–258). London: Lawrence Erlbaum Associates.

Barnard, P. (1991). Bridging between basic theories and the artefacts of human–computer interaction. In: J. M. Carroll (Ed.), *Designing Interaction: Psychology at the Human–Computer Interface* (pp. 103–127). Cambridge: Cambridge University Press.

Barnard, P. (2004). Bridging between basic theory and clinical practice. *Behaviour Research and Therapy,* 42(9), 977–1000.

Barnard, P. & deLahunta, S. (2017a). Mapping the audit traces of interdisciplinary collaboration: Bridging and blending between choreography and cognitive science. *Interdisciplinary Science Reviews,* 42(4), 359–380.

Barnard, P. & deLahunta, S. (2017b). Intersecting shapes in music and in dance. In: D. Leech-Wilkinson & H. M. Prior (Eds.), *Music and Shape* (pp. 328–350). Oxford: Oxford University Press.

Barnard, P., deLahunta, S., & McGregor, W. (2008). A summary: Principles of choreographic thinking. *Report from Symposium at the Squire Bancroft Studio, Royal Academy of Dramatic Art, London.* 14–15.

Baron, F., Montuori, A., & Baron, A. (1997). *Creators on Creating: Awakening and cultivating the imaginative mind.* New York: Penguin.

Blackwell, A., deLahunta, S., McGregor, W., & Warwicker, J. (2004). Transactables. *Performance Research, On The Page Issue,* 9(2), 67–72.

Campitelli, G., Connors, M. H., Bilalić, M., & Hambrick, D. Z. (2015). Psychological perspectives on expertise. *Frontiers in Psychology,* 6, 258.

Cooke, N. J. (1994). Varieties of knowledge elicitation techniques. *International Journal of Human-Computer Studies,* 41: 801–849.

deLahunta, S. (2008). The choreographic language agent. *Proceedings of the World Dance Alliance Global Summit.* http://ausdance.org.au/articles/details/the-choreographic-language-agent (accessed March 2018).

deLahunta, S. (2013). Publishing choreographic ideas: Discourse from practice. In: M. Wilson & S. van Ruiten (Eds.), *SHARE: Handbook for Artistic Research Education* (pp. 170–177). Amsterdam, Netherlands: ELIA.

deLahunta, S. & Barnard, P. (2005). What's in a Phrase? In: J. Birringer & J. Fenger (Eds.), *Tanz im Kopf / Dance and Cognition* (pp. 253–266). Münster, Germany: LIT Verlag.

deLahunta, S., Barnard, P. J., & McGregor, W. (2009). Augmenting choreography: Insights and inspirations from science. In: J. Butterworth & L. Wildschut (Eds.), *Contemporary Choreography: A critical reader* (431–448). London: Routledge.

deLahunta, S., Clarke., G., & Barnard, P. (2011). A conversation about choreographic thinking tools. *Journal of Dance and Somatic Practices,* 3(1&2), 243–259.

Gantt, H. L. (1910). *Work, Wages and Profit.* New York: the Engineering Magazine. Republished in 1974 as *Work, Wages and Profits.* Easton, PA: Hive Publishing Company.

Kaufman, J. C. & Sternberg, R. J. (2010). *The Cambridge Handbook of Creativity.* New York: Cambridge University Press.

Kirsh, D. (2006). Distributed cognition: A methodological note. *Pragmatics and Cognition,* 14(2), 249–262.

Kirsh, D., Muntanyola, R., Jao, J., Lew, A., & Sugihara, M. (2009). Choreographic methods for creating novel, high quality dance. *Design and Semantics of Form and Movement: DESFORM 2009 in Taipei, Taiwan.*

Leach, J. (2006). Extending contexts, making possibilities: An introduction to evaluating the projects. *Leonardo*, 39(5), 447–451.

Leach, J. & deLahunta, S. (2015). Dance 'becoming' knowledge. https://curve.coventry. ac.uk/open/file/cce782d9-6cde-4726-819a-92b58f6b2489/1/becomingcomb.pdf (accessed March 2018).

Long, J. B. & Dowell, J. (1989). Conceptions of the discipline of HCI: Craft, applied science and engineering. In: A. Sutcliffe & L. Macaulay (Eds.), *People and Computers* (Vol. V, pp. 9–32). Cambridge: Cambridge University Press.

May, J., Calvino-Merino, B., deLahunta, S., McGregor, W., Cusack, R., Owen, A., Veldsman, M., Ramponi, C., & Barnard, P. (2011). Points in mental space: An interdisciplinary study of imagery in movement creation. *Dance Research*, 29(2), 402–430.

McGregor, W. & Barnard, P. (2013). *Thinking with the Body: Process and concept tracking.* Video. http://wellcomecollection.org/files/thinking-body-process-and-concept-tracking-wayne-mcgregor-random-dance (accessed March 2018).

McGregor, W., Barnard, P., deLahunta, S., Wilson, J., & Douglas-Allen, G. (2013). *Mind and Movement – Choreographic thinking tools.* London: Wayne McGregor | Random Dance.

Root-Bernstein, R. & Root-Bernstein, M. (1999). *Sparks of Genius: The thirteen thinking tools of the world's most creative people.* Boston, MA: Houghton Mifflin Co.

Runco, M. A. (2014). *Creativity: Theories and themes: Research development and practice, Second Edition.* London: Academic Press.

Sawyer, R. K. (2006). *Explaining Creativity: The science of human innovation.* Oxford: Oxford University Press.

Stevens C., Malloch S., McKechnie S., & Steven, N. (2003). Choreographic cognition: The time-course and phenomenology of creating a dance. *Pragmatics and Cognition,* 11(2), 297–326.

Studio XO. (2013). *Studio XO Fashioning Technologies.* Video. http://tinyurl.com/oaq5pbw (accessed March 2018).

Van Imschoot, M. (2005). Rests in Pieces: On scores, notation and the trace in dance. Essay. http://olga0.oralsite.be/oralsite/pages/What's_the_Score_Publication/ (accessed March 2018).

Wellcome Collection. (2013). *Thinking with the Body: Mind and movement in the work of Wayne McGregor | Random Dance.* Exhibition. http://wellcomecollection.org/thinking withthebody (accessed March 2018).

Part II
The science perspective

6 Building blocks and architecture of dance

A cognitive–perceptual perspective

Thomas Schack

Introduction

Dance has been a functional element in evolution and the development of our culture since more than one million years. Furthermore, dance plays an important role in ontogenesis and therefore has an effect on our daily lives. I happily remember my first efforts in dancing as a child, or the more communicative function of dancing as a teenager. It has been a pleasure for me to do some vague steps in learning Mambo, Tango, Salsa or Swing. However, a new dimension of understanding the world opened up when we had the opportunity to observe our little daughter at the age of 2 or 3 years often dancing for more than 30 minutes without any obvious external reason and without music, but with an impressive (innate?) choreography. Not only for our personal and social development, but also for future cultural rules, dance plays an important role; for instance, in the context of traditional healing ceremonies (Schack and Schack, 2017). Very often joyful to perform or to observe, dancing can be very difficult to describe in scientific terms and to investigate in an appropriate manner. What could be described as *fusion of dance with environment and circumstance* occurs if dancers do not plan their movements or think about their limbs and body kinematics, but trust their coordination and their capacity for movement freely, with flexibility in space and time. The wish to experience this joyful stage over and over again could be the reason and motivation for human dancing in general.

In contrast, learning a specific movement technique in dance requires a lot of attention to individual movement elements and to the dynamics and the kinematics of the movement. This, of course, also applies to teaching dance: teaching dancing skills includes much technical and aesthetic preparation and expertise, and much work on movement details, as well as on mental and emotional states (see Chapter 1). In such dance-related interactions, teachers and dancers sometimes fail to understand each other, for a number of different reasons. First, they might be addressing different details of the movements, and/or they might be using different words to describe them. Second, coaches and dancers often differ strongly in age and expertise level. Third, coaches and dancers might have a different learning background or preference. To understand the cognitive and motivational reasons for such dance-related teaching and interaction problems, it is important to get a closer insight into the development and changes within the cognitive and bio-mechanical systems of dancers. In this light, science comes into play and may help practitioners to increase the understanding of the building blocks and the cognitive architecture of dance.

Experts from the field of dance often emphasize the function of the senses, experience and movement memory in a dancer's learning of movements. In many interesting discussions among the authors of this book we have learned that, in our common understanding, skill learning in dance is based on different building blocks, such as perceptual information, mental representation of movement elements in long-term memory ('movement memory bank'), and muscle and reflex control in the motor system. We agreed that researchers often refer to assumptions about the principles governing the combination and cooperation of such building blocks in dance, and that such building blocks and principles may have also informed the background of dance-theoretical and teaching systems developed by Rudolf Laban, Agrippina Vaganova and others.

Research from multiple disciplines has demonstrated that motor actions are based on modular structures, comprised of individual building blocks or motor primitives that are organized in a hierarchical way (see Schack et al., 2014a). Building blocks and principles of motor control in dance have been addressed from different perspectives and at different levels of granularity. Jola, Davis and Haggard (2011), for instance, have investigated basic processes of dancing performance focusing on the integration of perceptual information from different sensory modalities, such as visual and kinesthetic information. Other studies have investigated kinematic and dynamic components of dance from the perspective of biomechanics (see Krasnow et al., 2011, for an overview), attention and choreography-related timing (Minvielle-Moncla et al., 2008), or neurophysiological mechanisms of interaction and coordination in dance (Keller, Novembre and Hove, 2014). From an interaction-oriented perspective, not only basic processes or building blocks of dance at an individual level are of interest, but also shared action goals and shared knowledge of dance partners (see Keller, Novembre and Hove, 2014). Another line of studies has investigated neurocognitive processes in dance observers (e.g., Karpati et al., 2015; Jang and Pollick, 2011: see also Chapters 10 to 13).

For defining and understanding building blocks of dance, event segmentation theory has provided an interesting approach (Zacks et al., 2007), showing that the way in which a person spontaneously segments an observed action determines the understanding and later memorizing of this action (e.g., Zacks et al., 2009). This approach has been applied by Bläsing (2015) to study the expertise- and experience-dependent segmentation of movements in dance. The scientific definition and understanding of particular units or building blocks of action (e.g., motor primitives, events and basic action concepts) in dancing performance can be informed and framed by action theory. From an action-theoretical point of view, a fundamental action situation consists of three components: the person, the task and the environment (Nitsch and Hackfort, 2016; Schack and Hackfort, 2007). By considering these components, every action situation can be accounted for in detail.

Dance performance depends on the current physical and mental condition of the dancer (person), on the situational demand of the discipline (task), and on the conditions under which the task has to be carried out, for example in training or competition (environment). From this perspective, actions are organized intentionally in line with a person's subjective interpretation of a given person–task–environment constellation (action situation). Considering that dance is most often related to other persons and an audience, it could be addressed as an interaction, so that additional components of interpersonal coordination, like anticipating others' actions, come into play (Keller, Novembre and Hove, 2014).

This chapter, with a particular focus on action-related aspects of dance, presents a functional model that highlights the interplay between movement goals, mental representations and perceptual feedback. Using research from related fields, it is illustrated how this hierarchical model is composed of interdependent levels, of which goal-directedness is the highest level of action organization in dance. Considering that mental representations may have a functional role between the level of (shared) goals, perception and motor execution, this will become the starting point of a journey from dance to science, leading to a better understanding of motor control, learning and teaching in dance.

Mental representation in dance

Mental representations are important components of dancing performance and human motor actions in general (Schack and Mechsner, 2006; Bläsing et al., 2014; Schack et al., 2014a: see also Chapters 9 and 1). In dance, as in sports, mental representation makes it possible to select and combine effective sources of information. Regardless of the movement (whether a ballet dancer has to perform a pirouette, a Latin dancer has to select the appropriate Salsa movement for his partner, or a round dancer to choose with which member of the group to perform the next figure in a waltz), dancers use their mental representation as a foundation to identify possible and functionally relevant sensory input. Frequently, this identification has to be made under extreme time pressure. Hence, mental representation in dance has to be available quickly and has to provide clear criteria for selecting relevant pieces of information. At the same time, mental representation forms the functional basis for a meaningful and thereby task-related reduction in the large number of potential behaviors available to us, our partners in dance and the whole performance system. Mental representation in dance does not just facilitate information selection, but also more generally permits a target-related and purposeful adaptation of behavioral potentials to conditions in the environment. In other words, mental representation helps to *shape interaction patterns* in dance in purposeful ways. This also includes storing the cognitive–perceptual outcomes of learning processes in long-term memory.

The representational nature and functional role of the long-term memory structures involved in human movement control remains under much debate in movement science and cognitive psychology. One fundamental issue is the representational medium: Is there a special motor memory completely distinct from perceptual–cognitive structures and processes, or do movements, objects and external events have a common representational medium (Hommel et al., 2001)? One prominent theoretical position favours the first alternative, while assuming that motor performance basically means the selection and execution of muscle-related motor programs. Characteristic invariants of such motor programs may be stored in long-term memory. For example, Schmidt's theory of generalized motor programs (GMP; Schmidt and Lee, 1998) suggests that relative durations as well as relative forces in patterns of muscular activation define invariants of motor programs that are stored in long-term memory. This theory also posits that the absolute duration and absolute force need to be planned for motor performance, but that this is done in a situation-specific way.

An alternative view suggests that movements are organized and stored in memory as perceptible events through a mental representation of anticipated characteristic (e.g., sensory) effects, with the corresponding motor activity auto-matically and flexibly tuned to serve these effects. A number of scientists (e.g., Bläsing, Tenenbaum and Schack, 2009; Mechsner et al., 2001; Schack and Mechsner, 2006; Schack and Ritter, 2013) hypothesize that voluntary movements follow perceptual–cognitive (mental) representations. In a similar vein, different researchers (e.g., Ivry et al., 2004; Weigelt, Kunde and Prinz, 2006; Seegelke et al., 2013) have claimed that central costs and interference in bimanual actions depend solely on how these movements are represented on a cognitive level. Assuming that these hypotheses of a perceptual–cognitive control are correct, it seems plausible to generalize them to more complex tasks such as those performed by dancers (Bläsing, Tenenbaum and Schack, 2009; Geburzi, Engel and Schack, 2004: see also Chapter 9). In the same direction, David Rosenbaum assumes that the cognitive representation of intended body postures plays an important role in performing dance movements (see Chapter 7). Following this perspective, we could imagine that the represented body postures are guiding the dance movements towards the perceivable key elements of the performance. Emily S. Cross describes how the brain works when a human observes biological motion (see Chapter 11). The results of her studies support the idea of a perceptual–cognitive effect repre-sentation of complex dance movements in the brain. Furthermore, according to Beatriz Calvo-Merino, dancers perform internal simulation when they observe a complex dance action which is represented in the brain (see Chapter 10). If dancers indeed code external motor events through their own motor repertoire, they could do this most efficiently based on cognitive representation of perceptual effects in the context of body postures adopted while performing dance movement. Taken together, these approaches and studies corroborate that movement control in dancing is based on the representation of anticipated effects, leading to the establishment of a perceptual–cognitive control system.

To gain a better understanding of the functionality of representation and cogni-tive categorization in motor control, this chapter will present a model of the cognitive architecture of dance movement. I will then consider relevant issues in research methodology and methods that can be used to assess action-relevant knowledge structures experimentally. Furthermore, empirical studies based on these methods are described to show relations between cognitive representation and performance in different types of human movement. In addition to the cognitive background, emotions such as stage-fright, stress, anxiety or happiness are important when considering dance performance. Therefore, this chapter will integrate the concept of emotions into the dance-architecture model. Finally this chapter addresses mental training in order to open up a perspective for developing and stabilizing performance in dance.

Building blocks in memory and the architecture of dance

The fact that a 'model of the needed future' (Bernstein, 1967; Nadin, 2015), and thus anticipated movement effects, play a central role in the implementation and control of actions is easily understood by dancers. While performing movements, dancers address different effects in their own body. While performing the same moment in interaction with others, dancers 'speak' with their partners in terms of movement expressions and 'tingling senses', and they attempt to attract the audience with compositions of movement elements and well-defined movement expression. Therefore, it is of central relevance for dancers to anticipate keypoints (i.e., body postures) of dance movements, interaction patterns or whole choreographies.

The function of a 'model of the future' can be seen clearly in studies addressing the *end-state comfort effect* (Rosenbaum et al., 2007; Seegelke et al., 2013; Weigelt, Kunde and Prinz, 2006; Weigelt and Schack, 2010: see also Chapter 7). This research has shown that individuals are prepared to adopt uncomfortable positions with their hands and arms when initiating and executing object manipulations (movement constellations) as long as this leads to a comfortable position for the final (end) state of the movement. For example, to pick up a pencil that is pointing upwards in a cup, one initially uses an awkward underhand grip to ultimately hold the pencil in a comfortable writing posture. Such observations show clearly that movements are planned, controlled and performed with reference to the anticipated final position of the movement. Hence, they indicate the existence of a *mental model* (of the needed future) to which all control processes can be related.

As we know from everyday life, sports and dance, parts of our actions are sometimes unanticipated. We observe processes of automatization or direct activation of movements in the context of special stimuli (e.g., grasping pieces of chocolate when we see a chocolate bar). When dancers repeatedly make errors in special parts of a movement phrase, dancers and teachers can learn about the difference between anticipated and real effects. Often dancers and teachers spend much time in de-automatizing unadjusted movement elements. Therefore, it is useful to think about different levels of movement organization in complex movements in more general terms.

The idea that movement control is constructed hierarchically has been expressed by various authors (first by Bernstein, 1947). One set of studies focused on a hierarchy of different levels of representation (e.g., Keele, 1986; Perrig and Hofer, 1989; Rosenbaum, 1987), other studies emphasized the aspect of a hierarchical

Table 6.1 Levels of action organization

Code	Level	Main function	Subfunction	Tools
IV	Mental control	Regulation	Volitional initiation control strategies	Symbols; strategies
III	Mental representation	Representation	Effect-oriented adjustment	Basic action concepts
II	Sensorimotor representation	Representation	Spatial–temporal adjustment	Perceptual effect representation
I	Sensorimotor control	Regulation	Automatization	Motor primitives; routines

Source: Modified from Schack, 2004; Schack and Ritter, 2013

regulation of action execution (e.g., Greene, 1988; Hacker, 1998; Keele, Cohen and Ivry, 1990; Rosenbaum, 1987). In contrast, the model proposed here views the functional construction of actions (Schack and Bar-Eli, 2007; Schack and Hackfort, 2007; Schack and Ritter, 2013) on the basis of a reciprocal assignment of performance-oriented regulation levels and representational levels (see Table 6.1). These levels differ according to their central tasks on the regulation and representation levels; therefore, each level is assumed to be functionally autonomous.

The level of *sensorimotor control* (Level I) is linked directly to the environment. In contrast to the level of *mental control* (Level IV), which is induced intentionally, Level I is induced perceptually and is mainly responsible for processes of automation. It is built on functional units composed of perceptual effect representations, afferent feedback and effectors. The system is broadly autonomous; therefore, automatisms and routines emerge when this level possesses sufficient correction mechanisms to ensure the stable attainment of the intended effect.

The need for a level of *sensorimotor representation* (Level II) is apparent in this context. It can be assumed that this is where the modality-specific information representing the effect of the particular movement, among other information, is stored. Subsequently, relevant modalities change as a function of expertise in the learning process and as a function of the concrete task. For instance, when we learn to perform a Salsa movement at the beginning of the learning process, we first read much more optical information about body posture and movement timing. Later in the learning process, proprioceptive information about our movement postures and impulses garner increased meaning.

The level of *mental representation* (Level III) predominantly forms a cognitive workbench for Level IV, the level of *mental control,* as has already been sketched for voluntary movement regulation and the coding or the anticipated outcome of movement. Basic action concepts (BACs) have been identified as major representation units for such mental representation in motor control (Schack and Ritter, 2013; Schack et al., 2014a). BACs are created through the cognitive chunking of body postures and movement events in the realisation of action goals. They do not refer to behavior-related invariance properties of objects as is the case with object concepts; rather, they refer to perception-linked invariance properties of movements. Their characteristic set of features results from the perceptive and functional properties of action effects (i.e., they tie together functional and sensory features). Furthermore, BACs integrate sensory features of sub-movements of a complex motor action, for example, through chunking (see Verwey, Abrahamse and Jiménez, 2009) or event segmentation (see Bläsing, 2015). BACs can be viewed as mental counterparts of functionally relevant elementary components or transitional states of complex movements. They are characterized by recognizable perceptual features and can be described verbally as well as pictorially, and labelled with linguistic markers. For example, 'turning the head' or 'bending the knees' could be construed as basic action concepts of a complex floor exercise. (BACs for a *pirouette en dehors* in classical dance are described in Chapter 9; see also Bläsing, Tenenbaum and Schack, 2009).

This leads us to ask how we can conceive the mental structures responsible for complex movements. Is it possible to confirm mutual overlaps between representation structures and movement structures in humans? If so, how can we use such information for mental training? To answer these and other pertinent questions, this chapter will review extant lines of empirical research, beginning with studies of mental representation of movement in long-term memory.

Structures in action and memory

Simplification of cognitive operations and movement structures in dance is characterized by order formation. Such order formation in action knowledge reduces the cognitive effort required to activate relevant information. In general, cognitive structures have been shown to improve when more problem-solving-related classifications (concepts) are formed. From our perspective, we have to solve *movement tasks* purposefully and linearly within the framework of a voluntary organization of dance movements. Therefore, it is of interest to learn about the task-related order formation of action knowledge.

The structure of memory in dancers has been addressed by some interesting and elegantly designed studies. Smyth and Pendelton (1994) studied the ability of dance experts and novices to remember ballet-like movements and nonsensical movements. The authors found that dance experts remembered both types of movement for a longer duration than novices, using cognitive markers to bind the movements to other contents of their long-term memory. In a study by Starkes and colleagues (1987), participants had to recall movement sequences that were presented either verbally or executed by the participants themselves. Results showed that dance experts performed better than novices at recalling choreographically structured sequences, but not at recalling unstructured sequences. Combined, the results of these studies emphasize the importance of mental representations for the learning of dance movements and point towards the quality of these representations as providing vital markers of dance expertise.

Recent neuroscientific studies show that motor expertise and the expertise-dependent activation of the neurocognitive system are important factors for the valid prediction of an observed dance movement (Calvo-Merino et al., 2005; 2006;

Cross, Hamilton and Grafton, 2006). Together, these studies provide strong evidence for the notion that involvement of the neurocognitive system while observing complex movements depends on motor experience of performing the observed movements, and not merely on an observer's immediate visual experience. Thus, mental simulation involving respective cortical areas is only possible for movements belonging to the observer's own movement repertoire.

Following this line of argument, an important question is: What is the cognitive basis for mental simulation, for a quick and effective perception of action-related cues, and for producing stabile movements? The usual rating and sorting methods do not permit a psychometric analysis of the representational structure, so we have developed an experimental method for probing mental representation structures (Lander and Lange, 1996; Schack and Schack, 2005) that has later been modified for the analysis of action representation (structural dimensional analysis-motoric, SDA-M; Schack, 2004). This experimental approach has been documented in several publications (see Land et al., 2013, for a review). To learn about the relationship between memory and action structures in dance, Geburzi and colleagues (2004) have used the SDA-M method to evaluate the cognitive structure of dance movement representations in long-term memory. The authors compared the representation structure of different groups of Latin American dancers: 10 world-leading dancers, 10 dancers from the European Top 20, 15 beginners and 12 non-dancers. The investigation focused primarily on the Rumba forward step, allowing for consistency across groups. The results reflected that structure formation of mental representations in long-term memory depended on expertise: the higher the level of expertise, the higher the degree of hierarchy in their long-term memory structures. Furthermore, the results of this study showed an overlap between long-term memory structures and biomechanically defined functional movement structures in the experts. Further studies using the SDA-M method to investigate long-term memory structures of dance movements are presented in detail in Chapter 9 (see also Bläsing, Tenenbaum and Schack, 2009; Bläsing and Schack, 2012).

The SDA-M method consists of four steps. In the first step, participants are familiarized with the BACs by looking at pictures with verbal labels as printed headings. These pictures can remain positioned in front of each participant throughout the experiment. In order to determine subjective distances between the BACs, the participants perform the following splitting procedure: on a computer screen, one selected BAC is presented as an 'anchoring unit' at the top of a list containing the remaining BACs in randomized order. The participant decides whether each of the BACs in the randomized list is 'functionally related' (associated) to the anchor BAC 'while performing the movement' or not. This procedure produces two subsets of BACs (functionally related and not functionally related) that can then be submitted to the same procedure as the full list. Each BAC is used as anchor once; therefore this procedure results in as many decision trees per participant as BACs are used. In the second step of the SDA-M, the BACs are submitted to a hierarchical cluster analysis with distances based on the subjective distance judgments of all combinations of pairs of BACs obtained in the previous step, via the splitting procedure. This results in the individual partitioning of the BACs for each participant. In the third step, the dimensioning of the cluster solutions is performed using a factor analysis applied to a specific cluster-oriented rotation process, resulting in a factor matrix classified by clusters (see Schack and Mechsner, 2006; Schack and Schack, 2005). Finally, in the fourth step of the SDA-M, cluster solutions are tested for invariance both within and between groups (for details, see Hodges, Huys and Starkes, 2007).

To illustrate the SDA-M method in this chapter, we have chosen a special action from windsurfing: the front loop (end over). This complex movement seems well suited for an investigation of representational structures at different levels of expertise, as it is a technical challenge for both excellent hobby windsurfers and competitive professionals (many highly skilled windsurfers are unable to perform jumps involving forward rotations). The front loop has a finite, recognizable (and thereby flexible) action pattern with an overall structure that is well defined by biomechanical demands. Many degrees of freedom in the musculoskeletal system have to be controlled, and performance quality is influenced considerably by both training and expertise.

Until 1986, the possibility of performing an 'end over' (see Figure 6.1) was only speculative. Nobody knew for certain how the impulse for forward rotation might be generated from an ongoing forward motion. In 1987, Cesare Cantagalli became the first person to perform a forward rotation (which was named 'Cesare Roll', and later, 'Cheese Roll') in an international competition at Maui, Hawaii.

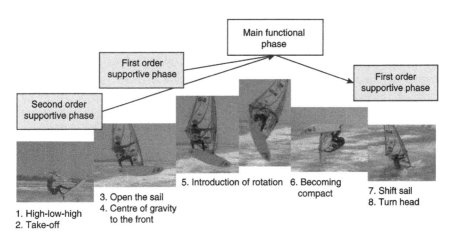

Figure 6.1 Movement phases of the front loop in windsurfing. The task-related basic action concepts (BAC) are allocated to the respective phases. In the take-off phase, the front loop can hardly be distinguished from a regular jump. The surfer waits until the angular point of the slope angle, and then abruptly pushes the sail's pressure point forward-down. Robby Nash entitled this time lag before the introduction of the front loop as the 'moment of shock for the spectator'.

This led to a boom of experimentation with highly complex movement actions among professional windsurfers. Mark Angulo turned this sideways rotation into the spectacular front loop (end over) with the characteristic rotation over the mast top. The front loop is executed through rotation around the horizontal and the longitudinal (vertical) axis.

In assessing the movement phases of the front loop in windsurfing, BACs were defined and allocated to the biomechanically (functionally) determined movement phases (see Figure 6.1). The BACs relevant for the front loop were gathered through a multi-stage process. First, a group of eight expert and seven novice athletes gave free descriptions of the front loop movement. Subsequently, they were interviewed individually with reference to the BACs from their point of view. This revealed that BACs were not just labelled verbally, but could also be demonstrated as specific movement patterns. The results were complemented or corrected through video-based self-confrontation and validated through allocation experiments (Schack, 2002). From this process, the following eight BACs for the front loop were acquired: (1) high-low-high; (2) take off; (3) opening the sail; (4) moving the centre of gravity to the front; (5) introduction of the rotation; (6) becoming compact; (7) shifting the sail; and (8) turning the head.

A total of 40 experts and novices participated in a study with the aim to develop new forms of technical preparation. The 20 experts (all male; mean age of 28.8 years; engaged in windsurfing for 15.8 years on average; performing front loops for 9.4 years on average; reported training for approximately 30 weeks per year) were counted among the world elite in windsurfing at that time and had participated in international competitions (World Cup, Grand Prix, etc.). A number of them were thought of as pioneers of windsurfing, having been involved in the creation of the front loop from its beginning. Each could perform the front loop reliably and variably in a competitive setting, some even as double front loop. The 20 novices (18 males, 2 females; mean age of 22 years; engaged in windsurfing for 8.2 years on average; performing front loops for 1.6 years on average; reported training for approximately 23 weeks per year) participated in national and international competitions, but had no relevant rankings, and were unable to perform the front loop under competitive conditions. Overall, their (potential) scope for development was comparable to that of the expert group. The minimum condition for acceptance in the novice group was to have performed the front loop at least twice (according to their own reports). One of the main assumptions of the study was that the novices mastered the technical execution of the front loop far less reliably than the experts. The results of this study are illustrated in Figures 6.2 and 6.3 (α is constantly set at .05, allowing for a d_{crit} value of 3.51).

Figure 6.2 displays the group structure of windsurfing experts based on cluster analysis in the form of a dendrogram and reports the factor matrix arranged according to the three clusters. The structures of mental movement representation in the expert group shows a remarkable resemblance to the biomechanical functional structure of the movement (Hossner, Schiebl and Göhner, 2015), according to which the *take-off* could be classified as a second order supportive phase,

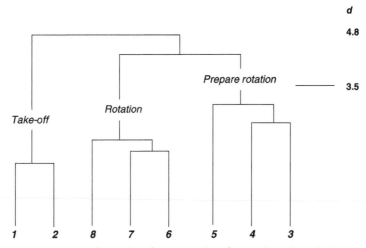

1. High-low-high; 2. Take-off; 3. Open the sail; 4. Centre of gravity to the front; 5. Introduction of rotation; 6. Becoming compact; 7. Shift sail; 8. Turn head

Figure 6.2 Results of the hierarchical cluster analysis of BACs for the front loop in the expert group. The lower the value of an interconnection between the study units (see the Euclidian distance scale on the right), the lower the distance of the concepts (n = 20; α = 5%; d_{crit} = 3.51).

preparation of rotation as a first order supportive phase, and *rotation* as the main phase (see Figure 6.1). The experts' superordinate concepts were acquired on the basis of clusters and are spatially distinct and organized in a temporal sequence. Therefore, we assume that they serve as a means to solve specific subordinate problems of the movement (e.g., energizing, introduction of impulse and rotation).

Whereas the experts' cluster solution followed a functional structure of the movement, no comparable structure could be found in the cluster solution for the novice group (see Figure 6.3). The novices' cluster solution reveals weak structural links between the elements (i.e., the BACs are connected slightly above the critical distance of d_{crit} = 3.51). Therefore, no clusters could be confirmed for the whole group, and neither a phase-related clustering nor a temporal–sequential structure could be identified.

Taken together, in the presented study, we were able to confirm the relation between cognitive representation and performance for a special movement technique in windsurfing. The cognitive structure of persons with high ability was more differentiated, and more strongly function-oriented than that of beginners (Schack, 2010). Subsequently, it can be argued that experts are better able to apply their knowledge in practice when aiming for optimal execution of a given movement. Furthermore, we have forwarded statements regarding cognitive structures that are directly relevant for training processes. These statements can help a coach to decide which cognitive context(s) athletes can understand and in which contexts they might work best. This statement is particularly relevant for

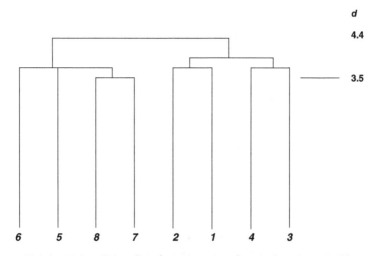

1. High-low-high; 2. Take-off; 3. Open the sail; 4. Centre of gravity to the front;
5. Introduction of rotation; 6. Becoming compact; 7. Shift sail; 8. Turn head

Figure 6.3 Results of the hierarchical cluster analysis of BACs for the front loop in the novice group (n = 20; α = 5%; d_{crit} = 3.51).

movements that have to be carried out under extreme time pressure, which is often the case in dance.

Are these long-term memory structures also functional for movement performance? At the present time, we consider this to be the case, because it is plausible that long-term memory structures exist within the context of a perceptual–cognitive or anticipatory control scheme, as hypothesized above. Indeed, we can see no other way of addressing the functional demands related to BACs other than by controlling the corresponding submovements directly through their anticipated perceptual effects. As we have emphasized, characteristic perceptual features of BACs relate meaningfully to corresponding functional features. For example, sensory feedback tells athletes whether or not they have performed a movement properly and effectively. Taken together, it is plausible that functionally successful movements require the use of an anticipatory control that draws on BAC networks. We conclude from this that the control system may well use the revealed cognitive BAC networks in long-term memory to construct situation-specific reference structures for anticipatory control.

Consequences for technical preparation and mental training can be derived from such analyses of the representational and biomechanical structures of a movement. This makes it possible to ascertain the phase of the movement in which representational problems are located. Subsequently, technical preparation and mental training can inform the movement sequence. A specific teaching method has been developed for this purpose: *Mental Training Based on Mental Representation* (MTMR) (Schack and Bar-Eli, 2007; Schack and Hackfort, 2007); we will come back to this topic later in this chapter.

Emotions in the architecture of dance

Experts in dance and sport who exhibit a high level of performance in practice might yet sometimes struggle under the stressful conditions in game situations, competition or on stage (see Beilock and Gray, 2007, for an extensive review). Though motor skills and mental representations of these skills are inherited and learned, a performer's access to them changes under emotional and temporal pressure. How, though, might the architecture of dance change under emotional pressure? What are the underlying cognitive mechanisms that permit or prevent an efficient course of action? Although sound theories and extensive research have been developed to explore this linkage, empirical efforts have yet to take an integrative approach. This chapter will now offer an initial road map to understand mental and motor operations in relation to emotions in dance performance.

The functioning of motion is based on both the cognitive and emotional components of motor control and performance; therefore, we must pay attention to the functional meaning of emotions and should therefore integrate the concept of emotions in our architecture model. From this point of view, we should understand negative emotions (e.g., anxiety) not only as having an undermining effect on performance, but also as a process of adaptation to specific events, or as a motivating factor for a particular action. A performer's anxiety at a particular moment of an action can reinforce his or her sensitivity for dangerous situations, prompting the adoption of defensive strategies, and engagement in more realistic decision making. Carver and Scheier's (1988) control process model of anxiety and performance posits that anxiety can have either facilitative or debilitative effects on performance, depending on a subject's expectation of being able to cope with anxiety and complete the action. Support for this contention in sport comes from the work of Jones and colleagues, where highly skilled swimmers (Jones, Hanton and Swain, 1994) and cricketers (Jones and Swain, 1995) interpreted both cognitive and somatic anxiety symptoms as more facilitative to their performance. Swimmers who had positive expectancies of goal attainment interpreted anxiety as more facilitative than swimmers who had negative expectations of goal attainment (Jones and Hanton, 1996). Thus, cognitive anxiety can improve motivation and facilitate appropriate attentional focus (Jones, Swain and Hardy, 1993).

The relationship between emotion and cognition from an action-oriented perspective is depicted in Figure 6.4. The appraisal of events, action effects, or stimuli in the environment is the first cognitive process in action organization. Subsequently, the result of one's appraisal is not only stored in memory, but is also of central meaning for eliciting emotions. Here, the level of mental control (Level IV, see Table 6.1) comes into play. Processing at this level begins with making a decision about a relevant course of action. The result of this decision-making process is the intention to achieve specific action effects. Based on this intention, an action plan is created, and the mental control processing runs to a module that is responsible for action execution. This module is linked to the level of sensorimotor control (Level I), and includes all motor components necessary for the production of goal-directed action effects. If action effects are not congruent with the intended

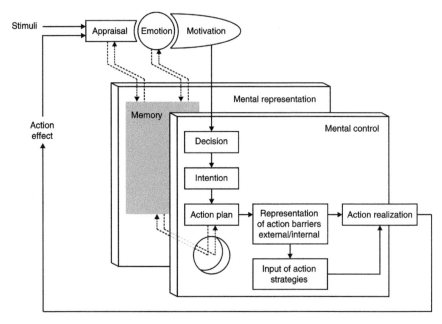

Figure 6.4 Interaction between cognitive and emotional processes and modules in the architecture of dance. Emotions are not only influenced by appraisal processes and related to memory, but also impact on components of motivation: part of the perception–action–effect cycle.

outcomes, or are not valid for coping with the actual situation, the appraisal system will read an insufficient action, and will evoke negative emotions.

In the case of problems in action realization (e.g., the real situation is much more difficult than the expected one – for example, in competition), mental control processing must take a different path, and the performer has to use action strategies such as control of attention, control of emotion or motivational control. Such strategies are supported by inner speech (self-talk), and are used to stabilize action realization. Performers who lack such strategies have no tools ready to control actions appropriately. Furthermore, if performers lack mental control, they will not realize their intentions and will miss intended action effects. This kind of information is negatively valued by the appraisal system, which influences the development of emotions dramatically. Thus, an important link between emotion and information storage is caused by the representation of emotionally induced action effects in long-term memory. From this point of view, emotions are a crucial part of information storage in general.

The model depicted in Figure 6.4 shows a functional relationship between the level of mental control (Level IV) and emotions. From this point of view, the development of emotions is functionally related to observed action effects. Of additional importance to the formation of emotions is the difference between intended and actual effects, and an individual's appraisal of this difference. For this reason, the model is in accordance with specific emotion theories. Mandler (1979; 1985) assumes that the abortion of a previously planned action can be seen as a central reason for anxiety development. According to Mandler's approach, task-relevant stimuli are perceived through the increased interruption of action. In turn, these stimuli demand their own attentional resources, and hence disturb action performance. Therefore, paradoxically, anxiety might not only be the reason for a performance interruption, but also its consequence. The models presented in this chapter (see Table 6.1 and Figure 6.4) are based on the assumption that the interruption of activated performance plans and the increasing inability to subordinate an action performance to an action program are attributed negatively and emotionally. Therefore different psychological training methods, like training of inner speech or stress-regulation techniques, are helpful to improve mental control and to reduce stage fright or anxiety.

Links between the architecture of dance and psychological training methods

Regarding the work of a dance teacher, theory provides a framework that commonly relates to practical problems. The crucial assumption is that a theory is primarily applied in connection with specific practical problems, and that its value is subsequently derived from evaluating its practical impact. However, practical applications (e.g., in training or intervention techniques) have to be attached to theory. In this respect, nothing would be more practical than a good theory!

From an applied perspective in dance, the theoretical concept of the construction of actions (see Table 6.1) is fundamental to both the development of suitable diagnostic procedures and the selection of appropriate training methods. It is therefore exceptionally important to understand that different action systems contribute to a dancer's performance. A frequently observed practical problem is that dancers are able to perform a certain movement optimally in practice, but fail to do so in competitive settings. When the movement structure is accessible under less stressful circumstances (e.g., in rehearsal), and appears to be optimally represented in the dancer's memory, the problem is likely to be rooted in mental control.

We have developed methods that allow a reliable diagnosis of how a movement is represented, which enables both researchers and practitioners (i.e., coaches) to control the goal-directedness of psychological training – see Figure 6.5 (Schack and Hackfort, 2007). Problems which may, for instance, be located in emotion regulation or motivation result from deficits in mental control and are allocated to the level of mental control (Level IV). Psychological training procedures which intervene at this level, particularly those targeting attention control, optimization of self-talk, and stress and anxiety control aim to improve *basic regulation*. In contrast, the structure of a movement – and therefore its optimal technical execution – is largely determined by the level of mental representation (Level III). Consequently, training procedures designed to optimize *process regulation* have to be allocated on Level III. The term 'process regulation' refers to the execution-related organization of an action, whereas 'basic regulation' describes the generation of emotional and motivational conditions for the action and is produced at Level IV.

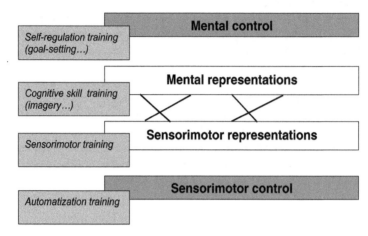

Figure 6.5 Levels of action regulation and related psychological training methods.

Theoretical considerations regarding the construction of complex and integrated actions in dance are helpful when trying to identify suitable psychological training methods. As stated previously, it is most appropriate to start by using specific diagnostic procedures to investigate the systems involved in the organization of action. In this context, it is important to note that investigators also apply such diagnostic tools in the consulting process so that athletes or patients in rehabilitation receive feedback about their action-related memory structures (Braun et al., 2007; 2008; Land et al., 2013; Schack and Hackfort, 2007). This diagnosis is important when deciding whether an athlete possesses a good disposition for optimal process regulation. Problems regarding the capacity to perform optimally in competitive settings may be located in process regulation and basic regulation. We have applied appropriate diagnostic tools to test components such as stress regulation, competition anxiety, self-talk or different components of volition. Results of such diagnostic tests are given to the athlete as a mental profile that can be used to help practitioners make better decisions regarding psychological training methods for the individual athlete (Schack and Hackfort, 2007). Appropriate training methods and strategies to strengthen mental control may include exercises to optimize self-talk, relaxation methods, and procedures for optimizing stress regulation. If problems concerning movement memory and motor coordination on the level of mental representation are diagnosed, appropriate training methods include imagery training or technical preparation. The advantage of the synthesis of mental training and memory analysis lies in the fact that the individual athlete's memory structures are integrated into the mental training, providing sufficient consideration regarding individual dispositions.

New paths in mental training

Studies carried out during the first half of the twentieth century indicate that performing motor tasks as mental simulation leads to an improvement in subsequent physical task performance (Sackett, 1935). More recent studies in sports psychology have shown mental practice alone can be effective in improving the execution of movements in individual athletes and helps with the acquisition of novel skilled actions (e.g., Gould, Damarjian and Greenleaf, 2002; Morris, Spittle and Watt, 2005), but these effects may be less significant than those of physical exercise alone, or physical exercise in combination with mental practice (Driskell, Copper and Moran, 1994; Frank et al., 2014).

Various theories have been used to explain the effects of mental training (e.g., Heuer, 1985; Driskell, Copper and Moran, 1994; Frank et al., 2014). The major explanatory models based on recent scientific findings can be differentiated according to whether they consider effects to be due to physically peripheral (neuromuscular) processes or central mechanisms (e.g., symbolic codes or programs). Recent findings on the architecture of action have extended the work on ideomotor action (e.g., Koch, Keller and Prinz, 2004). These, in combination with neurophysiological findings (Jeannerod, 1995; 2004), open up a new explanation for the effects of mental training: the *perceptual–cognitive* hypothesis. This hypothesis posits a representation system in which strong cognitive representation units are linked to perceptual representations (e.g., kinaesthetic, visual or acoustic effect codes). Due to their spatiotemporal structure, these representations can be translated directly into movement. This makes additional motor, spatial-pictorial or other representations unnecessary for movement control. Another basic assumption of the perceptual–cognitive model is that imaging a movement and performing it are based on the same representations (Jeannerod, 1995; 2004; Schack et al., 2014b). This assumption can explain the impact of mental training by proposing that it internally activates and stabilizes the representation system. Mental simulations of a movement may forge, or strengthen, links between the cognitive representation of intermediate states of that movement and the accompanying perceptual effect codes.

This theoretical background makes the methods developed here (e.g., SDA-M) directly significant for developing new forms of mental training. The main disadvantage of traditional procedures is that they try to optimize performance through repeatedly imagining the movement without taking an athlete's mental representation of the technique into account (i.e., they are representation-blind). If the movement's cognitive reference structure has structural gaps or errors, these will be stabilized rather than overcome by repeated practice. The alternative procedure proposed here is to measure the mental representation of the movement before initiating mental training, and then integrate the results into that training. This method, called Mental Training Based on Mental Representations (MTMR), has now been applied successfully for several years in professional and amateur sports such as golf, volleyball, gymnastics, windsurfing and soccer (Schack and Bar-Eli, 2007; Schack and Hackfort, 2007; Schack et al., 2014b). Additionally, MTMR has been applied in the rehabilitation of stroke patients to stabilize and gradually improve their grasping movements (Braun et al., 2007; 2008). After injury, mental training offers a helpful means of training even when active movement execution is still severely impaired. As a result, new opportunities for the use of mental training have come to fruition in medical and orthopaedic–traumatologic rehabilitation. In this context, mental training has proved to be of great use for regaining lost movement patterns after joint operations or joint replacements. Thus, beyond the world of dance and elite sports, mental training provides a general means to link together imagery and movement in various areas of life.

Conclusion: When we dance . . . then we take a chance

To support various techniques used by dancers and dance coaches, this chapter has presented methods that focus on precisely defined components of motor actions. It is clearly advantageous for a coach to know how mental structures form, stabilize and change during the course of a specific dance movement. A coach who possesses such knowledge might also be better able to support the individual dancer on his or her current level of learning and performance, and therefore shape specific instructions appropriately. The methods presented in this chapter make it possible to take essential information regarding the underlying cognitive–perceptual action system into account, while addressing the individual needs of a dancer in an effective way. Furthermore, the theoretical perspective on the construction of dance movements developed here and the presented methods are not just relevant for optimizing the daily work of sport psychologists and dance coaches, but are also useful to open up new perspectives for teaching dance, including technical preparation and mental training.

References

Beilock, S. L. & Gray, R. (2007). Why do athletes choke under pressure? In: G. Tenenbaum & R. C. Eklund (Eds.), *Handbook of Sport Psychology, Third Edition* (pp. 425–444). Hoboken, NJ: Wiley.

Bernstein (Bernštejn), N. A. (1947). *O postrojenii dviženij (On the Structure of Movements)*. Leningrad, USSR: Medgiz Publishers.

Bernstein, N. A. (1967). *The Coordination and Regulation of Movement.* London: Pergamon Press.

Bläsing, B. (2015). Expertise in dance: Effects of visual familiarity, motor experience and music on movement segmentation. *Frontiers in Psychology,* 5, 1500.

Bläsing B., Güldenpenning, I., Köster, D. & Schack, T. (2014). Effects of expertise on the categorization of climbing holds and activation of associated grasp actions. *Frontiers in Psychology,* 5, 1008.

Bläsing B. & Schack, T. (2012). Mental representation of spatial movement parameters in dance. *Spatial Computation and Cognition,* 12(2–3).

Bläsing, B., Tenenbaum, G., & Schack, T. (2009). Cognitive structures of complex movements in dance. *Psychology of Sport and Exercise,* 10, 350–360.

Braun, S. M., Beurskens, A. J., Schack, T., Marcellis, R. G., Oti, K. C., Schols, J. M., & Wade, D. T. (2007). Is it possible to use the Structural Dimension Analysis of Motor Memory (SDA-M) to investigate representations of motor actions in stroke patients? *Clinical Rehabilitation,* 21(9), 822–832.

Braun, S. M., Kleynen, M., Schols, J. M., Schack, T., Beurskens, A. J., & Wade, D. T. (2008). Using mental practice in stroke rehabilitation: A framework. *Clinical Rehabilitation, 7,* 579–591.

Calvo-Merino, B., Glaser, D. E., Grezes, J., Passingham, R. E., & Haggard, P. (2005). Action observation and acquired motor skills: An FMRI study with expert dancers. *Cerebral Cortex,* 15, 1243–1249.

Calvo-Merino, B., Grezes, J., Glaser, D. E., Passingham, R. E., & Haggard, P. (2006). Seeing or doing? Influence of visual and motor familiarity in action observation. *Current Biology,* 16, 1905–1910.

Carver, C. S. & Scheier, M. F. (1988). A control-process perspective on anxiety. *Anxiety Research,* 1, 17–22.

Cross, E. S., Hamilton, A. F. D. C., & Grafton, S. T. (2006). Building a motor simulation de novo: Observation of dance by dancers. *Neuroimage,* 31(3), 1257–1267.

Driskell, J. E., Copper, C., & Moran, A. (1994). Does mental practise enhance performance? *Journal of Applied Psychology,* 79(4), 481–492.

Frank, C., Land, W. M., Popp, C., & Schack, T. (2014). Mental representation and mental practice: Experimental investigation on the functional links between motor memory and motor imagery. *PLOS ONE,* 9(4), e95175.

Geburzi, E., Engel, F., & Schack, T. (2004). Mentale Repräsentation von Grundbewegungen in den lateinamerikanischen Tänzen (Mental representation of basic movements in Latin-American dance). In: O. Stoll & A. Lau (Eds.), *Belastung und Beanspruchung (Stress and Strain).* (Abstractband zur 36. Jahrestagung der Arbeitsgemeinschaft für Sportpsychologie [asp], S. 84–85). Halle: asp.

Gould, D., Damarjian, N., & Greenleaf, C. (2002). Imagery training for peak performance. In: J. Van Raalte & W. B. Brewer (Eds.), *Exploring Sport and Exercise Psychology* (pp. 49–74). Washington, DC: American Psychological Association.

Greene, P. H. (1988). The organisation of natural movement. *Journal of Motor Behavior,* 20, 180–185.

Hacker, W. (1998). *Allgemeine Arbeitspsychologie (General Work Psychology).* Bern, Switzerland: Huber.

Heuer, H. (1985). Wie wirkt mentale Übung? (How does mental training take effect?). *Psychologische Rundschau,* 4, 191–200.

Hodges, N., Huys, R., & Starkes, J. (2007). Methodological review and evaluation of research in expert performance in sport. In: G. Tenenbaum & R. C. Eklund (Eds.), *Handbook of Sport Psychology,Third Edition* (pp. 161–183). Hoboken, NJ: Wiley.

Hommel, B., Muesseler, J., Aschersleben, G., & Prinz, W. (2001). The Theory of Event Coding (TEC): A framework for perception and action planning. *Behavioral and Brain Sciences,* 24(5), 849–878.

Hossner, E. J., Schiebl, F., & Göhner, U. (2015). A functional approach to movement analysis and error identification in sports and physical education. *Frontiers in Psychology,* 6.

Ivry, R., Diedrichsen, J., Spencer, R., Hazeltine, E., & Semjen, A. (2004). A cognitive neuroscience perspective on bimanual coordination and interference. In: S. Swinnen & J. Duysens (Eds.), *Interlimb Coordination.* Nowell, MA: Kluwer Academic Publishing.

Jang, S. H. & Pollick, F. E. (2011). Experience influences brain mechanisms of watching dance. *Dance Research,* 29(supplement), 352–377.

Jeannerod, M. (1995). Mental imagery in the motor context. *Neuropsychologia,* 33(11), 1419–1432.

Jeannerod, M. (2004). Actions from within. *International Journal of Sport and Exercise Psychology,* 2, 376–402.

Jola, C., Davis, A., & Haggard, P. (2011). Proprioceptive integration and body representation: Insights into dancers' expertise. *Experimental Brain Research*, 213(2–3), 257.

Jones, G., Hanton, S., & Swain, A. (1994). Intensity and interpretation of anxiety symptoms in elite and non-elite sports performers. *Personality and Individual Differences*, 17(5), 657–663.

Jones, G. & Hanton, S. (1996). Interpretation of competitive anxiety symptoms and goal attainment expectancies. *Journal of Sport and Exercise Psychology*, 18, 144–157.

Jones, G. & Swain, A. (1995). Predispositions to experience debilitative and facilitative anxiety in elite and non-elite performers. *The Sport Psychologist*, 9, 201–211.

Jones, G., Swain, A., & Hardy, L. (1993). Intensity and direction dimensions of competitive state anxiety and relationships with performance. *Journal of Sports Sciences*, 11, 1–15.

Karpati, F. J., Giacosa, C., Foster, N. E., Penhune, V. B., & Hyde, K. L. (2015). Dance and the brain: A review. *Annals of the New York Academy of Sciences*, 1337(1), 140–146.

Keele, S. W. (1986). Movement control in skilled motor performance. *Psychological Bulletin*, 70, 387–403.

Keele, S. W., Cohen, A., & Ivry, R. (1990). Motor programs: Concepts and issues. In: M. Jeannerod (Ed.), *Attention and Performance 13: Motor representation and control* (pp. 77–110). Hillsdale, NJ: Lawrence Erlbaum Associates.

Keller, P. E., Novembre, G., & Hove, M. J. (2014). Rhythm in joint action: Psychological and neurophysiological mechanisms for real-time interpersonal coordination. *Philosophical Transactions of the Royal Society B*, 369(1658), 20130394.

Koch, I., Keller, P. E., & Prinz, W. (2004). The ideomotor approach to action control: Implications for skilled performance. *International Journal of Sport and Exercise Psychology*, 2(4), 362–375.

Krasnow, D., Wilmerding, M. V., Stecyk, S., Wyon, M., & Koutedakis, Y. (2011). Biomechanical research in dance: A literature review. *Medical Problems of Performing Artists*, 26(1), 3–23.

Land, W. M., Volchenkov, D., Bläsing, B. E., & Schack, T. (2013). From action representation to action execution: Exploring the links between cognitive and biomechanical levels of motor control. *Frontiers in Computational Neuroscience*, 7.

Lander, H. J. & Lange, K. (1996). Untersuchung zur Struktur- und Dimensionsanalyse begrifflich-repräsentierten Wissens (Studies in structural and dimensional analysis of representational knowledge). *Zeitschrift für Psychologie*, 204, 55–74.

Mandler, G. (1979). Thought processes, consciousness, and stress. In: V. Hamilton and D. A. Warburton (Eds.), *Human Stress and Cognition: An information processing approach*. London: John Wiley & Sons.

Mandler, G. (1985). Consciousness, imagery, and emotion – with special reference to autonomic imagery. *Journal of Mental Imagery*, 8, 87–94.

Mechsner, F., Kerzel, D., Knoblich, G., & Prinz, W. (2001). Perceptual basis of bimanual coordination. *Nature*, 414, 69–72.

Minvielle-Moncla, J., Audiffren, M., Macar, F., & Vallet, C. (2008). Overproduction timing errors in expert dancers. *Journal of Motor Behavior*, 40(4), 291–300.

Morris, T., Spittle, M., & Watt, A. P. (2005). *Imagery in Sport*. Champaign, IL: Human Kinetics.

Nadin, M. (Ed.). (2015). *Anticipation: Learning from the Past: The Russian/Soviet contributions to the science of anticipation*. New York: Springer.

Nitsch, J. R. & Hackfort, D. (2016). Theoretical framework of performance psychology: An action theory perspective. In: M. Raab, B. Lobinger, S. Hoffmann, A. Pizzera, &

S. Laborde (Eds.), *Performance Psychology: Perception, action, cognition, and emotion* (pp. 12–26). Amsterdam, Netherlands: Elsevier.

Perrig, W. J. & Hofer, D. (1989). Sensory and conceptual representations in memory: Motor images that cannot be imaged. *Psychological Research*, 51, 201–207.

Rosenbaum, D. A. (1987). Successive approximations to a model of human motor programming. *Psychology of Learning and Motivation*, 21, 153–182.

Rosenbaum, D. A., Cohen, R. G., Jax, S. A., Van Der Wel, R., & Weiss, D. J. (2007). The problem of serial order in behavior: Lashley's legacy. *Human Movement Science*, 26, 525–554.

Sackett, R. S. (1935). The relationship between amount of symbolic rehearsal and retention of a maze habit. *The Journal of General Psychology*, 13(1), 113–130.

Schack, T. (2002). Zur kognitiven Architektur von Bewegungshandlungen – modelltheoretischer Zugang und experimentelle Untersuchungen (The cognitive structure of actions – model-theoretical approach and experimental studies.) Unpublished Habilitation. Psychological Institute, German Sportsuniversity Cologne.

Schack, T. (2004). The cognitive architecture of complex movement. *International Journal of Sport and Exercise Psychology*, 2(4), 403–438.

Schack, T. (2010). *Die kognitive Architektur menschlicher Bewegungen: Innovative Zugänge für Psychologie, Sportwissenschaft und Robotik (The Cognitive Architecture of Human Movements: Innovative approaches to psychology, sports science and robotics).* Aachen, Germany: Meyer & Meyer Verlag.

Schack, T. & Bar-Eli, M. (2007). Psychological factors in technical preparation. In: B. Blumenstein, R. Lidor, & G. Tenenbaum (Eds.), *Psychology of Sport Training* (pp. 62–103). Oxford, UK: Meyer & Meyer Sport.

Schack, T., Bläsing, B., Hughes, C., Flash, T., & Schilling, M. (2014a). Elements and construction of motor control. In: A. G. Papaioannou & D. Hackfort (Eds.), *Routledge Companion to Sport and Exercise Psychology: Global perspectives and fundamental concepts* (p. 308). London: Routledge.

Schack, T., Essig, K., Frank, C., & Koester, D. (2014b). Mental representation and motor imagery training. *Frontiers in Human Neuroscience*, 8.

Schack, T. & Hackfort, D. (2007). An action theory approach to applied sport psychology. In: G. Tenenbaum & R. C. Eklund (Eds.), *Handbook of Sport Psychology, Third Edition* (pp. 332–351). Hoboken, NJ: Wiley.

Schack, T. & Mechsner, F. (2006). Representation of motor skills in human long-term memory. *Neuroscience Letters*, 391, 77–81.

Schack, T. & Ritter, H. (2013). Representation and learning in motor action – Bridges between experimental research and cognitive robotics. *New Ideas in Psychology*, 31(3), 258–269.

Schack, T. & Schack, E. (2005). In- and outgroup representation in a dynamic society: Hong Kong after 1997. *Asian Journal of Social Psychology*, 8, 123–137.

Schack, T. & Schack, E. (2017). Anticipation in traditional healing ceremonies: The call from our past. In: M. Nadin (Ed.), *Anticipation and Medicine* (pp. 323–335). New York: Springer International Publishing.

Schmidt, R. & Lee, T. (1998). *Motor Control and Learning, Fifth Edition.* Champaign, IL: Human Kinetics.

Seegelke, C., Hughes, C. M., Knoblauch, A., & Schack, T. (2013). Grasp posture planning during multi-segment object manipulation tasks – Interaction between cognitive and biomechanical factors. *Acta Psychologica*, 144(3), 513–521.

Smyth, M. M. & Pendleton, L. R. (1994). Memory for movement in professional ballet dancers. *International Journal of Sport Psychology,* 25(3), 282–294.

Starkes, J. L., Deakin, J. M., Lindley, S., & Crisp, F. (1987). Motor versus verbal recall of ballet sequences by young expert dancers. *Journal of Sport Psychology*, 9(3), 222–230.

Verwey, W. B., Abrahamse, E. L., & Jiménez, L. (2009). Segmentation of short keying sequences does not spontaneously transfer to other sequences. *Human Movement Science,* 28, 348–361.

Weigelt, M., Kunde, W., & Prinz, W. (2006). End-state comfort in bimanual object manipulation. *Experimental Psychology,* 53(2), 143–148.

Weigelt, M. & Schack, T. (2010). The development of end-state comfort planning in preschool children. *Experimental Psychology*, 57(6), 476–482.

Zacks, J. M., Kumar, S., Abrams, R. A., & Mehta, R. (2009). Using movement and intentions to understand human activity. *Cognition*, 112(2), 201–216.

Zacks, J. M., Speer, N. K., Swallow, K. M., Braver, T. S., & Reynolds, J. R. (2007). Event perception: A mind-brain perspective. *Psychological Bulletin*, 133(2), 273.

7 Shall we dance again?

Action researchers and dancers can move together

David A. Rosenbaum

Introduction

Dance, an art form, and action research, a scientific enterprise concerned with the analysis of perceptual–motor behaviours, have had little contact. This is not surprising considering the usual separation of the arts and sciences. However, the gap between these two lines of activity need not persist. Filling the gap holds great promise. Dancers and dance instructors face technical as well as artistic challenges, and action researchers may be able to help dancers address these concerns. Action researchers, on the other hand, may benefit from the inclusion of artistic and emotional expression in their portfolio of research interests. By recognizing the challenges of acting gracefully or of acting in ways that convey emotions in musical contexts, action researchers may broaden the scope of their investigations to embrace artistic expression as well as more traditionally studied topics in action research, such as efficiency and maximum speed of movement (Fitts, 1954).

My own research, some of which is reviewed here, has been similar to much action research in that it has largely ignored the artistic side of physical expression. In my own case, this is ironic considering that my interest in perceptual–motor control stems largely from my long-standing interest in, and dedication to, violin playing. The cross-disciplinary approach pioneered here by Bettina Bläsing and her colleagues can help investigators like me feel freer to cross the science– art divide.

When I think about dance, two people leap to my mind: Fred Astaire and Ginger Rogers. Regardless of how these two people may be viewed in the 'serious' dance world, I have always found them to be geniuses of their medium. Fred Astaire danced as if he were weight free. Ginger Rogers carried herself just as lightly, plus, as she famously quipped, she did so in high heels and going backwards. The great artistry of these two dancers, like the great artistry of other masters of dance, reflected years of practice. As dancers and other practitioners of physical and artistic expression get better and better at what they do, they learn to plan and control their movements more and more effectively. The nature of this process is what has interested me and my colleagues. Our main interest has been in motor planning. The question driving the research is: How do we plan the movements we make?

One way of asking this question is to pursue the problem of how particular movement patterns emerge when any given physical task is chosen. This matter instantiates the degrees-of-freedom problem, which arises whenever there are multiple possible solutions to a presented problem (see also Chapter 8). Motor-planning tasks epitomize the degrees-of-freedom problem because there are usually many possible ways to achieve a given physical task. Nevertheless, one single solution typically emerges. The solutions are usually efficient, reflecting implicit efficiency criteria for movement selection.

Representations

What are these implicit efficiency criteria and how are movements selected (or how do movements emerge) that are based on them? In addressing this question, my point of departure as a cognitive psychologist, is to focus on the *mental representations* guiding motor planning. Cognitive psychology is the study of mental function. At its heart is the concept of mental representations. Mental representations, as their name implies, are states of mind corresponding to experiences. In their simplest forms, mental representations are sensations arising from exposure to sensory stimuli. The mapping from measurable sensory stimuli to measurable sensory experiences or their reports (e.g., magnitude estimations, discriminations, or scaling of similarities or differences) is the subject of psychophysics. More complex mental representations may interconnect, with some representations exciting or inhibiting others. At any given time, a mental representation may also occupy the focus of attention while other mental representations may not. The study of attention is the study of such focusing; it includes the analysis of the dynamics of the transitions between mental representations. Finally, and most important for the discussion to come, mental representations refer to remote objects or events. For example, when light impinges on the retina, we do not 'see' the activity of our photoreceptors. Rather, we refer the photoreceptor activity to objects and events in the outer world. Sensations, therefore, are referred; they *represent* what is out there. The same is true of other representations.

Representations of what is out there in the world need not just refer to present events. They can also refer to events in the past – what we call 'memories' – and to events expected to occur in the future – what we call 'predictions' or 'plans'. Plans for actions can be thought of as memories for the future. For cognitive psychologists interested in motor planning, the challenge is to understand how such memories are formed. How are these future-oriented memories structured and how are they assembled over time? (See Chapter 9 for a study that investigates mental representations for dance movements in particular.)

A core concept in the study of mental representations, including the mental representations comprising plans for physical actions, is the notion of *hierarchy*. Governing relations exist among mental representations. If one representation, A, excites or inhibits another representation, B, more than the opposite relationship, A can be said to control B. This observation has an important corollary. It is often said that there are *levels* of representations. For example, in the study of speech production, it is generally acknowledged that there are distinct levels of representation for speech (Levelt, 1989). These levels have been inferred from a variety of sources, a prime one being slips of the tongue. Mistakes made in speaking are usually systematic and suggest distinct levels: a semantic (meaning) level, a syntactic (word order) level, a phonological (sound) level, a vocal execution level, and so on. Each level is suggested by characteristic errors that can be attributed to the mixing or missing of elements within the hypothesized tiers. For example, verbs tend to exchange (switch) with other verbs but not with nouns, nouns tend to exchange with other nouns but not with verbs, and so on. Such exchanges bespeak a syntactic (word order) level where grammatical class (e.g., verb versus noun) has functional importance and is not just the figment of some grammarian's imagination. It is thought that distinct levels of representation arise or are utilized during the process leading from thought to language production (Levelt, 1989).

Goal postures

My colleagues and I have sought to elucidate the levels of planning for non-linguistic behaviours. The main contribution we have made is to suggest that there is a level of representation for motor planning between the identification of physical goals for movement and the planning of movements *per se*. This intermediate level of representation is the *goal posture*. Our idea is that when positioning movements are planned, as in directing one's hand to a target in space, a goal posture is planned before a movement to that goal posture is planned. The goal posture can be reassessed based on the movement planning, so the process need not be unidirectional (i.e., goal-posture selection first, movement planning second). However, in the theory that my colleagues and I have developed, we have limited ourselves to the case of goal-posture selection followed by movement planning without re-evaluation of the goal posture based on movement planning (Rosenbaum et al., 1993; 1995; 2001).

A goal posture is an intended body position. It includes the joint angles of all the joints in the body as well as the forces and torques of the body's muscles (or concomitant variables). Several lines of evidence have led to the view that goal postures, as just defined, are specified before movements are specified. These lines of evidence will be summarized below, except for noting beforehand that an important clue about the validity of the posture-based motion planning view comes from dance. When dancers pirouette, they are instructed by their coaches to turn from one key position to another, directing their attention to a steady landmark in the external environment in successive spins. (For a movement description, see Chapter 9.) When this method is implemented, the dancer looks as if he or she is spinning continuously, but from the perspective of the *control* of dance, what the dancer is actually doing is aiming for a goal position over and over again. Aiming for goal positions not only applies to pirouettes; it also applies to other dance moves. Dance, for its appearance of being a continuous activity, is actually controlled, or is supposed to be controlled, by aiming for one target position after another. Insofar as this method is endorsed by dance coaches and also proves useful for dancers, it probably reflects a deeper principle about the control of physical action. That deeper principle, according to the posture-based motion planning theory developed by my colleagues and me, is that a reference condition for goal postures is established for positioning movements before movements to goal postures are planned.

What are the additional arguments for the goal-posture approach? One argument stems from consideration of the degrees of freedom associated with *positions* on the one hand versus *movements* on the other. The position of an object in three-dimensional space has six degrees of freedom: the x, y, and z values of its centre, plus its pitch, roll and yaw angles. The position of the human body, expressed in terms of joint angles, is the number of joint angle values required to uniquely characterize a posture. For the arm, there are seven such angle values: the shoulder has three degrees of freedom, the elbow has two degrees of freedom, and the wrist has two degrees of freedom (for a simplified arm model with only three degrees of freedom, see Chapter 8). Other joints add still more degrees of freedom. When muscle force and torques are added, still more degrees of freedom are needed to fully characterize a posture. If movement is brought into the picture, even more degrees of freedom add to the mix. For movement, all the degrees of freedom for each posture on the way from the start posture to the goal posture must be added, plus the times of their occurrence. The number of degrees of freedom for an entire movement path is huge. The number of degrees of freedom for a single position, such as a goal position, is much smaller. This implies that it is easier to specify a goal posture before specifying a movement (compare to the passive motion paradigm described in Chapter 8).

Another reason why it makes sense to plan goal postures before movements is that in the case of positioning movements, the main task to be achieved is attainment of a position. For example, the task of touching an elevator button is defined with respect to applying an adequate amount of pressure at a location in external space. How one gets to the button is typically less important than pressing it. In terms of feedback control theory, the reference condition is closure of the button. This is the highest-level goal, so it makes sense that it should be the highest-level goal in motor planning.

According to the posture-based motion planning theory, positioning movements are planned by first specifying goal postures that satisfy the requirements of bringing one or more parts of the body, or extensions of the body, to target locations. From among the possible postures that achieve this aim, the one that is chosen is the one that satisfies the most task constraints. These constraints range from those that are most important (e.g., touching the elevator button), down to those that are least important (e.g., moving the hand in a path of minimum curvature). The relative importance of the constraints can vary for different tasks. For example, the shape of the hand path may be relatively unimportant in an unoccupied elevator, but may be very important in an elevator that is occupied, especially if one of the other occupants is carrying a wet paint brush or a sharp object. It may also be important in a dance movement in which the curvature of the hand path should elicit a specific impression. The process of selecting the goal posture is achieved, in posture-based motion planning theory, through a two-stage process. The first is finding a goal posture from the set of recently performed and stored goal postures that survives a winnowing procedure in which each posture is accepted only if it satisfies successively lower constraints (Tversky, 1972). The second is a 'tweaking' process in which the one accepted, previously adopted, stored posture is varied as time permits to allow for an even better goal posture for the immediate task requirements. Once a goal posture is selected, a movement to it is selected via the same constraint-satisfaction scheme (see Rosenbaum et al., 2001, for details.)

The foregoing scheme is a typical memory-search and decision process within cognitive psychology. Accepting candidate-stored postures based on how well they satisfy ever lower constraints is an example of a process known as 'elimination by aspects' (Tversky, 1972). Here, candidates are rejected if they fail to satisfy the most important requirement, and the remaining candidates are rejected if they fail to satisfy the second-most-important requirement, and so on. If there is more than one remaining candidate at the end of the winnowing process, the choice is made at random. This method is familiar to anyone who has been involved in making hiring decisions, making mating decisions or making shopping decisions. In making hiring decisions – for example, in deciding who to hire for a faculty position in a research-oriented academic department – highest priority is generally given to some area of research, second-highest priority is given to productivity, third-highest priority is given to teaching ability, and so on. Only if more than one candidate remains who satisfy all the main requirements can a preference be given for someone who happens to possess a fairly unimportant criterion, for example someone who also likes to spend one evening per week taking Tango lessons for fun. Elimination of aspects turns out to be an efficient means of choosing among alternatives when there are multiple constraints (Tversky, 1972).

The second step in the goal-posture selection process is also familiar in cognitive psychological models. Tweaking values – that is, injecting variations into candidate options – is often used as a memory-search method and, relatedly, as a spur to creativity (this is illustrated for the process of choreography in Chapter 4: repeatedly trying out a movement in new ways until it fits). Adding variations for the sake of achieving better fits is a well-known component of Darwinian natural selection.

Movies

After considering the logical or principled reasons for the posture-based approach, we examine next how well the approach does in practice. In keeping with the idea that science has much to learn from the arts, it is relevant that the posture-based approach has long proven useful in the arts, or more specifically in animation. From the early days of generating animated cartoons, it was realized that the process of making such movies could best be pursued in a hierarchical fashion. At the highest level is the person with the idea for the story line. At the next lower level is the person responsible for generating key frames. At the lowest level is the person responsible for connecting the key frames. Key frames, as their name implies, are critical moments. For cartoon animators animating cartoon characters, and by extension for creatures animating their own bodies (for instance, in dance), these critical moments are goal postures (leaving out the outside events). Even if goal postures do not seem to be explicitly required (e.g., because there is no external target to which motion is explicitly required), they are essential for providing direction to the next lower level, to the production of movement. Without a key frame to which movement is made, it is almost impossible to know which of the infinite number of possible movements should be generated from the last critical position. By contrast and more positively, key frames provide rich information for movements. (This principle is also applied in a pedagogical concept presented in Chapter 2: the students first create a 'shape bank' for postures or key frames, and then, in a second step, a 'transition bank' for movements.)

Having key frames or goal postures makes it possible to transition between them with minimal-path algorithms. Computer-based animation methods that rely on such algorithms yield convincingly realistic movement patterns. Furthermore, computer files that only store key frames and which are then read by programs that employ those minimal-path interpolation algorithms (files in so called .mpg format) take up much less memory storage than files that only store series of complete images (files in so called .avi format). Of course, it does not follow that if computers do well with .mpg files then biological animation relies on an analogous approach. However, the possibility is alluring. A number of lines of evidence, summarized below, support the idea that, in general, biological movement may be cognitively controlled much as are computer animated .mpg files.

Anticipation

One line of evidence bears out the expectation that if goal postures are represented in advance, features of movement to the goal postures should reflect anticipation of the goal postures' characteristics. Indeed, this is the case. Speeds of movements tend to grow with the distance to be covered, and this scaling of movement speed is apparent even within the first few milliseconds of movement initiation (Gordon and Ghez, 1994). This result suggests that the distance to be covered is known in advance. Directions of movement also differ from the start of movement depending on where one is heading, and often in subtle ways. Brown and colleagues (2002) observed that when people began moving the hand toward a screen to place a hand-held object up against an image on the screen, the orientation of the hand-held object as it left the start gate was measurably different depending on which final orientation the hand-held object would have to occupy. In reaching out to grasp an object, grasps likewise reflect anticipation of future positions. For example, if a horizontal cylinder is grasped with the right hand and the cylinder will be turned 90° counterclockwise, people show a strong tendency to grasp the cylinder with an underhand grasp. Such a grasp affords a comfortable or easy-to-control thumb-up grasp when the cylinder is brought to its final position. Conversely, if the same horizontal cylinder is grasped with the right hand and the cylinder will be turned 90° clockwise, people show a strong tendency to grasp the cylinder with an overhand grasp. This grasp also affords a comfortable or easy-to-control thumb-up grasp when the cylinder is brought to its terminal position. This pattern of results – the end-state comfort effect (see Rosenbaum et al., 2012, for a review) – again suggests that advance information influences how forthcoming movements will be completed.

Even at more macroscopic levels of behavioural description, one sees evidence for anticipation of future positions. Recent work in my lab has focused on the coordination of reaching and walking, two activities that have seldom been considered together despite the extensive body of research on prehension, on the one hand, and locomotion, on the other (Rosenbaum, 2008; 2012; van der Wel and Rosenbaum, 2007). When people decide between walking to the left or right of a table from which they are supposed to lift a bucket and carry it to a site varying distances from the left or right sides of the table, the participants are adept at selecting the side of the table that affords an expedient combination of walking and reaching. If the bucket is on the left edge of the table and requires a long reach from the right edge, participants tolerate the long reach if it permits a short walk to the goal site. By contrast, if the bucket is on the left edge of the table and requires a long reach from the right edge, participants do not tolerate the long reach from the right edge if it requires a long walk to the goal site. In general, the likelihood that participants will walk along the left or right edge of the table to pick up a bucket on the left, middle or right edge of the table depends on how far participants must reach relative to how far must walk. The estimated cost of reaching over some unit distance, such as one meter, is much greater than the estimated cost of walking over that same unit distance (Rosenbaum, 2008). The orderliness of the data and the data's susceptibility to a good fit with the model just sketched suggests that forthcoming movement sequences can be well represented in advance and that the entire body can be represented this way. This is what would be expected if goal postures play a role in movement planning.

Posture neurons

Another line of evidence for the representation of goal postures comes from neurophysiology. Graziano and colleagues (2002) showed that sustained electrical stimulation of the motor cortex and premotor cortex in monkeys causes the monkeys to adopt characteristic postures. This is what would be expected if one subscribed to the functional reality of goal postures for motor control. Even when the monkeys were in different initial postures, the electrical stimulation applied at the same site elicited the same posture. By contrast, when the stimulation was applied at different sites, different postures were adopted. The latter result indicates that different whole-body equilibrium positions are represented in the brain, as would be required if specification of goal postures were important for moving to goal postures.

Memory for positions versus memory for movements

If goal postures are more important than movements, one would expect memory for postures to be better than memory for movements. This prediction follows on from research in cognitive psychology, where the longevity of a memory is often taken as a sign of the importance of the coded experience. Memory for stories, for example, tends to preserve the gist over the long term. Details such as the exact words used by the characters, the names of the characters, and so on, fade much more rapidly. Information importance is not simply defined by information longevity, however, for that would be circular. Rather, information importance is defined by a range of factors such as how vital the information is explicitly judged to be by the participants, how memory for one kind of information affects memory of another kind of information (higher levels should affect lower levels but not vice versa), and how long it takes to remember the information initially (more important information generally takes longer to remember initially than does less important information).

Consistent with the view that goal-posture information is more important than movement information, it has been found in many studies that memory for position is better than memory for movement (for a review, see Smyth, 1984). For example, as shown by Marteniuk and Roy (1972), people have difficulty reproducing distances they just covered, but they are adroit at reproducing final positions they adopted. The benefit of position memory over movement is not just due to better memory for extrinsic rather than intrinsic coordinates, for when body positions (postures) are experimentally dissociated from external locations, there is a clear contribution of posture memory *per se* (Rosenbaum, Meulenbroek and Vaughan, 1999).

Simulation

The final source of evidence for the posture-based view is the ease with which movements can be simulated. Based on the theory, it is possible to simulate such activities as reaching for objects with straight-ahead movements, reaching for objects while circumventing obstacles, handwriting, reaching for objects with hand-held tools, reaching at different speeds and using effectors in different ways to maximize biomechanical efficiency, and compensating for changes in the mobility of different joints (see Meulenbroek et al., 1996; 2001a; Meulenbroek, Rosenbaum and Vaughan, 2001b; Rosenbaum et al., 1995; 2001; Vaughan, Rosenbaum and Meulenbroek, 2001; 2006: see also Chapter 8). All of these simulation results are achieved with the concepts and methods outlined above. They are achieved by specifying goal postures that satisfy task constraints and then by specifying movements to those goal postures that satisfy task constraints. The quality of the simulations is judged by their visual similarity to observed behaviour and, in some of our studies, by the quantitative degree of fit to actually measured behaviour. Meulenbroek and colleagues (1996) pursued the data-fitting approach for handwriting; Meulenbroek and colleagues (2001a; b) and Rosenbaum and colleagues (2001) pursued the data-fitting approach for hand and finger paths during reach-and-grasp moves; and Vaughan, Rosenbaum and Meulenbroek (2001; 2006) pursued the data-fitting approach for hand paths around obstacles both in two-dimensional (planar) and three-dimensional (depth) tasks, respectively.

All the comparisons were encouraging. In all cases, the simulated motions were as similar to actual behaviour of individual human participants as was the actual behaviour of the other human participants to the human data being studied. In other words, the model's fit to the behaviour of person A was no worse than the fit of the behaviour of person B to the behaviour of person A, and so on. Meanwhile, it was possible to reject versions of the model by using parameters that rendered it unlike what any person actually did. The latter outcome implies that the model was not simply too powerful to be rejected.

Conclusions

A few further comments are worth making about the simulation results that have been obtained and, indeed, about the status of the posture-based approach in general. First, although my colleagues and I have found the approach to be psychologically intuitive and powerful, the approach is only one of many, and it has limitations. Other theoretical approaches have been developed for the generation of movement patterns (e.g., Butz, Herbort and Hoffmann, 2007; Cruse, Steinkühler and Burkamp, 1998; Guigon, Baraduc and Desmurget, 2007; Erlhagen and Schöner, 2002; Guenther, Hampson and Johnson, 1998). Comparing the posture-based theory to these other approaches goes beyond the scope of this chapter. However, the papers just cited, like the papers by my colleagues and me (Rosenbaum et al., 1993; 1995; 2001), have generally included comparisons of relevant theoretical positions, as is always required for responsible scholarship.

Second and in the spirit of full disclosure, the posture-based approach has many limitations. The theory is not yet cast in neurally specific terms; it only handles moving with the body rooted to a particular place in the world (i.e., the model does not yet walk, let alone dance); it has limited learning abilities; and the model is entirely kinematic (i.e., it has not yet been extended to force and torque production). These limitations imply the need for caution in claiming that the approach is 'the answer'. In all likelihood, some idea or set of ideas from the approach will join with ideas from other models to permit a more comprehensive account.

A third comment concerns the simulation of dance. Dance has not been simulated with the posture-based theory, nor, as far as I know, has it been simulated with any other theory that generates movements on its own (autonomous motor planning). Artificial dancers have been developed in robotics, but they rely on observation of other dancers rather than autonomous generation of dance moves. The challenge in autonomous generation of dance is to make an artificial movement system, such as a robot, dance in ways that are lifelike. This is a tall challenge, for it opens the domain of movement simulation from merely 'getting the job done' to moving *stylistically*. Being able to move with different styles is likely to be a basic feature of motor control even though this has seldom been acknowledged in traditional, engineering-oriented research in this area. An animal or a person who needs to impress an antagonist with his or her seeming might, or who needs to impress a prospective mate with his or her suitability for parenting, must be able to move 'in style'. Dance can be viewed as a form of such stylized motor behaviour. The fact that ethologists speak of mating dances conveys this idea (see Brown et al., 2005). If we reach the point where robots dance as people dance, based on their own movement planning, this will indicate that we not only understand how to plan and control basic movements, but that we also understand how to plan and control the more nuanced features of movement that make activities like dance a natural activity for humans and animals, where the manner of moving as well the sheer capacity for movement are equally important.

References

Brown, L. E., Moore, C. M., & Rosenbaum, D. A. (2002). Feature-specific processing dissociates action from recognition. *Journal of Experimental Psychology: Human perception and performance, 28*, 1330–1344.

Brown, W. M., Cronk, L., Grochow, K., Jacobson, A., Liu, K., Popoviç, Z., & Trivers, R. (2005). Dance reveals symmetry especially in young men. *Nature, 438*, 1148–1150.

Butz, M. V., Herbort, O., & Hoffmann, J. (2007). Exploiting redundancy for flexible behavior: Unsupervised learning in a modular sensorimotor control architecture. *Psychological Review, 114*, 1015–1046.

Cruse, H., Steinkühler, U., & Burkamp, C. (1998). MMC – A recurrent neural network which can be used as manipulable body model. In: R. Pfeifer, B. Blumberg, J.-A. Meyer, & S. Wilson (Eds.), *From Animal to Animats 5* (pp. 381–389). Cambridge, MA: MIT Press.

Erlhagen, W. & Schöner, G. (2002). Dynamic field theory of movement preparation. *Psychological Review, 109*, 545–572.

Fitts, P. M. (1954). The information capacity of the human motor system in controlling the amplitude of movement. *Journal of Experimental Psychology, 47*, 381–391.

Gordon, J. & Ghez, C. (1994). Accuracy of planar reaching movements: I. Independence of direction and extent variability. *Experimental Brain Research, 99*, 97–111.

Graziano, M. S., Taylor, C. S. R., & Moore, T. (2002). Complex movements evoked by microstimulation of precentral cortex. *Neuron, 34*, 841–851.

Guenther, F. H., Hampson, M., & Johnson, D. (1998). A theoretical investigation of reference frames for the planning of speech movements. *Psychological Review, 105*, 611–633.

Guigon, E., Baraduc, P., & Desmurget, M. (2007). Computational motor control: Redundancy and invariance. *Journal of Neurophysiology, 97*, 331–347.

Levelt, W. (1989). *Speaking*. Cambridge, MA: MIT Press.

Marteniuk, R. G. & Roy, E. A. (1972). The codability of kinesthetic location and distance information. *Acta Psychologica, 36*, 471–479.

Meulenbroek, R. G. J., Rosenbaum, D. A., Jansen, C., Vaughan, J., & Vogt, S. (2001a). Multijoint grasping movements: Simulated and observed effects of object location, object size, and initial aperture. *Experimental Brain Research, 138*, 219–234.

Meulenbroek, R. G. J., Rosenbaum D. A., Thomassen, A. J. W. M., Loukopoulos, L. D., & Vaughan, J. (1996). Adaptation of a reaching model to handwriting: How different effectors can produce the same written output, and other results. *Psychological Research/ Psychologische Forschung, 59*, 64–74.

Meulenbroek, R. G. J., Rosenbaum, D. A., & Vaughan, J. (2001b). Planning reaching and grasping movements: Simulating reduced movement capabilities in spastic hemiparesis. *Motor Control, 5*, 136–150.

Rosenbaum, D. A. (2008). Reaching and walking: Reaching distance costs more than walking distance. *Psychonomic Bulletin and Review,* 15, 1100–1104.

Rosenbaum, D. A. (2012). The tiger on your tail: Choosing between temporally extended behaviors. *Psychological Science,* 23, 855–860.

Rosenbaum, D. A., Chapman, K. M., Weigelt, M., Weiss, D. J., & van der Wel, R. (2012). Cognition, action, and object manipulation. *Psychological Bulletin,* 138, 924–946.

Rosenbaum, D. A., Engelbrecht, S. E., Bushe, M. M., & Loukopoulos, L. D. (1993). Knowledge model for selecting and producing reaching movements. *Journal of Motor Behavior,* 25, 217–227.

Rosenbaum, D. A., Loukopoulos, L. D., Meulenbroek, R. G. M., Vaughan, J., & Engelbrecht, S. E. (1995). Planning reaches by evaluating stored postures. *Psychological Review,* 102, 28–67.

Rosenbaum, D. A., Meulenbroek, R. G., & Vaughan, J. (1999). Remembered positions: Stored locations or stored postures? *Experimental Brain Research,* 124, 503–512.

Rosenbaum, D. A., Meulenbroek, R. G., Vaughan, J., & Jansen, C. (2001). Posture-based motion planning: Applications to grasping. *Psychological Review,* 108, 709–734.

Smyth, M. M. (1984). Memory for movements. In: M. M. Smyth & A. M. Wing (Eds.), *The Psychology of Human Movement* (pp. 83–117). London: Academic Press.

Tversky, A. (1972). Elimination by aspects: A theory of choice. *Psychological Review,* 79, 281-299.

van der Wel, R. P. & Rosenbaum, D. A. (2007). Coordination of locomotion and prehension. *Experimental Brain Research,* 176, 281–287.

Vaughan, J., Rosenbaum, D. A., & Meulenbroek, R. G. J. (2001). Planning reaching and grasping movements: The problem of obstacle avoidance. *Motor Control,* 5, 116–135.

Vaughan, J., Rosenbaum, D. A., & Meulenbroek, R. G. J. (2006). Modeling reaching and manipulating in 2- and 3-D workspaces: The posture-based model. *Proceedings of the Fifth International Conference on Learning and Development, Bloomington, IN.*

8   Getting cognitive

Holk Cruse and Malte Schilling

What do I see when I watch somebody dance? Obviously, a dance expert or a dancer himself would see the dance in a very different way than I do: he would pay attention to the relevant features, he would be able to predict the next movements and therefore would know where to look next and would recognise a surprising move or a simple fault, while I only see a series of elaborated movements, being surprised by their order and hopefully pleasured by their aesthetic expression.

What do our brains see and do while watching the dance? Is there any difference between the function of my brain and that of a professional dancer when going to the ballet? There is now a large amount of data supporting the notion that our brains process such visual experiences differently. In particular, studies of Calvo-Merino and colleagues (2005; 2006: see also Chapter 10) analysed activations in dancers' brains while watching familiar movements that they could easily perform in contrast to equally skilled demanding movements used in a different style of dance that they had never learnt. Major differences were found in brain activation while viewing these two kinds of movements. Our repertoire of movements and our abilities to act influence the way in which we perceive. This is in accord with many other neurological or behavioural studies (Jeannerod, 1999; Prinz, 1997; Fogassi et al., 2005) and the idea has been put forward that our own action system constrains our way of perceiving other's actions (Loula et al., 2005; Schütz-Bosbach and Prinz, 2007; Schubotz, 2007). Observing a dance is activating the same neuronal circuits I would use to dance myself – I am dancing along in my head. Hence, perceiving is a way of re-enacting the watched dance.

In this chapter, we will explain how a simple (re-)action system can become a system that perceives its environment in a meaningful way. We propose a simple system that is limited to walking behaviour. With this example, we want to demonstrate, on the one hand, how these simple control structures have to take into account the body of the walker and information about the environment and, on the other hand, how a body model can be used for perception and as a next step – by decoupling the body and only acting on the body model – for planning ahead.

The details of the reactive system introduced here are based on insect studies. This is done because: (1) motor control of complex behaviours has been studied in insects in great detail on both the behavioural and neurophysiological level; and (2) there is evidence that the basic control structures of insects and mammals are well comparable (Pearson, 1993). Any complex behaviour, including dance, does however not only rely on reactive structures, but includes higher level, cognitive aspects like planning a movement or imagining a movement. Concerning such questions, the insect system is presumably not suited. Therefore in the second part of this chapter we complement the reactive, low-level system by an expansion that covers cognitive aspects. This part is necessarily speculative, but still inspired by biological knowledge and supports the idea that the cognitive system does not form a separate system being independent from the reactive part, but relies on the reactive system by exploiting its properties.

This chapter is therefore to be understood as a short introduction to basic properties of motor-control systems and to provide a description of one side of the bridge addressed by Chapter 7 that may help to close the gap between science and art.

Motor control and cognition

In any organism, the basic task a brain has to solve is to control body movements. Some brains are, in addition, able to show cognitive abilities like thinking, imagining or feeling. Traditionally, questions related to how these different capabilities may be realised are considered to concern quite separate domains of research. However, more and more evidence has been collected, and we will argue that both aspects are not only tightly coupled, but may be hardly separable on the neural level. Both motor control and thinking (as well as imagining) appear to be produced by the same neuronal mechanisms; a result which has great impact for the understanding of our brains.

The control of tasks like a cheetah chasing an antelope, a goat jumping on steep rocks, or a spider spinning a web and later walking on it, is considered to be quite difficult. Nevertheless, the ability to cope with these tasks appears to be of quite different character compared to abilities underlying cognition, in particular human cognition that enables us to imagine future situations, to communicate using a complex language, to draw inferences, and to find proofs for mathematical problems. Such cognitive tasks concern very recent evolutionary inventions (in evolutionary terms) and human beings usually feel positive to have these capabilities available in contrast to other animals. Although it is not yet clear whether the 'invention' of typical human cognitive abilities can really be considered an advantage in the long run, to a scientist, cognition is quite an interesting phenomenon representing a challenge in order to understand the underlying principles. Trying to understand the underlying mechanisms can be considered a progress with respect not only to our cultural development, but also as regards improved healthcare and, for use in engineering, the construction of more intelligent machines.

As already mentioned, we will argue that the apparent gap between both domains – motor control and cognition – is much smaller than usually assumed. To this end, we begin with a description of what we know about control of simple movements. By simple movements, we mean movements that are called reactive or reflex-controlled movements. The corresponding movement controllers may be learned or may be innate, but in any case are characterized by representing a well-defined neuronal system that receives sensory input and uses these inputs to determine the motor output. Simple cases are avoidance reflexes. As has been studied in insects for example, there might also be quite complex motor behaviours that still can be considered as sensory driven or reactive. Insect walking – although seemingly being far away from human motor control – has been considered to be a typical case of reactive behaviour. We will start by describing what is known concerning walking and climbing in insects.

While control of walking might appear quite simple, it includes many problems solved by nature that are not fully understood by biologists and engineers. There is still a huge gap between the movements shown by robots and those of real insects (for an overview, see Berns, 2008). We will therefore summarize what is known about insect walking and what are the associated problems (for details, see Schilling et al., 2013).

For an insect that has six legs, each with three joints, the movements of 18 joints have to be controlled simultaneously. When we consider – as a simplification – each of these joints as a simple hinge joint, each joint position can be characterized by one real valued number defining the angle of this joint. Thus, the central nervous system (CNS) of the insect has to specify 18 numbers in order to determine the position of the body in space (called 'degrees of freedom': DoF). So the question can be reformulated as: How does the CNS control these 18 DoF (joint angles) when the insect is walking? To describe a simple hypothesis concerning the neural system that controls movement of the legs, we have to refer to some details of the anatomy of the insect leg. An insect leg contains essentially 3 segments: the coxa, the femur and the tibia (see Figure 8.1). The three hinge joints connecting these segments are termed α joint, β joint and γ joint. To simplify matters, we assume that each joint is controlled by one single information channel, the output value of a single 'motor neuron' (this assumption is justified for a robot that has one motor per joint, but represents a simplification for animals that have at least two muscles per joint; each muscle usually being driven by many motor neurones.) In addition, each joint is equipped with one sensor, measuring the actual joint angle. How could a neuronal system looking like this control sensory driven movements?

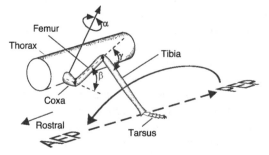

Figure 8.1 Leg morphology of an insect: leg angles, swing movement and stance movement. AEP: anterior extreme position; PEP: posterior extreme position.

We begin with a simple behavioural element required for walking; the so-called 'swing' movement.

A reactive system: Control of swing movement

When walking, a leg can be regarded as applying two behavioural elements in alternation. The first is the stance movement, during which the leg supports the body while moving from front to rear in order to propel the body (during forward walking). Of course, there is a rear position of the leg (called posterior extreme position: PEP) where the leg must be lifted off the ground and moved forward. This return movement starting at the PEP and ending at the anterior extreme position (AEP) is called the 'swing movement' (the curved arrow in Figure 8.1). Thus, the complete behavioural element requires lifting the leg off the ground, moving it forward, and then moving it downward in an appropriate spatial and temporal manner. How might a neural controller look; one that is able to move the leg (i.e., the three leg joints) in order to perform such a swing movement?

Before showing such a hypothetical controller based on a network consisting of artificial neurons, we are going to introduce our artificial neurons (see Figure 8.2). A typical neuron consists of an input (dendrite), a cell body, and an output element (axon). The output signal is transmitted to the input of the next neuron - its dendrite - via a synapse indicated by a black circle in Figure 8.2. In the case of a motor neuron, the output signal drives the muscles (not shown). In the case of a sensory neuron, the input is given by a physical measure (e.g., a leg joint angle) transmitted to an activation of the neuron. This transmission is symbolized by a semicircle in Figure 8.2.

Of course, in a realistic neuronal network, there is not just one sensor, one synapse and one output neuron, but many of each. Figure 8.3 shows a (still simple) network containing nine neurones. Three are motor neurones, which determine the motor output (α_m, β_m, γ_m) to the three leg joints; three are sensor neurones, which measure the actual joint angle values (α, β, γ); and three further neurones specify the angles (α_{ref}, β_{ref}, γ_{ref}) that, for each joint, should be approached at the end of the swing movement (see Rosenbaum's discussion regarding a level of

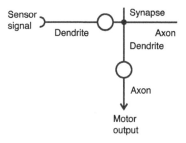

Figure 8.2 Connection between a sensor unit and a motor unit. Somata of the neurons are marked by open circles; the connecting synapse is marked by a small black circle. The transmission of a sensor signal (input) is symbolized by a semicircle.

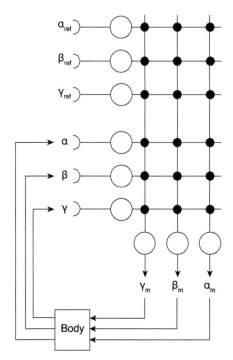

Figure 8.3 Swing net; controlling the swing movement of an insect leg (represented
by the box 'body'). α_m, β_m, γ_m : motor output driving the three joints α, β,
γ, the actual values of which are measured by sense organs. α_{ref}, β_{ref}, γ_{ref} :
the angle values that should be reached at the end of the swing movement.
Synapses are marked by small black circles.

representation – called the 'goal posture' – for motor planning between the identification of physical goals for movement and the planning of movements *per se,*
in Chapter 7). Now we have a network containing nine neurons connected by
18 synapses. Each synapse is characterized by a given number which represents
the strength of this synapse. This number represents a factor, by which the signal
coming from the axon of the first, presynaptic, neuron is multiplied and then given
to the dendrite of the second, postsynaptic, neuron. Each dendrite simply sums all
its input values.

For this given structure of the net, we can find a combination of weights that
when connected to a leg can produce a swing movement. Therefore this network is
called a swing net. When activated, the network moves the leg up, forward and then
down again. In this way, it produces a specific behaviour and may therefore be
called a memory element.

Further memory elements are necessary to control walking. First of all, each leg
needs a 'stance net' to be able to control the other important behavioural element,
the stance movement. We will not describe the stance net in detail (see Schilling
et al., 2012; Schmitz et al., 2008). However, given such a network, there is now a

kind of competitive situation, because both networks, the controller for the stance movement and that for the swing movement 'want' to control the same joints. Therefore, a third neural network is required that decides which of the two behaviours, swing or stance, should actually be performed. This network is called a selector net. The selector net again receives sensory input on the basis of which decisions are made – for example, the actual leg position or the leg having ground contact or not. Figure 8.4a schematically depicts these three networks plus a further one, called a target net. The target net determines the position the leg should adopt at the end of swing. This network receives sensory input from another leg, the anterior neighbour, in order to allow the swing net to move the swinging leg near the actual position of the anterior leg. This is quite helpful when climbing in branches, because the position of the anterior leg guarantees the ability to find support. All four networks mentioned receive sensory input from leg sensors, i.e., from body parts, measuring position and velocity, for example. Another important sensory input refers to ground contact of a leg (GC: see Figure 8.4a). In Figure 8.4a, information flow is depicted by bold arrows pointing from 'body' to sensory input

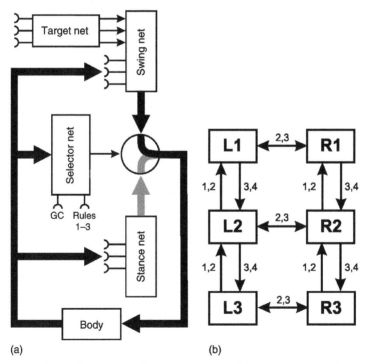

(a)   (b)

Figure 8.4 Walknet; *(a)* single leg controller; and *(b)* coupling of the six legs. The selector net decides whether swing net or stance net can control the body (leg). Selector net receives as input whether the leg has ground contact (GC) or not, as well as information concerning leg position, the latter signal being influenced by information from other legs (rules 1-3: see Schilling et al., 2013). Numbers in *(b)* refer to these rules. Rule 4 is realized by the target net shown in *(a)*.

of these networks. Swing net and stance net, in turn, provide motor output to move body elements, i.e., leg segments (bold arrow pointing to 'body'). The ability of the selector net to decide on stance or swing is indicated by the two arrows shown in black or grey, respectively. As our model has six legs, we need six of these controllers. Naturally, these six controllers have to be coupled to allow for coordination of leg movement during walking. Behavioural studies have indicated that a small number of local rules govern the coordination between the six legs (Schilling et al., 2013). Figure 8.4b illustrates the pathways of rules 1 to 4, each acting between a pair of neighbouring legs. As indicated, rules 1 to 3 influence the selector nets, and rule 4 describes the effect of the target net.

Thus, Figure 8.4 depicts, in a graphical form, a quantitative hypothesis on how the neural system of an insect able to control walking might look. How can we show that this network, called Walknet, is actually able to control walking, in particular walking in a difficult environment?

The only way to investigate and test the properties of such a model is to simulate it. This can be done, on the one hand, as a software simulation which requires not only to simulate the network (Walknet), but also to simulate the body and the environment, e.g., obstacles to be negotiated. On the other hand, a more realistic test for the hypothesis is to perform a hardware simulation in which the neural network is still simulated on a computer, but a physical robot is also controlled that acts in the real, physical world. In this way, the hardware simulation avoids errors due to inappropriate simplifications unavoidable by the abovementioned software simulations. Walknet has been tested successfully by both kinds of approaches and has been shown to produce different types of walking patterns observed in walking insects, in order to negotiate obstacles and curves and to cope with different disturbances (Schilling et al., 2013). Simple expansions of the network allow to cope with loss of legs, as do the insects (Schilling, Arena and Cruse, 2007) and, in particular, to climb over very large gaps (Bläsing, 2006), the latter requiring complex searching behaviour as well as specific adjustment of leg stepping.

To summarize, quite complex behaviour can be controlled by a reactive, i.e., strictly sensory driven, neural network. However, two aspects have to be stressed. The network represents a completely decentralized structure. Apart from the specification of walking velocity and the tightness of a curve to be negotiated, there is no information from 'higher' centres. All decisions are made locally, including the coordination between the six legs and the reactions to any unexpected disturbances. Thus, Walknet forms an example of self-organization of complex behaviour. The second important aspect concerns the fact that the existence of the body (plus the environment) is an essential element of the 'computation' necessary to control the behaviour. The movement of the individual leg is not only driven by its own muscles, but also by the influences of the other legs, to which this leg is mechanically connected via the body and via the various physical properties of the ground. This aspect is often characterized by the terms 'embodiment' and 'situatedness', stressing the important contributions of the body and the properties of the environmental situation, respectively. Taking embodiment and situatedness into account allows for unexpected high 'motor intelligence' in spite of a comparatively simple neuronal structure.

Central pattern generators, i.e., systems that produce rhythmic motor output without sensory feedback, have been considered as an alternative approach. Yet both approaches appear complementary. On one hand, central motor programs have been studied in investigations on fast walking or running and appear viable only when the environment is highly predictable (e.g., Pfeifer, Lungarella and Iida, 2007). On the other hand, studies of animals walking slowly and in cluttered environment show that sensory feedback is applied in these cases (Cruse, 2002).

Cognitive systems: Why use internal models?

Proponents of the behaviour-based approach (e.g., Brooks, 1991) have argued that the CNS does not require a representation of the own body or the environment, as was typical for the traditional artificial intelligence, but that, relying on embodiment and situatedness, the world as such can serve as 'its own best model'. This view opposed the strong influence of the later-termed 'good old fashioned artificial intelligence'. However, an increasing multitude of experimental results clearly indicates that humans and other 'higher' animals possess some kind of internal models of the world, including a model of their own body. The latter, seen from the brain's point of view, has been regarded the most important part of the world (Cruse, 2003). These results raise questions as to how such internal models might be realized neutrally, and what purpose such models may serve.

Internal models may serve several purposes. One aspect is that knowledge about the geometrical properties of the body may be used to improve the quality of the sensory input. Sense organs, for example those monitoring the joint angles, always show limited accuracy of measurement. Therefore, it is possible that only incorrect information concerning the actual position of the legs and the body may be available, based on raw sensor data. In addition, the interpretation of these data may lead to geometrically inconsistent results (see the Pinocchio example below). However, running these partly incorrect data through such a body model can provide corrected sensor data. Such a body model could not only improve the sensor data, but may even restore information, if, due to defect sense organs, some data are completely missing.

Shiffrar and colleague (1990; 2001) gives an example to show that humans appear to apply body models for perception. These experiments exploit the so-called phi-phenomenon. When a subject is confronted with two successive images, for example one with a point on the left side immediately followed by one with a point on the right, we have the impression that there is only one point that moves from left to right. It is usually assumed that the brain constructs such an apparent motion in order to move along the shortest path between the two objects. Shiffrar confronted subjects with pictures showing a person with two different arm positions (see Figure 8.5). According to the hypothesis, the arm should move along a straight vertical line as shown by the bold arrow. This was actually the case when both pictures were presented within a very short time interval. However, when this

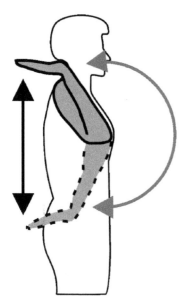

Figure 8.5 Shiffrar's experiment. Subjects are shown two pictures in temporal
            sequence; one with the arm in upper position, and the other with the arm
            in lower position (dashed lines). For short delays between viewing the
            pictures, an apparent motion is perceived as indicated by the black arrow;
            for longer delays, the apparent motion follows the curved grey arrow.

period was prolonged and corresponded to the time needed to move a real arm
from the first position to the second, subjects perceived a movement as indicated
by the curved arrow in Figure 8.5 – a movement which, in contrast to the result of
the first experiment, could be performed by a human body.

These findings strongly suggest that the brain does not interpret the visual input
on a 'pixel level', but feeds it into its body model. If the match is sufficiently realistic, this interpretation is given to higher levels leading to subjective experience.
The result that the body model cannot match the very fast movements shows
that our body models also represent dynamic properties of the (physical) world.
(A possible brain site responsible for recognition of biological movements is
described in Chapter 11.)

A second, and completely different, way to exploit a body model concerns motor
control, in particular when the task is to control a body with extra DoF, which is the
rule and not the exception. For example, think of the task to point with the hand to
a dot marked on a table in front of you. The position of the dot in three-dimensional
space can be described by three coordinate values: x, y and z of a Cartesian
coordinate system (the task is defined by three DoF). However, the mechanics of
the human arm are characterized by seven DoF (not counting the finger joints: see
also Chapter 7 for a description of further types of degrees of freedom). Therefore,
there are 7–3 = 4 extra DoF, which allow for many different arm positions when

solving the task. This has the advantage that we can select a specific arm position that is more comfortable than others, for example. However, the disadvantage is that this requires the brain to solve a computationally difficult problem, called inverse kinematics. The solution is especially difficult for the underdetermined case where the brain has to select one of many possible solutions. However, if a body model is available, there is a comparatively easy way to solve this task. Intuitively, this solution has already been recognized by H. von Kleist (1987/1810). In his essay 'Über das Marionettentheater' (see also Chapter 1) the protagonist, a ballet dancer, states that movements performed by puppets, simply moved by threads fixed to the hands, are highly comparable with the elegant movements of animals or naturally moving humans. (Von Kleist contrasts these natural movements, assumed to be controlled by such a 'puppet principle', with consciously controlled movements, where the actor vainly attempts to perform elegant movements.)

In modern times this principle has been termed 'passive motor paradigm' (Mussa Ivaldi, Morasso and Zaccaria, 1988). The underlying idea is that the extra degrees-of-freedom problem can be solved if a body model is used like a puppet: the tip of the puppet's/the body model's hand is pulled to the position of the target, whereby the other segments of the arm necessarily follow, thereby solving the problem. To control the real arm, the joint movements of the model arm can be read off the model and then used as signals to control the real arm. Even constraints, such as the mechanical limits of specific joints, can be introduced into the model. Therefore, it has been hypothesized (Steinkühler and Cruse, 1998) that body movement is controlled by application of a neuronal model of one's own body, which becomes particularly helpful when the body to be controlled contains extra DoF.

As a combination of perception and motor control, a body model may be suited for the imitation of an observed movement, if activation of the motor output is not switched off (which is apparently the case for patients suffering from echopraxia). Perception, when directly connected to the motor-control system, may immediately lead to an understanding of the action observed, because perceiving that action means to stimulate the viewer's own neuronal system that would be used when actively performing the action (e.g., Rizzolatti et al., 1996; Gallese and Lakoff, 2005).

The third reason to use internal models represents a crucial step beyond the capability of reactive systems as described so far. Internal models could be used to simulate a behaviour in order to test possible consequences of that behaviour without actually performing it. For example, the walker may test whether it is possible to lift three specific legs without loosing stability. To this end, the internal body model can be driven by the reactive controller while its connections to the motor output are switched off. The 'internal', i.e., simulated, behaviour of the body model feeds sensor information back to the reactive controller, as would the real body in the reactive system discussed above. Therefore the behaviour can be internally realized – and even dangerous behaviours can be tested – without harming the body. Thus, a system using a body model in this way is able to plan ahead, which, according to the definition of McFarland and Bösser (1993) can be characterized as being able to show cognition. Freud introduced the term 'probehandeln', an ability, which, according to Freud, corresponds to thinking. Of course, for such a system to be cognitive, further mechanisms are required, as is the ability to judge the resulting outcomes of the simulated behaviour (see Schilling and Cruse, 2017; 2008). The ability to simulate new movements may not only be exploited for testing new behaviours, but also for training a specific behavioural sequence (e.g., 'mental training'). This may be advantageous as internal simulation can be faster and does not have to cope with unexpected disturbances or compensation of erroneous movements, as is the case when performing physical training in the real world. Metzinger (2006) used the term '2nd order embodiment' for this concept because a body model that represents the physical properties of the real body in sufficient detail is required for such simulations.

To study this application of a body model in more detail, we have to return to the question: How can such a body model be realized by means of a neuronal network? Recall that this body model has to be 'manipulable' like a puppet. It must be able to represent all geometrically possible body positions and movements. A concept for the construction of such a body model has been proposed that is based on a specific recurrent neural network (RNN) (Steinkühler and Cruse, 1998; Schilling et al., 2012). To allow the reader to develop an intuitive idea of the functional properties of such RNN, the basic principle will be explained using a simple version (Kühn, Beyn and Cruse, 2007). Consider three vectors *A*, *B* and *C* forming a triangle (see Figure 8.6a). Vectors *A* and *B* may be interpreted as describing the upper arm and the lower arm, respectively, while vector *C* points from the basis (the shoulder) to the hand. This geometrical arrangement can be represented by an RNN (see Figure 8.6b: also shown in more detail in Appendix A).

In the network depicted in Figure 8.6b, each artificial neuron, or unit, receives an input from sense organs (the semicircles), and shows an output as is the case for the neurons shown in Figures 8.2 and 8.3. Different to the earlier networks, each neuron also receives input from the other neurons belonging to this net and its own output (recurrent input), thus forming a recurrent net. What are the properties of such a network? At the beginning the activations of the three neurons are set by the sensory input given for one iteration. If this input value describes a geometrically consistent situation (i.e., a closed triangle as in Figure 8.6a), the activation of the

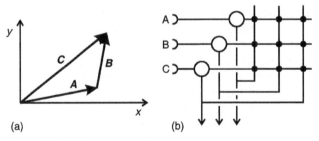

(a)   (b)

Figure 8.6 *(a)*Three vectors that represent a two-segment arm (vectors *A* and *B*) that point to a position determined by vector *C*. *(b)* A recurrent neural network structure that can represent all possible vector positions.

net remains stable, even after this input is switched off. Such a network represents a memory for the actual position of the arm. An important property of this network is that, after any disturbance given at the input, the network always relaxes to a new stable state that is again characterized by a geometrically sensible position of the arm. This means that the three vectors again form a closed triangle, in general different from the first triangle. In this way, the network is able to represent geometrically possible body configurations. The sensory (for example, visual) input describing vector C sets the status of the network, i.e., determines the position of the arm segments; and the output drives the muscles/motors controlling the joints to adopt the corresponding position of the arm. To control a movement of the arm, this net could be exploited in the following way: If the input to neuron C is changed, for example by a spoken command ('move your hand to the dot'), vector C is changed – it now points to the target position – and, as a consequence of the recurrent connections, vectors A and B are changed too, until they fulfil the geometrical condition determined by the externally determined vector C. These changes in the model can be used to move the joints of the real arm. Thus vector C has an effect like the thread pulling the hand of a puppet.

The individual neuron, being part of a recurrent network, cannot be classified as either a sensory unit or a motor unit as was possible in the example of the feed-forward network, shown in Figure 8.3. This is reminiscent of the properties of canonical or mirror neurons, found within the premotor cortex of monkeys and described by Rizzolatti and colleagues (1996) and Gallese and Lakoff (2005). Mirror neurons are active when the animal performs a specific movement, but also when the animal observes the same movement being performed by another subject. Thus they appear at the same time to be both motor-related units and sensor-related units. This is also the case for the units of our RNN. Thus, observation of the body movement of another subject and controlling the corresponding movement of the own body appear to be performed by one and the same neural network. Together with Shiffrar's result reported earlier that perception of a body movement of another subject requires a neural body model (see Figure 8. 5), this leads to the speculation that mirror neuron and canonical neuron-like units are part of this body model and that this model is not only used for perception, but is also used for controlling the movement of the own body. This is in agreement with Loula and colleagues (2005) studies, which show that videos of movements of the own body can better be recognized than movements of other human subjects.

A functionally similar model has been proposed by Rosenbaum (see Chapter 7). Both models are able to deal with extra DoF. The most important difference between both models refers to the fact that our model is based on an RNN structure that determines the position dynamically, whereas Rosenbaum's model uses look-up tables that can be learned.

We will now briefly indicate how these ideas could be implemented in order to expand a reactive motor system, for example Walknet, to become a cognitive system. Figure 8.7a shows an abstracted version of Walknet (the fact that there are many leg controllers is indicated here by showing stacked swing nets and stance nets). The motor output drives the body that, by influencing the sense organs, closes the loop and stimulates the neurons of Walknet, allowing for complex behaviours. In contrast to this basic version, the sensory input is already provided to a body model to improve perception. Figure 8.7b shows a further expansion. A switch (the circle, lower right) is introduced that allows the motor output to be directed either to the body or, instead, to the body model. The latter case allows for a simulation of body movements. We assume that the switch is triggered in emergency situations, i.e., when a situation occurs that cannot be handled by the reactive controller. Specific 'problem sensors' are, of course, required to identify such a situation. To be able to plan ahead, the system is further equipped with the ability to invent new behaviours which then can be tested using this body model. If by such simulations a solution is found that no longer activates the emergency sensors, this solution appears to be a sensible one and should therefore be tested in reality. This requires the switch to be moved back into its original position. In addition,

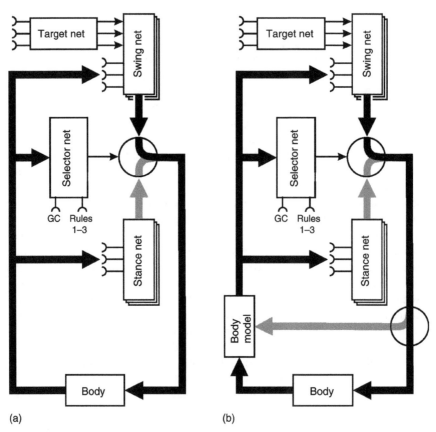

(a)   (b)

Figure 8.7 *(a)* Walknet: the fact that there are six leg controllers is indicated by plotting several stacked stance nets and swing nets. *(b)* Expansion of Walknet by introduction of a body model. A switch (circle, lower right) is sited to decouple the controller from the motor output to the body, and to drive the body model instead.

a new successful solution should be stored in long-term memory. This concept, representing a realisation of more general ideas proposed by different authors, for example the 'simulation theory' of Jeannerod (1999) or the 'common coding concept' of Prinz (1997), is actually being tested by expanding Walknet to reaCog (Cruse and Schilling, 2015; Schilling and Cruse, 2017).

Internal aspect

In the preceding sections we have considered neuronal mechanisms that might be responsible for the control of reactive and cognitive behaviour. However, by concentrating on the neuronal mechanisms, we have completely neglected the intriguing fact that some neural activities lead to the phenomenon of subjective experience whereas others do not (Cruse and Schilling, 2015; Schilling and Cruse, 2016).

Ansorge and colleagues (1998) have performed a masking experiment. A subject has learned to press a button as fast as possible with the right hand when a square is presented on a screen, and to press another button with the left hand when a circle is shown. After learning is finished in the experiment, the circle is shown, but only for about 30 ms, and is followed by a square shown for a longer time. Interestingly, the subjects report to have seen only the square, but nevertheless press the left button, i.e., the button belonging to the circle. Thus, the square was subjectively experienced, but not the circle, although the latter stimulus has triggered the relevant neuronal system leading to a behavioural reaction.

The phenomenon of some neural activities leading to subjective experience raises questions. A simple question concerns the anatomical and physiological properties of those neural networks that are leading to subjective experiences. Also a more difficult question: How can we, or can we at all, understand that a neuronal mechanism creates such a 'miraculous' property as is subjective experience? This question is directly related to the mind–body problem and some philosophers assume that the answer to this question is beyond human capabilities. Chalmers (1996) has called this the 'hard problem'.

Concerning the first question, sensible answers might be possible. Different observations support the assumption that some activities of neural networks, in detail yet unknown, form at least necessary conditions for subjective experience to occur. It is, for example, clear that the naive assumption 'we experience what our sense organs provide' is not justified. We do not perceive the image projected to our retina, but perceive a much more elaborated image which means that at least some neuronal 'computation' is required before a state is reached that allows for subjective experience. Furthermore, patients with an amputated arm report subjective experiences of this nonexistent arm, the so-called 'phantom-limb sensation', and this observation shows that sensory input is not necessary. Patients with brain damage who are suffering from Hemi-neglect syndrome experience only half of the world although their sensory systems are intact, and this may provide hints towards the neuronal structures that are responsible for subjective experience.

Although details concerning the responsible structures for subjective experience are not known, imaging studies and other experiments strongly indicate that the same neuronal systems are responsible for control of action, for planning an action and for imagining an action (e.g., Gallese and Lakoff, 2005). These results led us to the speculation that the RNNs suggested above to represent the body models required for control of action and for planning ahead, also form the neuronal substrate that is the prerequisite for our capability to have subjective experiences (Cruse and Schilling, 2015). This assumption has led Metzinger (2006) to the notion of the '3rd order embodiment'. Cruse (2003) has specifically speculated that the phenomenon of subjective experience appears when the corresponding RNN is near the end of its relaxation. According to this hypothesis, the RNN approaching its attractor state might be the necessary and sufficient condition for subjective experience to occur.

At first sight, a test of this hypothesis appears to be impossible, because we cannot decide whether a neural network constructed according to the hypothesis actually creates subjective experience. We can only register subjective experiences by introspection or by relying on reports of other human subjects. Nevertheless, an indirect approach appears to be possible. Basically, the idea to test this hypothesis is to search for artificial neural networks that (i) can simulate the observed behaviour and (ii) approach an attractor state when, in the corresponding experiment with humans, the latter report to have the corresponding subjective experience. We have carried out this test for the masking experiment explained above. In principle, such a simulation was also possible for another experiment called the 'Pinocchio illusion' (Lackner, 1988). In this experiment, a human subject is asked to hold his/her nose between index finger and thumb of the right hand. Then the biceps muscle of the right arm is mechanically stimulated with a high frequency signal. This stimulus has the effect that the subject has the impression that the elbow joint is extended, although it is fixed. During this treatment, some subjects have the subjective experience that their nose is elongated up to 30 cm (hence the reference to Pinocchio). In the body model proposed, elongation of the nose may actually occur when the attractor state is being reached (Schilling and Cruse, 2008).

Another experiment has been reported by Ramachandran and colleagues (2002). A patient suffering from a phantom sensation of the amputated left arm felt that this arm always remained in a fixed position. Ramachadran placed a mirror before the patient such that the mirror image of the patient's right arm appeared at a position where an intact left arm could have appeared. So the patient saw two arms, but still felt his left (phantom) arm was in the fixed position. Now Ramachandran asked him to move both arms in the same way, say up and down. Although the patient first reported not to be able to move his left arm for many years, he followed the proposal and announced excitedly that suddenly he felt his left arm moving. This subjective experience disappeared when the mirror was taken away. According to our interpretation, the patient's body model received new sensory input, the visual one, which stimulated the arm model to match the external stimulus (corresponding to the C vector in our simple model shown in Figure 8.6). Approaching this new attractor state also led to the corresponding subjective experience.

So, for all three examples, the behaviour of the artificial network is in agreement with the behavioural observations and with the report of subjective experiences, thus supporting our hypothesis. For a further examination of Chalmers' 'hard problem', see Cruse (1999; 2003). In short, we have argued that this question will not be explicitly answered, but will simply disappear. This is in accordance with a question that was intensively discussed at the beginning of the last century: Is there a specific entity that causes a physical system to become a living one? Today, it is generally assumed that there is no necessity for such an entity as a *vis vitalis* – rather, the state of living is considered a system property.

Conclusion

In summary, results of a broad range of experimental investigations and of simulation studies support the idea that human brains contain neural networks that are simultaneously responsible for motor control, perception of movement, and imitation, planning and imagining movements. The ability to plan ahead characterizes the system as a cognitive one; and the ability to imagine refers to the phenomenon of having subjective experience, eventually also considered as an essential prerequisite for the system to be termed cognitive.

Simulations performed to understand these capabilities are based on a body model using a specific recurrent neural network, the units of which show relations to mirror neurons. The body model is assumed to be used for perception, in particular for improvement of partly incorrect or even missing sensor data, but also for understanding the meaning of an action observed as well as for motor control, motor imitation and motor planning ('probehandeln'), the latter three relying on the 'passive motion paradigm' or von Kleist principle. According to this principle, control of movement (in particular when extra degrees of freedom have to be controlled) corresponds to moving a puppet being pulled by an imaginary thread. The network shows a relatively simple structure, but nevertheless allows for an interpretation of how subjective experiences may result.

Appendix A: The realization of a body model by means of a neuronal network

As mentioned in the text referring to Figure 8.6, the vectors A, B and C are considered, with A and B representing the upper and the lower arm, respectively, and C the connection between shoulder and tip of the hand. How could such a situation be represented by a neural network? This geometrical situation can be described by the vector equation $A + B = C$. This equation can be used to determine the following system of equations:

$$A = -B + C$$
$$B = -A + C$$
$$C = A + B$$

If we consider these vectors as time-dependent variables – necessary, for example, because the position of the arm may vary over time – the system can be reformulated as:

$$A(t+1) = -B(t) + C(t)$$
$$B(t+1) = -A(t) + C(t)$$
$$C(t+1) = A(t) + B(t)$$

This can be further expanded by introduction of a factor $d > = 0$:

$$A(t+1) = (d*A(t) - B(t) + C(t))/(d+1)$$
$$B(t+1) = (-A(t) + d*B(t) + C(t))/(d+1)$$
$$C(t+1) = (A(t) + B(t) + d*C(t))/(d+1)$$

This equation system describing the temporal change of vectors A, B and C can be split into two systems of equations each describing scalar values, the x-components and the y-components of the corresponding vectors. As the coefficients are the same for the x-component system and the y-component system, only the x-system will be shown:

$$Ax(t+1) = d/(d+1)*Ax(t) - 1/(d+1)*Bx(t) + 1/(d+1)*Cx(t)$$
$$Bx(t+1) = -1/(d+1)*Ax(t) + d/(d+1)*Bx(t) + 1/(d+1)*Cx(t)$$
$$Cx(t+1) = 1/(d+1)*Ax(t) + 1/(d+1)*Bx(t) + d/(d+1)*Cx(t)$$

The coefficients of this system, describing the matrix,

$$d/(d+1) \ -1/(d+1) \ 1/(d+1)$$
$$-1/(d+1) \ d/(d+1) \ 1/(d+1)$$
$$1/(d+1) \ 1/(d+1) \ d/(d+1)$$

can be interpreted as representing the strengths of the synapses of the RNN. These synapses are shown in Figure 8.6b by small closed circles in the same format as given by the matrix. The output values for time $t+1$ are used as input to the next iteration, thus forming a recurrent system.

This network shows the properties mentioned earlier. By changing the input (vector C), the output of the units representing vectors A and B can be used to control the movement of the arm to the new position. As the network can be easily expanded to represent limbs with more joints, such a system with extra degrees of freedom allows for an infinite number of solutions (arm positions) when pointing to a given position in space. The simple network introduced here is, however, not able to maintain the length of a vector representing a body segment constant. To represent a realistic body with fixed segment lengths, more complex networks, called MMC nets with nonlinear expansions, are necessary (see Steinkühler and Cruse, 1998).

References

Ansorge, U., Klotz,W., & Neumann, O. (1998). Manual and verbal responses to completely masked (unreportable) stimuli: Exploring some conditions for the metacontrast dissociation. *Perception*, 27, 1177–1189.

Berns, K. (2008). Walking machine catalogue. http://www.walking-machines.org (accessed September 2008).

Bläsing, B. (2006). Crossing large gaps: A simulation study of stick insect behaviour. *Adaptive Behavior*, 14(3), 265–285.

Brooks, R. A. (1991). Intelligence without representation. *Artificial Intelligence*, 47, 139–159.

Calvo-Merino, B., Glaser, D. E., Grèzes, J., Passingham, R. E., & Haggard, P. (2005). Action observation and acquired motor skills: An FMRI study with expert dancers. *Cerebral Cortex*, 15(8), 1243–1249.

Calvo-Merino, B., Grèzes, J., Glaser, D. E., Passingham, R. E., & Haggard, P. (2006). Seeing or Doing? Influence of visual and motor familiarity in action observation. *Current Biology*, 16, 1905–1910.

Chalmers, D. J. (1996). *The Conscious Mind.* New York: Oxford University Press.

Cruse, H. (1999). Feeling our body – the basis of cognition? *Evolution and Cognition*, 5, 162–173.

Cruse, H. (2002). The functional sense of 'central oscillations' in walking. *Biological Cybernetics*, 86, 271–280.

Cruse, H. (2003). The evolution of cognition – A hypothesis. *Cognitive Science*, 27, 135–155.

Cruse, H. & Schilling, M. (2015). Mental states as emergent properties – From walking to consciousness. In: T. Metzinger & J. M. Windt (Eds.), *Open Mind.* Frankfurt am Main: MIND Group.

Fogassi, L., Ferrari, P. F., Gesierich, B., Rozzi, S., Chersi, F., & Rizzolatti, G. (2005). Parietal lobe: From action organization to intention understanding. *Science*, 308(5722), 662–667.

Gallese, V. & Lakoff, G. (2005). The brain's concepts: The role of the sensory-motor system in conceptual knowledge. *Cognitive Neuropsychology*, 22(3–4), 455–479.

Jeannerod, M. (1999). To act or not to act: Perspectives on the representation of actions. *Quarterly Journal of Experimental Psychology*, 52A, 1–29.

Kühn, S., Beyn, W. -J., & Cruse, H. (2007). Modelling memory functions with recurrent neural networks consisting of input compensation units. I: Static situations. *Biological Cybernetics*, 96, 455–470.

Lackner, J. R. (1988). Some proprioceptive influences on the perceptual representation of body shape and orientation. *Brain*, 111, 281–297.

Loula F., Prasad S., Harber K., & Shiffrar M. (2005). Recognizing people from their movement. *Journal of Experimental Psychology: Human perception and performance*, 31, 210–220.

McFarland, D. & Bösser, T. (1993). *Intelligent Behavior in Animals and Robots.* Cambridge, MA: MIT Press.

Metzinger, T. (2006). Different conceptions of embodiment. *Psyche*, 12(4).

Mussa Ivaldi, F. A., Morasso, P., & Zaccaria, R. (1988). Kinematic networks – A distributed model for representing and regularizing motor redundancy. *Biological Cybernetics,* 60, 1–16.

Pearson, K. G. (1993). Common principles of motor control in vertebrates and invertebrates. *Annual Review of Neuroscience,* 16, 265–297.

Pfeifer, R., Lungarella, M., & Iida, F. (2007). Self-organization, embodiment, and biologically inspired robotics. *Science,* 318(5853), 1088–1093.

Prinz, W. (1997). Perception and action planning. *European Journal of Cognitive Psychology,* 9, 129–154.

Ramachandran, V. S., Rogers-Ramachandran, D., & Cobb, S. (2002). Touching the phantom limb. *Nature,* 377, 489–490.

Rizzolatti, G., Fadiga, L., Gallese, V., & Fogassi, L. (1996). Premotor cortex and the recognition of motor actions. *Cognitive Brain Research,* 3, 131–141.

Schilling, M., Arena, P., & Cruse, H. (2007). Hexapod walking: An expansion to walknet dealing with leg amputations and force oscillations. *Biological Cybernetics,* 96, 323–340.

Schilling, M. & Cruse, H. (2008). The evolution of cognition – From first order to second order embodiment. In: I. Wachsmuth & G. Knoblich (Eds.), *Modeling Communication with Robots and Virtual Humans* (pp. 77–108). Berlin: Springer.

Schilling, M. & Cruse, H. (2016). Avoid the hard problem: Employment of mental simulation for prediction is already a crucial step. *Proceedings of the National Academy of Sciences (PNAS).*

Schilling, M. & Cruse, H. (2017). ReaCog, a minimal cognitive controller based on recruitment of reactive systems. *Frontiers in Neurorobotics,* 11, 3.

Schilling, M., Hoinville, T., Schmitz, J., & Cruse, H. (2013). Walknet, a bio-inspired controller for hexapod walking. *Biological Cybernetics,* 107(4), 397–419.

Schilling, M., Paskarbeit, J., Schmitz, J., Schneider, A., & Cruse, H. (2012). Grounding an internal body model of a hexapod walker – Control of curve walking in a biological inspired robot. *Proceedings of IEEE/RSJ International Conference on Intelligent Robots and Systems.* 2762–2768.

Schmitz, J., Schneider, A., Schilling, M., & Cruse, H. (2008). No need for a body model: Positive velocity feedback for the control of an 18-DOF robot walker. *Applied Bionics and Biomechanics,* 5(3), 135–147.

Schubotz, R. I. (2007). Prediction of external events with our motor system: Towards a new framework. *Trends in Cognitive Sciences,* 11(5), 211–218.

Schütz-Bosbach, S. & Prinz, W. (2007). Perceptual resonance: Action-induced modulation of perception. *Trends in Cognitive Sciences,* 11(8), 349–355.

Shiffrar, M. (2001). Movement and event perception. In: B. Goldstein (Ed.), *The Blackwell Handbook of Perception* (pp. 237–272). Oxford: Blackwell Publishers.

Shiffrar, M. & Freyd, J. J. (1990). Apparent motion of the human body. *Psychological Science,* 1, 257–264.

Steinkühler, U. & Cruse, H. (1998). A holistic model for an internal representation to control the movement of a manipulator with redundant degrees of freedom. *Biological Cybernetics,* 79, 457–466.

von Kleist, H. (1987). Über das Marionettentheater [On the Marionette Theatre]. In: H. Sembdner & H. von Kleist (Eds.), *Sämtliche Werke und Briefe* [*Complete Works and Letters*], Bd 2, pp. 338–345. Munich: Verlag. (Originally published in Berliner Abendblätter, 1, 1810.)

9 The dancer's memory

Learning with the body from the remembered, the perceived and the imagined

Bettina Bläsing

As humans, we have inherited many different ways of moving and interacting with our environment. At some point in evolution, we have even acquired the ability to move in a deliberate and rhythmic way, to communicate and express emotions and ideas through our body, to mimic and imitate the movement of other humans and animals, and to assign abstract qualities like beauty to such movements. We have learnt to use these exceptional abilities to tell stories, and we have started to create movement styles to serve this purpose. In short: we have learnt to dance!

To study complex movements in humans we can gain access to different levels of movement information by observing the kinematic features of movement via motion capture, measuring the activations of muscles via electromyography (EMG), or by recognizing the movement-related activity in the central nervous system, applying methods such as electroencephalography (EEG), functional magnetic resonance imaging (fMRI) or positron emission tomography (PET) (see Box 9.1 for further information regarding these methods of investigation). These methods have also been used for studying effects related to expertise in dance. Motion capture and EMG have been applied to measure muscle activation and body kinematics during ballet movements in dancers (Krasnow et al., 2011). Brain imaging techniques and EEG have been used to study brain activation in dance experts and novices while watching dance (Calvo-Merino et al., 2005; 2006; Cross, Hamilton and Grafton, 2006; Orgs et al., 2008: see also Chapters 10–13), and even while dancing (Brown, Martinez and Parsons, 2005). In addition to the described methods, we can apply behavioural methods from experimental psychology through which we can gain access to cognitive processes related to attention, memory, decision making or creativity (e.g., Chapters 6 and 7).

In this chapter, I will focus on the behavioural approach and on cognitive aspects of dance expertise, in particular relating to long-term memory and learning. The research I present here is motivated by the questions: How are complex full-body movements represented on a higher cognitive level? Also: How is such representation linked to motor control and learning? According to current perspectives in the cognitive sciences, internal representations co-evolve together with corresponding actions, and become vehicles for higher mental functions such as thinking and planning ahead (see Steels, 2003). The view that a mind, or a cognitive system, can only evolve through the interaction with the physical world is referred

***Box 9.1*   Methods in brain and movement science**

Electroencephalography (EEG) is a method of recording the activity of neurons, mainly in the cerebral cortex, using a set of electrodes placed on the scalp. Potentials of single neurons are summed, and the resulting brain waves can be used to monitor the activity of the cortex over a longer period of time, or to measure evoked potentials that occur in response to specific events. In studies of cognitive science, event-related potentials are recorded, for example, to gain information about the processing of distinct signals in the brain (e.g., following the perception of unfamiliar words, pictures or sounds). The study of brain waves is an important measure in sleep research and neurological diagnostics, as different states of sleep, alertness or attention are characterized by brain waves of specific frequencies and amplitudes. Another important field of application is clinical diagnostics, as several neurological diseases (e.g., epilepsy) can be identified on the basis of specific brain-wave patterns.

Electromyography (EMG) is a method of recording the activity of muscles, usually using surface electrodes fixed on the skin above the muscle. Muscle activation is generated by electrical potentials from nerve cells (motor neurons) that each innervate a group of muscle fibres called a motor unit. Activation of a motor unit that leads to muscle contraction is accompanied by electrical potentials in the muscle fibres. Surface EMG measures the electrical activity in several motor units at the same time.

Functional magnetic resonance imaging (fMRI) is a method of measuring the blood flow in the brain. As active neurons need increased levels of oxygen, the blood flow is dynamically regulated to supply oxygenated haemoglobin to active brain areas. Brain activity can thus be measured as relative difference between levels of haemoglobin before oxygen release (oxyhaemoglobin) and after oxygen release (deoxyhaemoglobin). As oxy-haemoglobin and deoxyhaemoglobin differ characteristically in their magnetic susceptibility, activated brain areas show a different magnetic resonance from less active brain areas. This effect, the BOLD (blood oxygen level dependent) response, is measured in fMRI. Results are achieved by statistical methods being applied to the magnetic signals recorded during many repetitions of the action performed by the person in the scanner (e.g., reading sentences or seeing pictures or movie clips).

Magnetoencephalography (MEG) is a method of measuring cortical activity via the magnetic fields produced by electrically active neurons. MEG resembles EEG in many respects, but instead of electrodes, very sensitive measuring devices called SQUIDs (superconducting quantum interference devices) are applied to the scalp. Compared to EEG, MEG has better spatial resolution and very high temporal resolution, but a smaller operating distance, detecting only superficial cortical signals. It is therefore often used in addition to other methods such as EEG, fMRI or PET.

Motion capture is a method of recording movements of a (human) body and of translating them into a digital model of the moving body. One well-established method is to fix reflecting markers on the body of an actor and to sample the movement by a set of infra-red cameras simultaneously from different sides. The recorded data are mapped onto a digital three-dimensional body model that can then be made to perform the same movements. Joint angles can be calculated from this model, which gives scientists the opportunity to calculate movement kinematics. This method is used by scientists to analyze the movement of humans and animals, for example in sports, but also by film makers and computer game designers in order to generate virtual characters that move in a natural way.

Positron emission tomography (PET) is a method of recording three-dimensional pictures of metabolic processes in the human body by use of a radioactive tracer. A short-lived radioactive isotope embedded into a carrier molecule is injected into the bloodstream and transported via the blood circulation to the area of interest, for example the brain. As the tracer decays, it emits positrons, anti-particles of electrons. When a positron meets an electron in the body tissue, both particles are annihilated, and a pair of gamma photons is emitted. These gamma particles are recorded by a luminescent material in the PET scanner. As the blood flow is increased in brain areas with high activity levels, the gamma radiation measured from these areas will also be higher as compared to less active areas. In a different approach, the tracer can be carried by molecules that bind directly to receptors for specific neurotransmitters in order to monitor the activity of these receptors, for example in neuropsychiatric patients. Even though PET involves the incorporation of a radioactive tracer, it is not dangerous because the dose of radiation involved is very small.

Transcranial magnetic stimulation (TMS) is a non-invasive method of influencing neuronal activity in the brain. Rapidly changing magnetic fields applied with high precision by a figure-eight shaped electrical coil induce weak electric currents in the brain tissue. These electric currents interfere with the neuronal activity in the target areas, temporarily 'knocking them out', which can lead to measurable effects on task performance, such as increased reaction times. Whereas methods like EEG or fMRI can only help to detect the correlation of neuronal activity in a brain area with a specific task, TMS can give stronger evidence for a *causal* relationship between task performance and brain activity, by showing that suppressing a specific brain area results in deterioration of task performance.

to as 'embodiment' (see Wilson, 2002; Barsalou, 2008; Metzinger, 2006: see also Chapter 8), and has been discussed intensively among scientists and philosophers in recent years. Perception is never independent of action (Prinz, 1997; Schütz-Bosbach and Prinz, 2007a; b): it is always shaped by the body and its spatiotemporal conditions. Therefore, memory in its most immediate form is embodied in the world via our bodily self (Glenberg, 1997). This connection enables us to perceive through memory, to learn by adapting and forming memories, or to recall memories. For dancers, the idea that thinking, understanding and learning begins with the body is not at all astonishing. How should it be otherwise? In my view, this is one of the reasons why the art of dance and cognitive science form a very fruitful alliance.

Complex movement in long-term memory

When it comes to memory and learning, dancers stand out as experts, because for them, memory skills themselves are a fundamental part of their expertise. Dancers who perform live on stage have to master not only the performative skills of their discipline, but also how to manage vast amounts of material that is to be learnt, stored, recalled, adapted, modified and used for new creative processes. Dancers hold hour-long sequences of complex movement in their memory in order to perfectly reproduce and re-create them on stage, and to adapt them to the spatial and temporal requirements of the performance and to the ongoing interactions with other dancers and the audience. By ways of memorizing, recalling and creatively adapting and modulating, the learned movement material is repeatedly enacted and embodied by the dancer, and thus becomes his/her individual artistic property.

In his standard work on classical dance, Nikolai I. Tarassow indicates that the dancer's memory is the major source of competence that holds the technical and artistic score of the dramatic action (Tarassow, 2005). As Tarassow reports; 'A well-trained memory assures the mental anticipation of the following dramatic action at any time and leads the dancer safely to success'. According to Tarassow, the dancer's memory consists of three parts: auditive, visual and motor memory:

> These different qualities of memory are inextricably linked. They allow the dancer to move in a technically and artistically correct way and to form the movement creatively.
>
> (Tarassow, 2005: translated from the German)

Psychologists distinguish different parts of memory primarily according to the duration the content is stored. Short-term or working memory acts as a gate or filter through which only relevant information is passed on to long-term memory, in which information can be stored for a longer time, and up to a lifetime, and from which it can be retrieved for various purposes (Squire and Zola, 1996). All information stored in long-term memory can potentially be drawn back into working memory, where it can be compared to, merged with or modified by, novel information from current processes of action-based perception (Baddeley, 2000). Working memory capacity is described as up to seven items held up to a few minutes, but it can be extended by training to several more minutes and a larger amount of inform-ation. Chunking techniques that help organize information into meaningful units can contribute largely to its efficacy. In cognitively demanding situations, working memory plays a crucial role in controlling and allocating attentional resources (Burgess, 2000). In their comprehensive working memory model, Baddeley and Hitch (1974) have ascribed the latter function to a sub-system termed 'central executive' in which information from lower level sub-systems is integrated and processed. These sub-systems are specific to vision (the 'visuospatial sketchpad') and audition (the 'phonological loop') and hold small amounts of modality-specific information for a few milliseconds, like an after-image or echo. Later versions of Baddeley's model include a fourth compartment, the 'episodic buffer', in which multimodal information can be held, modified and linked to long-term memory content (Baddeley, 2000).

Scientists differentiate between two basic types of long-term memory: the consciously accessible declarative memory that comprises personal experiences (episodic memory) and knowledge of facts (semantic memory); and procedural memory, which includes motor skills as well as cognitive skills that have typically been acquired implicitly through practice, or trial and error. The contents of proce-dural memory (Squire, 1992; Squire and Zola, 1996) are typically neither con-sciously accessible nor immediately available for verbal expression, but underlie all the skills we master, from riding a bike or using a tool to dancing Kitri's solo from *Don Quixote*. In contrast, declarative memory contains all explicitly learned and verbally expressible knowledge about the world; its content is consciously accessible and can be modulated by thought and language. Events we have encoun-tered, and relevant information related to them, are stored in episodic memory; whereas facts that are not linked to specific events, such as poems learnt by heart, or names of capital cities, are stored in semantic memory (Tulving, 1972; 2002). Episodic and semantic memory can be understood as processing stages, as most facts have at some point during the learning process been linked to episodes, before they are generalized by frequent repetition and retrieval.

Although this differentiation between long-term memories can be helpful for analyzing and diagnosing memory (dys)functions, complex learning situations in the real world typically require a combination of different types of memory. In movement learning, both declarative and non-declarative memory act in conjunc-tion, building up the individual's specific motor repertoire. An artist learning to dance a complex series of movements will achieve the best results when combining implicit and explicit means of learning and memory. Let us imagine a dancer who learns a difficult movement phrase as part of a new choreography. The novel move-ments are demonstrated and to some part explained verbally by the choreographer and then adapted by the dancer and his/her colleagues using their own creative and bodily workspace. The situation in the dance studio, the face and voice of the cho-reographer, the images given to illustrate or generate the movement, and the others' comments and responses, are all stored in the dancer's episodic memory. After some time, the dancer will likely forget the details of this experience, and only the relevant facts will remain as part of semantic memory. Whilst the dancer observes and practises the movement, all sensorimotor information is stored in his/her non-declarative memory. With repeated practice, the movement becomes more and more automatized and thereby more deeply anchored and independent of attention, which gives him/her increasing freedom to focus on other aspects and work creatively with the newly acquired movement material. As it is this automated movement knowledge he/she will rely on when performing the piece, it is crucial that it contains as much relevant and flawless information as possible. For modifying or adapting the sequence, or for correcting learnt mistakes, language can provide clarity and help to make implicit movement knowledge explicit before linking it to new episodic, semantic and procedural content.

The close interaction of procedural and declarative memory becomes obvious when we try to apply corrections to already automatized movements. The first useful step in 'un-learning' an old mistake is often to find a verbal description for what is going wrong and what should be done instead. Language can provide clarity to thoughts and can be used as a tool to manipulate implicit knowledge. The process of making implicit movement knowledge explicit by linking it to new (episodic, declarative and procedural) content in order to improve it and automatize it again in its new corrected form, is often more challenging than simply learning a new movement from scratch. Another situation in which learned and potentially automatized movements have to be made explicit, and thereby accessible for intentional modification, is improvisation in contemporary dance. In the creation process for the piece *Theatrical Arsenal* in October 2009, the dancers of The Forsythe Company were asked to turn the movement phrase on which they were working into its opposite (Elizabeth Waterhouse, personal communication). This task is particularly interesting from a cognitive–science perspective, as it lends itself to being solved in a top–down manner involving the conceptual level. Kinematically, the movement phrase has too many degrees of freedom to be consciously perceived in completion: it therefore has to be defined on the conceptual level and assigned characteristics that have opposites. Only then can it be treated as a compound of the characteristics and be re-created, after selected characteristics have been replaced by their respective assumed opposites. Skilled dancers can rise to this challenging task by creating meaningful outcomes even without making this process conscious.

From a science perspective, we argue that such complex processes of re-creating learnt material are closely linked to embodied cognitive representations in long-term memory, in which all sensory modalities are integrated and merged into one entity that is perceived as consistent and meaningful. According to recent theoretical and empirical evidence, motor learning includes the integration of multimodal (visual, auditive, verbal, haptic, kinaesthetic and proprioceptive) information into a holistic mental representation of the learnt action (Barsalou, 2008; Zacks et al., 2007; Rosenblum, Dias and Dorsi, 2017). We have come to understand that such representations in long-term memory are not purely procedural or declarative, not learnt either implicitly or explicitly, but that they comprise procedural, semantic and episodic aspects that are integrated and updated with every new access, and that they underlie the execution as well as the imagination of the learnt actions (Land et al., 2013). Kate Stevens, a cognitive psychologist who has been one of the first in the field working with professional dancers and musicians, adds to this perspective by proposing that extensive dance training can render procedural memory of implicitly learned movement material explicit and declarative even without verbal articulation, leading to a 'heightened capacity for conscious control of procedural memory concerning the body and motor skills' (Stevens, 2017).

Furthermore, dancers apply specific techniques, such as marking, to support their learning and memorizing of complex movements or movement sequences. Marking is typically used as shorthand for choreography and movement learning through which experienced dancers indicate sections, transitions and directions typically with hand or foot gestures, with reduced full-body movement or by turning to directions in space, instead of dancing 'full-out'. Marking can be considered a cognitive tool that makes use of the same cognitive functions and brain structures as executing, observing and mentally simulating motor actions (Jeannerod, 1995; 2004), and thus it is used by dancers to learn, recall, modify, adapt, create or communicate movement. In collaboration with Wayne McGregor's contemporary dance company, David Kirsh (2011) assembled a taxonomy of marking practices, and analyzed their cognitive function as landmarks for memorization and tools for choreographic thinking. A common function identified was the production of landmarks for memorization. Warburton and colleagues (2013) tested the effectiveness of marking for memorization and recall and found that dancers' recall of newly learnt choreography was superior when marking in comparison to dancing full-out. Kirsh also studied the function of marking as a tool for choreographic thinking: experienced dancers can mentally image one version of a choreography whilst marking another version in order to compare the movements and to develop new ideas (Kirsh, 2011).

Studying cognitive structures of dance movement

In my research, I have addressed different aspects of memory in dance, based on theoretical conceptions. Studies investigating memory and learning in dance show that dancers indeed possess enhanced memory skills compared to non-dancers, and that they acquire specific techniques for facilitating movement learning and recall (Bläsing et al., 2012; Sevdalis and Keller, 2011). In this section, I will refer to a selection of studies that were motivated by, and conducted in collaboration with, dance professionals, to investigate processes of memory and learning in dance.

According to the theoretical perspective applied, complex movements are stored in long-term memory as a network of sensorimotor information (Schack, 2004: see also Chapter 6). The nodes within this network contain perceptual effects that have been associated during movement learning and movement performance. With reference to the *pirouette en dehors*, the node *'plié'*, for example, includes bending and stretching the knees while maintaining control of the position of hips and shoulders and the distribution of body weight, felt as pressure on the soles of the feet. Furthermore, the movement representation includes spatiotemporal features such as the downward and following upward movement of the centre of mass, and the antagonistic pulling of the knees into the opposite directions, etc. The movement knowledge of a complex movement such as a *pirouette en dehors* can be regarded as a network of such nodes in long-term memory. The better a dancer can perform such a movement, the more orderly the network is organised, and vice versa. The higher the degree of order the network features, the better the knowledge can be accessed, the better the movement can be performed, and the less attention and concentration are necessary for completing the task correctly.

We applied the structural dimensional analysis-motoric (SDA-M) method (described in detail in Chapter 6) to analyze the structure of such networks of movement knowledge in the long-term memory of dancers of different skill levels. A crucial first step was to define the basic action concepts (BACs) that were understandable and meaningful for novices as well as experts. This was accomplished with the help of dancers, amateurs and experienced ballet teachers, as well as standard references on classical dance training (Lörinc and Merényi, 1995; Tarassow, 2005; Vaganova, 2002). Classical ballet is particularly well suited for a study that uses verbal labels for movement concepts, as all movements that form the canon of classical ballet are named and associated with verbal labels for those who train in the dance discipline. Many of these verbal labels are commonly used in training, both with beginners and experts: they refer to movement elements that can be combined into a hierarchical structure – thereby, they are already closely related to BACs. It is hardly possible to define BACs without extensive feedback given by persons who master the task on different skill levels. Furthermore, it is important to take the experience of teachers into account, and also to look at the way in which the task is actively structured during learning and training, as concepts that emerge during training are likely to remain intact as scaffolding in long-term memory. 'Expert' BACs might not be experienced by the individual before reaching a sufficient level of performance and, subsequently, might not be integrated into the task-specific memory structure of a beginner; 'beginner' BACs, however, might cease to exist for an expert or might branch into several new concepts.

As reference for the group mean cluster solutions, we used the movement structure as revealed by functional movement analysis (Hossner, Schiebl and Göhner, 2015). According to this practice-based approach, a complex movement can be considered as a solution to a given movement task; each functional phase then serves the purpose of solving one of its sub-goals, and the interplay between phases leads to the solving of the task in completion. Functional phases are sorted according to their importance for reaching the overall movement goal during the main functional phase. Assisting (auxiliary) functional phases lead to the completion of sub-goals that support and prepare for reaching the main goal, with primary assisting phases being more important for, and closer to, the overall goal than secondary assisting phases, etc. For the *pirouette en dehors,* we defined four functional phases, with the actual turn taking place during the main functional phase (see Figure 9.1). The turn is initialised during the preparation, predominantly by the *plié,* which is regarded as the main component of the primary assisting phase. The primary function of this phase is to build up spring tension for the turn.

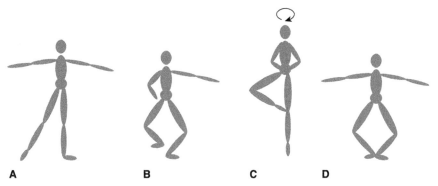

Figure 9.1 Functional phases of a *pirouette en dehors*. A – second order assisting functional phase: body alignment and pose; B – first order assisting functional phase: build-up of elastic forces for the turn; C – main functional phase: turn; D – final assisting functional phase: catching the turn and pose. The following BACs have been used in the study: phase A – (1) stand, right foot in front; (2) open arms for preparation; (3) right foot slides to side; phase B – (4) move right arm to front; (5) move right foot back; (6) bend knees; (7) locate eye focus; phase C – (8) stabilize body axis; (9) close arms; (10) push left leg into ground; (11) move right foot up to left knee; (12) turn head; phase D – (13) relocate eye focus; (14) close right foot behind left; (15) open arms after turn; (16) bend knees, stretch. (Modified from Bläsing, Tenenbaum and Schack, 2009).

During the first part of this preparation, in the secondary assisting phase, the body is aligned, and the attention of both the dancer and the audience are focused on the following turn. During the final assisting phase, the turn is halted and the body is shaped into a pose. We expected that the cluster solution of expert dancers would involve their implicit knowledge of the movement structure, reflecting a rich experience of performing the movement, and would therefore intrinsically correspond to the functional phases. Correspondingly, we expected the representation structure of less experienced dancers to be less consistent with the functional phases, due to the lack of reliable movement-related information and the lower degree of order in their knowledge network.

The results, displayed in Figure 9.2, confirmed our hypotheses in general, but also offered surprising aspects. The professional dancers' cluster solution of the *pirouette* indeed corresponded to the functional phases, but so too did that of the advanced amateurs. The main difference between these two groups concerned the BAC 'stabilize body axis' that was included into the primary assisting phase by the advanced amateurs, but singled out by the professional dancers. When we asked participants about this result after the study, the dancers agreed that this was not an action that was part of the *pirouette,* but an actual state they were in 'all the time, anyway'. Amateurs, by contrast, reported that they focused their attention on the body axis right before initiating the turn. As expected, the beginners' results showed far less consistency with the functional phases, and the results of

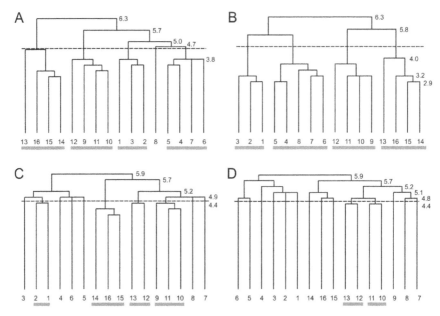

Figure 9.2 Results of the study regarding a *pirouette en dehors*, displayed as dendrograms:
A – professional dancers; B – advanced amateurs; C – beginners; D – novices.
The numbers on the bottom line mark the BACs, see Figure 9.1. The numbers
on the right relate to the horizontal bars in the dendrogram, which indicate
the Euclidean distances between the BACs: the lower the horizontal bar, the
smaller is the distance between the corresponding BACs in long-term memory.
The dashed horizontal line indicates the critical value of 4.b: only structural
links between BACs with distances below this value are considered relevant.
(Modified from Bläsing, Tenenbaum and Schack, 2009).

the non-dancers showed hardly any clusters at all, reflecting a highly inconsistent
sorting behaviour during the experimental task.

Pirouettes on the computer screen

Participants of our study included active professional dancers from Ballett
Dortmund, Tanztheater Bielefeld and Aalto Ballett Theater Essen; amateur dancers
from different ballet schools; and a control group of sport students who had never
been trained in dance. Amateurs varied to a great extent regarding their training
experience, quantitatively as well as qualitatively, and were therefore divided into
two groups: advanced amateurs who had trained in classical ballet for between 8
and 20 years and beginners who had trained for less than 5 years. Most of the
dancers regarded the experimental task with a mixture of curiosity, interest and
suspicion. Several of them had previously been interested in scientific questions
related to dance, or had read about studies on movement control and learning. Most
of the dancers, however, were new to our improvised lab situation and 'reductionist'

approach. Common questions included: 'Will I be judged personally here?' and 'What if I fail in this test?' Also: 'What can I gain from this?' and 'Will this improve my dancing?' Even though the subject of the tasks were movements that were very familiar to the dancers and belonged to their daily routine, the mode of thinking about these movements during the experiment seemed quite peculiar for most of them. Dancing a *pirouette* is, in fact, very different from sorting its parts, in verbal description, on a computer screen!

Initially, participants found this task rather confusing, as the lists of BACs were constantly shuffled and presented repeatedly. As they carried on with the task, however, they discovered a way to shed light onto the apparent thicket of abstract terms by recalling implicit movement knowledge from their long-term memory via the mental simulation, or imagery, of the movement. To make the experimental situation equally acceptable for experienced dancers and non-dancers, we allowed all participants to try out the movements both before and during the experiment, to activate their knowledge or try out 'what the movement felt like'. Novices tried the new movement several times before the experiment, until they felt that they understood how it worked, and many of them also interrupted the experiment to get up and try again. Most experts and amateurs marked the movement repeatedly during the experiment, often without getting up, to assist its retrieval from long-term memory.

The interest dancers took in our work, especially after they had finished the experiment and had thereby already gained an impression of what our work was about, led to vivid and fruitful discussions about body and mind, movement and thought, their work and our work, so that we hardly found enough time to answer each of the participants' questions and to have our own questions answered. For many of the dancers, the experimental procedure had already generated its own light-bulb moment, and participants considered this explicit way of thinking about movements as rather uncommon but beneficial for their work. Several expressed that they had never thought about their dance movements in such detail before. 'Now I should finally understand what I do every day' one dancer said, 'I wonder if that will show during my next training!'

In a complementary study, we investigated the contribution of spatial features (spatial parameters in an egocentric frame of reference) associated to the skill-based mental representations of classical dance movements in dancers of different skill levels and non-dancers. Dancers often use spatial directions in an egocentric frame of reference, relative to their own body, as mental cues for supporting movement performance and for shaping movement quality. The aim of this practice is to support the stability and quality of movements, as well as their artistic expression, for example, by associating opposing directions to give maximal stretch to the dancer's body. We used the *pirouette en dehors* with the first set of BACs and applied the same method as in the first study already described. This time, however, participants did not have to associate the BACs to one another, but were asked to relate them to spatial directions, such as: front, back, left, right, up, down, close and far.

In the first study, we had found that the mental representation of the *pirouette en dehors* showed a high degree of order formation reflecting the functionality of skillful movement execution in professional dancers and advanced amateurs, whereas beginners and novices did not possess such functionally structured movement representations (Bläsing, Tenenbaum and Schack, 2009). Interestingly, only the professional dancers, and not the advanced amateurs, showed similarly functional results when the same movement was addressed via associated spatial directions in an egocentric frame of reference (Bläsing and Schack, 2012). Specifically, for the *pirouette*, the dancers clustered movement concepts of the main functional phase via the spatial parameters 'up' and 'close', which can be interpreted as reflecting actions involved in stabilizing the turning axis. The findings from this study suggest that dance experts indeed possess embodied representations of dance movements that include information about spatial parameters in an egocentric frame of reference. These mental representations of action-related body-centred spatial parameters provide a valuable tool, especially for, and probably exclusively to, skilled dancers (Bläsing and Schack, 2012). The question as to how dancers achieve such rich movement representations can be related to their extensive training, as well as to the application of imagery techniques that often refer to spatial parameters.

Watching and parsing dance movement

Another aspect of dance expertise in which we were interested is linked to the visual perception of movements. Several studies showed differences in brain activation of dance experts and novices while watching dance (Calvo-Merino et al., 2005; 2006; Cross, Hamilton and Grafton, 2006: see also Chapters 10 and 11). It has been shown for many sports disciplines that skilled performers are better at predicting forthcoming actions and recognizing performers' intentions than novices (Aglioti et al., 2008; Abernethy and Zawi, 2007; Allerdissen et al., 2017; Müller and Abernethy, 2006; Sebanz and Shiffrar, 2009). Results of these studies support the idea that we perceive actions we have previously ourselves performed in a different way from actions we have never performed, even if we have watched them frequently (Schütz-Bosbach and Prinz, 2007b). This means that movement experts with a high skill level in action performance differ from purely visual experts with extensive observational experience and knowledge on the level of action perception (Calvo-Merino et al., 2006; Aglioti et al., 2008).

In a project that links action perception and memory in an expertise-related context, we applied Zacks' event segmentation paradigm (Zacks et al., 2007) to study how observers of different levels of dance expertise segment a choreographed sequence of contemporary dance movement (Bläsing, 2015). In their Event Segmentation Theory, Zacks and colleagues propose that observers spontaneously parse actions or scenes into small segments, and, crucially, that this subconscious segmentation is fundamental for the understanding and later recall of the observed scene (Zacks et al., 2007). Zacks and colleagues applied their event segmentation paradigm to different types of scenarios and participants, showing for example that patients suffering from memory dysfunctions (e.g., Alzheimer's disease) differ significantly from healthy persons in the parsing of observed events (Zacks et al., 2006). In close relation to the event segmentation approach, Rubin and Umanath

(2015) have proposed event memory as a complementary concept of long-term memory. They argue that the memory of prototype events (as a mental construction of scenes that have often been experienced personally, via reports or observation) has more potential to explain real-world memory phenomena and experimental findings than episodic memory.

Most of these studies focus on everyday activities typically involving the manipulation of one or more goal objects, such as assembling a musical instrument, erecting a tent or washing the dishes. Results of these studies suggest that different grains of segmentation refer to different levels of cognitive processing, with broad parsing into segments of approximately 30–60 seconds typically reflecting interactions with the goal objects, and fine-grained parsing into 10–20 second segments reflecting characteristics of the movement itself (Zacks et al., 2009). Interestingly, the event segmentation paradigm has hardly been applied to dance movements. The few exceptions include studies that investigated the brain activity underlying the parsing of classical ballet and Indian Bharatanatyam (Noble et al., 2014; Pollick et al., 2012). In their work with Wayne McGregor | Random Dance, deLahunta and Barnard (2005) applied a similar 'viewing and parsing exercise' to their choreographic process. After watching and segmenting selected movement material from video clips, the dancers were asked to comment on their decisions in detail in order to gain insight into the underlying cognitive frameworks.

In the study I want to present here, Zacks' segmentation paradigm was applied to examine how observers of different levels of dance expertise segment a sequence of contemporary dance choreographed and performed by Ilona Paszthy (IP dance, Cologne). Furthermore, we wanted to know to what extent the way in which spectators' segmentation of dance movement is influenced by: their general dance expertise; their visual familiarity with the observed movement; their specific motor experience of dancing the movement phrase they were watching in the experiment; and by accompanying music. In two consecutive experiments, participants watched a 90-second video clip showing the dancer and choreographer performing a sequence from her dance piece in a training studio. All participants watched the clip 20 times on a computer screen, and only the last five presentations were accompanied by music. They were instructed to press the space bar of the computer each time they perceived that a part of the movement ended and a new one began. The first experiment was conducted with two groups of participants, 10 professional dancers and 12 non-dancers, focusing mainly on effects of expertise. The second experiment was conducted with a group of eight amateur dancers and investigated effects of the participants' experience of dancing the phrase themselves; therefore the participants of the second experiment carried out the experimental task twice, once before learning the dance sequence, and a second time after they had learned it as part of a choreography in their training.

Results of the first experiment comparing dancers and non-dancers revealed that experts in general defined less segment boundaries – and thereby longer segments – than novices. This finding can be interpreted in relation to claims made by Zacks and colleagues (2007), who propose that high success in anticipating and predicting forthcoming movement trajectories reduces the number of segment boundaries. The amateurs in the second experiment defined less segmentation boundaries than the non-dancers, and their segmentation did not differ significantly from that of the experts. Interestingly, the difference between the amateurs' and the non-dancers' results increased from the amateurs' pre-leaning to their post-learning condition, suggesting that their definition of segment boundaries became 'more expert' with increasing motor experience of the dance sequence. The professional dancers also defined less segment boundaries in early, as opposed to later, trials, showing an effect of visual familiarity.

Music affected segmentation in different ways: professional dancers and amateurs defined less segment boundaries when the dance sequence was accompanied by music, whereas non-dancers defined more segment boundaries in the music trials than in previous trials. Interestingly, in the amateurs this effect was only found before learning the phrase, whereas no effect of music was found after they had danced the phrase themselves. The contradictory effect of music is rather hard to interpret, but we assume that the character of the music might play a crucial role. The music applied in our study consisted of slowly falling and rising chords, without a metric rhythm or pulse. According to the applied post-experimental questionnaires, experts and amateurs perceived that the music had a binding and harmonizing effect, whereas the non-dancers found the music that lacked a clear supporting rhythm or pulse rather irritating. These findings pose questions for a more systematic investigation of the relationship between movement and music (or sound in general) in dance. As listening to music on its own has been found to be sensitive to event segmentation (Sridharan et al., 2007), it can be assumed that accompanying music affects the segmentation of observed movement depending on its characteristics (i.e., its metrics, pitch, rhythm, pulse, etc.). Other factors that warrant further study in this respect are the way in which movement and music or sound are temporally integrated; the dancers' entrainment with the music; and how the dancers react to musical cues and follow or deliberately counterpoint them.

When the participants were asked about their subjective segmentation criteria and strategies in a questionnaire they filled out after the experimental task, we found interesting similarities and differences between the groups. All groups named movement features such as change of direction and speed, or active body parts, as segmentation criteria, but only the amateur group added learning criteria (e.g., 'how the teacher would teach it'), and only the experts referred to dynamic movement features requiring advanced motor simulation (e.g., 'how much force would be needed'). The latter comment might reflect that dancers were particularly able to simulate the observed movement and thereby extract dynamical features more efficiently than non-dancers and amateurs. It might also reflect a general tendency of skilled dancers to pay more attention to intrinsic, functional movement features rather than to more compositional or structural ones.

The question of dance parsing is not only of theoretical interest for scientists interested in dance, but also of practical relevance. A dance pedagogue or choreographer who teaches a complex movement sequence is faced with the problem of breaking down the sequence into meaningful parts in order to facilitate students' or dancers' learning. This, however, might result in an unwanted segmentation that interferes with the flow of the movement during performance later on. To overcome this unwanted fragmentation, practitioners apply approved methods, such as practising the transitions between former fragments separately, or varying the length of the parts to change transition points. The efficiency of these methods and their effect on the representation of the learnt movement material in long-term memory would be a promising topic for scientific study.

What is the best way for learning dance?

The final study I want to present here has been initiated and planned together with two renowned dance pedagogues from the Palucca Hochschule für Tanz Dresden: Jenny Coogan and José Biondi. Motivated by questions deriving from contemporary dance training on professional level (BA dance, 2nd year), we compared the success of observational learning from a human model to learning from verbal movement description presented acoustically (Bläsing et al., 2014).

From a scientific perspective, observational learning is considered to be primarily implicit and based on the activation of shared neural correlates of action execution, observation and simulation (Jeannerod, 1995; 2004). Learning from observation has found to be most successful in terms of the time spent learning and the accuracy of the outcome (see Chapter 11). Research investigating motor learning has shown that a human model demonstrating the movement is helpful (Cross et al., 2009), and that moving along with the movement demonstration (e.g., marking) warrants better results than just watching (Badets, Blandin and Shea, 2006; Warburton et al., 2013). The use of language (e.g., verbal cues for imagery, explanation of complex moves, or error correction), on the other hand, can facilitate or enhance motor learning by guiding attention towards relevant features of the movement and making them explicit (Wulf and Prinz, 2001), or by adding semantic content to support the creative adaptation or expressive quality.

As has been argued, a dancer learning to dance a complex movement will achieve the best results when combining implicit and explicit means of learning and memory. In dance training, a clearly defined movement phrase is commonly learnt through observation, by watching a human model (e.g., the teacher) execute the phrase. This implicit learning mode is commonly supported by language, gesture and body language providing kinematic, spatiotemporal and performative cues. In contemporary dance training, dancers are expected not only to reproduce movement material, but also to shape and develop movement material on their own, in order to achieve a more personal expression and higher artistic quality. Dance pedagogues educating future professional dancers, in particular in contemporary dance, emphasize the importance of their students achieving skills that enable them not only to dance a learned phrase correctly but to interpret it with their own artistic quality, thus claiming ownership of the novel movement material rather than simply reproducing it.

The assumption that has evolved in the context of dance training practice is that even though observational learning of dance movement has proved to lead to the best results in terms of correct movement reproduction, the presence of the visual model also interferes with the dancers' sense of movement ownership, which can become visible in the expression of the performance. Based on this argument, we aimed to compare observational learning of a dance phrase to a way of learning that did not involve visual observation of a model. Based on practical considerations, we decided to implement the complementary learning task as verbal description of a movement phrase that included detailed kinematic instructions and spatial cues, while neglecting temporal and rhythmic aspects as well as imagery and associations.

In our study, we compared observational learning from a human model presented in a video clip to learning from a verbal movement description presented as audio recording. The to-be-learnt movement material consisted of two dance phrases that had been choreographed by Jenny Coogan and José Biondi for comparability in terms of duration, complexity and presence of certain elements, such as turns, jumps, walks, changes of direction and height level (see Figure 9.3). Eighteen dance students (BA dance, 2nd year) of the Palucca Hochschule für Tanz Dresden participated in the study. The learning session was conducted with each student separately and lasted approximately one hour in which the student first learned one movement phrase either from observation or from the verbal description, with the other learning mode added in a second step, and then the other movement phrase in the opposite way. The order of the movement phrases and their assignment to the learning modes were balanced over the group. For each movement phrase, the student was allowed to listen or watch up to five times while moving freely to

Figure 9.3 Still images of the two dance phrases in our study (choreography: Jenny Coogan (upper panel) and José Biondi (lower panel); dancer: Robin Jung). The verbal description of the first five images in the upper panel: 'Stand facing the front left diagonal of the room in first position. At the same time extend your left leg forward and your two arms sideways to the horizontal. Allow your right hand to continue moving until it arrives to a high diagonal. Gradually let the shape melt back into its beginning position as you shift your weight into the right hip, bending both knees, sinking your head to the left to make a big C-curve. Continue into falling, then catch the weight with a step of the left leg crossing to the right. Follow with two steps sideward, in the same direction, while throwing both arms in front of your shoulders. Keeping your arms close to you, spiral to the right diagonal, then, kick your right leg, left arm and head forward as you throw your right arm behind you. Bring the energy back into you quickly, bending both elbows and the right knee close to the body, spine vertical.'

support learning, then he/she was recorded performing the learned material. In a second learning step, the complementary mode was applied (the video clip for the movement phrase initially learned from verbal description, and vice versa), followed by another recording of the student's performance. Two weeks after the learning session, a retention test was carried out to evaluate long-term effects of the learning processes. For this test, the students were individually and unexpectedly called to a free dance studio and asked to perform both learned phrases from memory while being recorded. After the initial learning session and the retention test, all students were asked to fill out questionnaires regarding their impressions of the learning tasks, the movement phrases, their own performance and their general learning preferences.

The recorded video material showing the students' performances was evaluated in two different ways. To evaluate movement recall, two annotators rated the completeness of the movement phrases according to a pre-defined schema that regarded the absence or presence of 11 individual movement elements and their spatiotemporal order. Additionally, two independent dance pedagogues who had not been involved in the experiment and not informed about the learning conditions rated the recordings with respect to the artistic quality of the dance performance and the accuracy of the presented movement in comparison to the choreographed model phrases.

The completeness scores showed that after the first learning step, the students were able to recall and reproduce the phrase they had initially learned from observation more completely than the one they had first learnt from verbal description. After the second learning step, they were able to reproduce the phrases more completely than after the first step, for both leaning modes. Crucially, in the retention test, the material initially learned from observation was reproduced more completely than the material initially learned from verbal description. The latter finding clearly indicates that the observation mode was more beneficial for movement recall than the verbal description mode. According to the experts' ratings, the students reproduced the movement more accurately when they had learned from observation than from verbal description in the first learning step, whereas no difference was found between the two modes after the second step. As expected, accuracy was higher in general after the second than the first learning step. Interestingly, the experts' ratings for performance quality did not differ for any of the four conditions, and no correlation was found between accuracy and artistic quality. Instead, individual performance ratings were highly consistent over all conditions, showing that the students who danced well did so throughout the study independent of their learning patterns. Our study corroborated previous findings regarding observational movement learning, but also added new aspects. In contrast to the dance pedagogues' expectations, the students did not dance the material learned initially from verbal description with better quality or expression, nor did they express a preference or stronger feeling of ownership for the verbally learned material in the questionnaires.

As this study was conducted in an interdisciplinary team of scientists and dance pedagogues based on a research question that was inspired by teaching practice rather than theory, the insights and implications go beyond scientific publication.

We gained qualitative insight into the students' individual learning strategies and preferences, as well as their individual approaches to learning complex dance material under time-restricted conditions. Fruitful discussions arose during the course of the study regarding different strategies and approaches to learning and teaching, the use of language in dance education, and possible applications of scientific results to dance practice in general. Taking an applied science perspective, the study represents one of the still rather rare examples of interdisciplinary experimental research initiated and conducted by mixed teams of scientists and dance practitioners.

Conclusions

In this chapter, I have strived to illustrate approaches that psychologists, cognitive and neuro-scientists apply to study complex motor actions on different levels. I have presented several studies investigating mental representations in long-term memory and their relevance for dance, as well as the perception and segment-ation of dance movements by observers of different skill levels; and learning of dance sequences through different modalities. These studies refer to features of cognitive expertise in dance that I find particularly fascinating because dancers are, indeed, experts in learning complex movement material, and their specific memory skills are suited to challenge and to extend established models of memory in cognitive psychology.

Another aim of this chapter has been to demonstrate why studying dance is such a fascinating issue for those interested in cognitive aspects of movement, and in particular learning and memory, and how the cognitive effort put into learning and optimizing movement can serve to elaborate dance. To achieve this goal, it is neces-sary to conduct more studies that are motivated by questions of shared interest for dancers, dance pedagogues and scientists, instead of only serving one side or the other. In recent years, we have managed to conduct several studies that were initiated, planned and carried out by interdisciplinary teams including members of scientific, artistic and pedagogical expertise. One of these studies has been pre-sented in this chapter in some detail (Bläsing et al., 2014). Another example is currently being carried out by an interdisciplinary team of cognitive and computer scientists, artists, dance scholars and dancers from The Forsythe Company. In this project, our aim is to investigate developmental processes involved in the staging of William Forsythe's dance piece *Duo* (Waterhouse, Watts and Bläsing, 2014: see also Chapter 3). Both studies have been sparked from collaborations within the Dance Engaging Science network (http://motionbank.org/de/content/dance-engaging-science).

Through these collaborations and discussions, we have become aware that interdisciplinary or multidisciplinary work that integrates empirical sciences and the art of dance is a difficult task that requires effort and patience on both sides. The reason why I consider this challenging and time-consuming process to be promising and worthwhile is that I am convinced of the significance of this work in promoting the understanding of human minds and their unique abilities and accomplishments.

Interdisciplinary research, however, cannot be achieved just by lecturing – and hopefully listening – to each other. It is also crucial to go a step further, to accept the existing differences and make serious effort to understand and overcome their origin. This might at times be hard, for example, when basic concepts in the different disciplines describe different content (see Chapter 13) – and it might then be beneficial to take a step backwards and re-evaluate definitions and conceptions in order to achieve common ground on which meaningful communication is possible. Even if differences seem trivial at first, their clarification might be crucial for a fruitful collaboration in order to avoid frustration based on misconceptions on both sides.

I would like to finish this chapter with a few suggestions regarding the further study of learning and memory in dance. First, I strongly encourage research planned and conducted by multidisciplinary teams; and to spend time talking and listening to each other, in making an effort to find a shared language and shared points of interest, and moving together – after all, dance is about movement of the body, and a deeper understanding of dance-related cognitive processes will have to include the experience of physical movement. Second, I recommend the application of both quantitative and qualitative methods in combination when investigating dance-related questions in order to: support the interpretation and understanding of results that verify or falsify given hypotheses; consider individual participants' characteristics, preferences and strategies; and to explore what might be relevant for future research of any kind. Third, there are certain aspects that are specific to dance, or more generally to the performing arts, that have the potential to challenge or expand our concepts and knowledge of memory processes and learning (see Hansen and Bläsing, 2017). Several of these aspects have been touched upon in this chapter, and their study might help to increase our understanding of how memory works in both theory and practice. Finally, research in this field is well suited to be motivated and guided by questions from applied fields including (but not restricted to) education, rehabilitation and therapy. The benefits that multi-disciplinary, well informed research can have for these fields can be large, and should be considered from the start, to place neurocognitive research in dance in a richer context.

Acknowledgements

I would like to thank the Aalto Ballett Theater Essen, Ballett Dortmund, Tanztheater Bielefeld, Theaterballettschule Bielefeld, Staatsballett Berlin, The Forsythe Company, Gymnasium Essen Werden, and all other participants for supporting this work and participating in our studies. Special thanks to Martin Puttke, Gregor Zöllig, Maria Haus, Ilona Paszthy, Jenny Coogan, José Biondi, Liane Simmel, Elizabeth Waterhouse, Freya Vass-Rhee, Scott deLahunta and Thomas Schack for their collaboration and stimulating discussions. Our work was kindly supported by Tanzplan Essen 2010 (Tanzplan Deutschland, Kulturstiftung des Bundes), the Volkswagen Foundation and the Center of Excellence Cognitive Interaction Technology (CITEC) at Bielefeld University.

References

Abernethy, B. & Zawi, K. (2007). Pickup of essential kinematics underpins expert perception of movement patterns. *Journal of Motor Behavior,* 39(5), 353–367.

Aglioti, S. M., Cesari, P., Romani, M., & Urgesi, C. (2008). Action anticipation and motor resonance in elite basketball players. *Nature Neuroscience,* 11(9), 1109–1116.

Allerdissen, M., Güldenpenning, I., Schack, T., & Bläsing, B. (2017). Recognizing fencing attacks from auditory and visual information: A comparison between expert fencers and novices. *Psychology of Sport and Exercise,* 31, 123–130.

Baddeley, A. (2000). The episodic buffer: A new component of working memory? *Trends in Cognitive Sciences,* 4(11), 417–23.

Baddeley, A. D. & Hitch, G. J. (1974). Working memory. In: G. A. Bower (Ed.), *Recent Advances in Learning and Motivation 8* (pp. 47–90). New York: Academic Press.

Badets, A., Blandin, Y., & Shea, C. H. (2006). Intention in motor learning through observation. *Quarterly Journal of Experimental Psychology,* 59(2), 377–386.

Barsalou, L. W. (2008). Grounded cognition. *Annual Review of Psychology,* 59, 617–645.

Bläsing, B. (2015). Expertise in dance: Effects of visual familiarity, motor experience and music on movement segmentation. *Frontiers in Psychology,* 5, 1500.

Bläsing, B., Calvo-Merino, B., Cross, E., Jola, C., Honisch, J., & Stevens, K. (2012). Neurocognitive control in dance perception and performance. *Acta Psychologica,* 139(2), 300–308.

Bläsing, B., Coogan, J., Biondi, J., Simmel, L., & Schack, T. (2014). Motor learning in dance using different modalities: Visual vs. verbal models. *Cognitive Processing,* 15(1), 90–93.

Bläsing, B. & Schack, T. (2012). Mental representation of spatial movement parameters in dance. *Spatial Computation and Cognition,* 12(2-3), 111–132.

Bläsing, B., Tenenbaum, G., & Schack, T. (2009). The cognitive structure of movements in classical dance. *Psychology of Sport and Exercise,* 10(3), 350–360.

Brown, S., Martinez, M. J., & Parsons, L. M. (2005). The neural basis of human dance. *Cerebral Cortex,* 16(8), 1157–1167.

Burgess, P. W. (2000). Real-world multitasking from a cognitive neuroscience perspective. In: S. Monsell & J. Driver (Eds.), *Control of Cognitive Processes: Attention and performance* (Vol. 18, pp. 465–472). Cambridge, MA: MIT Press.

Calvo-Merino, B., Glaser, D. E., Grèzes, J., Passingham, R. E., & Haggard, P. (2005). Action observation and acquired motor skills: An FMRI study with expert dancers. *Cerebral Cortex,* 15, 1243–1249.

Calvo-Merino, B., Grèzes, J., Glaser, D. E., Passingham, R. E., & Haggard, P. (2006). Seeing or doing? Influence of visual and motor familiarity in action observation. *Current Biology,* 10, 1905–1910.

Cross, E. S., Hamilton, A. F. de C., & Grafton, S. T. (2006). Building a simulation de novo: Observation of dance by dancers. *Neuroimage,* 31, 1257–1267.

Cross, E. S., Kraemer, D. J., Hamilton, A. F., Kelley, W. M., & Grafton, S. T. (2009). Sensitivity of the action observation network to physical and observational learning. *Cerebral Cortex,* 19(2), 315–326.

deLahunta, S. & Barnard, P. (2005). What's in a phrase? In: J. Birringer & J. Fenger (Eds.), *Tanz im Kopf – Dance and Cognition* (pp. 253–266). Berlin: LitVerlag.

Glenberg, A. M. (1997). What memory is for? *Behavioral and Brain Science,* 20(1), 1–19.

Hansen, P. & Bläsing, B. (2017). Introduction: Studying the cognition of memory in the performing arts. In: P. Hansen and B. Bläsing (Eds.), *Performing the Remembered Present: The cognition of memory in dance, theatre and music.* London: Methuen.

Hossner, E. J., Schiebl, F., & Göhner, U. (2015). A functional approach to movement analysis and error identification in sports and physical education. *Frontiers in Psychology*, 6.

Jeannerod, M. (1995). Mental imagery in the motor context. *Neuropsychologia*, 33(11), 1419–32.

Jeannerod, M. (2004). Actions from within. *International Journal of Sport and Exercise Psychology*, 2, 376–402.

Kirsh, D. (2011). How marking in dance constitutes thinking with the body. *Versus: Quaderni Di Studi Semiotici*, 113–115, 179–210.

Krasnow, D., Wilmerding, M., Stecyk, S., Wyon, M., & Koutedakis, Y. (2011). Biomechanical research in dance: A literature review. *Medical Problems of Performing Artists*, 26(1), 3.

Land, B., Volchenkov, D., Bläsing, B., & Schack, T. (2013). From action representation to action execution: Exploring the link between mental representation and kinematic structure. *Frontiers in Computational Neuroscience*, 7, 127.

Lörinc, G. & Merényi, Z. (1995). *Methodik des klassischen Tanzes*. Berlin: Henschel.

Metzinger, T. (2006). Different conceptions of embodiment. *Psyche*, 12(4).

Müller, S. & Abernethy, A. B. (2006.) Batting with occluded vision: An in situ examination of the information pick-up and interceptive skills of high- and low-skilled cricket batsmen. *Journal of Science and Medicine in Sport*, 9, 446–458.

Noble, K., Glowinski, D., Murphy, H., Jola, C., McAleer, P., Darshane, N., Penfield, K., Kalyanasundaram, S., Camurri, A., & Pollick, F. E. (2014). Event segmentation and biological motion perception in watching dance. *Art Perception*, 2, 59–74.

Orgs, G., Dombrowski, J. -H., Heil, M., & Jansen-Osmann, P. (2008). Expertise in dance modulates alpha/beta event-related desynchronization during action observation. *European Journal of Neuroscience*, 27, 3380–3384.

Pollick, F., Noble, K., Darshane, N., Murphy, H., Glowinski, D., McAleer, P., Jola, C., Penfield, K., & Camurri, A. (2012). Using a novel motion index to study the neural basis of event segmentation. *i-Perception*, 3, 225–225.

Prinz, W. (1997). Perception and action planning. *European Journal of Cognitive Psychology*, 9, 129–154.

Rosenblum, L. D., Dias, J. W., & Dorsi, J. (2017). The supramodal brain: Implications for auditory perception. *Journal of Cognitive Psychology*, 29(1), 65–87.

Rubin, D. C. & Umanath, S. (2015). Event memory: A theory of memory for laboratory, autobiographical, and fictional events. *Psychological Review*, 122(1), 1.

Schack, T. (2004). The cognitive architecture of complex movement. *International Journal of Sport and Exercise Psychology*, 2, 403–438.

Schütz-Bosbach, S. & Prinz, W. (2007a). Prospective coding in event representation. *Cognitive Processing*, 8(2), 93–102.

Schütz-Bosbach, S. & Prinz, W. (2007b). Perceptual resonance: Action-induced modulation of perception. *Trends in Cognitive Sciences*, 11(8), 349–355.

Sebanz, N. & Shiffrar, M. (2009). Detecting deception in a bluffing body: The role of expertise. *Psychonomic Bulletin and Review*, 16(1), 170–175.

Sevdalis, V. & Keller, P. E. (2011). Captured by motion: Dance, action understanding, and social cognition. *Brain and Cognition*, 77, 231–236.

Squire, L. R. (1992). Declarative and nondeclarative memory: Multiple brain systems supporting learning and memory. *Journal of Cognitive Neuroscience*, 4(3), 232–243.

Squire, L. R. & Zola, S. M. (1996). Structure and function of declarative and nondeclarative memory systems. *Proceedings of the National Academy of Sciences USA.* 93, 13515–13522.

Sridharan, D., Levitin, D. J., Chafe, C. H., Berger, J., & Menon, V. (2007). Neural dynamics of event segmentation in music: Converging evidence for dissociable ventral and dorsal networks. *Neuron*, 55(3), 521–532.

Steels, L. (2003). Intelligence with representation. *Philosophical Transactions: Mathematical, physical and engineering sciences*, 361(1811), 2381–2395.

Stevens, C. (2017). Memory and dance: 'Bodies of knowledge' in contemporary dance. In: P. Hansen & B. Bläsing (Eds.), *Performing the Remembered Present: The cognition of memory in dance, theatre and music* (pp. 39–68). London: Methuen Drama.

Tarassow, N. I. (2005). *Klassischer Tanz. Die Schule des Tänzers* (pp. 39–68). Berlin: Henschel.

Tulving, E. (1972). Episodic and semantic memory. In: E. Tulving & W. Donaldson (Eds.), *Organization of Memory* (pp. 381–403). New York: Academic Press.

Tulving, E. (2002). Episodic memory: From mind to brain. *Annual Review of Psychology*, 53, 1–25.

Vaganova, A. G. (2002). *Grundlagen des klassischen Tanzes*. Berlin: Henschel.

Warburton, E. C., Wilson, M., Lynch, M., & Cuykendall, S. (2013). The cognitive benefits of movement reduction: Evidence from dance marking. *Psychological Science*, 24(9), 1732–1739.

Waterhouse, E., Watts, R., & Bläsing, B. (2014). Doing duo – a case study of entrainment in William Forsythe's choreography 'Duo'. *Frontiers in Human Neuroscience*, 8, 812.

Wilson, M. (2002). Six views of embodied cognition. *Psychonomic Bulletin and Review*, 9(4), 625–636.

Wulf, G. & Prinz, W. (2001). Directing attention to movement effects enhances learning: A review. *Psychonomic Bulletin and Review*, 8, 648–660.

Zacks, J. M., Kumar, S., Abrams, R. A., & Mehta, R. (2009). Using movement and intentions to understand human activity. *Cognition*, 112, 201–216.

Zacks, J. M., Speer, N. K., Swallow, K. M., Braver, T. S., & Reynolds, J. R. (2007). Event perception: A mind-brain perspective. *Psychological Bulletin*, 133(2), 273.

Zacks, J. M., Speer, N. K., Vettel, J. M., & Jacoby, L. L. (2006). Event understanding and memory in healthy aging and dementia of the Alzheimer type. *Psychology and Aging*, 21(3), 466.

Part III

Neurocognitive studies of dance

10 Neural mechanisms for seeing dance

Beatriz Calvo-Merino

Introduction

The art of dance involves body movement as a way of expression. We would like to start this chapter by elaborating on four strands of dance performance. First, a dance performance typically involves several elements, including, but not limited to, narrative, costumes, music or lighting. These may vary among different dance styles, cultures and societies. However, there is a core element (that may extensively vary in its form) that is shared among all dance styles: the *movement*. Second, these movements are performed by an agent, who often requires specific motor and mental training in order to execute the movements with precision and fluency: the *dancer*. Third, dance is the process or product of deliberately arranging these elements (movements, dancers, scenario and music) in a way that appeals to the senses or emotions of the audience, and is thus strongly connected to an *aesthetic experience*. Finally, the aesthetic experience is often the result of the participation of an *observer* in a performance setting. In this chapter, the three elements of movement, dancer and observer are discussed in the context of cognitive neuroscience. The concept of aesthetic experience is introduced here, but is further developed in Chapter 12.

Specifically, this chapter will focus on several issues that concern dance and science. Here, we leave aside the training and the execution components of a dance performance, and instead focus on dance observation, i.e., when it is being watched. Using neuroimaging techniques, we will illustrate what may be occuring in the human mind and brain when we see movements, and in particular, when we watch dance. We will also consider a key aspect of dance: the motor skills of the dancers. These extraordinary acquired abilities not only change the way dancers perform, but also the way they see. Finally, we will briefly introduce a concept that will be extended in Chapter 12, which is a property tightly connected to dance: the aesthetic property of a movement, and how the observer represents aesthetic experience. To conclude, we will summarize how science and art can develop ways of successful interaction in order to learn from each other.

The core element of dance: The movement

Movement is a physical displacement in time and space of the location of a body, or body part. Humans possess an extraordinary motor system that allows us to use movement as a means of interaction with the environment and with other individuals. Through movements we express our emotions, intentions and many needs. Classical motor neuroscience has studied in detail the human motor system, and its anatomical and physiological properties are well known (Berthoz, 2002). Recently, cognitive neuroscience has further investigated how different brain regions of the motor system participate not only in the observable movement execution, but also in internal action processes, such as having the intention to move, planning a movement or a sequence of movements, and finally, implementing this order by sending appropriate commands to the muscles and effectors (for a review, see Jeannerod, 1997).

In this chapter, we will concentrate on actions, rather than movements. Action can be defined as a voluntary movement directed to a goal (Jeannerod, 1997). Moving our arm forward and backward might be just a movement, but if we move our arm forward in order to reach a cup of tea, this reaching gesture is no longer a mere movement, but a motor act. This simple motor act might be part of a more complex action plan to achieve a final goal or intention, in this case, to drink tea. This goal can be a physical external stimulus or an internally generated intention or need. Similarly, actions can be oriented towards an object, so-called transitive actions, like grasping a cup of tea, or intransitive actions, like waving our hand to say hello. Dance, for example, is mostly composed from intransitive actions, as often there are no (physical) objects required to drive the movement. However, dance cannot be that easily classified, and each style or even performance might have its own action properties. The movements might be completely guided by the rhythm of the music, or, in some dance styles such as Tango or Swing, there is a person who initiates the movement, the leader, while the partner performs a complementary movement in its response, the follower. Nevertheless, the concept of action as a voluntary goal-directed movement can be applied to most dances (see also Chapter 7).

Human motor repertoire

The Oxford Dictionary defines 'repertoire' as: 'the body of pieces known or regularly performed by a performer or a company'. The term is originally French, but it derives from the Latin *reperire*, which means 'to find' or 'to discover'. Cognitive neuroscience has studied the very similar concept of 'motor repertoire', which can be defined as a summary or storage of all motor knowledge that we have acquired during our life. The single piece or unit of this repertoire is called 'motor representation' or 'action representation'. The concept of motor representation has evolved since William James suggested 'an idea of movement' that generates some motor act, and Bastian's proposition (Bastian, 1880) that every time we execute a movement we generate motor traces or 'kinetic *images*' that will be used every time we do that same movement. Nowadays, a motor representation is understood as a dynamic unit that can be modified by experience. This representation is the core of an assembly of relationships between different sensory and motoric components. An action representation encompasses internal or mental content related to intention to act, action goals, or the knowledge of either physical or more general consequences of a given action, as well as the covert neural operations that are supposed to occur before an action begins, and the physical implementation of motor commands into the muscles (see also the cognitive architecture model presented in Chapter 6). Therefore, an action is the observable outcome of previous internal information processing stages (Jeannerod, 1997). Finally, the elements that compose action representation should not really be considered as independent components, but as a network of different nodes where all are related at cognitive and neural levels (in Chapters 6 and 9, these nodes are termed Basic Action Concepts).

We would like to draw attention to two factors that constrain the content of the human motor repertoire: physical properties of the basic musculoskeletal system, and personal and individual motor history. The first factor constrains our body through the limited number of flexions and extensions that our joints and muscles allow us to perform – we can only bend our arms and legs to a certain degree, and certain movements will always remain physically impossible, even after training. Therefore, the number of movements that a human can perform is limited by the physical properties of his or her body. The second factor is related to motor learning. From the moment we are born, we learn new motor skills by moving around our environment and physically interacting with other humans and objects. Most of these acquired motor skills are common movements (such as walking, running, reaching and grasping objects, and hand gestures). However, life allows us to become *motorically unique,* by shaping the content of our motor repertoire when acquiring specific motor skills through a particular motor training. Therefore, each individual motor repertoire will be comprised of common actions (shared by a large part of the human population) and specific or personal actions (only shared by those individuals trained in the same actions). For example, an individual trained in classical ballet has a motor repertoire of all the common movements we all know, plus those specific to the acquired technique (i.e., the canon of classical ballet: *pirouette, pas de chat, arabesque,* etc.).

Action and perception: Two merged systems

During a live dance performance, there are two fundamental processes that occur in absolute synchrony: the dancer *acting* on the stage and the spectator *seeing* the movements. Although it is difficult to dissociate the dance from the dancer, in a very broad sense, dance performers and dance observers focus on the same element: the movement. This common space between someone *doing* and someone *seeing* has been the focus of study for philosophers, psychologists and neuroscientists.

For a long time, action and perception have been considered to be two independent processes in the human brain. The perceptual system is formed by the different components that secure the processing of sensory information. By contrast, the action system comprises those components that participate in the different stages of producing motor acts. Descartes emphasised the difference between action and perception in the *Traitee de l'Homme* (1980), using two different metaphors for describing the two processes. However, other groups of philosophers and academics such as Lotze, James or Munsterberg have underlined the concept of a continuum between action and perception, suggesting the idea of a shared content between motor and perceptual representations. The neuropsychologist, neurobiologist and Nobel laureate Roger W. Sperry suggested that one basic function of the perceptual system is to prepare the system to act (Sperry, 1952). Later, Konorski (1967) proposed that when we perceive a movement, our brain automatically executes the corresponding voluntary movement. More recently, Berger described the relationship between the perception of different body part movements and the innervations of the corresponding muscles (Berger et al., 1979). Psychologists have also produced a large set of literature supporting common or shared mechanisms for action and perception as well as theoretical models. One example is the common coding model, which proposes that codes related to action and perception are shared in a common representational domain (Prinz, 1997). Finally, from an evolutionary perspective, the human brain will not be more than the result of evolutionary changes, and among them, the action perception cycle has a fundamental role. Definitively, action influences perception and perception influences action (Gibson, 1979). However, although a level of significant interaction between both perception and action systems is accepted, there is a lack of understanding about how this could be implemented in the human mind, and, more importantly, in the human brain.

Mirror neurons: The link between action and perception

The key answer for a common action and perception mechanism was found by neurophysiology studies in the monkey brain. Giacomo Rizzolatti and his colleagues, working in a neurophysiology laboratory in Parma (Italy), described for the first time a set of neurons in the premotor cortex of the monkey brain that responded when the monkey was doing a simple action (i.e. grasping), and also when the monkey was watching the experimenter or another monkey performing that same action (di Pellegrino et al., 1992; Gallese et al., 1996; Rizzolatti et al., 1996). Neurons with similar properties were subsequently also found in the parietal cortex (Gallese et al., 1996; Rozzi et al., 2008). It was already known that these regions had motor properties and respond during action execution; however, it was a completely novel discovery to see how the same neuron also responded to visual presentations of the action. This meant that the same neuron can have both visual and motor properties, and can potentially code information related to executing an action and seeing the same action. These types of neurons were called 'mirror neurons' because they seemed to reflect the observed action (like a mirror) onto the action that we have in our motor repertoire.

Since this initial discovery, a series of studies has been undertaken to describe in more detail the properties of mirror neurons (for a recent mirror neuron review, see Rizzolatti and Sinigaglia, 2016). One of the most interesting properties of the mirror neurons is their congruency between visual and motor responses (Gallese et al., 1996). Physiological studies have described neurons in the primate premotor cortex that specifically participate in actions such as grasping, reaching or holding.

Each neuron is principally 'specialized' in participating in the execution of a determinate action. The concept of congruent mirror neurons means that those neurons that are specialized in executing one action, may be also engaged in the observation of that same action. For example, neurons activated during a grasping movement are also engaged during *seeing* grasping. In premotor and parietal cortex, we can find neurons with different levels of congruency. There are high levels of congruency among neurons that participate in execution and observation of the same action, and lower levels in neurons that participate in execution of several actions and observation of other similar ones. These mirror neurons are the first direct evidence linking together perception and action mechanism. Their localization in a set of regions classically regarded as motor areas, such as premotor cortex, and also in parietal regions, indicates the importance of our motor system for the observation of actions. However, although monkeys are our very close relatives, the existence of a similar system in the human brain still needed to be demonstrated.

The first evidence of mirror neurons in humans came from a study using Transcranial Magnetic Stimulation (TMS: see Box 9.1). Fadiga and colleagues found that muscle excitability patterns during observation of simple grasping movements were congruent with those found during execution of the same actions (Fadiga et al., 1995). This was the first step to suggest that a mirror-neuron-like mechanism also existed in the human brain. While other studies using the same technique confirmed these results (Strafella and Paus, 2000; Baldissera et al., 2001), a different group of studies aimed to localize brain regions with mirror properties in the human brain. These studies suggest that there is a set of regions that consistently participate during observation of an action performed by another agent. Among these areas (shown in Figure 10.1), we find the ventral and dorsal

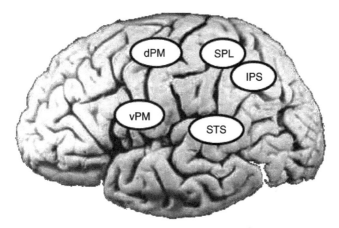

Figure 10.1 Schema of brain regions that participate in perception of movements. These areas are known to form part of the human mirror neuron system because they respond during both action execution and action observation: vPM, ventral premotor cortex; dPM, dorsal premotor cortex; SPL, superior parietal lobe; IPS, intraparietal sulcus; STS, superior temporal sulcus (only active in action observation).

premotor cortex (vPM, dPM), as well as several regions in the parietal cortex, such as intraparietal sulcus (IPS), superior parietal lobe (SPL) and superior temporal sulcus (STS) (Decety et al., 1997; Grafton et al., 1996; Grèzes and Decety, 2001; Iacoboni et al., 1999; Rizzolatti, Fogassi and Gallese, 2001). The supplementary motor area (SMA) and motor cortex are typically not activated, unless an element of movement preparation is also involved, for example in cases of action observation for delayed imitation (Grèzes and Decety, 2001). These areas are considered part of an action observation network that participates in several aspects related to action execution and observation (see Chapter 11). Motor simulation theory takes these results into account and suggests that during action observation, there is an automatic activation of high-order motor representations. However, initial TMS studies did show that there is a direct correspondence between observed and executed action (Fadiga et al., 1995), suggesting that brain processes for motor simulation are based on direct correspondence between the neural codes for action observation and for execution, rather than a mere recovery of higher order abstract or multimodal action representations.

A later series of neuroimaging studies investigated the properties of the human mirror system, and how it responds to biological actions. First, these mirror regions were not activated during observation of mechanically impossible actions (Stevens et al., 2000). Second, activation was stronger when humans saw actions performed by a biological agent rather than an artificial one (a robot arm) (Perani et al., 2001; Tai et al., 2004). Third, mirror regions seem to follow a somatotopic organization during action observation similar to the one that can be observed during action execution (Buccino et al., 2001). This means that observation of motor acts performed with different effectors, like the hand, mouth or foot, leads to activation of specific parts of the premotor and parietal cortices that resemble the classical somatotopic organization described by Penfield in the motor cortex during action execution (Penfield and Rasmussen, 1950). Although some of these studies are controversial and follow-up studies have suggested alternative explanations (Gazzola et al., 2007), overall they suggest that the human mirror system might be highly sensitive to a degree of correspondence between the observed action and the internal motor representation of the observer.

There are several issues that remain to be elucidated. First, most of these studies followed initial primate work on grasping execution and observation and used relatively simple and restricted sets of hand actions (Grafton et al., 1996; Rizzolatti et al., 1996; Grèzes and Decety, 2001). These studies reported brain responses during action observation, but have not directly tested whether observing a particular action involves activating our own motor programs for that action. Buccino et al. (2004) performed an elegant study by comparing brain activation during observation of biological actions performed by a human and by a non-conspecific agent, like a dog or monkey, and found that actions belonging to the motor repertoire of the observer showed stronger resonance in the mirror system regions. However, these activations did not fully account for the level of familiarity observers have with the acting agent, or the differences in kinematics between human and non-conspecific agents.

As we have described in previous sections, humans have a motor repertoire that far exceeds these simple hand–object-oriented actions. In this way, motor skills are a powerful tool in studying the tuning of the mirror neuron mechanism. A particular action might exist in the motor repertoire of a trained expert, but not in the motor repertoire of someone who has not been trained. We conducted a couple of studies that used this difference between people's motor repertoire to test the assumption that watching an action automatically involves a simulation of their own internal motor representation of that same action. Following this idea, any internal simulation should be stronger if the observer knows and can perform the observed motor act.

When mirror neuron theory meets dance

Neurophysiology studies in non-human primates and human neuroimaging studies have provided evidence that observing a simple movement activates the same neural regions used when we perform these movements ourselves. In order to directly test the hypothesis of a direct match between observed and executed actions, we have devised a novel paradigm that combines different levels of expertise (Calvo-Merino et al., 2005). We studied groups of people with different acquired motor skills to investigate whether regions of the putative mirror neuron system are tuned to the individual's acquired motor repertoire. If this is true, the classical mirror neuron regions, such as the premotor and parietal cortices, should exhibit stronger brain responses while watching actions that the observer has learnt to perform, compared to those that are novel or unfamiliar. However, a couple of important issues about this approach are worth considering. First, one needs to find two separate groups of motor experts that differ in the specific acquired motor skills. Second, these different skills should be kinematically similar (with respect to speed, direction of movement, or involved effectors in whole-body movements) in order to avoid obvious differences in visual processing of both types of actions.

Dance offers a great opportunity to realise these experimental affordances. Many dance styles (including classical styles such as ballet) involve arbitrary and intransitive movements of the whole body. Besides, they are composed of a well-established and distinct set of movements that can be easily classified: a vocabulary of movements (see Chapter 1). Each movement can be perfectly characterised by both its name and its dynamics. Therefore, professional dancers are the perfect motor experts for studying the influence of expertise on observing actions, as they have acquired the motor skills to perform a series of dance-specific movements in a highly coordinated way. Some dancers have been highly trained in only one dance discipline, acquiring its entire motor repertoire to perfection. In knowing the dance style in which a dancer has been trained therefore allows characterisation of his/her motor repertoire. For example, a professional classical ballet dancer has acquired the motor representation of practically all defined canonical classical ballet movements.

We selected two types of dance disciplines that are comparable with respect to the kinematics of their movements, yet in which the movement shared little or no overlap with the movement of the other dance discipline. Classical ballet and capoeira are two dance styles that share this characteristic. With the assistance of dance choreographer Tom Sapsford we selected from all movements of the ballet and capoeira repertoire a list of those movements that matched according to criteria such as body parts used, direction of the movements or movement speed. Most dance performances are more than a dancer performing a series of movements; they are the result of the interaction of, among other factors, movements, music and costumes. However, in order to experimentally address the question of interest, we deconstructed the dance to its core element and focussed on the movements *per se* (for complementary studies that integrate other dance components such as motor execution and music, see Brown and Parsons, 2008). Additionally, in order to minimize the visual difference between the two dance sets of video clips, performing ballet and capoeira dancers were morphologically similar and dressed in similar clothes.

We used functional magnetic resonance (fMRI: see Box 9.1) to measure brain activity of ballet and capoeira dancers who were watching video clips of 3 seconds each showing ballet and capoeira movements. At this stage of the experiment, both ballet dancers and capoeristas participated as mere observers, and they were required to lie still in the scanner room while watching the video clips and performing an easy task to ensure that they were paying attention (i.e., after each video clip, participants had to rate on a scale 1–3 'how tiring' the movement appeared). The results showed that when we observe a dance movement that we have learnt before (e.g. ballet dancers seeing ballet movements), there is a set of neural regions that are more active than when we watch a kinematically similar movement that we have never performed before (e.g. ballet dancers seeing capoeira movements). Among these brain regions were the vPM, dPM, SPL, IPS and STS (see Figure 10.1). These regions belong to what previously has been described as the action representation system or the action observation network (Decety et al., 1997; Grafton et al., 1996; Grèzes and Decety, 2001: see also Chapter 11). These results suggest that when we observe a familiar action, we retrieve information related to that action by recruiting it from the action representation network. In this way, by observing a movement, we can access previously stored information related to that movement. This includes motor information related to the specific motor commands to perform the action, sensory information, and semantic information associated with that action (e.g. movement name and memories related to that movement; see also Chapter 9).

This study supports the idea that we perform an internal simulation when we observe an action and that this simulation is represented in the brain, as evidenced here by stronger activity in regions involved in the action observation network. However, there is a question that remains unanswered: Which component of the action representation network is retrieved during observation? More specifically: Does action observation predominantly engage purely motoric mechanisms, over and above the visual representation of the action, semantic knowledge of the action, or its aesthetic experience? In order to answer these questions, we needed to disentangle the different components of the action representation. After a year of interactions with dancers and choreographers, we became aware of an important factor through which classical ballet movements are classified. In classical ballet there are gender-specific movements (i.e. movements that are mostly trained and performed by either male or female dancers, but not both), and gender-common movements (trained and performed by both genders). Therefore, female dancers trained in classical ballet will have acquired motor training of female-specific moves, and vice versa for male dancers. However, as female and male dancers train and perform together, both genders will acquire visual familiarity and semantic knowledge about all the movements, regardless of their gender. We therefore conducted a subsequent experiment that allowed us to dissociate visual and motor familiarity, and test for neural regions that are more responsive to an internal simulation of the action in motor terms, over and above any associated visual or semantic representations (Calvo-Merino et al., 2006).

Again, the experiment used an action/observation task. Now female and male classical ballet dancers watched 3-second video clips of gender-specific dance movements. These movements were performed by a female dancer and a male dancer, dressed in black clothes. We also used a set of dance movements commonly performed by both genders, in order to rule out any possible effects related to observing a female or a male dancer. In order to dissociate purely motor and visual representations during observation of gender movements, it was essential that only classical ballet dancers trained specifically in their corresponded gender (and not in the opposite gender moves) participated in the study. We controlled dancers' motor training using a preliminary questionnaire enquiring about how often they enact and see the movements used in the experiment in their professional training. This questionnaire showed that male dancers were visually familiar with both male and female movements, but only motorically familiar with the male ones, and the opposite for the female dancers. This control is particularly important nowadays, where rules of classical dance are broken in order to create novel performances where male dancers perform ballet moves classically associated with females (for examples, see *Les Ballets Trockadero de Monte Carlo*, www.trockadero.org or Matthew Bourne's *Swan Lake*, www.swanlaketour.com).

The results of this study are very straightforward and conclusive. To summarize, we looked for brain activity changes related to gender and gender-specific and common classical ballet movements, in order to find areas tuned by purely motor resonance with the observed action, rather than other action-related information such as visual or semantic knowledge. We found that brain activity was higher in three regions for observation of movements with a strong motor familiarity, compared to observation of movements with only visual familiarity. These areas are the premotor cortex in left hemisphere, and the superior parietal lobe and cerebellum bilaterally (Figure 10.2). The fact that our experimental design controlled for visual familiarity and other information associated to the action meant that we could relate the activation in these areas to an internal motor resonance with our own motor system codes action, specifically actions that we are observing. One can generalize and conclude that when we observe a familiar action that we have previously performed ourselves and therefore motorically learnt, the human brain

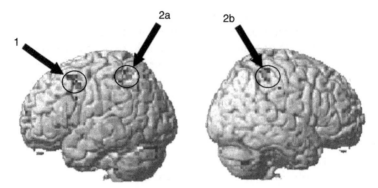

Figure 10.2 Effect of motor expertise on action observation. Activations shown represent the activation associated with seeing an action for which the observer possesses the motor representation. These areas are the core of the mirror system and seem to sustain a network for internal motor simulation during observation: (1) left dorsal premotor cortex, (2a) left intraparietal sulcus and (2b) right intraparietal sulcus. (Modified from Calvo- Merino et al., 2006.)

evokes an automatic response and employs a code for motor execution that enables *seeing* the action. We seem to code external motor events through our own motor repertoire.

   In general, these series of studies combining acquired motor skills, such as dance, and action observation paradigms may provide some useful insight not only for the cognitive neuroscience community, but also for the dance community. On the one hand, these studies show for the first time neural responses to action observation of whole-body intransitive actions, and how this activity is modulated by the observer's motor experience. On the other hand, these studies illustrate how dancers are specialists not only in the way they *move* thanks to their motor training, but also in the way they *see* other people's movements. These studies using dancers' expertise (Cross, Hamilton and Grafton, 2006: see also Chapters 9, 11 and 13) illustrate that the motor knowledge and training that dancers acquire during their career is shaping the way their mind and brain process information related to movements, further than the mere motor execution – such as simple observation of dance movements.

Aesthetic perception of dance

The term 'aesthetic' derives from the Greek word *Aesthesis* and was re-defined by Baumgarten in the eighteenth century as the gratification of the senses or sensuous delights (Goldman, 2001). The term 'aesthetic experience' is defined as a particular psychological state elicited by a type of sensory stimulus that is, often but not exclusively, a work of art. Philosophy, psychology and several other disciplines have produced a large number of essays and studies on aesthetic experience.

Among them, two classical perspectives have led researchers to focus mainly on two elements of aesthetics: the perceived stimuli and the observer. Most aesthetics studies have used artwork such as music or static stimuli like paintings, and very little research has been undertaken in other art disciplines. Dance is one of the performing arts that uses the dynamics of human movement as a form of expression, and often associates it with an aesthetic value. Here we revisit some of the classical aesthetics theories from psychology and new studies developed from neuroscience in the new discipline of neuroaesthetics. Finally, we will focus on a special way of seeing actions: the aesthetic perception of dance.

The psychology and neuroscience of aesthetics processing

Psychology of aesthetics has produced two main theories that focus on different components associated with the concept of evaluation: objective theory and subjective theory. The objective theory focuses on the intrinsic properties of the evaluated object ('this is a beautiful item'), while the subjective theory focuses on the individual experience or attitude of the observer ('I like it').

Objectivist theories emerged from early psychophysical studies that focused on identifying particular stimulus properties or arrangements of attributes that induced aesthetic experience, such as symmetry, balance, complexity and order of stimuli. One such example is the 'golden cut' that will induce an aesthetic feeling in any observer and will be preferred to any other composition of stimuli (Livio, 2002). These studies have used a wide range of stimuli, from simple geometrical figures to more complex stimuli such as paintings (McManus and Weatherby, 1997; Jacobsen, 2004; Jacobsen et al., 2004; Jacobsen and Hofel, 2002; McManus, 1980). A common finding is that aesthetic experience depends on compositional arrangements between parts of the stimulus, and between individual parts and the whole, and that all observers share a common perceptual mechanism for seeing these attributes (Leder et al., 2004). In conclusion, the objectivist theories suggest that the perceptual system of an observer will treat beauty and other aesthetic properties of our environment like any other attribute. On the other hand, subjective theories support the common saying 'beauty lies in the eye of the beholder'. This perspective completely counters the objectivist viewpoint by giving larger importance to individuals' preferences, taste and attitudes. In this way, each individual is special and unique, and his/her preference should be the product of interaction between idiosyncratic factors such as personal experience and cultural environment (Zajonc, 1968). Psychology has tried to create models that unify individual's behaviour, but the subjectivity of aesthetic behaviour has increased the difficulty of this task, and only one model has been developed to integrate psychological states in a neuropsychological model of aesthetics (Chatterjee, 2004; Chatterjee and Vartanian, 2014).

However, with the advance of neuroscience and modern neuroimaging techniques such as fMRI and magnetoencephalography (MEG: see Box 9.1), a new discipline, called neuroaesthetics, has emerged. It focuses on investigating the neural mechanisms underlying the internal processes associated with aesthetic experience, such as aesthetic evaluation, aesthetic judgment, and aesthetic perception

(Cela-Conde et al., 2004; Kawabata and Zeki, 2004; Vartanian and Goel, 2004). In general, most early studies in neuroaesthetics aimed to describe the brain mechanisms involved in aesthetic evaluation *per se*, regardless of the physical properties of the preferred item. These studies recorded brain activity while participants explicitly evaluated the aesthetic properties of static images such as paintings, objects, casual scenes or geometrical figures (Cela-Conde et al., 2004; Kawabata and Zeki, 2004; Jacobsen et al., 2006; Vartanian and Goel, 2004). As often in the early stages of a new discipline, there has been little consensus on the concepts, predictions or methodologies required for studying neuroaesthetics, which has produced a mix of both converging and divergent results (for a review, see Nadal et al., 2008). Nevertheless, the overall present literature suggests that the neural mechanism of the aesthetic processing (and more particular, aesthetic evaluation) might be distributed along at least three types of networks or processes. These are a perceptual, a cognitive, and an emotional mechanism.

The first mechanism refers to an early sensory or perceptual component. It is through these components that a piece of art or stimulus reaches the human mind. The mechanisms underlying audition and vision are well studied in the scientific literature. For example, a network of visual cortical areas independently processes multiple features of visual stimuli, such as colour, form, motion and depth independently (Zeki and Lamb, 1994). Several recent studies have reported more brain activity in visual areas during the perception of stimuli that were going to be aesthetically evaluated (Jacobsen et al., 2006; Kawabata and Zeki, 2004; Vartanian and Goel, 2004). Among these regions, extrastriate areas (Jacobsen et al., 2006) and the occipital and fusiform gyri (Vartanian and Goel, 2004) are repeatedly reported as active when subjects see stimuli that they like, as opposed to dislike. Similar regions show responses while evaluating different degrees of attractiveness of faces (Iidaka et al., 2002; Paradiso et al., 1999). Although it is still unclear whether these activations are related to preference or show a merely functional specialized processing and perception of the category of stimuli being judged (Moutoussis and Zeki, 2002; Zeki et al., 1991), it is highly accepted that 'all visual art must obey the laws of the visual system' (Zeki and Lamb, 1994).

A second cognitive or semantic component can be defined as part of aesthetic processing. Several neuroaesthetics studies have shown activity in areas related to cognitive processes such as memory or social cognition during positive evaluation of beauty. Cela-Conde and colleagues, for example, have shown stronger activity in the prefrontal dorsolateral cortex when participants were watching and evaluating their preference for different paintings (Cela-Conde et al., 2004). This region has also been described as the centre of the perception–action interface and is critical for the monitoring and comparison of multiple events in working memory (Cela-Conde et al., 2004; Petrides, 2000). Activity in another frontal region, the fronto-median cortex, joint with activity in prefrontal regions, as well as temporal–parietal brain areas, has been found in another study that compared brain responses during aesthetic judgments and perceptual judgments, like symmetry (Jacobsen et al., 2006). Interestingly, these same set of regions are involved while performing other judgements about human nature, such as social and moral judgments (Cunningham et al., 2003). Overall, this might indicate that aesthetic processing involves the combination of specific mechanism for aesthetic evaluation, as well as those common to general judgments.

Finally, we can describe a hedonic or emotional component associated with the reward of the stimuli regardless of their aesthetic properties. This assumption is supported by studies showing brain responses in the orbitofrontal region of the prefrontal cortex during the observation of stimuli rated as beautiful compared to those that were less liked (Kawabata and Zeki, 2004; Kirk et al., 2009). There are no studies comparing the temporal dynamics of the cognitive and hedonic components during aesthetic response; however, it is likely that cognitive processing and hedonic or reward mechanisms work in parallel during the perception of sensory stimuli, linking systems for individual preference behaviour, and basic pleasure and emotion.

The previously described aesthetic components clearly suggest that seeing beauty involves at least three separate stages or mechanisms, including perceptual processing, cognitive processes related to memories, and emotional processes associated with reward. Neuroaesthetics is a new field, and some of the neural activations described here are not fully consistent across studies; however, this might be due to the use of different paradigms rather than to the lack of a specific neural processing for the aesthetic response. Overall, it can be concluded that a dedicated set of regions participate in the explicit aesthetic evaluation of beauty, although the role of each component and the stage of its participation on the general aesthetic response is still to be determined. Other important aspects to consider are the following. First, previous studies have mainly focused on subjective approaches and have compared different sets of stimuli according to individual preferences, allowing for a general view of the brain responses of the observer during the aesthetic evaluation process. However, they have given little attention to the physical properties of the selected stimuli. This provides little information about which physical properties of stimuli are responsible for the aesthetic experience of a participant. Second, most of these studies have used paintings as the art form to be aesthetically rated, and although some new research has been done on ancient sculptures (Di Dio, Macaluso and Rizzolatti, 2007) and architecture (Kirk et al., 2009), there is a blank space waiting to be filled by dynamic artistic expressions such as dance. Therefore, we propose a new approach for studying neuroaesthetics.

Most importantly, our research complements a number of studies that focus on static stimuli such as paintings (Cela-Conde et al., 2004; Kawabata and Zeki, 2004; Vartanian and Goel, 2004) or music (Blood and Zatorre, 2001), by focusing on a specific dynamic stimulus from the performing arts never studied before: dance. We move away from the classical explicit evaluation of beauty to study implicit processing embedded in the automatic perception of stimuli. Finally, we use a consensus approach, which, compared to the individual and subjective approach, allows us to identify brain responses for an average observer. This last issue is particularly important because it allows us to project the results from the activated brain regions back into stimulus space and to describe physical properties of the dance movements that have an associated neural response. Other aproaches to the neuroaesthetics of dance are described in Chapter 12.

Neural correlates of implicit aesthetic responses to watching dance

The way we perceive the external word is modulated by intrinsic factors such as our current mood or previous experience. Aesthetic processing is similarly affected by these factors. Kant (cited by Crawford, 1970) stated that observers need to be in a certain state to have an aesthetic experience. Therefore, every time we walk into an art gallery or a performance theatre, we prepare our senses for an aesthetic experience. Neuroimaging studies have tried to grasp the essence of this specific *mood for aesthetics,* also called 'aesthetic attitude' (Cupchik and László, 1992), by evoking this attitude under laboratory conditions, while measuring brain activity that may correlate with this process. Later, different neural responses for positive judgements ('I like this image') were compared to negative ones ('I do not like it'). However, one would expect that there is more to aesthetic experience than the explicit judgment of beauty. Otherwise, no spontaneous aesthetic pleasure could arise unless we have placed ourselves in the appropriate mood.

We prepared a study with two main aims: First, we aimed to investigate neural responses that correlate with implicit aesthetic experience, extending previous work on aesthetics of static stimuli to the performing arts, in this case, dance (a complete description of this study can be found in Calvo-Merino et al., 2008). Second, we aimed to analyse the data so that we could look back into stimulus space, and identify the stimuli that produced the strongest aesthetic responses, both at a subjective level and at a neural level. We divided the study into two sessions. In the first session, we measured brain responses in naïve participants with no formal dance experience while they watched dance movements and performed a dummy task (to ensure they paid attention to the stimuli). It is important to note that no explicit aesthetic question was asked during the viewing inside the brain scanner. As in previous studies, we worked closely with a choreographer in order to select a range of dance movements from different cultural backgrounds (classical ballet and capoeira). Combining responses for both dance disciplines allowed us to evaluate general responses to dance perception, irrespective of dance style. The selected movements were classified on the basis of four kinematic properties: speed, used body part, direction of movement, and vertical and horizontal displacement. This pre-classification is important to later produce a physical description of the movements that elicited different aesthetic response (see Figure 10.3). In a separate second session, participants were shown the same dance video clips and were asked to rate them individually in an aesthetics questionnaire that contemplated five dimensions (Berlyne, 1974). These were liked–disliked, simple–complex, interesting–dull, tense–relaxed, and weak–powerful. From this questionnaire, the only dimension that showed significant levels of correlation with neural activity was liked–disliked. We therefore focused on this dimension during the analysis and discussion.

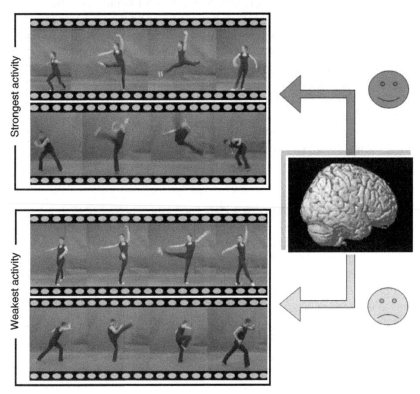

Figure 10.3 Sensorimotor aesthetic tuning during observation of dance movements. The brain areas that responded to movements on a consensus scale between 'like' and 'dislike' are the premotor cortex in the right hemisphere and visual cortex bilaterally. Footage of the dance movements that activate strongly are in the top box, and include horizontal and vertical displacement (jumping); whereas the movements in the bottom box, which activated weakly, involve mainly one limb and little displacement. (Modified from Calvo-Merino et al, 2008.)

We analysed brain activity using standard procedures (for a full description, see Calvo-Merino et al., 2008). The subjective ratings for each movement were first normalized within each subject and then averaged across subjects to create a consensus rating of the group of participants for each movement. We then divided the movements into two halves: the highest scores (more liking), and the lowest scores (more disliking). We then used the group average of all subjects' ratings to identify brain areas sensitive to whether they were watching a generally high or low rating in this aesthetic dimension, as determined by the consensus scores (see Figure 10.3). We found two specific brain regions showing significant neuroaesthetic tuning. These regions were more activated when subjects viewed movements that, on average (in the consensus), they liked, compared to movements that, on average, they disliked. These aesthetics-sensitive areas are localized in the early visual cortex, in the medial region, and in the premotor cortex of the right hemisphere. These areas therefore may be relevant for implicit positive aesthetic experience of dance. No significant results were found for the opposite comparison, i.e., when looking for brain regions sensitive to viewing less-preferred rather than preferred movements. This result suggests that an automatic sensorimotor response underlying our current mechanism for seeing actions (or dance in particular) is sensitive to implicit positive aesthetic feeling. Similar activation in the premotor cortex has been found in the previously described studies during action observation. Therefore, the results from the present aesthetics study are in agreement with previous statements that underlie the relation between perceptual mechanism for perceiving the stimuli and aesthetics processing (Zeki and Lamb, 1994).

Back to movement

The subjective approach has been widely used in most previous neuroaesthetics studies, where brain analysis was often driven by individual responses and aesthetics ratings. This approach allows for identifying brain areas that participate in aesthetics decisions, but it does not allow for making any inferences about the stimuli that evoke this response. The consensus approach that we have presented here (for details, see Calvo-Merino et al., 2008) does not allow for generalizing the result to the general population, as we eliminate differences between individuals when generating the consensus average. However, it does allow us to identify individual stimuli that specifically modulate the aesthetics-related brain areas described in the group of subjects that participated in this study. Since the movements were selected on the basis of four criteria, we can produce a physical description of those dance movements that preferentially target these aesthetics-sensitive areas. We then identified which specific dance movements were responsible for maximal and minimal activation for the two aesthetically responsive brain areas (visual and premotor cortices). Figure 10.3 shows an example of the movements that achieve highest and lowest neural responses for the occipital area in the left hemisphere and the equivalent stimuli for the right premotor activation. This result suggested that, on average, these aesthetics-sensitive areas preferred whole-body movements, such as in jumping in place or with a significant displacement of the entire body in space, like horizontal jumps. When we performed the same type of analysis based only on the behavioural data, we observed that the kinematic properties of the movements that received the highest and lowest consensus liking scores in the subjective rating show clear correspondence with the moves that target the brain areas revealed as aesthetically relevant in the functional imaging analysis. These two latest results suggest a correlation between subjective liking and neural liking. It is of course impossible to determinate (within the setting of the present experiment) which process precedes which. Does a strong sensorimotor resonance produce a stronger feeling of beauty in movements? Or does the way we feel beauty modulate the level of the sensorimotor response? Or is positive aesthetic feeling the result of the perfect interaction of both subjective and neural response? These questions raise the possibility of continuing research on neuroaesthetics of performing arts using a sensorimotor framework.

Conversations between neuroscience and dance

Scientific research, as well as dance production, are processes that involve several stages and different people with different abilities and responsibilities. For example, a dance performance requires at least the participation of choreographers, dancers, and an audience to observe the final product. During our research, we have mainly focussed on dance perception rather than the creative process of dance or dance execution. In particular, we studied how neurocognitive mechanisms involved in observing dance movements are sensitive to different factors, such as the observer's experience with the observed movement and implicit aesthetic experience. However, despite focusing on the dance observer, during some stages of the research process there was an inestimable contribution of the dance execution section of the performance team, and this was comparable to the one needed in a dance performance setting. Our experience told us that in order to create an efficient communication between artist and scientist and to avoid a Babel tower, there is a need to embrace the different views of each world (art and science) and synthesize a common language. Once this is done, ideas can flow and fertilize all approaches and knowledge for a common matter of interest: in this case, dance.

Although all collaborations are unique and can develop in their own ways, our experience has shown us two pathways. The first one: Involves a full collaboration and interaction between scientist and artist along the entire path of a study. This helps to address questions of common interest, leading to a common and shared output. While this may be a desired and ideal scenario, in reality it is often difficult to pursue (see also Chapter 13). The second path is mostly unilateral, and can work for both scientists and artist. From the scientist perspective we have here reported a series of studies that use dance or dancers as model participants, in order to address specific experimentally driven questions – this can include dance itself (Calvo-Merino et al., 2005; 2006; Cross, Hamilton and Grafton, 2006; Brown, Martinez and Parsons, 2006: see also Chapters 9, 11 and 13). In this type of inter-action, the artist–science collaboration might be necessary only at some stage of the research, even if it is a key factor. In our own studies, it was the experimenters' role to define stimulus requirements to test the experimental hypotheses (e.g., kinematics properties, length, colours, etc.). We then discussed this information and the aim of the study with an experienced choreographer, who, being familiar with our experimental framework and approach, made a final selection of move-ments appropriate for the experiment, and guided the dancers while performing the steps in the video-recording session. Although this collaboration was essential for the success of the research, as well as the participation of professional dancers as subjects, this collaboration was limited to the early stages of the research time-line, and was developed *ad hoc* to fit into the original experimental hypothesis. From the artist's perspective, there is the possibility of benefit from science as a source of inspiration for choreographing new movements or whole performances (for an example, see Wayne McGregor, *AtaXia*, 2004: www.choreocog.net/ataxia. html). However, this side of the collaboration is better discussed by other writers with intrinsic knowledge from the dance world (deLahunta and Barnard, 2005; Hagendoorn, 2004: see also Chapter 13).

Another issue to consider in science–art collaborations regards the different methods that both disciplines use to pursue their final aim. Only after this has been understood, can one start to share work-in-progress and outputs. The researcher and the artist aim to: generate support for a theory; find out whether a hypothesis regarding a specific phenomenon is correct; or produce a final work of art. Yet whatever their shared aim, they pursue the same target from different angles. Basically, the differences are due to different views on two extremes; the whole and the part. The approach of science is to understand a phenomenon (here: a dance performance) by performing an analytical deconstruction of its parts or elements. Then each component is investigated in isolation. This initial segmentation is essential to study independent contributions of each independent component and their participation in individual process (see Chapter 9). Artists, on the other hand, manipulate parts and units to compose the whole. For example, in order to create a dance performance, one has to combine individual elements such as movements, as well as considering the performing dancers, scenario and costume (as described in Chapter 4). All these elements merge together in perfect harmony to create the dance performance we see from the other side of the dance theatre.

Considering this last point, the logical question to ask is: Can the artist collect the information about the individual elements that science can provide and put them back together into a piece of art? The studies presented here have illustrated the human neural mechanism that participates in the observation of movements in general, and dance movements in particular. In order to conduct this research and isolate the elements of interest, we reduced dance movements to their minimal expression, by using short video clips and minimizing variability between dancers' bodies and costumes. This allowed us to identify a neural network that participates during the observation of dance. This network could be the basis of an internal motor simulation mechanism that matches the actions we watch with internal action representations stored in our own motor repertoire. More importantly, we also showed that this sensorimotor mechanism is sensitive to the nature of familiarity – visual or motor – that the observer has with an action (Calvo-Merino et al., 2005; 2006), and to the level of implicit liking during mere observation in non-familiar observers (Calvo-Merino et al., 2008). Interestingly, because we previously described the physical properties of individual movements, each video clip can be conceived as an independent movement unit whose properties are known. We also know the level of preferences that each of these movement units elicit in the sensorimotor network of the observer. Therefore, it would be interesting to see how choreographers collect these movement units, and develop a performance or choreography *à la carte* that stimulates specific brain regions required for an aesthetic experience. Thinking ahead, and envisaging that research following this approach will increase over the years, one can start to imagine how it may be possible to create a performance that effectively stimulates different components of the aesthetics-processing network.

Here we propose a new tool, namely the use of knowledge about the neural mechanisms underlying action observation in an observer. Taking into account the properties of the system that is going to perceive and probably judge the final production – the brain – might help to control the quality or quantity of an observer's experience. It is difficult to distinguish the piece of art from the observer (for a recent example, see Anthony Gormley's Fourth Plinth Commission entitled 'One and other': www.antonygormley.com/show/item-view/id/2277). Even if researchers have used theories and methods of cognitive science to describe aspects of dance, such as choreographic thoughts and creativity (Stevens and McKechnie, 2005), only time will tell how much cognitive psychology and neuroscience knowledge about the way humans see dance and feel pleasure will influence the way dance is produced, or how much of these disciplines will be considered by the choreographer in the artistic creation process.

Acknowledgements

This chapter was part of a larger set of studies performed at University College London with Professor Patrick Haggard. We are grateful to all the ballet dancers and capoeristas for their participation in the studies, to Deborah Bull of the Royal Opera House (ROH2), Emma Maguire of the Royal Ballet and Giuseppe Vitolo (Professor Polvo – Capoeira Abolicao) for assistance with preparing the stimuli, and to Tom Sapsford for choreography. We thank Daniel Glaser, Julie Grèzes, Corinne Jola and Dick Passingham for help with planning and analyzing the imaging studies. Finally, we thank Sven Bestmann and Matthew Longo for their useful comments and earlier version of the manuscript. This work was supported by a Leverhulme Trust Research Grant, Economical Social Research Council (ESRC) and City University Fellowship (City, University of London).

References

Baldissera, F., Cavallari, P., Craighero, L., & Fadiga, L. (2001). Modulation of spinal excitability during observation of hand actions in humans. *Eur. J. Neurosci.*, 13, 190–194.

Bastian, H. C. (1880). *The Brain as an Organ of Mind.* London: Kegan Paul.

Berger, S. M., Carli, L. L., Hammersla, K. S., Karshmer, J. F., & Sanchez, M. E. (1979). Motoric and symbolic mediation in observational learning. *J. Pers. Soc. Psychol.*, 37, 735–746.

Berlyne, D. E. (1974). *Studies in the New Experimental Aesthetics: Steps toward an objective psychology of aesthetic appreciation.* Washington, DC: Hemisphere Publishing.

Berthoz, A. (2002). *The Brain's Sense of Movement.* Cambridge, MA: Harvard University Press.

Blood, A. J. & Zatorre, R. J. (2001). Intensely pleasurable responses to music correlate with activity in brain regions implicated in reward and emotion. *Proc. Natl. Acad. Sci. U.S.A,* 98, 11818–11823.

Brown, S., Martinez, M. J., & Parsons, L. M. (2006). The neural basis of human dance. *Cereb. Cortex,* 16, 1157–1167.

Brown, S. & Parsons, L. M. (2008). The neuroscience of dance. *Scientific American Magazine,* July, 78–83.

Buccino, G., Binkofski, F., Fink, G. R., Fadiga, L., Fogassi, L., Gallese, V., Seitz, R. J., Zilles, K., Rizzolatti, G., & Freund, H. -J. (2001). Action observation activates premotor and parietal areas in a somatotopic manner: An fMRI study. *Eur. J. Neurosci.,* 13, 400–404.

212   *Calvo-Merino*

Buccino, G., Lui, F., Canessa, N., Patteri, I., Lagravinese, G., Benuzzi, F., Porro, C. A., & Rizzolatti, G. (2004). Neural circuits involved in the recognition of actions performed by nonconspecifics: An FMRI study. *J. Cogn. Neurosci.,* 16, 114–126.

Calvo-Merino, B., Glaser, D. E., Grèzes, J., Passingham, R. E., & Haggard, P. (2005). Action observation and acquired motor skills: An FMRI study with expert dancers. *Cereb. Cortex,* 15, 1243–1249.

Calvo-Merino, B., Grèzes, J., Glaser, D. E., Passingham, R. E., & Haggard, P. (2006). Seeing or doing? Influence of visual and motor familiarity in action observation. *Curr. Biol.,* 16, 1905–1910.

Calvo-Merino, B., Jola, C., Glaser, D. E., & Haggard, P. (2008). Towards a sensorimotor aesthetics of performing art. *Conscious. Cogn.,* 17, 911–922.

Cela-Conde, C. J., Marty, G., Maestu, F., Ortiz, T., Munar, E., Fernandez, A., Roca, M., Rosselló, J., & Quesney, F. (2004). Activation of the prefrontal cortex in the human visual aesthetic perception. *Proc. Natl. Acad. Sci. U.S.A,* 101, 6321–6325.

Chatterjee, A. (2004). The neuropsychology of visual artistic expression. *Neuropsychologia,* 42, 1568–1583.

Chatterjee, A. & Vartanian, O. (2014). Neuroaesthetics. *Trends Cogn. Sci.,* 18(7), 370–375.

Crawford, D. (1970). Reason-giving in Kant's aesthetics. *J. Aesthet. Art Crit.,* 28, 505–510.

Cross, E. S., Hamilton, A. F., & Grafton, S. T. (2006). Building a motor simulation de novo: Observation of dance by dancers. *Neuroimage.,* 31, 1257–1267.

Cunningham, W. A., Johnson, M. K., Gatenby, J. C., Gore, J. C., & Banaji, M. R. (2003). Neural components of social evaluation. *J. Pers. Soc. Psychol.,* 85, 639–649.

Cupchik, G. C. & László, J. (1992). *Emerging Visions of the Aesthetic Process: In psychology, semiology and philosophy.* Cambridge, UK: Cambridge University Press.

Decety, J., Grèzes, J., Costes, N., Perani, D., Jeannerod, M., Procyk, E., Grassi, F., & Fazio, F. (1997). Brain activity during observation of actions. Influence of action content and subject's strategy. *Brain,* 120(10), 1763–1777.

deLahunta, S. & Barnard, P. (2005). What's in a phrase? In: J. Birringer & J. Fenger (Eds.), *Tanz im Kopf: Dance and Cognition* (pp. 253–266). Munich: Verlag.

Descartes, R. (1980). *Traitee de l'Homme.* Madrid: Editora Nacional.

Di Dio, C., Macaluso, E., & Rizzolatti, G. (2007). The golden beauty: Brain response to classical and renaissance sculptures. *PLOS ONE,* 2(11), 1–9.

di Pellegrino, G., Fadiga, L., Fogassi, L., Gallese, V., & Rizzolatti, G. (1992). Understanding motor events: A neurophysiological study. *Exp. Brain Res.,* 91, 176–180.

Fadiga, L., Fogassi, L., Pavesi, G., & Rizzolatti, G. (1995). Motor facilitation during action observation: A magnetic stimulation study. *J. Neurophysiol.,* 73, 2608–2611.

Gallese, V., Fadiga, L., Fogassi, L., & Rizzolatti, G. (1996). Action recognition in the premotor cortex. *Brain,* 119 (2), 593–609.

Gazzola, V., Rizzolatti, G., Wicker, B., & Keysers, C. (2007). The anthropomorphic brain: The mirror neuron system responds to human and robotic actions. *Neuroimage.,* 35(4), 1674–1684.

Gibson, J. J. (1979). *The Ecological Approach to Visual Perception.* Boston, MA: Houghton Mifflin.

Goldman, A. (2001). The aesthetic. In: B. Gaut & D. McIver-Lopes (Eds.), *The Routledge Companion to Aesthetics* (pp. 181–192). London: Routledge.

Grafton, S. T., Arbib, M. A., Fadiga, L., & Rizzolatti, G. (1996). Localization of grasp representations in humans by positron emission tomography. 2. Observation compared with imagination. *Exp. Brain Res.,* 112, 103–111.

Grèzes, J. & Decety, J. (2001). Functional anatomy of execution, mental simulation, obser-vation, and verb generation of actions: A meta-analysis. *Hum. Brain Mapp.,* 12, 1–19.

Hagendoorn, I. G. (2004). Some speculative hypotheses about the nature and perception of dance and choreography. *J. Conscious. Stud.,* 11(3/4), 79–110.

Iacoboni, M., Woods, R. P., Brass, M., Bekkering, H., Mazziotta, J. C., & Rizzolatti, G. (1999). Cortical mechanisms of human imitation. *Science,* 286, 2526–2528.

Iidaka, T., Okada, T., Murata, T., Omori, M., Kosaka, H., Sadato, N., & Yonekura, Y. (2002). Age-related differences in the medial temporal lobe responses to emotional faces as revealed by fMRI. *Hippocampus,* 12, 352–362.

Jacobsen, T. (2004). Individual and group modelling of aesthetic judgment strategies. *Br. J. Psychol.,* 95, 41–56.

Jacobsen, T., Buchta, K., Kohler, M., & Schroger, E. (2004). The primacy of beauty in judging the aesthetics of objects. *Psychol. Rep.,* 94, 1253–1260.

Jacobsen, T. & Hofel, L. (2002). Aesthetic judgments of novel graphic patterns: Analyses of individual judgments. *Percept. Mot. Skills,* 95, 755–766.

Jacobsen, T., Schubotz, R. I., Hofel, L., & Cramon, D. Y. (2006). Brain correlates of aesthetic judgment of beauty. *Neuroimage.,* 29, 276–285.

Jeannerod, M. (1997). *The Cognitive Neuroscience of Action.* Oxford: Blackwell.

Kawabata, H. & Zeki, S. (2004). Neural correlates of beauty. *J. Neurophysiol.,* 91, 1699–1705.

Kirk, U., Skov, M., Christensen, M. S., & Nygaard, N. (2009). Brain correlates of aesthetic expertise: A parametric fMRI study. *Brain Cogn.,* 69, 306–315.

Konorski, J. (1967). Some new ideas concerning the physiological mechanisms of perception. *Acta Biol. Exp. (Warsz.),* 27, 147–161.

Leder, H., Belke, B., Oeberst, A., & Augustin, D. (2004). A model of aesthetic appreciation and aesthetic judgments. *Br. J. Psychol.,* 95, 489–508.

Livio, M. (2002). *The Golden Ratio: The story of Phi, the extraordinary number of nature, art and beauty.* London: Headline Book Publishing.

McManus, I. C. (1980). The aesthetics of simple figures. *Br. J. Psychol.,* 71, 505–524.

McManus, I. C. & Weatherby, P. (1997). The golden section and the aesthetics of form and composition: A cognitive model. *Empir. Stud. Arts,* 15, 209–232.

Moutoussis, K. & Zeki, S. (2002). The relationship between cortical activation and perception investigated with invisible stimuli. *Proc. Natl. Acad. Sci. U.S.A,* 99, 9527–9532.

Nadal, M., Munar, E., Capo, M. A., Rossello, J., & Cela-Conde, C. J. (2008). Towards a framework for the study of the neural correlates of aesthetic preference. *Spat. Vis.,* 21, 379–396.

Paradiso, S., Johnson, D. L., Andreasen, N. C., O'Leary, D. S., Watkins, G. L., Ponto, L. L., & Hichwa, R. D. (1999). Cerebral blood flow changes associated with attribution of emotional valence to pleasant, unpleasant, and neutral visual stimuli in a PET study of normal subjects. *Am. J. Psychiatry,* 156, 1618–1629.

Penfield, W. & Rasmussen, T. (1950). *The Cerebral Cortex of Man: A clinical study of localization of function.* New York: Macmillan.

Perani, D., Fazio, F., Borghese, N. A., Tettamanti, M., Ferrari, S., Decety, J., & Gilardi, M. C. (2001). Different brain correlates for watching real and virtual hand actions. *Neuroimage.,* 14, 749–758.

Petrides, M. (2000). The role of the mid-dorsolateral prefrontal cortex in working memory. *Exp. Brain Res.,* 133, 44–54.

Prinz , W. (1997). Perception and action planning. *Eur. J. Cogn. Psychol.,* 9, 129–154.

Rizzolatti, G., Fadiga, L., Gallese, V., & Fogassi, L. (1996). Premotor cortex and the recognition of motor actions. *Brain Res. Cogn. Brain Res.,* 3, 131–141.

Rizzolatti, G., Fogassi, L., & Gallese, V. (2001). Neurophysiological mechanisms
underlying the understanding and imitation of action. *Nat. Rev. Neurosci.,* 2, 661–670.

Rizzolatti, G. & Sinigaglia, C. (2016). The mirror mechanism: A basic principle of brain
function. *Nat. Rev. Neurosci.,* 17(12), 757–765.

Rozzi, S., Ferrari, P. F., Bonini, L., Rizzolatti, G., & Fogassi, L. (2008). Functional organization of inferior parietal lobule convexity in the macaque monkey: Electrophysiological
characterization of motor, sensory and mirror responses and their correlation with cytoarchitectonic areas. *Eur. J. Neurosci.,* 28, 1569–1588.

Sperry, J. A. (1952). Neurology and the mind brain problem. *Amer. Scientist,* 40,
291–312.

Stevens, J. A., Fonlupt, P., Shiffrar, M., & Decety, J. (2000). New aspects of motion
perception: Selective neural encoding of apparent human movements. *Neuroreport,*
11, 109–115.

Stevens, C. & McKechnie S. (2005). Minds and motions: Dynamic Systems in choreography, creativity and Dance. In: J. Birringer & J. Fenger (Eds.), *Tanz im Kopf / Dance
and Cognition* (pp. 241–252). Munich: Verlag.

Strafella, A. P. & Paus, T. (2000). Modulation of cortical excitability during action
observation: A transcranial magnetic stimulation study. *Neuroreport,* 11, 2289–2292.

Tai, Y. F., Scherfler, C., Brooks, D. J., Sawamoto, N., & Castiello, U. (2004). The human
premotor cortex is 'mirror' only for biological actions. *Curr. Biol.,* 14, 117–120.

Vartanian, O. & Goel, V. (2004). Neuroanatomical correlates of aesthetic preference for
paintings. *Neuroreport,* 15, 893–897.

Zajonc, R. B. (1968). Attitudinal effects of mere exposure. *J. Pers. Soc. Psychol,* 9, 1–27.

Zeki, S. & Lamb, M. (1994). The neurology of kinetic art. *Brain,* 117(3), 607–636.

Zeki, S., Watson, J. D., Lueck, C. J., Friston, K. J., Kennard, C., & Frackowiak, R. S.
(1991). A direct demonstration of functional specialization in human visual cortex.
J. Neurosci., 11, 641–649.

11 Building a dance in the human brain

Insights from expert and novice dancers

Emily S. Cross

As humans, we have an unparalleled ability to coordinate our bodies to perform an endless number of skilled actions. As dancers, this ability is even more impressive, as a dancer's motor repertoire comprises movements that are not only highly skilled, but also remarkably precise, complex and coordinated. An intriguing feature of the human brain is how a network of seemingly disparate cortical regions and subcortical nuclei can give rise to dance movements, from the razor-sharp precision of 32 *fouettés en tournant* performed by Odile in *Swan Lake* to the contorted, convulsive and seemingly out-of-control whole-body flings and gyrations that typify the choreographic vocabulary of Twyla Tharp's *Torelli*. Of particular interest to neuroscientists is the remarkable plasticity of the human brain to integrate different types of physical and perceptual experiences in order to learn new movements. Such abilities are quite pronounced in dancers, whose livelihood depends on rapid and adept movement production and reproduction. How does the brain accomplish this feat? The network of brain regions comprised of the cortical regions and subcortical nuclei works together when we observe someone else performing an action and then learn how to perform it ourselves.

Neuroscientists first found evidence of a neural system that matches action with perception in the brains of non-human primates (see Chapter 10). Subsequent research revealed that these particular neurons do indeed respond preferentially to actions that are either observed or performed, which led researchers to name them 'mirror neurons'. As such, mirror neurons appear to compose a cortical network that matches observation of actions with execution of those same actions (Grafton et al., 1996). These specialized neurons have prompted researchers to propose that action perception and production processes form a bidirectional, interactive loop within the primate brain.

Since the discovery of mirror neurons in monkeys, many studies have investigated similar functional regions within the human brain, providing evidence for a human mirror-neuron system (e.g., Rizzolatti and Craighero, 2004), or, more broadly, an 'action observation network' (Cross et al., 2009b). For the purposes of this chapter, the term 'action observation network' (AON) is used instead of 'mirror-neuron system', since this term is more general and encompasses all of the brain regions involved in action-observation processes, not simply the two main mirror neuron regions (i.e., the inferior parietal and premotor cortices).

As illustrated in Figure 11.1, the brain regions that comprise the AON include the ventral premotor cortex (PMv), the inferior parietal lobule (IPL), the superior temporal sulcus (STS) and the supplementary and pre-supplementary motor areas (SMA and pre-SMA) (Binkofski et al., 2000; Decety, 1996; Grafton et al., 1996; Rizzolatti et al., 1996b; Stephan et al., 1995). Increasing evidence from behavioral, neuroimaging and neurostimulation procedures suggests that action understanding might be explained by covert simulation of another's movements by an observer (Decety, 1996; Fadiga et al., 1995; 1999; Jeannerod, 2001; Rizzolatti and Craighero, 2004).

The challenge for researchers investigating the relationship between action perception and production is to determine the explanatory power and generalization

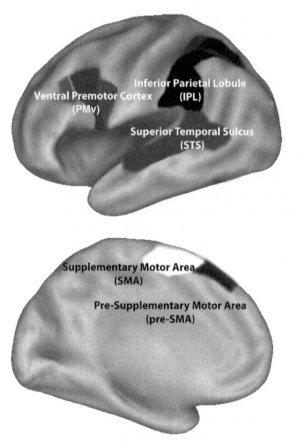

Figure 11.1 A representation of the action observation network (AON), using the
PALS data set and Caret visualization tools (http://brainvis.wustl.edu/
wiki/index.php/Caret:Download), which render brains to appear slightly
inflated, therefore enabling better visualization of activations deep
within sulci and on the cortical surface. The AON is represented
bilaterally, but for visualization purposes, the medial and lateral
surfaces of the left hemisphere only are illustrated here.

of this network and to define its relationship with new action learning and motor expertise. It is the hope of researchers in this field to eventually explore applications for the recovery of function after neurological injury, as well as improved learning and teaching practices. The focus of this chapter will be on work my team and I have performed on the neural and behavioral mechanisms and consequences of people learning to perform complex actions, specifically dance. First, I will introduce work we have performed with expert dancers that probed questions of the neural representation of whole-body action expertise. Next I will discuss findings from several studies performed with novice dancers through which we addressed questions concerning how different types of learning (i.e., physical vs. observational), as well as different cues to learning (i.e., watching a person vs. a series of symbolic cues), shape action perception. I will conclude with a brief discussion of the broader implications for this work and I will suggest several directions for future research.

Placing the dancer's brain in a scientific context

My colleagues and I have turned to populations of expert and novice dancers to help us address questions of action cognition for several reasons. Dance requires a great degree of coordination not only between the different limbs of the body, but also between perception and action, and time and space. As an example, most dancers can relate to the experience of arriving at a technique class in a new studio, progressing with ease through the warm up or *barre* exercises, and then being expected to perfectly perform long and complex sequences of steps that have been rapidly demonstrated in the most cursory manner. Dancers' ability to transform scant visual or verbal information into highly sophisticated movements has great potential value to scientists. Significant utility exists in examining both novice and expert dancers in order to investigate how complex movements are learned, remembered and reproduced. Not only can scientists learn about the coordination and expression of complex actions by quantifying dancers' behavioral performance, but careful measurement of how such skilled actions are represented at the neural level can shed additional light on how the human body is capable of learning and performing such complex movements with limited information.

In line with research from my laboratory, which has studied *de novo* dance learning in both expert and novice dancers, elegant work by a growing number of other laboratories has substantiated the feasibility of using dance learning and observation as a paradigm for investigating the properties of the AON (Brown, Martinez and Parsons, 2006; Calvo-Merino et al., 2005; 2006; 2008: see also Chapters 10, 12 and 13).

Early studies (Brown, Martinez and Parsons, 2006; Calvo-Merino et al., 2005; 2006) using expert ballet, capoeira and tango dancers, were among the first to provide robust evidence for changes within the AON with the presence (or emergence) of execution competency. My colleagues and I built upon this foundation by addressing open questions regarding the establishment of motor and perceptual expertise, the sensitivity of this network to different kinds of learning experience, and how embodiment and aesthetic preferences might be intertwined. The studies discussed below address these objectives mostly through use of training experiments performed with expert and novice dancers. By tackling such questions about the function of the AON through use of both behavioral and neuroimaging measures that build upon dance paradigms, we aim to better characterize the processes that underlie the various ways in which people acquire new movements and perceive others in action.

What can expert dancers' brains teach us?

The first study our laboratory performed with dancers aimed to address three objectives (Cross, Hamilton and Grafton, 2006). First, we sought to characterize how the human brain represents expertise for complex whole-body actions (in this case, dance sequences). Second, we wanted to determine whether the neural signature for newly learned complex dance sequences differs from kinematically similar sequences that remained untrained. Finally, we aimed to determine if neural activity was related to individuals' perceived mastery of the dance movements that they learned. We hoped that by tackling these questions, we might add a measure of clarity to a continuing debate in the study of action simulation concerning the relationship between physical embodiment of actions (i.e., those actions that an individual can and has performed) and neural activity when observing such actions.

In this study, we asked expert dancers to observe a dancer's movements and at the same time to imagine themselves performing these movements. In this situation, the visual stimulus guides and constrains the motor simulation. Since our task involved action observation, we were considering how visual stimuli depicting human actions are able to drive motor regions of the brain. As mentioned previously, numerous neuroimaging studies implicate the motor and premotor areas that are classically associated with movement preparation as also being engaged when simply observing the actions of others (Buccino et al., 2001; Grafton et al., 1996; Grèzes and Decety, 2001; Iacoboni et al., 1999; Johnson-Frey et al., 2003; Rizzolatti et al., 1996b). Behavioral studies have further demonstrated interactions between action perception and execution (Brass et al., 2000; Brass, Bekkering and Prinz, 2001; Brass, Zysset and von Cramon, 2001; Hamilton, Wolpert and Frith, 2004; Kilner, Paulignan and Blakemore, 2003), and thus lend additional credence to the idea of overlapping neural processes for action observation and execution. Meta-analyses of studies on action representations provide converging evidence that extensive overlap exists between brain regions active during action observation, simulation and execution (Grèzes and Decety, 2001; Molenberghs, Cunnington and Mattingley, 2012). Together, these findings suggest that a broad collection of sensorimotor brain regions compose the AON, most of which are active both when observing and when performing actions.

In our study, we recruited 10 expert modern dancers who were learning the movement vocabulary for Laura Dean's seminal modern dance work, *Skylight* (Dean, 1982). The dancers spent over 5 hours per week learning the *Skylight* vocabulary as part of their company's reparatory. Importantly, this was a longitudinal study in which the dancers' brains were scanned once a week across 6 weeks of learning the new dance work. Such a method enabled us to effectively take snap-shots of the expert dancers' brains as they progressed from unfamiliarity with the new movement vocabulary to an expert level of performance proficiency. During the weekly scanning sessions, the dancers watched 18 video clips of *Skylight* movements, and 18 videos of kinematically similar but unfamiliar and unrehearsed dance movements. The dancer in the video clips was filmed from behind as she moved in front of a mirror. This not only enabled our participants to see nearly 360° of visual information about the movements, but it also provided an ecologically valid viewing context, since dancers are accustomed to observing and practicing movements in front a mirror in a studio context. While the participants watched each video clip in the scanner, they were asked to imagine themselves performing each dance sequence. Following each video, the dancers were asked to rate their perceived performance ability for each sequence, at that particular point in time.

The behavioral and neuroimaging procedures yielded several exciting results about the representation of expertise in dancers' brains. Unsurprisingly, we found that the dancers rated their ability to perform the rehearsed *Skylight* movements as progressively greater across the 6 weeks of training, while their ratings of their ability to perform the control movements remained relatively unchanged (Cross, Hamilton and Grafton, 2006). The neuroimaging results corroborated and extended previous work on expert dancers in several capacities. First, in line with what was reported by Calvo-Merino and colleagues (2005), we saw greater activation across a broadly defined AON, including parietal, premotor, supplementary motor and superior temporal regions, when dancers watched dance movements compared to at rest, and when they watched movements they had physically rehearsed com-pared to unrehearsed control movements (see Figures 11.2a and b). The critical contribution of this study was that as the dancers' expertise with the rehearsed dance sequences increased, activity within PMv and IPL in the left hemisphere also increased with their perceived expertise (see Figure 11.2c).

This study provided evidence for rapid and targeted changes in engagement of two core AON regions within the brains of expert dancers learning new choreography. In just 6 weeks, dancers progressed from novices to experts with the *Skylight* choreography (as evidenced by their subjective evaluations of performance ability). While watching the movements they were most expert at performing, greater neural responses were observed in the left premotor cortex and the left IPL, the two regions that form the crux of the putative mirror-neuron system in humans (Rizzolatti and Craighero, 2004). By studying dancers who were in the midst of intensive rehearsals to learn a new work, we were optimally poised to discover what happens in the brain as individuals build movement expertise. However, one major shortcoming of this study is that the dancers were not scanned prior to beginning rehearsals for *Skylight*. Thus, while we were able to take snapshots of their brains across the rehearsal process, we did not have a clear measure of how the AON responded to rehearsed movements before they were ever seen in the studio. With the next set of studies, we attempted to overcome this issue, as well as

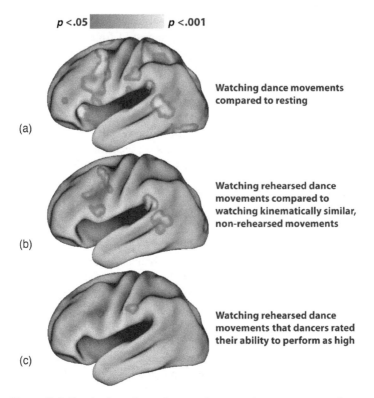

p <.05   *p* <.001

(a)   **Watching dance movements compared to resting**

(b)   **Watching rehearsed dance movements compared to watching kinematically similar, non-rehearsed movements**

(c)   **Watching rehearsed dance movements that dancers rated their ability to perform as high**

Figure 11.2 Results from the study on action expertise among expert dancers. (Modified from Cross, Hamilton and Grafton, 2006.)

the limitation of using subjective performance ratings, through investigation of novice dancers learning simple dance sequences.

What can novice dancers' brains teach us?

While research with expert dancers has shed light on the neural correlates of highly skilled action embodiment (e.g., Calvo-Merino et al., 2005; Cross, Hamilton and Grafton, 2006), a look into the brains of novice dancers learning to integrate visual and auditory cues with coordinated whole-body movements can be equally instructive for our understanding of complex action learning. We know that many avenues exist for learning new dance movements. To return to the dance class example introduced earlier, if an instructor wants her students to perform a particular combination of steps, she could accomplish this in a number of different ways. She could verbally name or describe the sequence of individual steps; she could indicate or gesture the movements with her hands; she could show her students a string of symbols that denotes the combination in Laban movement notation; or she could perform the desired sequence herself.

To parse how different methods of learning might influence performance, we have performed two studies with individuals who previously had no previous dance experience or training (Cross et al., 2009b; Kirsch and Cross, 2015). In both studies, we controlled how novice dancers learned new dance movements and examined resulting changes in participants' brains. In the first study, we measured dance performance accuracy and neural activity within a group of participants as they learned simple dance stepping sequences in an interactive video game context. In order to address our experimental objectives, we used a three-by-two factorial experimental design (see Figure 11.3a). We explored two separate, but

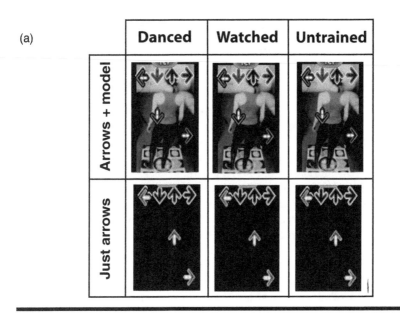

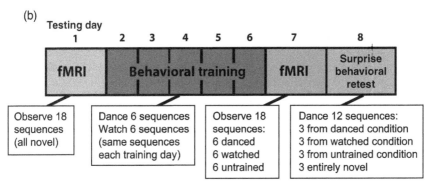

Figure 11.3 Experimental design and time course for study with novice dancers:
(*a*) represents the 3 (training experience: danced, watched or untrained) by 2 (action cue: dancer with arrows or just arrows) study design; and
(*b*) depicts the 4 phases of the study in chronological order.

related, avenues of new action learning in novice dancers: observational learning and learning from human vs. symbolic action cues. This study was carried out over 8 consecutive days, as illustrated in Figure 11.3b. Our first objective was to examine how observational learning, such as when one simply watches a dance instructor without imitating the movements and then tries to reproduce the movements at a later point in time, is represented within the AON (Cross et al., 2009b). The second objective was to determine how movement training influences activity within the AON – both while observing and copying an expert model accurately performing the actions (such as when one dances in step with a dance instructor while observing her movements), and when relying on purely symbolic cues (such as when one follows a diagram or symbolic notation of step patterns: see Cross et al., 2009a). Even though both questions were investigated with a single study, for the sake of clarity, each objective is considered in turn.

Learning from observation

When we learn to walk, use a fork or drive a car, we learn by first observing others do the task, and then practicing it ourselves. It is thus unsurprising that a wealth of behavioral research suggests that the quickest and most accurate learning results from observing and simultaneously reproducing another individual's movements (e.g., Badets, Blandin and Shea, 2006; Bandura, 1977; 1986; Blandin, Lhuisset and Proteau, 1999; Blandin and Proteau, 2000; Schmidt, 1975; Sheffield, 1961). This research has demonstrated that not only is observation helpful for learning (Blandin, Lhuisset and Proteau, 1999), but that physical practice is more beneficial than mere observation of new movements (Badets, Blandin and Shea, 2006). One aim of our study with novice dancers was directed at further exploring the separate and combined contributions of these factors on acquiring novel movement sequences. Additionally, using functional neuroimaging, we aimed to characterize the neural underpinnings of observational learning with or without the added benefit of physical practice.

One of the primary explanations as to why observational and physical learning share so many of the same features is that they both engage similar cognitive processes (Barzouka, Bergeles and Hatziharistos, 2007; Blandin, Lhuisset and Proteau, 1999; Bouquet et al., 2007). For instance, a study combining psychophysical and electromyographic (EMG) measures demonstrated that participants' learning of a novel complex motor task is facilitated if they previously observed another individual learning to perform that same task, as compared with watching another individual perform the task without learning or learning to perform an unrelated task (Mattar and Gribble, 2005). However, as Blandin and colleagues note (1999), such findings do not mean that physical and observational learning are *identical* cognitive processes; particular features are unique to each kind of learning.

Behavioral research establishes a solid foundation for exploring areas of overlap and divergence between observational and physical learning. However, it is difficult to determine with only behavioral experimentation the degree to which cognitive processes underpin these two types of learning. Behavioral and EMG studies alone cannot satisfactorily address the underlying neural mechanisms. Here we benefit from using functional neuroimaging, which can identify the neural mechanisms engaged during observational and physical learning. If both types of learning engage the same areas of the brain, then we can infer that both observational and physical learning engage comparable cognitive processes. Conversely, the emergence of different areas of neural activity based on learning would imply that distinct cognitive processes underlie these two types of learning.

We investigated observational learning by training novice dancers to perform complex dance movement sequences while manipulating training elements. Specifically, we sought to determine whether observational and physical learning result in quantitatively similar or different behavioral performance and patterns of neural activity. Due to the complexity and unfeasibility of having participants physically perform dance sequences in the scanner (but see Brown, Martinez and Parsons, 2006, for an innovative approach to this problem involving tango dancing in a PET scanner), we instead chose to train participants to perform the movement sequences with music videos outside the scanner, and then asked them to observe the training videos during the scanning sessions. The focus of this portion of the study was on the differences between the three training conditions; danced, watched and untrained (Figure 11.3a).

Seventeen young adult participants with no dance experience first came into the laboratory to participate in an fMRI session while they watched and listened to 18 upbeat music videos. Half of these videos featured a person 'dancing' along with arrows that scrolled upwards on the screen, and the other half had only the arrows scrolling on the screen. This first scanning session was followed by five consecutive days of dance training, where participants spent approximately 1 hour in the laboratory each day, practicing dancing six music videos (henceforth to be referred to as the 'danced' condition), and resting while passively viewing, but not dancing to, another set of six music videos (henceforth to be referred to as the 'watched' condition). We used StepMania software (www.stepmania.com), in conjunction with a dance pad connected via USB to a desktop computer, to display the dance videos and record participants' dance performance. We chose to use an interactive video game in order to precisely quantify dance performance, instead of relying upon subjective ratings, as we did in the Cross and colleagues (2006) study, while also maintaining participants' attention and interest across the lengthy training procedures.

Following 5 days of dance training, participants returned for a second fMRI session where they observed the same 18 music videos from the first week of scanning. This time, however, six of those videos were highly familiar from having been physically practiced; another six videos were visually familiar from having been passively viewed during each training day; and the remaining videos had not been seen since the first week of scanning. In contrast to the instructions given to our expert dance participants in the study discussed above (Cross, Hamilton and Grafton, 2006), participants in this study were instructed to simply observe the videos. Following the second scanning session, participants returned to the laboratory to perform a surprise dance retest of a selection of the dance sequences they had practiced dancing, a selection of dance sequences they had passively observed, and a selection of untrained and entirely novel dance sequences.

Behavioral findings indicated that participants' performance of the sequences from the 'danced' condition significantly improved across training days. Moreover, results from the surprise behavioral retest show that participants were able to perform the dance sequences they passively observed during the week of training at an intermediate level (between those sequences they danced and the untrained and novel sequences).

The imaging analyses were designed to accomplish three objectives. The first objective was to determine which brain regions were active when participants observed the dance music videos before ever stepping foot into the training room. This was achieved by identifying regions that showed a greater response while observing all music videos (task) compared to watching a static black screen with a white fixation cross in silence (baseline) from the pre-training scanning session. This contrast revealed broad activation within the AON. This pattern of activity was used as a mask for the next two imaging analyses from the post-training scanning session, in order to limit the search volume for the effects of interest. The next analysis identified neural regions that showed distinct response profiles when observing videos that were danced or watched. Here we found evidence that physical practice engages select components of the AON above and beyond passive observation. Specifically, participants showed heightened activity in the right precentral gyrus when presented with videos they had danced, and did not recruit this same area when viewing videos they had only passively viewed during training. This pattern of findings is consistent with the notion that physical practice engages select components of the AON above and beyond passive observation (Aglioti et al., 2008; Calvo-Merino et al., 2006).

This is not to suggest that observational learning relies on an entirely different system than physical learning. Indeed, a conjunction analysis revealed that both physical and observational learning engaged activity in select areas of the AON (see Figure 11.4). Further statistical analyses (detailed in Cross et al., 2009a) indicated that the neural responses within these two regions did not differentiate between videos that were danced or watched, but responded more strongly to videos that had been trained in either of these manners compared to videos that were untrained and observed only during scanning. When considered together, the imaging analyses from this study suggest that, at least among our sample of novice dancers, physical and observational learning share more commonalities than differences at a neural level.

In a new study, we attempted to further explore how different kinds of experience shape perception (Kirsch and Cross, 2015). Using an updated approach to our previous study (Cross et al., 2009b), we again recruited novice dancers and this time we taught them far more sophisticated dance sequences using the *Dance Central 2* video game for Xbox, and the Xbox Kinect motion-tracking system to quantify full-body dance performance. In this study we specifically sought to investigate the additive effects of combining training modality, and thus focused on comparisons between: sequences with which participants had no experience; sequences for

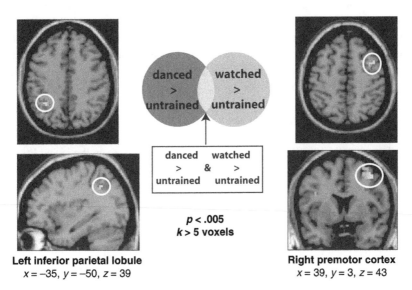

danced > untrained
watched > untrained

danced > untrained & watched > untrained

$p < .005$
$k > 5$ voxels

Left inferior parietal lobule
$x = -35, y = -50, z = 39$

Right premotor cortex
$x = 39, y = 3, z = 43$

Figure 11.4 Brain regions that respond to physical and observational learning in
novice dancers. Two regions of particular interest that demonstrated
similar patterns of activity when novice dancers watched dance
videos they had trained on throughout the week, or merely passively
observed, are illustrated here on a rendered cortical surface of a
standard brain from the Montreal Neurological Institute (MNI).

which they had heard the soundtrack only (unimodal experience); sequences they
watched and listened to the music (bimodal experience); and sequences they saw,
listened to the music, and physically practiced (multimodal experience). Echoing
the findings we reported in the earlier study (Cross et al., 2009b), we found that
participants learned best when all three modalities were present during practice, and
that responses within three core AON regions (left premotor cortex, left superior
temporal gyrus and right intraparietal cortex) were stronger the more modalities
participants used to learn. In other words, these brain regions displayed: the most
engagement when participants watched sequences that they had physically practiced
that also included audiovisual information; less engagement when watching
sequences that they had previously only watched and listened to the music; less
engagement again when watching sequences they had only heard the soundtrack to
during training; and least engagement when watching sequences that were entirely
untrained/unfamiliar. Moreover, we extended previous findings by demonstrating
that the magnitude of response within the left premotor cortex (and to a lesser
extent, the left intraparietal cortex) was positively correlated with how well participants learned during the bimodal and multimodal training conditions (Kirsch
and Cross, 2015).

The converging evidence from behavioral and brain data from both of these
studies (Cross et al., 2009b; Kirsch and Cross, 2015) serves to link the rich history

of behavioral research on observational learning with the burgeoning field of neuroimaging inquiry into action cognition. We found it especially noteworthy that such clear evidence emerged for observational learning in light of the fact that participants were never explicitly told to try and learn the sequences they watched during each training day. Indeed, evidence from other studies suggests that the amount of observational learning we reported in this study could have been markedly increased if we had explicitly instructed participants to try and learn the sequences they watched during the training procedures (e.g., Hodges et al., 2007; Mattar and Gribble, 2005).

These results are generally in agreement with findings from the extant literature on complex action representations in the brain (e.g., Cross, Hamilton and Grafton, 2006; Calvo-Merino et al, 2005; Brown, Martinez and Parsons, 2006), which suggest that the AON, particularly parietal and premotor components of this network, is modulated by experience. The two studies described here make several novel contributions to this literature through inclusion of two critical control conditions, namely, the use of an 'untrained' experimental condition in addition to the danced and watched conditions (and the music-only condition in the most recent study), and the inclusion of a pre-training scanning session. The inclusion of the pre-training scan is an especially valuable contribution, as it enabled us to quantify the effects of the dance training manipulation with greater precision than we were able to do in the study by Cross and colleagues (2006).

Of course, these findings are not without their limitations. The most serious limitation stems from our use of a within-subjects experimental design. A valid criticism of this design is that observational learning does not occur in a purely observational context, since all of our novice dance participants were also learning to dance particular sequences during the same sessions that they passively observed different sequences. However, we believe that our results are not invalidated by this criticism, as evidenced by dance performance scores and neural responses to stimuli from the untrained experimental condition. Put simply, if the skills participants were learning in the training condition that included physical practice broadly generalized to all similar kinds of tasks, then we would have expected participants to be able to physically perform the dance sequences in *all* the training conditions that did not include physical practice equally well (including the audio-visual-experience training condition, auditory-experience-only training condition and the untrained conditions). The behavioral and neuroimaging findings from both studies demonstrate that this was clearly not the case: instead, several regions of the AON responded in a similar manner to learning achieved by physical practice and by audiovisual experience alone, and this pattern was also reflected in the behavioral findings. At present, myriad avenues remain open for future research to explore regarding the parameters that influence how different kinds of visual, physical (and auditory) learning shape behavioral and brain responses, including: how motivation or intention to learn shapes learning; which part of the physical model provides the most information for learning a new skill; and how different kinds of instructions might influence observational learning.

Learning from human vs. non-human cues

Another feature of action cognition that we examined with the same novice dancers from one of the studies described in the previous section (Cross et al., 2009b) was the specificity of the AON to learning from other humans, as compared to learning from abstract symbols. In the past, several different functions have been proposed for the AON, including; action prediction (Kilner, Friston and Frith, 2007; Prinz, 1997; 2006; Schütz-Bosbach and Prinz, 2007), action understanding (Rizzolatti and Fadiga, 1998; Rizzolatti et al., 1996b; Rizzolatti, Fogassi and Gallese, 2001), inferring the intention of others (Fogassi et al., 2005; Hamilton and Grafton, 2006; Kilner, Marchant and Frith, 2006), and social cognition (Iacoboni and Dapretto, 2006). Previous imaging studies have not directly compared these functions within the same experiments in order to determine whether different components of this network might serve specific, individual functions. One particularly unsettled issue is whether or not this network responds exclusively, or even preferentially, to observation of actions performed by other humans. For example, one could imagine that it is simpler to learn how to dance the *Macarena* from watching another person perform it than by following stick figure depictions, Laban notation or a computer simulation of the movements. One factor that can help determine whether the AON responds to the actions cued by other humans, *per se*, is whether it responds when actions are cued symbolically or only to observation of another person performing the action. Moreover, if the AON tracks the correspondence between observed and executable actions, then manipulating the degree to which an observed action can be readily mapped onto an observer's body should also affect the level of activity in the AON. One way this can be evaluated is by varying the amount of direct experience one has with performing an observed action, as well as the physical stimuli used to cue particular actions. To accomplish this, we used the same novel dance training paradigm introduced above to determine the extent to which activity within the AON is driven by an observer's prior experience with an action, as compared to how readily an action cue can be mapped onto an observer's body.

If the AON tracks the similarity between an observed agent or action and the observer, we might expect it to show a preference for biological motion stimuli, as some data from manual action studies suggests (e.g., Kessler et al., 2006; Tai et al., 2004; Brass et al., 2000). Kessler and colleagues (2006) showed that left premotor and bilateral parietal and superior temporal cortices were more active while participants performed a finger tapping movement cued by a video of a finger tapping compared to a dot moving over the specific digit in a still photograph of a hand. It was suggested that these regions are likely working together (along with several other subcortical regions) to prime the brain to respond faster when imitating biological movement compared to symbolically cued movement. Tai and colleagues observed greater activity within the left premotor cortex when participants watched grasping actions performed by a human actor rather than a robot model, which led them to conclude that the AON is specifically tuned to observation of biological movements (Tai et al., 2004).

The notion that the AON responds preferentially to human, biological action cues compared to non-biological action cues remains controversial, however. For example, several studies demonstrate that the AON responds to non-biological stimuli in a similar manner as to biological stimuli (Gazzola et al., 2007; Press et al., 2005). In one such study, participants were shown videos of dance movements that featured either smooth, human-like motion or rigid, robotic-like motion, each performed by a human or a Lego robot (animated through the use of stop motion cinematography). We were interested in the extent to which human vs. robotic form and motion cues influenced perception. Somewhat surprisingly (and in contrast to what the majority of studies examining familiarity and AON engagement had shown), we found that the AON was clearly more engaged when participants watched robotic motion compared to smooth human motion, and that parietal portions of the AON also responded preferentially to robotic compared to human-form cues (Cross et al., 2012).

The inferences that can be drawn from this study, and indeed, a number of similar studies (e.g., Brass et al., 2000; Gazzola et al., 2007; Kessler et al., 2006; Press et al., 2005; Tai et al., 2004), are somewhat limited by participants' dissimilar amounts of experience or familiarity with the human and non-human action cues that they observe within the task. For example, participants in these previous studies were most likely very familiar with observing hands grasping objects in everyday life, but were probably less likely to come across robots grasping objects or abstract symbols cuing actions in their daily lives. In a training study performed by my team, we avoided confounding biological motion with familiarity through the use of intensive training procedures. Using this approach, participants were taught to perform novel dance sequences with both a human model and with symbolic action cues (see Figure 11.3a). Such a methodology enabled precise control of participants' familiarity and physical experience with the action stimuli that they observed while being scanned. This permitted a measure of brain responses during action observation where human vs. non-human motion could be studied independently from experience.

The objective of this study was to clarify the contributions of several key components of the AON to observation of action cues both with and without a human agent. Specifically, we tested whether the AON is driven by observation of other humans, or whether it is driven by observation of familiar or executable actions. We directly manipulated both the presence of a human dancer and participants' physical experience with the dance sequences. If the AON responds uniformly as a function of observing humans or experiencing, then we would expect stronger responses across all components of the AON when observing biological motion compared to non-biological motion (e.g., Kessler et al., 2006; Tai et al., 2004), and when observing trained compared to untrained sequences (e.g., Calvo-Merino et al., 2005; Cross, Hamilton and Grafton, 2006). However, if it is the case that individual components of the AON are sensitive to different kinds of experience, we would predict that distinct components of this system should respond differently based on experience and the presence of a biological agent.

The experimental procedures were identical to those described for our previous observational learning study (Cross et al., 2009b). One critical feature of the training stimuli that merits restating is that for all categories of stimuli (danced, watched and untrained), half of the videos featured an expert human model dancing the sequences along with the arrows, and half of the videos had only the arrows denoting the sequences without a human model. Interestingly, when we reanalyzed the behavioral performance data across the 5 days of dance training, a small but significant effect emerged as regards the presence of a human model. Participants' dance scores were marginally higher for sequences that included a human dancing along with the arrows (Cross et al., 2009a).

The imaging analyses for this objective pursued two aims: to determine the effects of the presence of a human model on AON responses, and to determine the effects of training. The three-by-two factorial design (see Figure 11.3a) was essentially distilled to a two-by-two factorial design for this portion of the study, with training (trained vs. untrained) and presence of human (human present vs. human absent) as the two factors of interest. Functional imaging data from the post-training scanning session revealed a strong activation within bilateral posterior temporal cortices when participants observed videos that had a human model present (see Figure 11.5a). A robust main effect of training was observed in the right PMv (see Figure 11.5b), suggesting that this area was sensitive to the effects of

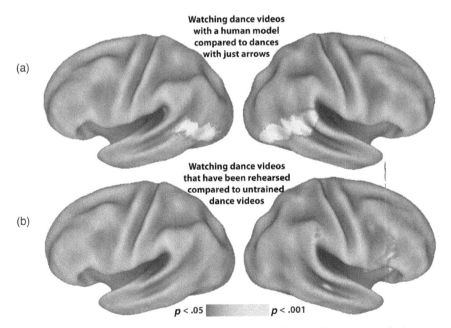

Figure 11.5 Brain regions in novice dancers that respond to: *(a)* the presence of a dancer on the screen (irrespective of dance training experience with the videos); and *(b)* the dance videos that the dancers have been trained to dance (independent of the presence or absence of a dancer on the screen).

training regardless of the training stimulus. However, bilateral posterior temporal cortices were uniquely sensitive to training stimulus.

Taken together, this pattern of results indicates that some parts of the AON respond preferentially to physical experience (PMv) while other parts respond specifically to the presence of a human model (posterior temporal cortex). The finding that PMv responds most strongly to cues for actions that have been physically experienced and not to the presence of a human model fits well with the subsequent data by our team investigating perception of human and robotic actions (Cross et al., 2012), and advances our understanding of what this region contributes to action cognition. Since the discovery of mirror neurons in an analogous region of monkey premotor cortex (Gallese et al., 1996; Rizzolatti et al., 1996a), several hypotheses have been put forward for the role of premotor cortex in motor and social cognition, including: predicting the ongoing actions of others (Kilner, Friston and Frith, 2007; Prinz, 1997; 2006; Schütz-Bosbach and Prinz, 2007; Wilson and Knoblich, 2005); inferring others' intentions (Fogassi et al., 2005; Hamilton and Grafton, 2006; Kilner, Marchant and Frith, 2006); and influencing social cognitive behaviors, including imitation and empathy (Iacoboni and Dapretto, 2006). A key question in distinguishing these hypotheses regards the responsiveness of PMv to biological and non-biological stimuli. For example, if it were the case that PMv plays a specific role in social cognition, then we would expect it to show stronger responses to observation of human actors. Results from previous studies of this issue have been mixed (Brass et al., 2000; Cross et al., 2012; 2013; Gazzola et al., 2007; Kessler et al., 2006; Press et al., 2005; Tai et al., 2004). Symbolically represented actions (e.g., using arrows as action cues) are an ideal way to separate human forms from action representations as the arrows do not resemble living agents but, following training, they are tied to specific motions. Thus, our data suggest that PMv does not respond specifically to human actions. Instead, PMv responses appear to be both flexible and dynamic, driven most strongly by action cues that are familiar from previous experience. This finding is in line with a theory advanced by Schubotz (2007), who suggests that activity within the premotor cortex during action observation serves to predict dynamic, ongoing and familiar events, regardless of whether or not they are performed by human bodies.

In contrast, temporal regions, including posterior superior temporal sulcus (pSTS) and inferior temporal gyrus (ITG), demonstrate an almost opposite response profile to PMv with respect to prior experience and the presence of a human model. These temporal regions responded most robustly to the presence of a human model, regardless of prior physical experience. A well-established literature has demonstrated robust activity within posterior temporal regions (including pSTS, pSTG and ITG) during observation of biological motion (Allison, Puce and McCarthy, 2000; Beauchamp et al., 2003; Grossman and Blake, 2002; Puce and Perrett, 2003). One interpretation is that pSTS and pSTG are critically involved in the automatic identification of animate entities in the environment at a very early level of visual processing (Schultz et al., 2005), which would have been particularly vital for our earlier ancestors in determining whether a flicker of movement might indicate the presence of a friend, foe or food. Reliable activation of STS during tasks designed to explore properties of action perception has resulted in the inclusion of STS as a component of the human mirror-neuron system (Gazzola et al., 2007; Iacoboni and Dapretto, 2006; Keysers and Gazzola, 2007; Kilner, Marchant and Frith, 2006). However, taking the present findings into account, it appears that STS's contribution to action resonance results from the observation of another human or biological form, not action cues. This result is consistent with recent data that demonstrate that observing and imagining moving shapes activates premotor and parietal components of the AON, but only observation of moving entities that participants construe as animate leads to STS activation (Wheatley, Milleville and Martin, 2007). We suggest that STS is involved in visual analysis of socially relevant conspecifics' actions, and this processing subsequently feeds into premotor and parietal mirror neuron areas. Therefore, we should not just consider STS to be an input to the AON, but should also recognize that it has distinct functions of its own, especially with regards to social cognition.

It is important to consider how these data relate to other studies that have reported contradictory results with respect to the AON's response to human and non-human action cues (Cross et al., 2012; 2013; Gazzola et al., 2007; Kessler et al., 2006; Tai et al., 2004). A persistent problem with previous studies examining questions of action resonance is the issue of familiarity or experience with the action being observed or cued (de Lange et al., 2008; Gazzola et al., 2007; Tai et al., 2004). Prior work performed with dancers has demonstrated that the more physically familiar an action is, the more the PMv responds when observing that action (Calvo-Merino et al., 2005; 2006; Cross, Hamilton and Grafton, 2006; Cross et al., 2009b). It is thus likely that the discrepant results concerning PMv activation in response to observation of actions featuring human and non-human cues are due to different degrees of experience with an action or action cue, and not the biological status of the agent, *per se*. In the study performed by my team (Cross et al., 2009a), we sidestepped this issue by training participants to perform complex sequences of dance movements that were entirely novel before the study began. Our findings that the premotor cortex responds more strongly to training than to the presence of a human model, and that posterior temporal areas respond to the presence of a human model but not to training, suggest that the AON comprises dissociable components involved in different aspects of action cognition. In particular, we suggest that activation of PMv does not necessarily reflect selective processing of human-related action stimuli, a finding further supported by our more recent work exploring the relationship between familiarity and AON engagement with dancing humans and Lego robots. Instead, the data reviewed in this section emphasize a role for motor familiarity in shaping AON, and also underscore the notion that the AON does not operate as a unitary network, but instead comprises individual nodes which contribute specialized functions to action cognition. Ongoing work by my team seeks to explore these ideas further by using connectivity-based analytical approaches to determine how observers' familiarity with observed dance sequences shapes the flow of information between the premotor, parietal and temporal nodes of the AON (e.g., Gardner, Goulden and Cross, 2015).

Implications and practical applications for dancers and beyond

At its essence, most of the research performed by my team is best described as basic science research seeking to delineate how experience shapes perception. However, we frequently turn to expert dancers as participants, or to dance-based paradigms to explore new learning, as dance requires highly adept sensorimotor integration and the ability to transform visual information into motor output. As such, for scientists, dance can be an extremely useful model for studying the perception and performance of 'movement for movement's sake'[1]. However, findings from this basic research might nonetheless inform the way dancers and dance instructors approach their work. With both expert and novice dancers, we observed that participants showed stronger and more finely tuned neural responses within sensorimotor areas of the brain when watching movements that had been previously physically experienced, or were rated as enjoyable to watch. These results are corroborated by data reported by Aglioti and colleagues (2008), who showed that only actual physical practice, which engenders embodied motor expertise, can transform an individual into a truly expert observer of skilled actions.

For teachers of dance, one suggestion might be to keep as active as possible in the instruction process, in terms of being able to perform all the desired movements at the most expert level possible. Although this suggestion might seem somewhat obvious and simple, it could facilitate an instructor's ability to more quickly and accurately diagnose and correct mistakes in dancers' movements. Intuitively, the research findings also suggest that dancers (particularly current dancers, as opposed to former dancers who have been out of the studio for years) might make the best dance instructors and evaluators, since their brains and bodies are highly (and regularly) practiced at matching action with perception.

For dancers, the research findings that could have the most appeal and potential for studio applications are those concerning physical, as compared to observational, learning (Cross et al., 2009a; Kirsch and Cross, 2015). Although it is the case that physical practice is more beneficial than mere observation for constructing neural and behavioral representations of new actions (e.g., Aglioti et al., 2008; Calvo-Merino et al., 2006; Frey and Gerry, 2006), it is nonetheless striking that simple observation can have significant effects on behavioral performance and activity within the AON (Cross et al., 2009b; Kirsch and Cross, 2015). This suggests that dancers can continue the learning process even while waiting at the side of the studio for a turn to execute a combination, or, more importantly, when unable to rehearse due to physical injury.

Indeed, Johnson-Frey (2004) presents a compelling case for speeded recovery from neurological injury (in this case, a cerebral vascular accident, or stroke) with the concomitant use of action observation and active action simulation, which is somewhat similar to the procedure we employed in our study with expert dancers. Recent work with healthy older adults learning to encode new motor memories lends additional support to the idea that observation of actions, in combination with physical performance, can lead to more robust memory traces and motor learning (Celnik et al., 2006). Considered together, this research suggests that observing can help dancers to maintain choreography in their bodies, and observing while simultaneously imagining themselves performing might aid this process even more, as well as potentially facilitate recovery from physical (or neurological) injury (see also Chapter 1).

Concluding remarks

As a final comment, it is important to note that 'dance neuroscience' research did not necessarily stem from a desire to investigate how the experience of being a dancer or watching dance influences the brain. Rather, neuroscientists have sought to work with dancers as they are an extremely valuable human resource in possession of a rich skill set that has often been honed for many years (if not decades), and whose expertise in the sensorimotor domain is a true asset for helping explore how the human brain negotiates the link between perception and action in new motor learning and skilled performance. More recently, exciting new interdisciplinary research ventures and funding opportunities are emerging that are opening new doors for more collaborative research between dancers and scientists from a number of different disciplines, many of which are explored in this book (see, for example, Chapter 13). Such interdisciplinary work holds great promise for advancing our understanding of the (neuro)science of art production, performance and evaluation, and ultimately what it means to be a member of a species that sees, feels, creates and is moved by movement.

Acknowledgements

The work described in this chapter was supported by the following funding for the author: a National Research Service Award from the National Institutes of Health, National Institute of Neurological Disorders and Stroke, a postdoctoral fellowship from the Alexander von Humboldt Foundation, a VENI award from the Netherlands Organisation for Scientific Research, a Marie Curie Career Integration Grant, and a Future Research Leader Award from the Economic and Social Research Council.

Note

1   Naturally I do not mean to imply that all dance is 'movement for movement's sake' – far from it! However, dance that is performed vs. dance that is studied in the (neuro)scientific research laboratory are often two very different things. Appreciating and articulating this distinction should hopefully lead to better understanding between dancers, scientists, and those of us who bridge these disciplines, in the future.

References

Aglioti, S. M., Cesari, P., Romani, M., & Urgesi, C. (2008). Action anticipation and motor resonance in elite basketball players. *Nat. Neurosci.,* 11(9), 1109–1116.
Allison, T., Puce, A., & McCarthy, G. (2000). Social perception from visual cues: Role of the STS region. *Trends Cogn. Sci.,* 4(7), 267–278.

Badets, A., Blandin, Y., & Shea, C. H. (2006). Intention in motor learning through observation. *Q. J. Exp. Psychol. (Colchester)*, 59(2), 377–386.

Bandura, A. (1977). *Social Learning Theory*. Englewood Cliffs, NJ: Prentice-Hall.

Bandura, A. (1986). *Social Foundations of Thought and Action: A social cognitive theory*. Englewood Cliffs, NJ: Prentice-Hall.

Barzouka, K., Bergeles, N., & Hatziharistos, D. (2007). Effect of simultaneous model observation and self-modeling of volleyball skill acquisition. *Percept. Mot. Skills*, 104(1), 32–42.

Beauchamp, M. S., Lee, K. E., Haxby, J. V., & Martin, A. (2003). FMRI responses to video and point-light displays of moving humans and manipulable objects. *J. Cogn. Neurosci.*, 15(7), 991–1001.

Binkofski, F., Amunts, K., Stephan, K. M., Posse, S., Schormann, T., Freund, H. J., & Seitz, R. J. (2000). Broca's region subserves imagery of motion: A combined cytoarchitectonic and fMRI study. *Hum. Brain Mapp.*, 11(4), 273–285.

Blandin, Y., Lhuisset, L., & Proteau, L. (1999). Cognitive processes underlying observational learning of motor skills. *Q. J. Exp. Psychol.: Hum. exp. psychol.*, 52A, 957–979.

Blandin, Y. & Proteau, L. (2000). On the cognitive basis of observational learning: Development of mechanisms for the detection and correction of errors. *Q. J. Exp. Psychol. A*, 53(3), 846–867.

Bouquet, C. A., Gaurier, V., Shipley, T., Toussaint, L., & Blandin, Y. (2007). Influence of the perception of biological or non-biological motion on movement execution. *J. Sports Sci.*, 25(5), 519–530.

Brass, M., Bekkering, H., & Prinz, W. (2001). Movement observation affects movement execution in a simple response task. *Acta Psychol. (Amst.)*, 106(1–2), 3–22.

Brass, M., Bekkering, H., Wohlschlager, A., & Prinz, W. (2000). Compatibility between observed and executed finger movements: Comparing symbolic, spatial, and imitative cues. *Brain Cogn.*, 44(2), 124–143.

Brass, M., Zysset, S., & von Cramon, D. Y. (2001). The inhibition of imitative response tendencies. *Neuroimage.*, 14(6), 1416–1423.

Brown, S., Martinez, M. J., & Parsons, L. M. (2006). The neural basis of human dance. *Cereb. Cortex*, 16(8), 1157–1167.

Buccino, G., Binkofski, F., Fink, G. R., Fadiga, L., Fogassi, L., Gallese, V., Seitz, R. J., Zilles, K., Rizzolatti, G., & Freund, H. J. (2001). Action observation activates premotor and parietal areas in a somatotopic manner: An fMRI study. *Eur. J. Neurosci.*, 13(2), 400–404.

Calvo-Merino, B., Glaser, D. E., Grèzes, J., Passingham, R. E., & Haggard, P. (2005). Action observation and acquired motor skills: An FMRI study with expert dancers. *Cereb. Cortex*, 15(8), 1243–1249.

Calvo-Merino, B., Grèzes, J., Glaser, D. E., Passingham, R. E., & Haggard, P. (2006). Seeing or doing? Influence of visual and motor familiarity in action observation. *Curr. Biol.*, 16(19), 1905–1910.

Calvo-Merino, B., Jola, C., Glaser, D. E., & Haggard, P. (2008). Towards a sensorimotor aesthetics of performing art. *Conscious. Cogn.*, 17(3), 911–922.

Celnik, P., Stefan, K., Hummel, F., Duque, J., Classen, J., & Cohen, L. G. (2006). Encoding a motor memory in the older adult by action observation. *Neuroimage.*, 29(2), 677–684.

Cross, E. S., Hamilton, A. F., & Grafton, S. T. (2006). Building a motor simulation de novo: Observation of dance by dancers. *Neuroimage.*, 31(3), 1257–1267.

Cross, E. S., Hamilton, A. F., Kraemer, D. J., Kelley, W. M., & Grafton, S. T. (2009a). Dissociable substrates for body motion and physical experience in the human action observation network. *Eur. J. Neurosci.,* 30(7), 1383–1392.

Cross, E. S., Kraemer, D. J., Hamilton, A. F., Kelley, W. M., & Grafton, S. T. (2009b). Sensitivity of the action observation network to physical and observational learning. *Cereb. Cortex,* 19(2), 315–326.

Cross, E. S., Liepelt, R., Hamilton, A. F. de C., Parkinson, J., Ramsey, R., Stadler, W., & Prinz, W. (2012). Robotic movement preferentially engages the action observation network. *Hum. Brain Mapp.,* 33(9), 2238–2254.

Cross, E. S., Stadler, W., Parkinson, J., Schutz-Bosbach, S., & Prinz, W. (2013). The influence of visual training on predicting complex action sequences. *Hum. Brain Mapp.,* 34(2), 467–486.

de Lange, F. P., Spronk, M., Willems, R. M., Toni, I., & Bekkering, H. (2008). Complementary systems for understanding action intentions. *Curr. Biol.,* 18(6), 454–457.

Dean, L. (1982). *Skylight.* Charleston, SC: Spoleto Festival USA.

Decety, J. (1996). Do imagined and executed actions share the same neural substrate? *Brain Res. Cogn. Brain Res.,* 3(2), 87–93.

Fadiga, L., Buccino, G., Craighero, L., Fogassi, L., Gallese, V., & Pavesi, G. (1999). Corticospinal excitability is specifically modulated by motor imagery: A magnetic stimulation study. *Neuropsychologia,* 37(2), 147–158.

Fadiga, L., Fogassi, L., Pavesi, G., & Rizzolatti, G. (1995). Motor facilitation during action observation: A magnetic stimulation study. *J. Neurophysiol.,* 73(6), 2608–2611.

Fogassi, L., Ferrari, P. F., Gesierich, B., Rozzi, S., Chersi, F., & Rizzolatti, G. (2005). Parietal lobe: From action organization to intention understanding. *Science,* 308(5722), 662–667.

Frey, S. H. & Gerry, V. E. (2006). Modulation of neural activity during observational learning of actions and their sequential orders. *J. Neurosci.,* 26(51), 13194–13201.

Gallese, V., Fadiga, L., Fogassi, L., & Rizzolatti, G. (1996). Action recognition in the premotor cortex. *Brain,* 119(Pt 2), 593–609.

Gardner, T., Goulden, N., & Cross, E. S. (2015). Dynamic modulation of the action observation network by movement familiarity. *J. Neurosci.,* 35(4), 1561–1572.

Gazzola, V., Rizzolatti, G., Wicker, B., & Keysers, C. (2007). The anthropomorphic brain: The mirror neuron system responds to human and robotic actions. *Neuroimage.,* 35(4), 1674–1684.

Grafton, S. T., Arbib, M. A., Fadiga, L., & Rizzolatti, G. (1996). Localization of grasp representations in humans by positron emission tomography. 2. Observation compared with imagination. *Exp. Brain Res. (Experimentelle Hirnforschung. Experimentation cerebrale),* 112(1), 103–111.

Grèzes, J. & Decety, J. (2001). Functional anatomy of execution, mental simulation, observation, and verb generation of actions: A meta-analysis. *Hum. Brain Mapp.,* 12(1), 1–19.

Grossman, E. D. & Blake, R. (2002). Brain areas active during visual perception of biological motion. *Neuron,* 35(6), 1167–1175.

Hamilton, A. F. & Grafton, S. T. (2006). Goal representation in human anterior intraparietal sulcus. *J. Neurosci.,* 26(4), 1133–1137.

Hamilton, A. D., Wolpert, D., & Frith U. (2004). Your own action influences how you perceive another person's action. *Curr. Biol.,* 14(6), 493–498.

Hodges, N. J., Williams, A. M., Hayes, S. J., & Breslin, G. (2007). What is modelled during observational learning? *J. Sports Sci.,* 25(5), 531–545.

Iacoboni, M. & Dapretto, M. (2006). The mirror neuron system and the consequences of its dysfunction. *Nat. Rev. Neurosci.,* 7(12), 942–951.

Iacoboni, M., Woods, R. P., Brass, M., Bekkering, H., Mazziotta, J. C., & Rizzolatti, G. (1999). Cortical mechanisms of human imitation. *Science,* 286(5449), 2526–2528.

Jeannerod, M. (2001). Neural simulation of action: A unifying mechanism for motor cognition. *Neuroimage.,* 14, S103–S109.

Johnson-Frey, S. H. (2004). Stimulation through simulation? Motor imagery and functional reorganization in hemiplegic stroke patients. *Brain Cogn.,* 55(2), 328–331.

Johnson-Frey, S. H., Maloof F. R., Newman-Norland, R., Farrer, C., Inati, S., & Grafton, S. T. (2003). Actions or hand-object interactions? Human inferior frontal cortex and action observation. *Neuron,* 39(6), 1053–1058.

Kessler, K., Biermann-Ruben, K., Jonas, M., Siebner, H. R., Baumer, T., Munchau, A., & Schnitzler, A. (2006). Investigating the human mirror neuron system by means of cortical synchronization during the imitation of biological movements. *Neuroimage.,* 33(1), 227–238.

Keysers, C. & Gazzola, V. (2007). Integrating simulation and theory of mind: From self to social cognition. *Trends Cogn. Sci.,* 11(5), 194–196.

Kilner, J. M., Friston, K. J., & Frith, C. D. (2007). Predictive coding: An account of the mirror neuron system. *Cogn. Process,* 8(3), 159–166.

Kilner, J. M., Marchant, J. L., & Frith, C. D. (2006). Modulation of the mirror system by social relevance. *Soc. Cogn. Affect. Neurosci.,* 1(2), 143–148.

Kilner, J. M., Paulignan, Y., & Blakemore, S. J. (2003). An interference effect of observed biological movement on action. *Curr. Biol.,* 13(6), 522–525.

Kirsch, L. P. & Cross, E. S. (2015). Additive routes to action learning: Layering experience shapes engagement of the action observation network. *Cereb. Cortex,* 25(12), 4799–4811.

Mattar, A. A. & Gribble, P. L. (2005). Motor learning by observing. *Neuron,* 46(1), 153–160.

Molenberghs, P., Cunnington, R., & Mattingley, J. B. (2012). Brain regions with mirror properties: A meta-analysis of 125 human fMRI studies. *Neurosci. Biobehav. Rev.,* 36(1), 341–349.

Press, C., Bird, G., Flach, R., & Heyes, C. (2005). Robotic movement elicits automatic imitation. *Brain Res. Cogn. Brain Res.,* 25(3), 632–640.

Prinz, W. (1997). Perception and action planning. *Eur. J. Neurosci.,* 9(2), 129–154.

Prinz, W. (2006). What re-enactment earns us. *Cortex,* 42(4), 515–517.

Puce, A. & Perrett, D. (2003). Electrophysiology and brain imaging of biological motion. *Philos. Trans. R. Soc. Lond. B Biol. Sci.,* 358(1431), 435–445.

Rizzolatti, G. & Craighero, L. (2004). The mirror-neuron system. *Annu. Rev. Neurosci.,* 27, 169–192.

Rizzolatti, G. & Fadiga, L. (1998). Grasping objects and grasping action meanings: The dual role of monkey rostroventral premotor cortex (area F5). *Novartis Found. Symp.,* 218, 81–95.

Rizzolatti, G., Fadiga, L., Gallese, V., & Fogassi, L. (1996a). Premotor cortex and the recognition of motor actions. *Brain Res. Cogn. Brain Res.,* 3(2), 131–141.

Rizzolatti, G., Fadiga, L., Matelli, M., Bettinardi, V., Paulesu, E., Perani, D., & Fazio, F. (1996b). Localization of grasp representations in humans by PET: 1. Observation versus execution. *Exp. Brain Res. (Experimentelle Hirnforschung. Experimentation cerebrale),* 111(2), 246–252.

Rizzolatti, G., Fogassi, L., & Gallese, V. (2001). Neurophysiological mechanisms underlying the understanding and imitation of action. *Nat. Rev. Neurosci.,* 2(9), 661–670.

Schmidt, R. A. (1975). A schema theory of discrete motor skill learning. *Psychol. Rev.,* 82, 225–260.

Schubotz, R. I. (2007). Prediction of external events with our motor system: Towards a new framework. *Trends Cogn. Sci.,* 11(5), 211–218.

Schultz, J., Friston, K. J., O'Doherty, J., Wolpert, D. M., & Frith, C. D. (2005). Activation in posterior superior temporal sulcus parallels parameter inducing the percept of animacy. *Neuron,* 45(4), 625–635.

Schütz-Bosbach, S. & Prinz, W. (2007). Prospective coding in event representation. *Cogn. Process.,* 8(2), 93–102.

Sheffield, F. D. (1961). Theoretical consideration in the learning of complex sequential task from demonstration and practice. In: A. A. Lumsdaine (Ed.), *Student Response in Programmed Instruction.* Washington, DC: National Academy of Sciences – National Research Council.

Stephan, K. M., Fink, G. R., Passingham, R. E., Silbersweig, D., Ceballos-Baumann, A. O., Frith, C. D., & Frackowiak, R. S. (1995). Functional anatomy of the mental representation of upper extremity movements in healthy subjects. *J. Neurophysiol.,* 73(1), 373–386.

Tai, Y. F., Scherfler, C., Brooks, D. J., Sawamoto, N., & Castiello, U. (2004). The human premotor cortex is 'mirror' only for biological actions. *Curr. Biol.,* 14(2), 117–120.

Wheatley, T., Milleville, S. C., & Martin, A. (2007). Understanding animate agents: Distinct roles for the social network and mirror system. *Psychol. Sci.,* 18(6), 469–474.

Wilson, M. & Knoblich, G. (2005). The case for motor involvement in perceiving conspecifics. *Psychol. Bull.,* 131(3), 460–473.

12 Knowing dance or knowing how to dance?

Sources of expertise in aesthetic appreciation of human movement

Guido Orgs, Beatriz Calvo-Merino and Emily S. Cross

A brief history of dance aesthetics

The study of how humans appreciate art has a long history in psychology. The first empirical investigations into aesthetic cognition were conducted in the late eighteenth century by Gustav Theodor Fechner (Fechner, 1876). Fechner studied optimal proportions in paintings ('the golden ratio') arguing that a 'bottom-up' scientific approach to aesthetics should aim to reveal general principles of human aesthetic judgement. Initially, the term 'aesthetics' was introduced by the philosopher Alexander Baumgarten. It is derived from the Greek word *aisthetikos* (meaning: 'I sense', 'I feel') and refers to 'sensual' as opposed to 'rational' cognition. Baumgarten believed that aesthetic judgements were entirely subjective and not accessible to empirical investigation (Hammermeister, 2002). Modern aesthetic science has primarily focussed on the visual arts and music (Berlyne, 1974; Shimamura and Palmer, 2012; Zajonc, 1968). Only a few attempts have been made to develop a theory of aesthetic perception in the performing arts, and more specifically, dance.

Kreitler and Kreitler (1972) argued that the aesthetic appeal of dance primary lies in 'remoteness from the habitual'. On this notion, dance movements are enjoyed because they are performed in such a way that people would not normally move. According to gestalt psychologist Rudolf Arnheim, aesthetic appreciations of dance should resemble the aesthetics of all other moving visual stimuli (Arnheim, 1974) and should depend on the gestalt laws of perceptual organisation, such as good continuation and symmetry. Importantly, he also emphasised the role of dynamic changes in movement speed and acceleration in movement aesthetics. In recent years, neuroaesthetics (Chatterjee and Vartanian, 2014; Pearce et al., 2016) have questioned such a purely visual approach to movement aesthetics. Even abstract visual art often makes references to human action and provides clues to the movements that were made by the artist to produce the artwork (Freedberg and Gallese, 2007; Sbriscia-Fioretti et al., 2013; Ticini et al., 2014). In the context of the performing arts, merely observing a dancer's movements evokes resonant brain activity in the brain of the spectator (Fadiga, Craighero and Olivier, 2005) that is indeed related to the aesthetic pleasure derived from watching other people move (Calvo-Merino et al., 2008; Jola et al., 2012; Kirsch, Dawson and Cross, 2015).

Dance as a social art form

Guido Orgs and colleaques (2016) have recently developed a neurocognitive model for studying human movement aesthetics that aims to combine different aspects of human movement in a single theoretical framework. The model emphasises the communication between a performer and a spectator as a key feature of dance and perhaps all performing arts. In any social interaction, information is exchanged between at least two people. In the context of conversation, Grice (1991) argues that this exchange of information requires cooperation between the speaker and the listener. In dance, information is primarily, though not exclusively, communicated through movement (Jola, Pollick and Calvo-Merino, 2014). Aesthetic appreciation of dance involves sharing ideas, feelings and intentions between performer and spectator via watching the performers' movements. Importantly, exchange of information in dance is often ambiguous and open to multiple interpretations. The pleasure derived from watching dance thus depends on the spectator's ability to perceive and understand the performers' intentions and emotions on the one hand, and the performer's ability to effectively express these intentions and emotions on the other hand (Hanna, 1983).

We can distinguish three components of the communicative process during a dance performance (Orgs, Caspersen and Haggard, 2016). The *dancer* transmits information to the *spectator* via the *movement message*. In turn the spectator acknowledges message transmission and understanding, for example by clapping at the end of the performance, or may even alter the course of the performance, for example in participatory contexts.

The performer

The performer conveys information to the audience by making body movements. The limits of what can be communicated through movement are set by the physical constraints of the human body. The increase in movement repertoire through dance training thus increases the number and quality of messages that can be communicated. As in conversation, the number of possible messages that can be exchanged non-verbally via movement can be termed the movement vocabulary (see Chapter 10). Dance styles are often characterised by fixed movement vocabularies, for example classical ballet. The movement vocabulary of the performer is expanded through training by adding new movements that were not previously possible or may involve perfecting movements that are made every day. In either case, the range of physical and emotional expression is increased (Christensen and Calvo-Merino, 2013). This idea resembles Rudolf Laban's specific exercises 'to develop the body as an instrument of expression' (Laban and Ullmann, 2011). Importantly, this definition of the purpose of dance training is not exclusive to any particular dance style or technique, but refers to a dancer's ability to effectively communicate intentions through movement. Becoming an effective transmitter of the message is thus an integral part of dance training, and perhaps all training in the performing arts.

The movement message

The movement message can be described in terms of its visual features, its action features and its social features. Visual, action and social features constitute the layers of the movement message and are associated with distinct neural processing mechanisms. Social features are derived from action features, and action features are derived from visual features of the movement message. Yet aesthetic appreciation of dance can occur at all three levels, depending on the appreciation style and the expertise of the spectator.

Visual, action and social features of movement

Visual features comprise the spatial organisation of dance movements of one or more dancers and how these spatial features unfold over time. Many of the visual features present in a dance performance are not necessarily specific to dance but are shared by all visual displays. As a visual stimulus, dance can be conceptualised as at least three levels of representation; the static postural level, the dynamic level and the structural level (Orgs, Hagura and Haggard, 2013). The static level comprises a set of body postures (see Chapter 7). Aesthetic perception of these static features will depend on the same principles that govern aesthetic perception of all visual stimuli. These include, for example, balance of composition and symmetry (Arnheim, 1974; McManus, 1980; 2005; McManus and Weatherby, 1997; Sammartino and Palmer, 2012) and posture geometry. For example, vertical ballet postures are preferred to more horizontal postures (Daprati, Iosa and Haggard, 2009). Next, the dynamic level comprises movements considered as transitions from one posture to another. Aesthetic evaluation at this level might depend on factors such as speed, movement direction and effort (Christensen and Calvo-Merino, 2013; Laban and Ullmann, 2011). For example, movements with a smooth, predictable movement path are preferred to jerky movement paths with changes of movement direction between every posture (Orgs, Hagura and Haggard, 2013). Other dynamic parameters of movement aesthetics include the speed at which turns are performed, movement amplitude and the presence of jumps (Calvo-Merino et al., 2008; Torrents et al., 2013). For groups of dancers, dynamic visual features will further include movement symmetry and synchrony between dancers (Brick and Boker, 2011; Vicary et al., 2017). Finally, at a structural level, individual movements can be arranged into longer phrases, following compositional rules (Opacic, Stevens and Tillmann, 2009; Orgs, Hagura and Haggard, 2013; Schiffer and Schubotz, 2011). Sequential symmetry is frequently used in the composition of dynamic artworks such as music (Koelsch et al., 2013; Kuhn and Dienes, 2005; Rohrmeier et al., 2015) and poetry (Jiang et al., 2012). In choreography, similar rules can be applied to arrange movement elements into longer sequences.

Action features include goals and intentions of the observed movement. Action features are inferred and predicted from movement kinematics (Giese and Poggio, 2003; Kilner and Lemon, 2013; Obhi and Sebanz, 2011; Sartori, Becchio and Castiello, 2011). For example, observers readily predict jumping height from the few steps that precede the jump (Ramenzoni et al., 2008) or use kinematic cues to detect deception (Sebanz and Shiffrar, 2009). Action features are thus perceptually inferred from visual features.

Movement also communicates *social features*. Emotions such as joy, sadness and anger can be accurately discriminated from the abstract movements of one arm only and are associated with distinct kinematic parameters (Pollick et al., 2001; Sawada, Suda and Ishii, 2003; Van Dyck et al., 2014). Emotion can be also recognised in dance (Christensen et al., 2014; 2016). Static body postures and visually impoverished point-light displays of a person moving provide reliable cues for specific emotions (Atkinson, Tunstall and Dittrich, 2007). In point-light displays, a human figure is reduced to a set of dots, typically positioned across joints. The configural motion of these dots gives a vivid impression of a person moving, in the absence of any available information about body shape. Interestingly, high intensity emotions are more easily identified from bodily, as compared to facial, expressions (Aviezer, Trope and Todorov, 2012). Moreover, observers readily distinguish between cooperative or competitive action goals based on movement kinematics (Obhi and Sebanz, 2011; Sacheli et al., 2012; 2013).

The social features of dance may play an important role in communicating social signals to other performers and spectators. For example, dancing in synchrony increases group affiliation (Reddish, Fischer and Bulbulia, 2013; Tarr et al., 2015; von Zimmermann et al., 2018) and memory for other group members (Woolhouse, Tidhar and Cross, 2016). Hagen and Bryant (2003) argue that dance and music fulfil an evolutionary function in 'coalition signalling'. Groups of performers moving in skilful synchrony signal to spectators that they are closely affiliated to each other and work together efficiently. A recent study (Vicary et al., 2017) directly measured the effect of movement synchrony on aesthetic perception of dance in live contemporary dance performances. In line with an evolutionary function of communicating social signals between groups of spectators and groups of performers, Vicary and colleagues (2017) indeed show that continuous rating of enjoyment are predicted by changes in movement synchrony among a group of dance performers. Importantly, *how* performers coordinated their movements was a better predictor of aesthetic judgements than *how much* the performers moved. These findings therefore support a layering of movement features. Visual and action features are the building blocks of the social features of dance.

The spectator

Visual, action and social features are processed by the spectator's brain. Aesthetic appreciation and aesthetic judgement thus require understanding of the psychological and brain mechanisms that process these different features of the movement message. One important constraint of communicating this information is the spectator's expertise with the movement that is being watched. In the case of dance, we can distinguish at least three sources of expertise. The first is the spectator's visual expertise with the observed movement: visual familiarity depends on how often the same or similar movements have been observed before. It also depends on experience with watching specific dance styles and vocabularies. For example, a regular spectator of ballroom dance will gain substantial visual experience with a specific set of partner dances such as the Viennese waltz, but will gain very little visual experience in watching other dances that are not part of this specific set, for example Indian Kathak. The second source of expertise is unique to aesthetic perception of bodies and human movement and relates to the motor familiarity with the observed movement. For example, a hiphop dancer who participates in a dance battle will not only have previously seen the movements that the other dancers are performing, but will also be able to perform the same or similar movements. The ability to perform observed actions alters how these actions are perceived and engages a distinct set of brain regions, as we will see in the next sections of this chapter.

Finally, the spectator's aesthetic response to a dance performance will depend on knowledge about how the specific dance piece was created. A dance piece that involves a specific series of fixed steps and a narrative will be judged not only based on the current performance that the spectator is watching, but also on other performances of the same piece that the spectator may have seen before. These specific realisations of choreographic score by a different cast or staged by a different choreographer may vary considerably. Frequent spectators may therefore have very specific expectations as to how a performance 'should look'. In contrast, a dance piece that is primarily composed of improvised movement does not easily allow for such comparisons. Dance making is a complex process and can involve a multitude of techniques, tools and compositional approaches (see http://motionbank.org for examples from contemporary choreography; see also Chapters 4 and 5). Novices to dance may not be aware of these varied approaches to dance making and choreography, and in contrast to much of visual art (Tinio, 2013), it is not possible to reconstruct the creative process of dance making by watching a performance of the choreographic work. Any movement observed may be either preconceived and form part of a fixed series of steps, or may be improvised or performance-specific and never be performed in the exact same way again.

Brain mechanisms relevant for movement aesthetics

Neuroaesthetics aims to link aesthetic perception to brain structure and function (Chatterjee and Vartanian, 2014; Zeki and Lamb, 1994). The neural mechanisms of aesthetic perception of dance are related to the neural correlates of perceiving others' movement. These involve a wide range of brain areas including the visual cortex, but also motor, premotor and parietal brain areas (Grosbras, Beaton and Eickhoff, 2012; Orgs et al., 2015). Neuroscientific research has identified specialised, yet overlapping, processing pathways for perception of; (a) static visual bodies, (b) human movement kinematics and (c) inferring intentions and emotions from other people's actions.

'Visual' areas for body and movement aesthetic perception

The human brain has dedicated areas for processing all kinds of moving stimuli, including both animate objects such as bodies, but also inanimate objects and abstract shapes. Semir Zeki (1998) argues that these mechanisms are also important for the aesthetics of (non-biological) motion. Specifically, some patterns of motion are particularly powerful in activating visual motion areas, such as V5/MT+. Zeki and Stutters (2012) showed that the preference for specific patterns of motion for abstract visual stimuli scales with the activation of motion-sensitive brain areas. Although this experiment was conducted using simple white dots moving on a black background, and did not contain any displays of the human body, similar principles of grouping dancers on stage are applied in choreography and are likely to contribute to the visual appeal of watching dance.

A number of brain areas have been shown to be important for neural processing of both static and dynamic features of human motor action. These include the Extra-striate Body Area (EBA) and the Fusiform Body Area (FBA) (Orgs et al., 2015; Orlov, Makin and Zohary, 2010; Urgesi et al., 2007). Whereas EBA primarily responds to body parts (Downing and Peelen, 2011; Vangeneugden et al., 2014), visual body representations in FBA are supposedly more configural and more closely related to the subjective percept (Bernstein et al., 2014; Ewbank et al., 2011; Orgs et al., 2015; Taylor and Downing, 2011). Moreover, activity in these body-specific areas is modulated by whether actions are neutral or display emotions (de Gelder, de Borst and Watson, 2015; Pichon, de Gelder and Grèzes, 2012). Specifically, angry body postures produce greater neural responses, presumably due to their evolutionary relevance for survival.

EBA and the ventral premotor cortex (vPMC) contribute to aesthetic preferences for body postures (Calvo-Merino et al., 2010b). In this study, pairs of body postures were presented while transcranial magnetic stimulation (TMS) was applied over both brain areas. For each pair, observers judged which body posture they preferred. Relative preferences were compared to an aesthetic baseline judgement for each body posture. Stimulating both EBA and vPMC independently altered aesthetic preferences relative to the baseline. Participants' aesthetic judgements were more consistent with their baseline ratings when EBA was stimulated relative to vPMC. In contrast to the study by Zeki and Stutters (2012), this pattern of results suggests that there is no simple linear relationship between the activity in one of these areas and aesthetic judgements. In the study by Calvo-Merino and colleagues (2010b), stimulating across both sites did not simply increase or decrease liking for these body stimuli. Instead, participants' preferences were less aesthetically sensitive, suggesting a more complex relationship between motor resonance and aesthetic judgements. This was the first study that employed TMS to modify aesthetic preference, and therefore shows a causal relationship between aesthetic judgement and processing of visual and action features in specific brain areas.

Aside from EBA and FBA, research using point-light walkers shows that the superior temporal sulcus (STS) is causally involved in recognising human movement (Blake and Shiffrar, 2007; Puce and Perrett, 2003; Vangeneugden et al., 2014). Similar to movement processing in EBA/FBA, activity in the posterior part of the superior temporal sulcus (pSTS) distinguishes between different emotions, suggesting an increased response of pSTS to expressive, as compared to non-expressive, movement (Grèzes et al., 2013; Pichon, de Gelder and Grèzes, 2012).

Further support for the role of STS in processing emotion comes from a recent study by Grèzes and colleagues, where the authors demonstrated structural connections between STS and the amygdala, one of the primary subcortical brain structures implicated in emotional processing (Grèzes et al., 2014). The STS is also associated with multisensory integration. Chen and colleagues (2009) suggest a close association between musical rhythm perception and movement coordination within the superior temporal gyrus, and identify this region as an important node for facilitating auditory–motor interaction in the context of rhythm (Chen, Penhune and Zatorre, 2009). A recent study that coupled sensorimotor dance training with pre- and post-training using functional magnetic resonance imaging (fMRI) scans to investigate how dance learning shapes observers' aesthetic preferences sheds further light on the role of this brain region in aesthetics (Kirsch, Dawson and Cross, 2015). The authors of this study found that a portion of the left STS showed greater engagement when participants watched movements they had not only observed but also practiced. Crucially, learning to perform these movements also increased aesthetic preference for these movements, relative to pre-training. Increased engagement of STS following training might reflect a binding of auditory, visual and motor experience to produce a more pleasurable and emotional experience for the perceiver.

'Motor' areas for body and movement aesthetic perception

Several brain areas traditionally associated with motor rather than perceptual functions are sensitive to observing other people's actions. Both premotor and motor areas are part of the classically defined human mirror-neuron system (MNS: see also Chapter 10). The MNS shows similar responses when observing and executing specific motor actions (Gazzola and Keysers, 2009; Rizzolatti and Sinigaglia, 2010). Such internal 'motor resonance' (Fadiga, Craighero and Olivier, 2005) fulfils a number of important functions and contributes to action understanding, action prediction and imitation learning (Keysers and Gazzola, 2014; Kilner, Friston and Frith, 2007). Recent studies have suggested that it may also participate during the aesthetic appreciation of dance (Calvo-Merino et al., 2008; Jola and Grosbras, 2013; Kirsch, Dawson and Cross, 2015).

Motor brain areas support action perception, for example when the movement stimulus is incomplete, lacking in information of bodily shape (Schütz-Bosbach and Prinz, 2007) or movement dynamics (Stevens et al., 2000; Orgs et al., 2015). Vivid perceptions of movement can result from watching purely static sequences of body postures (Orgs et al., 2011; Orgs and Haggard, 2011; Orgs, Kirsch and Haggard, 2013). In a recent imaging study, Orgs and colleagues (2015) showed that this reconstruction indeed involves primary and supplementary motor areas. Moreover, seeing such apparent biological motion was associated with increased functional connectivity between these motor areas and FBA. Motor resonance therefore does not only help to extract action features from the visual movement stimulus itself, but also reconstructs visual features based on existing motor representations of the observed movement.

Recent studies suggest a role of motor and premotor areas in aesthetic perception beyond dance. According to an embodied simulation account of aesthetics (Freedberg and Gallese, 2007; Sbriscia-Fioretti et al., 2013; Ticini et al., 2014; Umiltà et al., 2012), the simulation of actions, emotions and corporeal sensations provoked by a particular art form brings about an aesthetic experience. By allowing embodiment of the actions depicted on a canvas, sensorimotor brain regions contribute to the aesthetic evaluation of a given artwork and underpin a spectator's empathic response towards visual and performative art.

When considering further the role of the MNS in aesthetic evaluation, research investigating dance has contributed a number of important insights (Christensen and Calvo-Merino, 2013; Cross and Ticini, 2012; Jola, Ehrenberg and Reynolds, 2012; Orgs, Caspersen and Haggard, 2016). Calvo-Merino and colleagues were the first to use human neuroscience tools to investigate brain processes underlying an observer's aesthetic experience of watching dance (Calvo-Merino et al., 2008). They built on previous work using static images or limited body movement by investigating the relationship between activity within sensorimotor cortices and watching dance and giving aesthetic judgments. Functional MRI scans of non-dancers' brains were recorded while they viewed ballet and capoeira movements performed by professional dancers. Later, the same participants were invited back into the laboratory to rate each video stimulus on five aesthetic dimensions: complexity of the action, how interesting it was, whether it looked tense or relaxed, weak or powerful, and how much the participant liked or disliked the movement. The study found greater activation in bilateral occipital cortices and in the right premotor cortex while participants watched dance movements to which they later assigned high liking ratings (as an average group mean), in comparison to dance movements that received low average liking ratings. It is of note that no other dimension of aesthetics than liking was associated with differential neural responses during dance observation. The authors concluded that visual and sensorimotor areas play a role in an automatic aesthetic response to dance, in terms of how much spectators enjoy watching a movement. Furthermore, Cross and colleagues (2011) demonstrated stronger engagement of parietal portions of the MNS when dance-naïve observers watched dance movements they rated as both highly enjoyable to watch, and extremely difficult to reproduce (Cross et al., 2011). These findings emphasise the importance of action features in aesthetic appreciation of dance. Preferring movements that cannot be performed implies that the spectator performs aesthetic judgements in relation to his/her own motor repertoire. The spectator's experience of dance thus depends on prior knowledge and experience with both action and visual features of the movement message.

Aesthetics, expertise and brain plasticity

The neural mechanisms of perceiving and understanding other people's actions are not fixed, but depend on prior experience with the movements that are being observed (Calvo-Merino et al., 2006; Gardner, Goulden and Cross, 2015; Kirsch and Cross, 2015; Orgs et al., 2008). In the case of dance, this prior experience can take on at least three forms that constitute the spectator's expertise (as has been sketched at the beginning of this chapter). Firstly, they will depend on the viewer's visual experience, or expertise with the visual features of a movement. Secondly, brain mechanisms of motor simulation and action recognition will be shaped by the viewer's own motor repertoire. Actions that can be performed by the spectator will be processed differently than actions that cannot be performed by the spectator. Finally, aesthetic appreciation of a dance performance will depend on the spectator's conceptual expertise, his/her knowledge about dance making and its cultural history (Bullot and Reber, 2013; Leder and Nadal, 2014).

Perceptual familiarity

Aesthetic perception will depend on whether postures, movements and sequential structure are visually familiar to the spectator. The influence of perceptual familiarity on aesthetic judgement is well documented in the 'mere exposure effect' (Bornstein, 1989; Zajonc, 1968). Mere exposure increases the efficiency and speed of cognitive processing. Processing fluency theory states that the experience of cognitive fluency is pleasant; familiar stimuli should thus be preferred to unfamiliar stimuli (Reber, Schwarz and Winkielman, 2004). Movements that have been watched frequently should thus be preferred to movements that have been seen less frequently (Orgs, Hagura and Haggard, 2013).

The influence of perceptual familiarity on the spectator can explain why people prefer specific movement styles. This argument is particularly strong if a movement style relies on a relatively restricted movement vocabulary, as in classical ballet. This is because a restricted movement vocabulary will usually imply more repetitions of the same or similar movements, thereby increasing their perceptual familiarity. Initially unpopular dance styles may gain widespread recognition over time, the more often the artistic works are being staged and experienced. One example is Stravinsky's *Rite of Spring*, first staged by the Ballets Russes in 1913, which was rejected by the public when it premiered, but is now regarded as a masterpiece (Berg, 1988). Interestingly, such long-term changes in aesthetic appreciation also apply to specific visual features of dance movement. For example, ballet postures have become more extreme over the course of many years (Daprati, Iosa and Haggard, 2009). Changes in perceptual familiarity can thus partially explain long-term 'Zeitgeist' effects in aesthetic appreciation (Carbon, 2010). Using transcranial magnetic stimulation during live dance performances (Jola, Ehrenberg and Reynolds, 2012; Jola and Grosbras, 2013) showed that visual experience with a movement vocabulary such as ballet increases cortico-spinal excitability (see Chapter 13).

Perceptual familiarity does not only influence aesthetic appreciation for the exact same movements, but also for similar movements with a similar arrangement or structure. Studies on 'structural mere exposure' have shown that familiarity with visual and auditory sequence structure increases preference for the same sequences and new sequences that are arranged according to the same rules (Gordon and Holyoak, 1983; Kuhn and Dienes, 2005; Newell and Bright, 2001; Opacic, Stevens and Tillmann, 2009; Rohrmeier and Rebuschat, 2012; Zizak and Reber, 2004). In one of these studies (Orgs, Hagura and Haggard, 2013), participants were exposed to sequences of seven body postures. These body postures were either arranged to produce a smooth, predictable movement path or a jerky movement path with multiple reversals of movement direction. Additionally, body postures were either arranged in a symmetrical or asymmetrical sequential order. Following an initial exposure phase to either symmetrical or asymmetrical sequences, participants with no prior experience in dance judged how much they liked each movement sequence. In both exposure groups, fluent symmetrical movement sequences were preferred to all other sequences and their aesthetic appeal did not change depending on whether these sequences had been watched before. This finding suggests that simple stimuli are generally preferred to complex ones, and fits with aesthetic accounts of ease of processing fluency and gestalt principles. Smooth, symmetrical movements are preferred to complex, jerky and asymmetrical movements because they are more predictable and more easily perceived and recognised. However, for jerky and asymmetrical sequences, the study observed a 'structural mere exposure effect'. Liking for these movement sequences increased with prior experience, suggesting that movements that are initially disliked due to their high complexity and unpredictability become more enjoyable the more often they are seen. Importantly, observers in this study did not learn how to perform these movements. Repeated visual exposure only was sufficient to make these initially 'ugly' movement sequences more appealing. Unusual and more complex arrangements of movement therefore require repeated exposure to become enjoyable.

The brain has dedicated mechanisms that process stimulus structure and meaning of movement sequences. Electroencephalogram (EEG) studies using goal-directed everyday actions such as preparing coffee showed that expectation violation in the action domain are comparable to those in the language domain and are associated with similar neural correlates of semantic surprise (Maffongelli et al., 2015; Proverbio and Riva, 2009). Amoruso and colleagues (2014) showed that event-related potentials (ERPs) are sensitive to the perception of choreographic 'errors' in tango performance. Similarly, Ahlheim and colleages (2014) showed that observers are indeed sensitive to surprise in a function of the probability of action steps within an action sequence. In an fMRI experiment participants observed another person assembling objects according to a fixed set of arbitrary rules that were unknown to the observers. Following an exposure session, observers were able to predict movement transitions based on having acquired some knowledge of the underlying compositional rules. Importantly, activation in the anterior intra parietal sulcus (aIPS) scaled with the conditional surprise elicited by these action sequences, suggesting an involvement of the human MNS in learning and extracting sequential structure from action sequences. For observing dance movement, violations of the progression of the movement sequences have also been related to activity in the basal ganglia (Schiffer and Schubotz, 2011).

To summarise, the effects of familiarity with static, dynamic and sequential visual aspects of observed movement do not necessarily require that the spectator possesses action expertise with the movements that are being observed. Rather, surprise and aesthetic pleasure in this context depends on the spectator's prediction of 'what comes next'.

Motor familiarity

The size of the movement vocabulary in dance is set by the physical constraints of the human body and the stylistic and compositional decisions of the choreographer. Professional dancers have typically undergone years of specialised training in order to expand their motor repertoire. In dance performances that involve professional dancers, most spectators will not be able to perform the movements that they are observing. Typically, the spectator does not command the same motor repertoire as the dancer. However, if visual motion perception is an 'embodied process', in the sense of linking the observed actions of others to one's own motor repertoire, then the receiver must have the capacity to make the movement they observe (Aglioti et al., 2008; Calvo-Merino et al., 2005; 2006; Cross, Hamilton and Grafton, 2006; Gardner, Goulden and Cross, 2015; Kirsch and Cross, 2015; Orgs et al., 2008). Even though frequent spectators of dance performance may acquire substantial visual expertise with the observed movements, they will not acquire motor familiarity. To acquire motor familiarity, actions need to be performed (Casile and Giese, 2006; Catmur et al., 2011; Cook et al., 2014). Movements with low motor familiarity might therefore be less aesthetically pleasant than movements for which the observer has the corresponding motor representation (Beilock and Holt, 2007; Topolinski, 2010).

Interestingly, Calvo-Merino and colleagues (2010a) showed that experts and non-experts used a different style of visual processing during observing dance. Expert dancers familiar with the observed dance move perceived the movements in a holistic manner, while non-experts engaged in a more analytical visual analysis of the observed action. Despite the initially different visual processing of the perceived dance, everybody can enjoy a dance performance even if the type of visual processing they use may depend of their level of experience. Yet spectators clearly enjoy skill and virtuosity across dance styles, from breakdance to ballet. Indeed, some studies in movement aesthetics even suggest an inverse relation between motor familiarity and preference. The more spectacular a movement is, the more likely it is to be liked (Calvo-Merino et al., 2008). Similarly, contorted body postures are preferred to less contorted body postures (Cross et al., 2010). Aesthetic appreciation of movements that cannot be performed by the observer is in line with both the remoteness from the habitual as well as the artistic notion of virtuosity. Indeed, Cross and colleagues (2011) report an inverse relationship between the estimated ability to perform a movement and its preference. Movements that were rated low for feasibility were preferred to movements that scored higher on feasibility. Interestingly, mere exposure accounts of aesthetic experience predict the opposite: familiar and feasible movements should be preferred to unfamiliar movements, as greater familiarity with a movement is associated with increased processing fluency (Beilock and Holt, 2007; Topolinski, 2010). In two recent studies designed to directly test the relationship between movement familiarity or feasibility and aesthetic preference, Kirsch and colleagues found that participants who physically train to perform particular dance movements report liking those movements more after training, as compared to before training (Kirsch, Drommelschmidt and Cross, 2013; Kirsch, Dawson and Cross, 2015). When these findings are considered in light of those by Cross and colleagues (2011) that show more liking for less familiar movements, we start to see that the relationship between physical aptitude and aesthetic preferences is likely much more complex than any one theory can capture.

In summary, existing studies have produced mixed findings on the relationship between motor familiarity and preference. Whereas some studies show that knowing how to perform a movement correlates positively with aesthetic preference, other studies suggest that novel and complex movements outside of the motor repertoire of the observer are actually preferred to known movements. Two opposing influences seem to be important in aesthetic appreciation of dance. On the one hand observers enjoy watching movement that are simple and easily mapped onto existing motor representations. On the other hand, observers enjoy watching movements that exhibit a high level of skill and virtuosity.

Dance-making knowledge

In creating dance performances, performers and choreographers often engage in a prolonged and highly collaborative artistic process (Kirsh, 2011; Kirsh et al., 2009). Staged choreographies result from an extended period of artistic research, rather than linearly from a single idea or intention. Some compositional decisions or tasks to develop movement material will be deliberately applied, and others may be purely intuitive (see Chapters 4 and 5).

Dance performances vary considerably with respect to their reproducibility. Many traditional dance performances involve a fixed series of steps that are supposedly performed in a consistent and similar way every time the performance is staged. Many classical and modern dance pieces fall into this category of fixed-step choreographies. At the other end of the spectrum, dance performances may be fully improvised, with a movement vocabulary that is never repeated across different performances. In this case, choreographies are often characterised by more flexible rules and tasks governing the movements that the performers execute on stage. Such task-based choreographies (e.g., by William Forsythe or Deborah Hay, see http://motionbank.org/) sometimes involve direct participation of the audience, producing an interactive and dynamic environment that emphasis communication between performers and spectators in both directions.

Aesthetic appreciation of dance performances will therefore not only depend on perceptual and motor familiarity with the movements that are being performed, but also by the conceptual knowledge of the spectator. Complexity and originality of improvised dance movements can only be appreciated if the spectator is aware that these movements are in fact improvised on the spot and do not follow a set sequential structure. As in other art forms, many contemporary dance works are often characterised by the absence of a story, a conventional movement vocabulary, music or professionally trained performers (Siegmund, 2006). A choreography primarily consisting of performers walking or running across the stage may induce high levels of motor familiarity, but will not be appreciated if it does not comply with the spectator's definition of what dance is, or should be (Vicary et al., 2017). The expertise of the spectator is therefore characterised by perceptual and motor experience with the movement message on the one hand, and conceptual knowledge about dance making and its cultural and art–historical context on the other hand (Brieber, Nadal and Leder, 2015; Bullot and Reber, 2013; Gerger and Leder, 2015; Leder and Nadal, 2014).

Research on the role of context and conceptual knowledge for the aesthetic experience of dance is largely absent from the literature. Studies on appreciating the visual arts, however, show that these effects do have a pronounced impact on aesthetic judgements. For example, changing titles of paintings or experiencing art in museums, as compared to a psychological laboratory, alters aesthetic experiences. Indeed, Jola and Grosbras (2013) show that immersion in the performance and enjoyment are indeed increased for watching live, as compared to video-taped, dance performances. Such findings are in line with the notion of dance as an intrinsically social art form that involves direct communication between a spectator and a performer via movement.

Conclusion

The aesthetics of human movement and dance are still poorly understood. Yet in recent years our understanding of the psychological and brain mechanism involved in human movement perception has greatly improved. Framing dance aesthetics as communication via movement provides a flexible and inclusive approach to identifying the components of dance aesthetics. The components identified in this chapter may neither be independent nor combine in a simple and exhaustive way to fully explain why we enjoy watching performative art such as dance. Clearly more research with a strong focus on ecological validity is needed to see whether compartmentalising dance into visual, action and social features is a useful approach. Similarly, multisensory aspects of the dance experience, particularly in relation to the influence of music on movement aesthetics, have not received much attention in the existing research literature. However, a clear theoretical framework is needed in order to formulate predictions and testable hypotheses. Future studies will inform as to whether these predictions hold for live performances and other performing arts in which watching movement is an important aspect, such as acting, pantomime and musical theatre.

References

Aglioti, S. M., Cesari, P., Romani, M., & Urgesi, C. (2008). Action anticipation and motor resonance in elite basketball players. *Nature Neuroscience*, 11(9), 1109–1116.

Ahlheim, C., Stadler, W., & Schubotz, R. I. (2014). Dissociating dynamic probability and predictability in observed actions – An fMRI study. *Frontiers in Human Neuroscience*, 8, 273.

Amoruso, L., Sedeño, L., Huepe, D., Tomio, A., Kamienkowski, J., Hurtado, E., Ibáñez, A. (2014). Time to tango: Expertise and contextual anticipation during action observation. *NeuroImage*, 98, 366–385.

Arnheim, R. (1974). *Art and Visual Perception: A psychology of the creative eye.* (50th anniversary printing). Berkeley, CA: University of California Press.

Atkinson, A. P., Tunstall, M. L., & Dittrich, W. H. (2007). Evidence for distinct contributions of form and motion information to the recognition of emotions from body gestures. *Cognition*, 104(1), 59–72.

Aviezer, H., Trope, Y., & Todorov, A. (2012). Body cues, not facial expressions, discriminate between intense positive and negative emotions. *Science*, 338(6111), 1225–1229.

Beilock, S. L. & Holt, L. E. (2007). Embodied preference judgments: Can likeability be driven by the motor system? *Psychological Science*, 18(1), 51–57.

Berg, S. C. (1988). *Le Sacre du Printemps: Seven productions from Nijinsky to Martha Graham.* Ann Arbor, MI: UMI Research Press.

Berlyne, D. E. (1974). *Studies in the New Experimental Aesthetics: Steps toward an objective psychology of aesthetic appreciation.* Washington, D.C.: Hemisphere Publishing.

Bernstein, M., Oron, J., Sadeh, B., & Yovel, G. (2014). An integrated face–body representation in the fusiform gyrus but not the lateral occipital cortex. *Journal of Cognitive Neuroscience*, 26(11), 2469–2478.

Blake, R. & Shiffrar, M. (2007). Perception of human motion. *Annual Review of Psychology*, 58, 47–73.

Bornstein, R. F. (1989). Exposure and affect: Overview and meta-analysis of research, 1968–1987. *Psychological Bulletin*, 106(2), 265–289.

Brick, T. R. & Boker, S. M. (2011). Correlational methods for analysis of dance movements. *Dance Research*, 29(supplement), 283–304.

Brieber, D., Nadal, M., & Leder, H. (2015). In the white cube: Museum context enhances the valuation and memory of art. *Acta Psychologica*, 154, 36–42.

Bullot, N. J. & Reber, R. (2013). The artful mind meets art history: Toward a psychohistorical framework for the science of art appreciation. *The Behavioral and Brain Sciences*, 36(2), 123–137.

Calvo-Merino, B., Ehrenberg, S., Leung, D., & Haggard, P. (2010a). Experts see it all: Configural effects in action observation. *Psychological Research*, 74(4), 400–406.

Calvo-Merino, B., Glaser, D. E., Grèzes, J., Passingham, R. E., & Haggard, P. (2005). Action observation and acquired motor skills: An FMRI study with expert dancers. *Cerebral Cortex*, 15(8), 1243–1249.

Calvo-Merino, B., Grèzes, J., Glaser, D. E., Passingham, R. E., & Haggard, P. (2006). Seeing or doing? Influence of visual and motor familiarity in action observation. *Current Biology*, 16(19), 1905–1910.

Calvo-Merino, B., Jola, C., Glaser, D. E., & Haggard, P. (2008). Towards a sensorimotor aesthetics of performing art. *Consciousness and Cognition*, 17(3), 911–922.

Calvo-Merino, B., Urgesi, C., Orgs, G., Aglioti, S. M., & Haggard, P. (2010b). Extrastriate body area underlies aesthetic evaluation of body stimuli. *Experimental Brain Research*, 204(3), 447–456.

Carbon, C. -C. (2010). The cycle of preference: Long-term dynamics of aesthetic appreciation. *Acta Psychologica*, 134(2), 233–244.

Casile, A. & Giese, M. A. (2006). Nonvisual motor training influences biological motion perception. *Current Biology*, 16(1), 69–74.

Catmur, C., Mars, R. B., Rushworth, M. F., & Heyes, C. (2011). Making mirrors: Premotor cortex stimulation enhances mirror and counter-mirror motor facilitation. *Journal of Cognitive Neuroscience*, 23(9), 2352–2362.

Chatterjee, A. & Vartanian, O. (2014). Neuroaesthetics. *Trends in Cognitive Sciences*, 18(7), 370–375.

Chen, J. L., Penhune, V. B., & Zatorre, R. J. (2009). The role of auditory and premotor cortex in sensorimotor transformations. *Annals of the New York Academy of Sciences*, 1169, 15–34.

Christensen, J. F. & Calvo-Merino, B. (2013). Dance as a subject for empirical aesthetics. *Psychology of Aesthetics, Creativity, and the Arts*, 7(1), 76–88.

Christensen, J. F., Nadal, M., Cela-Conde, C. J., & Gomila, A. (2014). A norming study and library of 203 dance movements. *Perception*, 43(2), 178–206.

Christensen, J. F., Pollick, F. E., Lambrechts, A., & Gomila, A. (2016). Affective responses to dance. *Acta Psychologica*, 168, 91–105.

Cook, R., Bird, G., Catmur, C., Press, C., & Heyes, C. (2014). Mirror neurons: From origin to function. *The Behavioral and Brain Sciences*, 37(2), 177–192.

Cross, E. S., Hamilton, A. F. de C., & Grafton, S. T. (2006). Building a motor simulation de novo: Observation of dance by dancers. *NeuroImage*, 31(3), 1257–1267.

Cross, E. S., Kirsch, L., Ticini, L. F., & Schütz-Bosbach, S. (2011). The impact of aesthetic evaluation and physical ability on dance perception. *Frontiers in Human Neuroscience*, 5, 102.

Cross, E. S., Mackie, E. C., Wolford, G., & Hamilton, A. F. de C. (2010). Contorted and ordinary body postures in the human brain. *Experimental Brain Research*, 204(3), 397–407.

Cross, E. S. & Ticini, L. F. (2012). Neuroaesthetics and beyond: New horizons in applying the science of the brain to the art of dance. *Phenomenology and the Cognitive Sciences*, 11(1), 5–16.

Daprati, E., Iosa, M., & Haggard, P. (2009). A dance to the music of time: Aesthetically-relevant changes in body posture in performing art. *PLOS ONE*, 4(3), e5023.

de Gelder, B., de Borst, A. W., & Watson, R. (2015). The perception of emotion in body expressions. *Wiley Interdisciplinary Reviews. Cognitive Science*, 6(2), 149–158.

Downing, P. E. & Peelen, M. V. (2011). The role of occipitotemporal body-selective regions in person perception. *Cognitive Neuroscience*, 2(3–4), 186–203.

Ewbank, M. P., Lawson, R. P., Henson, R. N., Rowe, J. B., Passamonti, L., & Calder, A. J. (2011). Changes in 'top-down' connectivity underlie repetition suppression in the ventral visual pathway. *Journal of Neuroscience*, 31(15), 5635–5642.

Fadiga, L., Craighero, L., & Olivier, E. (2005). Human motor cortex excitability during the perception of others' action. *Current Opinion in Neurobiology*, 15(2), 213–218.

Fechner, G. T. (1876) *Vorschule der Ästhetik [Introduction to Aesthetics]*. Breitkopf: Leipzig, Germany.

Freedberg, D. & Gallese, V. (2007). Motion, emotion and empathy in esthetic experience. *Trends in Cognitive Sciences*, 11(5), 197–203.

Gardner, T., Goulden, N., & Cross, E. S. (2015). Dynamic modulation of the action observation network by movement familiarity. *The Journal of Neuroscience: The Official Journal of the Society for Neuroscience*, 35(4), 1561–1572.

Gazzola, V. & Keysers, C. (2009). The observation and execution of actions share motor and somatosensory voxels in all tested subjects: Single-subject analyses of unsmoothed fMRI data. *Cerebral Cortex*, 19(6), 1239–1255.

Gerger, G. & Leder, H. (2015). Titles change the esthetic appreciations of paintings. *Frontiers in Human Neuroscience*, 9, 464.

Giese, M. A. & Poggio, T. (2003). Cognitive neuroscience: Neural mechanisms for the recognition of biological movements. *Nature Reviews Neuroscience*, 4(3), 179–192.

Gordon, P. C. & Holyoak, K. J. (1983). Implicit learning and generalization of the 'mere exposure' effect. *Journal of Personality and Social Psychology*, 45(3), 492.

Grèzes, J., Adenis, M. -S., Pouga, L., & Armony, J. L. (2013). Self-relevance modulates brain responses to angry body expressions. *Cortex; a Journal Devoted to the Study of the Nervous System and Behavior*, 49(8), 2210–2220.

Grèzes, J., Valabrègue, R., Gholipour, B., & Chevallier, C. (2014). A direct amygdala-motor pathway for emotional displays to influence action: A diffusion tensor imaging study. *Human Brain Mapping*, 35(12), 5974–5983.

Grice, P. (1991). *Studies in the Way of Words*. Cambridge, MA: Harvard University Press.

Grosbras, M. -H., Beaton, S., & Eickhoff, S. B. (2012). Brain regions involved in human movement perception: A quantitative voxel-based meta-analysis. *Human Brain Mapping*, 33(2), 431–454.

Hagen, E. H. & Bryant, G. A. (2003). Music and dance as a coalition signaling system. *Human Nature*, 14(1), 21–51.

Hammermeister, K. (2002). *The German Aesthetic Tradition*. Cambridge, UK: Cambridge University Press.

Hanna, J. L. (1983). *The Performer-Audience Connection: Emotion to metaphor in dance and society.* Austin, TX: University of Texas Press.

Jiang, S., Zhu, L., Guo, X., Ma, W., Yang, Z., & Dienes, Z. (2012). Unconscious structural knowledge of tonal symmetry: Tang poetry redefines limits of implicit learning. *Consciousness and Cognition*, 21(1), 476–486.

Jola, C., Abedian-Amiri, A., Kuppuswamy, A., Pollick, F. E., & Grosbras, M. -H. (2012). Motor simulation without motor expertise: Enhanced corticospinal excitability in visually experienced dance spectators. *PLOS ONE*, 7(3), e33343.

Jola, C., Ehrenberg, S., & Reynolds, D. (2012). The experience of watching dance: Phenomenological–neuroscience duets. *Phenomenology and the Cognitive Sciences*, 11(1), 17–37.

Jola, C. & Grosbras, M. -H. (2013). In the here and now: Enhanced motor corticospinal excitability in novices when watching live compared to video recorded dance. *Cognitive Neuroscience*, 4(2), 90–98.

Jola, C., Pollick, F. E., & Calvo-Merino, B. (2014). 'Some like it hot': Spectators who score high on the personality trait openness enjoy the excitement of hearing dancers breathing without music. *Frontiers in Human Neuroscience*, 8, 718.

Keysers, C. & Gazzola, V. (2014). Hebbian learning and predictive mirror neurons for actions, sensations and emotions. *Philosophical Transactions of the Royal Society B: Biological Sciences*, 369(1644), 20130175.

Kilner, J. M., Friston, K. J., & Frith, C. D. (2007). Predictive coding: An account of the mirror neuron system. *Cognitive Processing*, 8(3), 159–166.

Kilner, J. M. & Lemon, R. N. (2013). What we know currently about mirror neurons. *Current Biology: CB*, 23(23), R1057–1062.

Kirsh, D. (2011). Creative cognition in choreography. *Proceedings of 2nd International Conference on Computational Creativity.*

Kirsh, D., Muntanyola, D., Jao, R. J., Lew, A., & Sugihara, M. (2009). Choreographic methods for creating novel, high quality dance. *Proceedings, DESFORM 5th International Workshop on Design & Semantics & Form.* 188–195.

Kirsch, L. P. & Cross, E. S. (2015). Additive routes to action learning: Layering experience shapes engagement of the action observation network. *Cerebral Cortex*, 25(12), 4799–4811.

Kirsch, L. P., Dawson, K., & Cross, E. S. (2015). Dance experience sculpts aesthetic perception and related brain circuits. *Annals of the New York Academy of Sciences*, 1337, 130–139.

Kirsch, L. P., Drommelschmidt, K., & Cross, E. S. (2013). The impact of sensorimotor experience on affective evaluation of dance. *Frontiers in Human Neuroscience*, 7, 521.

Koelsch, S., Rohrmeier, M., Torrecuso, R., & Jentschke, S. (2013). Processing of hierarchical syntactic structure in music. *Proceedings of the National Academy of Sciences of the United States of America.* 110(38), 15443–15448.

Kreitler, H. & Kreitler, S. (1972). *Psychology of the Arts*. Durham, NC: Duke University Press.

Kuhn, G. & Dienes, Z. (2005). Implicit learning of nonlocal musical rules: Implicitly learning more than chunks. *Journal of Experimental Psychology: Learning, Memory, and Cognition*, 31(6), 1417–1432.

Laban, R. & Ullmann, L. (2011). *The Mastery of Movement*. Alton, Hampshire, UK: Dance Books.

Leder, H. & Nadal, M. (2014). Ten years of a model of aesthetic appreciation and aesthetic judgments: The aesthetic episode – Developments and challenges in empirical aesthetics. *British Journal of Psychology*, 105(4), 443–464.

Maffongelli, L., Bartoli, E., Sammler, D., Kölsch, S., Campus, C., Olivier, E., D'Ausilio, A. (2015). Distinct brain signatures of content and structure violation during action observation. *Neuropsychologia*, 75, 30–39.

McManus, I. C. (1980). The aesthetics of simple figures. *British Journal of Psychology*, 71, 505–524.

McManus, I. C. (2005). Symmetry and asymmetry in aesthetics and the arts. *European Review*, (Suppl. S2), 157–180.

McManus, I. C. & Weatherby, P. (1997). The golden section and the aesthetics of form and composition. *Empirical Studies of the Arts*, 15(2), 209–232.

Newell, B. R. & Bright, J. E. H. (2001). The relationship between the structural mere exposure effect and the implicit learning process. *Quarterly Journal of Experimental Psychology Section A: Human Experimental Psychology*, 54(4), 1087–1104.

Obhi, S. S. & Sebanz, N. (2011). Moving together: Toward understanding the mechanisms of joint action. *Experimental Brain Research*, 211(3–4), 329–336.

Opacic, T., Stevens, C., & Tillmann, B. (2009). Unspoken knowledge: Implicit learning of structured human dance movement. *Journal of Experimental Psychology: Learning, Memory, and Cognition*, 35(6), 1570–1577.

Orgs, G., Bestmann, S., Schuur, F., & Haggard, P. (2011). From body form to biological motion: The apparent velocity of human movement biases subjective time. *Psychological Science*, 22(6), 712–717.

Orgs, G., Caspersen, D., & Haggard, P. (2016). You move, I watch, it matters: Aesthetic communication in dance. In: S. S. Obhi & E. Cross (Eds.), *Shared Representations: Sensorimotor foundations of social life*. Cambridge, UK: Cambridge University Press.

Orgs, G., Dombrowski, J. -H., Heil, M., & Jansen-Osmann, P. (2008). Expertise in dance modulates alphabeta event-related desynchronization during action observation. *European Journal of Neuroscience*, 27(12), 3380–3384.

Orgs, G., Dovern, A., Hagura, N., Haggard, P., Fink, G. R., & Weiss, P. H. (2015). Constructing visual perception of body movement with the motor cortex. *Cerebral Cortex,* 26(1), 440–449.

Orgs, G. & Haggard, P. (2011). Temporal binding during apparent movement of the human body. *Visual Cognition*, 19(7), 833–845.

Orgs, G., Hagura, N., & Haggard, P. (2013). Learning to like it: Aesthetic perception of bodies, movements and choreographic structure. *Consciousness and Cognition*, 22(2), 603–612.

Orgs, G., Kirsch, L., & Haggard, P. (2013). Time perception during apparent biological motion reflects subjective speed of movement, not objective rate of visual stimulation. *Experimental Brain Research*, 227(2), 223–229.

Orlov, T., Makin, T. R., & Zohary, E. (2010). Topographic representation of the human body in the occipitotemporal cortex. *Neuron*, 68(3), 586–600.

Pearce, M. T., Zaidel, D. W., Vartanian, O., Skov, M., Leder, H., Chatterjee, A., & Nadal, M. (2016). Neuroaesthetics: The cognitive neuroscience of aesthetic experience. *Perspectives on Psychological Science*, 11(2), 265–279.

Pichon, S., de Gelder, B., & Grèzes, J. (2012). Threat prompts defensive brain responses independently of attentional control. *Cerebral Cortex*, 22(2), 274–285.

Pollick, F. E., Paterson, H. M., Bruderlin, A., & Sanford, A. J. (2001). Perceiving affect from arm movement. *Cognition*, 82(2), B51-61.

Proverbio, A. M. & Riva, F. (2009). RP and N400 ERP components reflect semantic violations in visual processing of human actions. *Neuroscience Letters*, 459(3), 142–146.

Puce, A. & Perrett, D. (2003). Electrophysiology and brain imaging of biological motion. *Philosophical Transactions of the Royal Society of London. Series B, Biological Sciences*, 358(1431), 435–445.

Ramenzoni, V., Riley, M. A., Davis, T., Shockley, K., & Armstrong, R. (2008). Tuning in to another person's action capabilities: Perceiving maximal jumping-reach height from walking kinematics. *Journal of Experimental Psychology: Human Perception and Performance*, 34(4), 919–928.

Reber, R., Schwarz, N., & Winkielman, P. (2004). Processing fluency and aesthetic pleasure: Is beauty in the perceiver's processing experience? *Personality and Social Psychology Review*, 8(4), 364–382.

Reddish, P., Fischer, R., & Bulbulia, J. (2013). Let's dance together: Synchrony, shared intentionality and cooperation. *PLOS ONE*, 8(8), e71182.

Rizzolatti, G. & Sinigaglia, C. (2010). The functional role of the parieto-frontal mirror circuit: Interpretations and misinterpretations. *Nature Reviews Neuroscience*, 11(4), 264–274.

Rohrmeier, M. & Rebuschat, P. (2012). Implicit learning and acquisition of music. *Topics in Cognitive Science*, 4(4), 525–553.

Rohrmeier, M., Zuidema, W., Wiggins, G. A., & Scharff, C. (2015). Principles of structure building in music, language and animal song. *Philosophical Transactions of the Royal Society of London. Series B, Biological Sciences*, 370(1664), 20140097.

Sacheli, L. M., Candidi, M., Pavone, E. F., Tidoni, E., & Aglioti, S. M. (2012). And yet they act together: Interpersonal perception modulates visuo-motor interference and mutual adjustments during a joint-grasping task. *PLOS ONE*, 7(11), e50223.

Sacheli, L. M., Tidoni, E., Pavone, E. F., Aglioti, S. M., & Candidi, M. (2013). Kinematics fingerprints of leader and follower role-taking during cooperative joint actions. *Experimental Brain Research*, 226(4), 473–486.

Sammartino, J. & Palmer, S. E. (2012). Aesthetic issues in spatial composition: Effects of vertical position and perspective on framing single objects. *Journal of Experimental Psychology: Human Perception and Performance*, 38(4), 865–879.

Sartori, L., Becchio, C., & Castiello, U. (2011). Cues to intention: The role of movement information. *Cognition*, 119(2), 242–252.

Sawada, M., Suda, K., & Ishii, M. (2003). Expression of emotions in dance: Relation between arm movement characteristics and emotion. *Perceptual and Motor Skills*, 97(3 Pt 1), 697–708.

Sbriscia-Fioretti, B., Berchio, C., Freedberg, D., Gallese, V., & Umiltà, M. A. (2013). ERP modulation during observation of abstract paintings by Franz Kline. *PLOS ONE*, 8(10), e75241.

Schiffer, A. -M. & Schubotz, R. I. (2011). Caudate nucleus signals for breaches of expectation in a movement observation paradigm. *Frontiers in Human Neuroscience*, 5, 38.

Schütz-Bosbach, S. & Prinz, W. (2007). Perceptual resonance: Action-induced modulation of perception. *Trends in Cognitive Sciences*, 11(8), 349–355.

Sebanz, N. & Shiffrar, M. (2009). Detecting deception in a bluffing body: The role of expertise. *Psychonomic Bulletin and Review*, 16(1), 170–175.

Shimamura, A. P. & Palmer, S. E. (Eds.). (2012). *Aesthetic Science: Connecting minds, brains, and experience*. Oxford: Oxford University Press.

Siegmund, G. (2006). *Abwesenheit: Eine performative Ästhetik des Tanzes; William Forsythe, Jérôme Bel, Xavier Le Roy, Meg Stuart*. Bielefeld: Transcript.

Stevens, J. A., Fonlupt, P., Shiffrar, M., & Decety, J. (2000). New aspects of motion perception: Selective neural encoding of apparent human movements. *Neuroreport*, 11(1), 109–115.

Tarr, B., Launay, J., Cohen, E., & Dunbar, R. (2015). Synchrony and exertion during dance independently raise pain threshold and encourage social bonding. *Biology Letters*, 11(10), 20150767.

Taylor, J. C. & Downing, P. E. (2011). Division of labor between lateral and ventral extrastriate representations of faces, bodies, and objects. *Journal of Cognitive Neuroscience*, 23(12), 4122–4137.

Ticini, L. F., Rachman, L., Pelletier, J., & Dubal, S. (2014). Enhancing aesthetic appreciation by priming canvases with actions that match the artist's painting style. *Frontiers in Human Neuroscience*, 8, 391.

Tinio, P. P. L. (2013). From artistic creation to aesthetic reception: The mirror model of art. *Psychology of Aesthetics, Creativity, and the Arts*, 7(3), 265–275.

Topolinski, S. (2010). Moving the eye of the beholder: Motor components in vision determine aesthetic preference. *Psychological Science*, 21(9), 1220–1224.

Torrents, C., Castañer, M., Jofre, T., Morey, G., & Reverter, F. (2013). Kinematic parameters that influence the aesthetic perception of beauty in contemporary dance. *Perception*, 42(4), 447–458.

Umiltà, M. A., Berchio, C., Sestito, M., Freedberg, D., & Gallese, V. (2012). Abstract art and cortical motor activation: An EEG study. *Frontiers in Human Neuroscience*, 6, 311.

Urgesi, C., Calvo-Merino, B., Haggard, P., & Aglioti, S. M. (2007). Transcranial magnetic stimulation reveals two cortical pathways for visual body processing. *Journal of Neuroscience*, 27(30), 8023–8030.

Van Dyck, E., Vansteenkiste, P., Lenoir, M., Lesaffre, M., & Leman, M. (2014). Recognizing induced emotions of happiness and sadness from dance movement. *PLOS ONE*, 9(2), e89773.

Vangeneugden, J., Peelen, M. V., Tadin, D., & Battelli, L. (2014). Distinct neural mechanisms for body form and body motion discriminations. *The Journal of Neuroscience: The Official Journal of the Society for Neuroscience*, 34(2), 574–585.

Vicary, S., Sperling, M., Von Zimmermann, J., Richardson, D., & Orgs, G. (2017). Joint action aesthetics. *PLOS ONE*, 12(7), e0180101.

von Zimmermann, J., Vicary, S., Sperling, M., Orgs, G., & Richardson, D. C. (2018). The choreography of group affiliation. *Topics in Cognitive Science,* 10(1), 80–94.

Woolhouse, M. H., Tidhar, D., & Cross, I. (2016). Effects on inter-personal memory of dancing in time with others. *Frontiers in Psychology*, 7, 167.

Zajonc, R. B. (1968). Attitudinal effects of mere exposure. *Journal of Personality and Social Psychology*, 9(2, Pt.2), 1–27.

Zeki, S. (1998). Art and the brain. *Daedalus*, 127(2), 71–103.

Zeki, S. & Lamb, M. (1994). The neurology of kinetic art. *Brain*, 117(3), 607–636.

Zeki, S. & Stutters, J. (2012). A brain-derived metric for preferred kinetic stimuli. *Open Biology*, 2(2), 120001.

Zizak, D. M. & Reber, A. S. (2004). Implicit preferences: The role(s) of familiarity in the structural mere exposure effect. *Consciousness and Cognition*, 13(2), 336–362.

13 Choreographed science

Merging dance and cognitive neuroscience

Corinne Jola

Introduction: Dance–cognitive neuroscience research

Over the past 10 years, the number of art and science collaborations has steadily increased (Webster, 2005; Gibbs, 2014; Kemp, 2011; Shaughnessy, 2013). Here, the focus is specifically on collaborations that aimed at coupling dance and cognitive neuroscience (e.g., Jola, Ehrenberg and Reynolds, 2012); henceforth described as DCN (dance–cognitive neuroscience) projects. The recent advances in this field have been tremendous[1].

Evolution

At the base of cognitive neuroscience research into dance sits the seminal study on the brain activity of dancers during dance observation (Calvo-Merino et al., 2005). Earlier research on dance and cognition already existed at that time (see references in Jola and Mast, 2005a; Starkes, Helsen and Jack, 2001). However, the cognitive, perceptual and sensorimotor processes involved in dance gained the attention of many scientists through advances in brain imaging studies (see Chapters 10, 11 and 12: also reviews by Bläsing et al., 2012; Sevdalis and Keller, 2011). Further, the growing number of neuroscientific approaches to dance is predominantly rooted in the discovery of mirror neurons (see Chapters 10 and 11).

Overall, the functions of mirror neurons have been linked to processes related to sensorimotor learning (Catmur, 2013) and interpersonal communication (Keysers and Fadiga, 2008), such as action observation, motor simulation, imitation, action prediction, action understanding, and empathy as well as its dysfunctions. Watching dance is a special form of action observation. Dance does not require objects to be involved. Further, dance movements do not need a clear action goal but are typically crafted under the realms of aesthetic pleasure (for a more detailed discussion, see Christensen and Jola, 2015). Often, the movements are part of a movement 'vocabulary'. For example, traditional styles of dance, such as classical ballet, consist of specific formalised actions (e.g., *arabesques, pirouettes* and *jetés*). To summarise, dancers can be considered experts in executing complex stylised whole-body movements performed with exact efforts in order to achieve specific movement qualities. Dance thus allows investigating object-unrelated expert action observation on long movement sequences where the movement itself is the goal (Schachner and Carey, 2013). Thus, 'dance-like actions' challenged earlier assumptions of a mandatory interaction between an effector and an object as the basis of mirror neuron activity. As a result, the use of dance in cognitive neuroscience propelled in popularity as an informative tool in the research of mirror neurons and beyond (Sevdalis and Keller, 2011; Bläsing et al., 2012; Karpati et al., 2015).

Notably, the quality of dance employed as visual stimuli in the study of the human brain has not always been at the desired level for dance scholars (see Jola, Ehrenberg and Reynolds, 2012). However, as dance stimuli expanded in duration and complexity, research involving dance has significantly improved over the last 10 years (see Christensen and Jola, 2015). In earlier studies, the prevalent form of dance stimuli were short video clips (Calvo-Merino et al., 2005; 2006; Cross, Hamilton and Grafton, 2006; Orgs et al., 2008). More recently, professional live or choreographed performances have been employed with novel approaches, often driven by inter- and transdisciplinary research collaborations (Reason et al., 2016; Bachrach, Jola and Pallier, 2016; Herbec et al., 2015; Noble et al., 2014; Jola and Grosbras, 2013; Jola et al., 2013; Jola, Grosbras and Pollick, 2011; Grosbras, Tan and Pollick, 2012).

Without doubt, the mirror neuron theory has pushed forward the presence of dance in the scientific field while at the same time dance has pushed forward the understanding of mirror-neuron networks through its impending qualitative demands. The widespread proposed roles of the mirror-neuron system have since further accelerated the steady increase of research and theoretical frameworks (Rizzolatti et al., 2014; Casile, Caggiano and Ferrari, 2011), while healthy debates on the theoretical controversies of the mirror neuron system have surfaced (e.g., Gallese et al., 2011; Hamilton, 2013). Perhaps as a consequence of the presence of dance in neuroscientific research, dance is now acknowledged as a subject suitable for scientific study more than it has ever been before.

Nonetheless, it is vital to remember that dance touches upon a number of topics that are situated outside action observation and often beyond the territory of mirror neurons. Understanding the multifaceted cognitive and sensory processes involved in dancing and watching dance is important. It exemplifies the wide range of possibilities of using dance in science. For example, dance has been employed in brain imaging – as well as behavioural experiments – to study proprioception (Jola, Davies and Haggard, 2011; Golomer and Dupui, 2000), perspective taking (Jola and Mast, 2005b; Pilgramm et al., 2010), cognitive retention and rehabilitation (Kattenstroth et al., 2013; Niemann, Godde and Voelcker-Rehage, 2016), multisensory processing (Jola et al., 2013; Karpati et al., 2017), aesthetic appreciation (Bachrach, Jola and Pallier, 2016; Calvo-Merino et al., 2008; Kirsch, Dawson and Cross, 2015: for an overview, see Christensen and Calvo-Merino, 2013; Cross and Ticini, 2012; Kirsch, Urgesi and Cross, 2016; Orgs, Hagura and Haggard, 2013: see also Chapter 12), motor imagery (Golomer et al., 2008; Munzert et al., 2008), empathy (Jola, Pollick and Calvo-Merino, 2014; Jola and Grosbras, 2013; Jola et al., 2012), entrainment/synchronisation (Brown, Martinez and Parsons, 2006; Herbec et al., 2015: see also Chapter 3), motor learning and memory (Bläsing,

2015; Bläsing, Tenenbaum and Schack, 2009; Vicary et al., 2014; Warburton et al., 2013), and evolutionary research (Laland, Wilkins and Clayton, 2016; Brown et al., 2005; Bachner-Melman et al., 2005). Clearly, some of these topics (e.g., aesthetics, empathy and motor learning) are heavily discussed within the scope of mirror neurons. However, it is important to note that many of these mental processes are not purely mirror-neuron based and are thus also investigated within their own remits.

Challenges

Despite the increasing popularity of dance in scientific research, DCN projects still face numerous challenges. These lie predominantly in the methodological differences between the disciplines of dance and cognitive neuroscience. Before discussing five prototypical examples of methodological conflicts in more detail here (see Table 13.1), one has to consider issues surrounding the human body, probably the most significant denominator of science and dance.

The body is at the core of dance, often described as the 'instrument' of dance. The dance critic Walter (1942, p.16), for example, writes about dance:

> No paint nor brushes, marbles nor chisels, pianos nor violins are needed to make this art, for we are the stuff that dance is made of. It is born in our body, exists in our body and dies in our body.

Walter concludes that dance is thus the most personal of all art forms. Notably, dance is also described as being witnessed through the body. As Daly (2002) explains:

> Dance, although it has a visual component, is fundamentally a kinesthetic art whose apperception is grounded not just in the eye but in the entire body.

Partly due to religious, cultural and philosophical views on pleasure experienced with the human body (Dale, Hyatt and Hollerman, 2007), dance has been seen as sinful and subjected to censorship (Hanna, 2002). It is thus of no surprise that dance has been integrated into the academic curriculum much later than other art forms (e.g., visual art, music and poetry). Also, while functional neuronal activity underlying music or visual art perception were studied in the 1990s (e.g., Zatorre, Evans and Meyer, 1994; Zeki and Lamb, 1994), the seminal studies that examined observation of dance actions using brain imaging techniques have been published only in the early years of this millennium (Brown, Martinez and Parsons, 2006; Calvo-Merino et al., 2005; 2006; Cross, Hamilton and Grafton, 2006). Hence, the scientific enquiry of dance arguably still lags behind that of other art forms.

In addition, the body played a challenging part in psychology. Since the 'cognitive revolution' in the 1950s (Gardner, 1985), research in psychology has particularly focussed on cognitive processes of reasoning, thinking, language and vision. Psychology has *de facto* been regarded as the science of the mind, ignoring the role of the body as a source of information. Therefore, in cognitive neuroscience, the brain was, and still is to a large extent today, the focal point of study – until neuronal computing stressed the importance of the body as a vehicle that may influence thinking and behaviour. Today the body is recognised as being more relevant than a mere input tool with a clear sensory boundary where information about the environment is gathered by the body to be processed by the brain (see Chapter 8). Artificial intelligence has exemplified that the way the body functions and is organised has an effect on how we perceive and interact with the world around us (e.g., Pfeifer, Bongard and Grand, 2007). Motor-sensory aspects of the body and the integration of larger organism–environment considerations are slowly finding their place in cognitive neuroscience (e.g., Kiverstein and Miller, 2015).

Yet despite the changing attitudes towards the body in the sciences, dance still struggles to gain full recognition as an academic discipline (see Batson, 2012). Some of the underlying reasons are based in methodological differences between the two disciplines as listed below in Table 13.1. Considering the continuous inadequacy of funding structures and procedures that comprehensive studies using dance would require, organisational and ideological stumbling blocks deter researchers from conquering methodological differences up to the present day and effectively hinder reaching the full potential of DCN collaboration projects.

The *research practice* (see Table 13.1) in dance and in cognitive neuroscience deviate to such an extent, that their differences in methodologies and research cultures are often perceived as incommensurable (Dale, Hyatt and Hollerman, 2007). For example, in dance, a dancer's experience is recognised as providing valuable insights and is validly employed in research as practice endeavours. A view shared amongst many dance scholars is that dance practice provides the

Table 13.1 Prototypical instances of methodological oppositions between cognitive neuroscience and dance

	Cognitive neuroscience	*Dance*
Research practice	Shared consent of complying to a set of principles; objectivity is important; paradigm shifts are slow	Individualistic approaches; continued redefining; subjective experience is highly valued during creation
Type of knowledge	Shared, specific but generalizable; accessible, verifiable, replicable; based on empirical evidence	Individual, subjective; broad, based on empirical- or practice-based research
Chance procedures	High efforts for control; yet at times chance observations provide highly valued insights	Space provided to chance procedures; at times chance is the defining element of a work
Output forms	Peer reviewed manuscript; targeted audiences are expert scientists	Idiosyncratic performances; inclusive audience targeting
Aesthetic value	Frequently of low quality and generally not evaluated; occasionally even in the context of aesthetic perception	Valued highly; high importance

basis from which knowledge grows. For example, Batson (in Solano, 2016) debates that science does not have to validate practice in dance. Moreover, such knowledge through experience is not limited to the dance practitioner. During a dance performance, dancers can also evoke visual, kinaesthetic and emotional sensations within the observer. Sometimes, these sensory experiences might be processed consciously, combined with self-reflections. Together, they allow the observer to infer the performers' intended performative state as well as to gain insight into his/her own emotional states and cognitive processes (Reason and Reynolds, 2010). A dance performance can thus also be regarded as an external representation of complex mental processes. This has been proposed in particular for conceptual dance, where the dance often only comes together in the spectators' minds (e.g., Swoboda, 2013). Importantly though, it is often ignored that different types of practices offer different types of knowledge. Scientific research is not limited to confirming 'what dancers already know'. It gives insight into processes in a different form, which cannot be accessed by practice alone. Interestingly, participants' subjective insights have undergone an undulating role in the sciences, ranging from a form of assessing knowledge about the human mind to complete neglect (see Hurlburt and Heavey, 2001). Future studies could benefit from a middle ground by acknowledging the empirical valence of subjective experience through quantitative and introspection-based qualitative data (e.g., Jola, Grosbras and Pollick, 2011; Reason et al., 2016; Jola and Reason, 2016: for an overview, see Jola, 2016).

As stated above, the *type of knowledge* gained is dependent on the type of research practice. This applies also to different practices within dance, such as different styles of dance. While several dance styles have a rather strict formalised movement vocabulary (e.g., classical ballet: see Chapter 1), contemporary dance movements abide to continuous modification and invention. Contemporary choreographers seek the unknown, or as Cunningham presided: 'Every artist should ask . . . what is the point of doing what you already know?' (Bremser and Jowitt, 1999). Performances are often created through an extensive variety of practices with practically each choreographer developing his or her own individual creative approach (deLahunta, Clarke and Barnard 2012: see also Chapters 4 and 5). In addition, audiences' experiences are very individual and subjective (Hanna, 1983; Reason and Reynolds, 2010). In the sciences, research practice is confined (for more details, see, for example, Borgdorff, 2009). Novel methodical approaches are scrutinised by the community of researchers as to whether they allow systematic inquiries that fulfil specific principles of reasoning. As for DCN projects, it would be beneficial to make use of the full potential different types of dance styles offer, including those with contemporary, post-modern, social or conceptual features. This means that common scientific inquiries need to be examined each time in regards to their pertinence for an individual dance style, and eventually, different types of knowledge may need to be acknowledged.

An interesting element of differences in research practice is the role that is given to *chance procedures*. In many forms of dance, chance is an important part of the practice. For example, in contact improvisation, the dance evolves through playing with incidental occurrences. In the sciences, the focus is on minimising chance occurrences. Although chance observations have led to incredible findings in the sciences (such as the mirror neurons), high efforts are in place for gaining control (for more detail, see the discussion in Jola, 2013).

While the *output form* of dance is generally a performance, it is common knowledge and of reviewers' interest that to a general audience a performance reveals not only elements about the dance itself but also about perception, cognition, society and evolution (e.g., Daprati, Iosa and Haggard, 2009; Hanna, 1983; Hagendoorn, 2010a; 2010b; Stevens and McKechnie, 2005). In contrast to dance, researchers working in the field of cognitive neuroscience distribute their findings through peer-reviewed publications and conference contributions. A wider discourse on the scientific or social context of elements in the study is rarely part of the publication (although recently recognised more widely through the notion of the replication bias). Further, whether the scientists' work adheres to standards of scientific principles and whether the written manuscripts are publishable, are normally judged by an anonymous expert panel. In dance, performances can be staged without a review process: although many factors (e.g., where it is staged and how much funding it has received) also rely on critics' judgments (which in dance are generally not anonymous).

Clearly, the *aesthetic value* of dance works is of huge relevance. Thus, using dance in research for the purpose of creating experimental stimuli means that its aesthetic value has to be taken into account (see Christensen and Jola, 2015). While scientific research is in general not about 'liking' or 'disliking', the research could benefit from more attention given to the aesthetic value of stimuli used in scientific experiments. Since science aims to be objective, judgments of aesthetic qualities can be problematic. Notably, it has been shown that the visual representation in scientific publications has an effect on the reader's understanding of the study. For example, findings with colourful images of brains are seductive in the sense that they seem to attract more public interest, when in fact they are impeding people's judgments on the quality of the work (Weisberg et al., 2008; Weisberg, Taylor and Hopkins, 2015).

Collaborations in dance–cognitive neuroscience research

Creative collaborations between dance and science have existed for some time. Early documented versions focussed on using dance to make scientific discoveries more tangible (see, for example, Berg, 1971). More recent collaborations between dance and cognitive neuroscience can be classified into two main categories dependent on their output. In one type of collaboration, the intent is to create an artistic piece of work. In this case, it is predominantly artists that engage with the sciences in various forms and depths. One of the most widely known examples of this type of collaboration in the UK is Wayne McGregor's performances based upon his artist-in-lab residencies (see Chapter 5). In another example, the performance was in fact informed by the scientist, Nicky Clayton, who was the first scientist-in-residence at Rambert dance (Malina, 2015). In both cases, the output was a dance performance that does not claim to fully represent, explain or conduct science, but that was to some extent inspired by scientific ideas.

In the other more common type of dance–science collaborations, the focus is on publishing a peer-reviewed scientific paper. Therein, predominantly scientists employ a dancer to help create the visuals used in the experiments designed to study the human brain and behaviour (e.g., for an overview, see Bläsing et al., 2012; Sevdalis and Keller, 2011). It is important to note that dance professionals were only recently included as co-authors in the scientific publication (Reason et al., 2016; Waterhouse, Watts and Bläsing, 2014), potentially indicating that a shift in the focus of DCN research has commenced. Yet most collaboration studies of cognitive neuroscience and dance still predominantly explore neuronal activity of the passive observer during action observation. Partly due to technological challenges, dancers' neuronal activity during action execution is still studied less (Brown, Martinez and Parsons, 2006: see also Jola and Calmeiro, 2017; Karpati et al., 2015). For example, a measurement of brain activity is better accessible and more accurate of a motionless, passive participant compared to a moving person. In studies where the emphasis is on the scientific enquiry over and above concerns about the artistic creation, substantial methodological restrictions seem acceptable. Notably, the aesthetic experience has only recently received increased attention as being a crucial part of the scientific enquiry. For example, it has become more common to employ longer choreographed sequences of movements which are in some instances specifically choreographed for the experiment (Bachrach, Jola and Pallier, 2016; Herbec et al., 2015; Jola, Pollick and Calvo-Merino, 2014; Noble et al., 2014; Jola et al., 2012; 2013). Notably, in rare circumstances, attempts have been made to scientifically investigate the audiences' responses to an existing artistic performance (e.g., Reason et al., 2016; Jola, Grosbras and Pollick, 2011; Bachrach et al., 2015). Nonetheless, in all these cases, there is a definite scientific aim attached to the performance, which is the gathering of objective, quantitative data, to be analysed and published in a peer-reviewed scientific journal at a later point in time.

The two collaborative types of approaches described above have different perspectives on the output, which is either a performance or a research publication. To further elaborate the future of DCN projects, these two distinct collaboration types are discussed below under the two terms: *experimental choreography* and *embodied neuroscience*. Although neither term is established in the wider context of DCN projects, they remain a useful means to better describe the challenges DCN projects face; in particular, the validity and credibility of DCN research findings. Notably, the aim of these terms as used here is not to reinforce a boundary between two types of DCN projects. On the contrary, the ambition is to clarify the contexts under which the disciplines should step across their boundaries.

Experimental choreography

The term 'experimental choreography' was introduced in order to describe the use of choreography in studying the human brain and behaviour (Jola, 2006). From a scientific point of view, experimental choreography stands for a dance performance that entails a clear link to experimental studies. This link can be created either by referring to principles of experimental research designs, in particular by providing an element of contrasting variables (Jola, 2004), see Figure 13.1a, or by creating a dance performance that can be used in an experimental study (Reason et al., 2016), see Figure 13.1b.

(a)

(b)

Figure 13.1 Examples of experimental choreography. *(a)* Still from the performance of *Brainstorm*, both a performance and a study project examining how movement is transferred from the choreographers' mind to the audience. Movement instructions were verbally recorded and transformed into movements by the dancers. They met for the first time on stage at the opening night. The contrast between the interpretations of the two dancers provides a window into what the choreographers' intentions could have been. Performed at Tanzhaus in Zurich and at Dance Festival in Olten (Switzerland) in 2004. Concept and Choreography: Corinne Jola; Dancers: Ursula Ledergerber *(left)* and Andrea Schaerli *(right)*; Photograph: Franz Gloor. *(b)* Still from the rehearsal of *Double Points: 3x*. The piece is an adaptation from *Double Points: K* which in itself is an adaptation of Emio Grecco's *Double Points*. Kay's adaptation has a prelude and an ending, with three identical sections that are performed once to an electronic sound score, once to Bach, and once without music. This allowed comparison of how the same movement sequence is perceived when performed to different music. Choreography: Rosie Kay; Dancers: Morgan Cloud *(left)* and Rosie Kay *(right)*; Photograph: Frances Blythe.

Hence, the term 'experiment' in experimental choreography refers to its meaning in science, whereby an experiment is commonly the core of a purposefully controlled, designed study, conducted with a systematic approach. Over the last two centuries, in particular in academic psychological research, experimental practice has become a clearly defined method of scientific inquiry. It involves specific and shared protocols and requires following explicit codes of conduct. A central point of the experimental approach is the hypothesis, which is a precisely stated prediction of what the scientist expects to find with a particular study. Also, experimental practice has been associated with a reductionist approach up until recently, when it was highlighted that reductionism is not paramount.

Notably, the experimental procedure as a methodology is just one of five common guidelines for good academic research (see Table 13.2) and more complex live

Table 13.2 Five guidelines for good scientific practice in academia

1	*Originality*	Academic research has to be original; academic research is original if a new investigation is conducted in order to gain knowledge and understanding. One exemption to this rule are replication studies. Originality refers to the questions, problems and issues of the work, i.e., what is being investigated.
2	*Rationale*	The proposed research has to have a clear rationale. Research is rational if it is clearly stated why something is being investigated. This can be in relation to previous research or in relation to real life. It can be situated either within a discipline or reach beyond its own discipline.
3	*Methodology*	Research has to be methodological. While there is no exclusive method defined for research to be considered academically valid, meaningful research in any discipline should systematically follow a defined and transparent methodology that allows replication. Newton's rules of reasoning relate to the modern understanding of methodological needs, which is that a method should falsify a hypothesis, and allow universal and sufficient explanation. Currently the most common and widely acknowledged method that can also fulfil these criteria in cognitive neuroscience is the experimental approach. Interestingly, however, strong concerns have been raised in response to the failure of replicating findings in psychology (see Maxwell, Lau and Howard, 2015).
4	*Accessibility*	Research outputs – and nowadays also research data – need to be made accessible. Outputs can take many different forms. While written peer-reviewed publication and conference presentations are the most frequent and most acknowledged forms of dissemination in cognitive neuroscience, other forms are slowly finding their way into academic research; for example, performative outputs and/or digital documentation.
5	*Truthfulness*	Research should be truthful. Although truth and trustworthiness are regarded as highly important in academia, there is a growing understanding in the research community that more must be done to prevent falsification, fabrication and plagiarism, amongst other issues, that captivate the core of science; truth and trustworthiness.

experiments do not violate these. Also, these guidelines do not imply that other forms of research, in particular as present within the arts, are invalid (see also Hoogenboom, 2007). On the contrary, situating the arts within scientific research and Higher Education has been criticised as having a negative impact on the quality of the arts (see Elkins, 2011). There are indeed examples of artistic failures in attempts to link dance with scientific research, as I have experienced in my own works. Nevertheless, such attempts signify important steps towards improved practice (see Figures 13.2, 13.3 and 13.4). For DCN projects to be successful, it is important that all parties involved acknowledge discipline-specific standards and are prepared to subject these to an intrepid scrutiny. I argue that working within discipline-specific methodological guidelines is the most challenging aspect of DCN projects, requiring time and effort (predominantly due to ignorance, based on discipline-specific education). It is thus important that parties involved in DCN projects understand the meaning of scientific experimentation in both fields; dance and cognitive neuroscience (for more details on these, see Box 13.1).

Box 13.1 **'Experimental' terminologies**

Classical experimental paradigm: In a classical experimental paradigm, the relationship between a number of defined variables (elements of interest) is investigated by manipulating them with regards to the hypothesis while attempting to control any other factors that are suspected to have a systematic effect on the measurement. Thus forth, the experiment is designed to measure the effect of at least one (independent) variable on another (dependent) variable. For example, if one were to investigate whether training in dance improves mathematical abilities, the independent variables could be the type of training (dance training or a control condition like jogging) and the dependent variables could be measured as the number of correct answers in a mathematical test. The type of data analysis is subject to the experimental method chosen. Inferential statistics, as could be applied to the example above, allows the researcher to infer the causal role of the modified independent variables on the dependent variable within a certain level of confidence. Notably, inferring differences measured in the dependent variable as consequences of experimental variations in the independent variable, is described as a systematic differential approach. As such, it stands in contrast to 'experimental' work as normally encountered in the arts.

Experiment in dance and other art forms: In dance and other forms of art (e.g., visual arts and music), 'experiment' is generally used to describe a playful trial-and-error approach where variables are selected randomly or intuitively. Experimenting in dance is in fact close to its original form in Latin (*ex-periri*), which means 'to try out'. In dance, it is often used as a starting point to improvise. Moreover, to add to the confusion, experimental choreography is sometimes used to refer to a particular type of work that is unrelated to science, similar to other art forms (e.g., 'experimental music'). Usually, these works are abstract, non-narrative, and formal in nature, and arose by a practice constituent of 'try-outs', playing, improvising and exploring. This difference in the use of the terminology makes it particularly important to introduce the meaning of experimental choreography from a scientific point of view. On a side note, existing practice of 'try-outs' in sciences also exist. This is unfortunate, as 'try-outs' in the sciences can, for example, be in the form of 'data fishing', when a set of data is analysed in various ways until a desired result is found. This approach has been criticised because this use of data mining (i.e., looking for a pattern in data sets without first devising a specific hypothesis or by applying a statistical test of significance on a data set from which a pattern has already emerged) distorts the findings.

Figure 13.2 *(a) Aahh,* a solo performance by Natascha Ruegg with three projections representing the performer in different perspectives, aimed to interrogate how a three-dimensional representation of a performer is created in our minds. Informed by scientific knowledge on body representation and our sensory system, *Aahh* played with two ideas: first, the perception of bodies in relation to their orientation in space; and second, our body perception via the senses of touch, proprioception and vision, which informed the creation of the movement material. The stage design further represented an experimental situation. Despite elements of improvisation, the piece had a rigid and illustrative character due to the pre-recorded presentations. The audience also reported a sense of frustration at not being able to take a more active role (the stage design implied a three-dimensional participatory setting but prohibited them to 'participate'). Choreography: Corinne Jola; Stage design/Image: Erik Havadi. Performed at Laban Theatre London, 2008 (supported by Rebekka Skelton Fund). *(b)* The movement material of the original body representation work was further developed into an artistic site-specific performance *Ric and Elsa* at Deptford X Arts Festival in Deptford, London, 2008. This version had social but no scientific aims and was much more successful – potentially of higher artistic value. Choreography: Corinne Jola; Dancers: Riccardo Buscarini and Elsa Petit.

Figure 13.3 Stills from (*a*) *Setback* and (*b*) *Anna with Orange*, both examples where scientific research findings are presented in an artistic Way. In *Setback*, the performance was not choreographed according to an experimental approach, but ideas from physics were employed freely as a kinaesthetic inspiration for movement and choreography. Choreography: Corinne Jola; Performer: Jan Lee; Music: Nahum; Photograph: Alicia Clarke. Performed at Resolution at the Place, London, 2013. In *Anna with Orange*, a qualitative research approach was employed to explore the physical and mental transformation processes experienced in giving birth, as a metaphor for giving birth to new ideas.

Figure 13.4 'EVE' (Everybody moves) is an interactive installation that shows different immediate visual projections of participants and their movements, in order to provide a joyful means to explore movement (i.e., asking the participants to become investigators of their own movement traces). *(a)* Conference participants interacting with 'EVE' at the British Neuroscience Association Conference in Edinburgh, 2015; and *(b)* a dancer interacting with the system at the *Decoding Space* exhibition at the Hanna MacLure Centre in Dundee, 2015.

Based on disciplines' idiosyncrasies regarding what constitutes an experimental approach (as described in Box 13.1), I propose that confining 'experimental practice' to the systematic, scientific experimental approach in dance and in science will allow the identification of a particular form and stage of research in both disciplines. Other more specific terms, such as improvisation, intuition, trial-and-error, play, and exploration, should be used to describe non-systematic approaches. Notably, these activities are not confined to artistic practice. They can also happen during a systematic, scientific experimental approach. Further, scientific research demands for a variety of empirical approaches. Thus even in science, research practice and experimental practice are not interchangeable terms. A distinct use of terms that describes the actual actions would definitely help to clarify and potentially further strengthen artistic practice as research.

In addition to the different perspectives on what makes an experiment, it is important to note that the understanding of what is choreography may also not be shared (Durning and Waterhouse, 2013). In neuroscience, choreography has recently been used in the form of 'neural choreography', to describe the complex interplay of neuronal and related processes (Crotti and Glass, 2015; Molnár, Higashi and López-Bendito, 2003). However, neural choreography is not 'choreographed'. The original meaning of choreography comes from the ancient Greek and refers to the 'writing movement'. Hence, choreography involves the 'writing' of a reasoning instance, such as the person who acts in the role of the choreographer (e.g., Hagendoorn, 2010b). Choreographic works are creations that allow new organisational structures to be seen (see Palazzi and Shaw, 2009). Therefore, 'neural choreography' is a possibility when the researchers' influence in the drawing of the neural activity is recognised, as indicated by Akil and colleagues (2011). In analogy, 'choreographed science', the title of this chapter, emphasises the role dance has played in science over the last decade.

Embodied neuroscience

The term 'embodied neuroscience' emerged in response to a research project with the dance company Emio Greco | Pieter C. Scholten (Jola, 2013). In this project, I investigated the neuronal changes of dance students who learnt this company's dance style for the first time. Before designing the experiment, I participated in the company's training prior to meeting the dance students. I also accompanied the students to their workshops. The main objective for participating in the daily rehearsals was to inform the scientific research through the insights gained in the embodied practice. In other words, the participation in the company's workshop, called *Double Skin/Double Mind* (deLahunta, 2007), clarified on a physical level what characterises this company's work. Compared to other classical and contemporary dance movement 'warm-up' preparations, *Double Skin/Double Mind* is an uninterrupted 2-hour session (approximately), and is thus physically strenuous and cardiovascular challenging (for more details, see Bermúdez et al., 2011; Jola, 2013). Participation therefore allowed me to achieve a unique somatosensory experience – an embodied understanding – into the physical and cognitive demands of this dance style.

Embodied neuroscience thus specifically relates to the physical engagement of the researcher with the topic of inquiry in addition to the abstract, theoretical engagement. The assumption is that the embodiment of the practice to be studied allows the researcher to better understand the different factors impacting on what is to be investigated (see Jola, 2013), which may crucially inform the methodological approach while at the same time have the unfortunate effect of requiring more resources (e.g., time). In the above example, the embodied practice was decisive in the stimuli creation and the experimental design. Hence, embodied neuroscience can be of particular relevance for scientists, as their physical engagement – their embodiment with a subject – informs their inquiry. The underlying assumption is that in order to design a suitable study, the researcher has to physically and theoretically understand the subject. Without active participation, the researchers' understanding is restrained, and this can impede the research on a variety of levels.

Within the scientific community, 'embodiment' has become very popular over the last two decades. It is linked to scientists and philosophers, such as Varela, Thompson, Rosch, Damasio and Clark, who critiqued the sharp distinction between the body and the mind in the Cartesian mind–body dualism present in cognitive science at the time – pushing for a new view on the relationship of the body and the brain (Gallagher and Zahavi, 2008). It is important to note that the theoretical underpinnings of embodiment, or embodied cognition, are manifold. The ideas re-emerged from earlier psychological understanding of cognition (Wilson, 2002) and relocated the philosophically grounded concepts of Merlau-Ponty's or Heidegger's phenomenology (Loren and Dietrich, 1997). In general, embodied cognition encompasses the understanding that cognitive processes are deeply rooted in the body and its interactions with the environment (Beckes, IJzerman and Tops, 2015).

An extended perspective is embodied embedded cognition, where cognitive and physical states are regarded as one system of interacting components and where the brain, the body, and the world are of equal importance (Dijk et al., 2008). What is common across embodied viewpoints is that the brain should not be studied as an independent modular system, but as dependent upon and influenced by the body. Yet some theories on embodiment go further by assigning the environment an active role in shaping perception and cognition. According to radical embodied neuroscience (Kiverstein and Miller, 2015), the assumption is that neuronal functions are determined by the organism as a whole which includes its interaction with the environment. In order to better understand neuronal activity in relation to an individual's behaviour, the processes must be studied within the organisms' context. In the case of DCN projects, the proposition is therefore not just to observe the dancers' environment, but also to physically experience it, i.e., to embody it. Indeed, many of the researchers that employ dance in the study of the brain are keen dancers and/or passionate dance observers themselves. It may thus seem obsolete to specifically identify the need to embody dance. However, embodied neuroscience supports a strong link between dance and cognitive neuroscience within a particular DCN project, without making specific claims on how the brain functions, but how it needs to be studied in order to advance our understanding.

To summarise, embodied neuroscience questions the level of engagement of scientists with the subject of their investigation: Do scientists engage enough with the materiality of the stimuli they use in their experiments? Does the description of the experimental stimuli in a manuscript portray them accurately? One means of verifying the adequacy of stimuli is through subjective evaluation by participants, novices or experts. Another avenue is for the researcher to pursue an anthropological participatory study, such as embodied neuroscience or self-experimentation. Thus, the hope is that future DCN projects will follow the ideas on embodied cognition with dance not being a purely visual or cognitive art form, but embodied (e.g., Block and Kissell, 2001; Daly, 2002). Moreover, the idea is that embodied neuroscience can be employed beyond the field of dance into all aspects of cognitive neuroscience that can possibly be experienced through the senses. According to ideas on radical embodied cognition, novel methodological approaches are necessary. Embodied neuroscience is one possible approach to improve ecological validity of the experiment, as well as providing a situated inter-pretation of the objective and subjective data gathered. This means that in the design stages of an experiment, one does not exactly know what stimuli are needed, because experience (either participatory or research-based) with the set of stimuli is first required before a decision can be made. Notably, for choreographers, such circular states of refinement are a re-occurring issue when creating a performance (see also Chapters 4 and 5).

The landscape of dance–science research

If we think of a literal landscape for dance–science research, it would be 'hilly', if not 'craggy'. From a hierarchical point of view, in these projects, the rock-peaks would represent neuroscientific research. This can be explained partly through the hierarchy of scientific evidence, where expert opinion and individual case studies are situated at the bottom of the hierarchy, with randomised controlled experiments set higher up, and systematic meta-analyses sitting at the top. Such a model puts scientific research in general into a superior position over and above research or outputs from the arts (which are mostly qualitative and case-based studies). The awareness of this model is widespread. Thus, when dance and science come together, power imbalances are present and scientific evidence and disciplines' scepticisms bring internal and external tensions to DCN projects. Power imbalances can be felt in a number of aspects, such as the amount of governmental funding received. Notably, it has been shown that research funding applications that have a greater degree of interdisciplinary content are less likely to be successful (Bromham, Dinnage and Hua, 2016). Henceforth, DCN projects with a clear lead may receive a more appropriate evaluation. A project that is either research-led or art-led is more likely to be assigned to a panel of reviewers that can justify the funding application, thus a larger number of successful interdisciplinary projects potentially leading to a more varied landscape to be seen. Similar issues surface at later stages, when research outputs are being reviewed. Yet in order to move towards a complete amal-gamation of the disciplines, it is crucial that they should not be played against each other. While methodological differences should be recognised and acknowledged (see Table 13.1), the focus should shift towards opportunities.

Another crucial power imbalance is visible in the perspective of comparisons made between artistic and scientific research: the discourse is predominantly driven by a scientific perspective. Artistic research is often assessed as to whether it satisfies the criteria of scientific or academic research. Such an approach is clearly orchestrated by standards from scientific research and thus may ignore possible inputs from other research disciplines. Notably, experimental choreography (as described above) takes a similar stance. It is assumed to be inherently driven by the three scientific research principles: the aim of conducting original research; the use of a differential approach that would allow predictability of the factors investigated; and an increase in our understanding of the subject investigated. As such, embodied neuroscience is thought to act as a counterpart, by emphasising the importance of fully engaging with the other discipline. Hopefully, it was made clear that this was particularly addressed to scientists.

A change in perspective through learning from within the other discipline, as proposed in embodied neuroscience, could allow us to see further in the variety of research topics and means to conduct research. As indicated in the introduction, through seemingly incommensurable research in dance and science, dance has shown itself to be a driving force for scientific progress by pushing for a 'paradigm shift'. Borgdorff (2009) published a profound reflection upon the political perspectives of research in dance and the basic sciences. For example, artistic and scientific research have often been distinguished by the general view that research in basic science is hypothesis-led whereas research in the arts is discovery-led. However, as pointed out earlier, the unexpected, intuition and experience also play an important role in science. In particular, the central concept to DCN projects is the network of mirror neurons, which is itself paradoxically based on the coincidental, unpredicted finding of mirror neurons.

Although the tendency of DCN projects is moving increasingly towards more interdisciplinary research, the following two sections discuss examples of DCN projects that were either research-led (see Figure 13.5a) or art-led (see Figure 13.5b). The aim is to provide a better understanding of the intricacies and multitudes that occur at the points where layers of dance and cognitive neuroscience research meet.

Research-led projects

In research-led projects, the stimuli are typically created with a focus on the research question without taking artistic elements into much consideration. Earlier studies that employed dance predominantly aimed at a better understanding of how we perceive and mentally represent bodies and movements. These studies (see Figure 13.5a) generally compared data from novices with data from expert dancers (e.g., Calvo-Merino et al., 2010; Jola and Mast, 2005b; Stevens et al., 2010; Ramsay and Riddoch, 2001). For many of these studies, the stimuli were created 'in-house', with sufficient quality for the experiment (Figure 13.5a, number 1). Most of these studies also used the traditional moves of specific dance styles, such

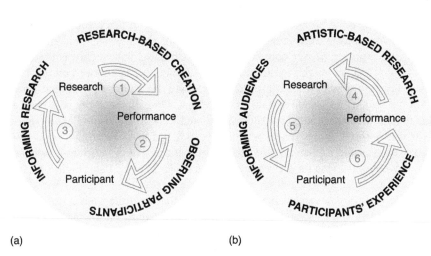

(a)   (b)

Figure 13.5 Turntable indicating bi-directional itinerary process in dance–cognitive neuroscience projects: *(a)* research-led creation; and *(b)* artistic-led research. 'Participant' describes an experimental participant, audiences or the researcher.

as ballet, capoeira or contemporary dance (Calvo-Merino et al., 2005; 2006; Cross et al., 2012; Kirsch, Drommelschmidt and Cross, 2013). Other studies employed existing steps from interactive technology games (Kirsch and Cross, 2015) or improvised actions (Gardner, Goulden and Cross, 2015). Only in a few cases did the research incite and support the creation of novel choreographed dance sequences either from scratch (Cross, Hamilton and Grafton, 2006; Orgs, 2016), or via adaptation of existing work (Jola et al., 2012; Reason et al., 2016). Yet, the pertinent part of research-led DCN projects is to aim for stimuli of high artistic quality that can stand as a performance event in its own right. This is important, as it affects spectators' experience and thus potentially influences the research findings (Figure 13.5a, numbers 2 and 3). Notably, the context of the stimuli presentation has also been found to be crucial. Recent studies have aimed at presenting dance live, in contexts where that particular style of dance would normally be seen. However, while live performance showed enhanced sensorimotor engagement of spectators, it does affect research as it provides less control, messier data, and more restricted use of measurement techniques (see Jola, Grosbras and Pollick, 2011; Jola et al., 2012 for more details).

Art-led projects

Typical artistic-led research is when the experimental practice is adjusted to assimilate with the constraints of existing performances (Figure 13.5b, number 4). For example, in Jola, Grosbras and Pollick (2011), the audiences' neuronal responses were measured during the two dress rehearsals of the ballet *Sleeping*

Beauty in the Theatre Royal in Glasgow. The method was informed by specific features of the already existing dance performance. For instance, the time-points of the measurements were strongly influenced by the narrative and dramaturgy of the piece. *Sleeping Beauty* contains movement phrases with highly emotional, highly physical, and highly gestural intensity. Hence, we categorised sections of this piece into these features in order to evaluate the effects of different types of movement sequences on spectators' responses. Overall, the entire data choice and method was constrained by the location and timing of the event. For example, as it was a formal dress rehearsal, the research had to work around rehearsal issues, such as interruptions and repetitions of sections. These constraints can lead to many complications for the research, in particular to noisy data (Figure 13.5b, number 5).

While there are several dance performances that lend themselves to art-led research projects, such as conceptual dances, there are only a few examples of an art-led research where the participant experiences the research kinaesthetically (Figure 13.5b, number 5). One of these is *Double Skin/Double Mind* (Bermúdez Pascual, 2013; deLahunta, 2007; deLahunta and Shaw, 2008), whereby research based on the company's movement practice informed the creation of an inter-active installation. The installation allows participants to sense the intentions through interaction, and consequently to allow them, as spectators, to perceive the performance in a more embodied manner. Moreover, artistic-led research ties in with embodied neuroscience, in the sense that researchers' experiences in the role of dance participation influences how the performance is seen and/or created for future research (Figure 13.5b, number 6: see also Jola, 2013). However, artistic research positioned in the same circle as science is still novel and, to date, only a few interdisciplinary art-driven research studies have been conducted (e.g., Waterhouse, Watts and Bläsing, 2014; Forsythe, 2009; deLahunta and Bermúdez Pascual, 2013: see also http://labo21.eu/)

Fused examples

According to the founder of Artscience Labs, David Edwards, it is possible to find ways of combining the aesthetic and the scientific to produce 'artscience' with what he calls a 'fused method'. In his words, fused method is:

> intuitive and deductive, sensual and analytical, comfortable with uncertainty and able to frame a problem embracing nature in its complexity and able to simplify to nature in its essence.
>
> (Edwards, 2008: p. 7)

In the framework described here, fusions have happened not only where both artistic and scientific approaches are present, but also where the distinction between research-led and art-led is less clear. At this moment in time, such fusions in DCN projects have yet to emerge and so far we can only describe DCN projects that move towards each other.

For example, in Jola et al. (2012), the stimuli were informed by artistic research whereas most parts of the experimental design were research-led. The overarching research question – whether visual expertise alone enhances spectators' engagement with the performance when they watch the dance style that they are visually familiar with – was informed by knowledge from both science and dance practice. Engagement was measured indirectly in the form of sensorimotor resonance of the spectators' hands and arms, through semi-structured interviews, and via questionnaires. To assess the effect of visual familiarity on sensorimotor resonance, participants watched different types of dances: ballet and Bharatanatyam, a classical Indian dance. In a typical ballet movement phrase, the hand muscle group remains relatively constant in activation intensity while the arm muscle groups change in activation according to large, extensive arm movements. In Bharatanatyam, the finger movements are part of the dance and thus the finger muscle activation changes throughout. The stimuli thus consistent of two solos concatenated from existing dance pieces from a classical repertoire in ballet and Bharatanatyam, respectively. In addition, a novel miming sequence was created in collaboration with an actor, who performed this sequence as a control condition. Arguably, the choreographic process was a necessary element for the findings of this study. The data showed that visually experienced ballet spectators (who have never physically trained in ballet) have enhanced sensorimotor resonance in expected muscle groups (i.e., the arm) during ballet-specific dance movements compared to the activity during Bharatanatyam-specific moves. This means that the dance-specific activity was apparent when the responses to ballet and Bharatanatyam were contrasted with the activity during the specifically choreographed control condition. Notably, the performances were adjusted based on participants' feedback to previous solos used in the pilot experiment, as well as aesthetic reasons (see Jola et al., 2012), meaning the research became partly research-led and partly art-led with a feedback loop between performance and research (Figure 13.5, numbers 1 and 4). It has to be added that this project was interdisciplinary from its outset, with researchers collaborating from different disciplines, and the stimuli were live performances with music and costumes aimed at matching as closely as possible the experience that visual spectators have in real life.

Reason and colleagues (2016) describe another example of a DCN project that was led by both art and research. The visual stimulation of this science is the performance *Double Points: 3x* by Rosie Kay (see Figure 13.1b). Until recently, this was a unique example where the research led to a novel professionally choreographed dance performance. In *Double Points: 3x*, the researchers' interest was to study the subtle differences in subjective experiences and neuronal responses when spectators watch dance with a changing sound scape. The argument here is again that in order to access specific processes relating to spectators' experiences, it is necessary to use not just any kind of stimuli, but dedicated choreographed works of high artistic quality. The choreographer Rosie Kay thus substantially modified an earlier existing work, in order to meet the requirements of both the experimental neuroimaging study and the qualitative research. The piece had the form of a performance while still containing the elements necessary for hypothesis testing. The experimental conditions contained three equal movement sections: once performed to Bach's *Concerto in A Minor*; once without music but audible breathing; and once to an electronic sound score. The results from the qualitative interviews showed more diverse responses in expressions of taste for the condition with no music, where the dancers' breathing was audible, than for both conditions with music. Audiences across levels of dance expertise reported that the no-music condition with audible breathing evoked a bodily presence, a sense of exertion, and physicality. However, while some enjoyed the physical intensity created by the audible breathing, others clearly disliked this section – they reported feeling uncomfortable with the perceived intimacy. This finding informed the design and interpretations of the neuroimaging research (Figure 13.5b, number 6). In one study (Reason et al., 2016), participants with a low level of dance experience watched the performances to Bach and to no music in an MRI scanner. The study showed wide overlap in the activity patterns that spectators shared in rural, parietal, temporal and premotor regions. Furthermore, when compared to the Bach condition, the no-music and breathing conditions showed more activity in rural areas as well as in areas in the vicinity of the extrastriate body area, known for processing bodily stimuli. This finding instigated new studies (see Figure 13.5a, number 3) that further explored the audiences' responses to the performers' presence (Jola, Pollick and Calvo-Merino, 2014; Jola and Reason, 2016). Both Jola and colleagues (2014), and Jola and Reason (2016), pointed towards conditions where spectators responded in specific ways to experiencing performers' physicality close up. These research findings, stimulated by audiences' observations of an artistic-led performance, showed that personality factors may need to be considered in cognitive neuroscience when studying audiences' embodied cognition and mirror neuron activity in response to action observation (see Figure 13.5a, number 2).

However, recent trends in dance may be particularly suitable to provide a platform for fused DCN projects where the individual disciplines melt into one. These performances, called 'conceptual' or 'non-dance', have strengthened the kinship of cognitive neuroscience and choreography. Husemann (2009) discusses conceptual dance in reference to Xavier Le Roy's and Thomas Lehmen's practice, describing it as:

> . . . a metadance, which critically reflects its own media through practice and offers the experience of this reflection to the spectator. Just as dance takes a critical look on itself, the spectator's perception gets an introspective dimension: He/she steps out of his/her watching and experiencing to reflect his/her own perception.

The author also suggests that non-dance has created a positive potentiality where production and reception can happen and reflect themselves, commonly through the withdrawal of dancing in dance. The choreographer Siobhan Davies compares her work to poetry:

> . . . it's the structure and attention to detail that allows the reader to be transformed into another mode of thought.
>
> (Winship, 2017)

Xavier le Roy's repertoire is probably the best known example of a skilful approach in the realms of experimental choreography, likely influenced by his practical experience in research prior to his career in performing. The choreographer understands choreography as the possibility to expose the choreographic working process, the reflection about the body, and its socio-cultural representation. In fact, many current works, such as those by Le Roy, Ivana Müller's *While We Were Holding It Together*, or the coherent research approach of the company Emio Greco | Pieter C. Scholten, entail a critical look at topics beyond dance itself. In this way, they enhance our understanding of the human mind. The spectators' insight into their perceptual, kinaesthetic and cognitive experience is, at times, further combined with research outputs in other formats. This combination is unique and facilitates art-led research.

Benefits of dance–cognitive neuroscience research

The benefits that DCN projects have to the sciences are evident: a significant element of employing dance in scientific studies has been that dance highlights the importance of ecological validity (e.g., Jola and Grosbras, 2013). Ecological validity produces increased applicability of research findings to real-life contexts. Hence, collaborations with dancers and dance scholars have pushed cognitive neuroscientists to critically reflect upon their rigorous scientific approaches (Christensen and Jola, 2015; Jola et al., 2012). Furthermore, researchers who engage thoroughly with the experience of dancing and watching dance have recognised numerous potentials for knowledge transfer, as well as for the creation of knowledge. In effect, several topics that are placed in the realm of other domains are now also studied in the terrain of dance. For example, Bachrach and colleagues (2016) found that a chain of 'dance-like' actions that participants rated as more coherent, led to enhanced brain activity in frontal and parietal brain areas, known to be part of the mirror-neuron network. The frontal areas are of particular interest, as they were previously linked to narrative comprehension in language and other domains (e.g., music). Hence, studies using specific elements of dance have the capacity to refine the understanding of the mirror-neuron network, amongst other processes.

In reverse, choreographers are aware that we are not always able to make good artwork when trying to achieve good science. However, scientific research has helped to increase the wider appreciation of the complexity of cognitive and sensory processes in which a dancer or a choreographer engages (e.g., Warburton et al., 2013; Brown, Martinez and Parsons, 2006; Bläsing et al., 2012; May et al., 2011). Moreover, through dance, DCN projects can reach a wider audience than neuroscience or dance could alone. For example, dance productions with a link to science target new audiences and neuroscientific studies on dance have fired a huge interest in the dance community. Unfortunately, as highlighted before, this does not mean that there is a better chance to attain funding. As a consequence, as has been highlighted by Batson (2012), a thorough coupling of the two disciplines is still relatively rare. To my knowledge, for example, all collaborations to date are forced to classify the research rationale as belonging to the one or the other discipline.

Also, the outputs are being forced into the one or the other category, having to align with the existing forms of publication and culture of dissemination. Similarly, the creation of new dance works with a clear link to empirical scientific research are not legitimised for funding applications to creative art councils in the UK. Yet with the present curiosity of many dance professionals in the workings of the human brain (see Foster, 2008), there is a huge potential for progressive DNC projects. Hopefully, these will raise the awareness that the question should not focus on 'Can dance inspire new scientific research?' but instead on 'Can a new type of scientific research and dance be established that satisfies the multiple demands (e.g., strands) of dance as well as science?' – or, to reach the full potential of DCN projects, one may ask: 'Can dance choreograph science?'

Conclusion

Dance–cognitive neuroscience (DCN) projects are inter- or transdisciplinary creative collaborations between dance practitioners and cognitive neuroscientists. DCN projects affect both the art of making dance as well as the art of conducting science. As a consequence, in meaningful DCN projects with equal partners, the outcomes of either discipline are affected. Based on the examples given in this chapter, it is clear that there is a long way to go until we can confidently say that the two disciplines have merged.

The aim of this chapter was to provide examples of how dance and cognitive neuroscience have been combined thus far. In its ideal form, dance and neuroscience in DCN projects share a topic of investigation whose questions can only be answered by addressing it using both fields. It is unfortunate that the full potential of DCN projects has not yet been exhausted, despite a shared interest over the last decade in the body and the brain as a constructive medium. For example, a choreographer may ask: Why not create a dance piece that also provides valuable empirical data? A scientist may question: Is a peer-reviewed publication really the best format to disseminate my findings?

Most present DCN projects can be distinguished as driven by either *experimental choreography* or *embodied neuroscience* and in most instances they are either research-led or art-led. The idea of experimental choreography is to pursue an empirical quest, meaning that conservative methodological approaches may not be sufficient to investigate the mechanisms involved in watching dance. In most instances, these projects are also research-led. If we want to acknowledge the importance of the complex real-life situation of a dance performance, new methodologies need to be considered and developed. This is currently happening (e.g., Bachrach et al., 2015; Reason et al., 2016; Herbec et al., 2015) and these changes can be considered art-led. While there are not yet many examples of experimental choreography, several funding bodies in the UK have recently supported projects combining the performing arts and science, such as Bloodlines, Imagining Autism, Watching Dance, Shared Creativity in Dance, In the Dancer's Mind, and synchronous movement cooperation. In future, the amalgamation of dance and neuroscience in the form of experimental choreographies will ultimately – if successful – impinge on our understanding of empirical research. Notably, with new spaces dedicated to art–science interactions, such as the LIVELab at McMaster University – a theatre space dedicated specifically to scientific research in/on the performing arts – it is likely that art-led research, as well as research-led performances, will become more common and fuse together to form a coherent whole.

The formation of a new type of scientific research with dance will hopefully help to receive the different kinds of resources that DCN projects require, as compared to the resources the disciplines have individually (see Batson, 2012). Hence, one could argue that DCN projects will continue to result in novel testable predictions in both the fields; dance and cognitive neuroscience. Importantly, these changes are in the early days and the full potential of DCN projects has arguably not yet been reached. Only the future will show how the expertise of artists, scholars and scientists in collaboration will advance and modify academic structures.

Some of the important steps towards fused DCN projects are:

- Involve experts from the practical side (i.e., choreographers, dancers and movement analysts) in scientific studies that employ movement or emotional expression, in particular if it is related to dance.
- Provide access to theatres that allow time, space and technical support (e.g., stage technologists) for empirical research.
- Increase the understanding of artistic professionals about gathering empirical evidence; for instance, by providing workshops on scientific research that target artists working outside university.
- Make stimuli available for others to view on online platforms.
- Conduct analysis of aesthetic value and appropriateness of the stimuli used, and make these public as part of the articles.

Note

1 In response to the substantial progresses made in this field, this new edition of my chapter contains a number of changes from the 1st edition. Most importantly, the section on effects of expertise has been removed. However, expertise is still acknowledged as a highly relevant characteristic in dance practice and dance-related research. A more thorough overview of the effects of expertise through dance participation and observation can now be found in Jola and Calmeiro (2017) as well as in Karpati and colleagues (2015).

References

Akil, H., Martone, M. E., & Van Essen, D. C. (2011). Challenges and opportunities in mining neuroscience data. *Science*, 331(6018), 708–712.

Bachner-Melman, R., Dina, C., Zohar, A. H., Constantini, N., Lerer, E., Hock, S., Sella, S., Nemanov, L., Gritsenko, I., Lichtenberg, P., Granot, R., & Ebstein, R. P. (2005). AVPR1a and SLC6A4 gene polymorphisms are associated with creative dance performance. *Public Library of Science Genetics,* 1, 42.

Bachrach, A., Fontbonne, Y., Joufflineau, C., & Ulloa, J. L. (2015). Audience entrainment during live contemporary dance performance: Physiological and cognitive measures. *Frontiers in Human Neuroscience*, 9, 179.

Bachrach, A., Jola, C., & Pallier, C. (2016). Neuronal bases of structural coherence in contemporary dance observation. *Neuroimage*, 1(124), 464–472.

Batson, G. (2012). *Ex-scribing the choreographic mind – Dance & neuroscience in collaboration.* SEAD white paper. https://seadnetwork.files.wordpress.com/2012/11/batson_final.pdf (accessed March 2018).

Beckes, L., IJzerman, H., & Tops, M. (2015). Toward a radically embodied neuroscience of attachment and relationships. *Frontiers in Human Neuroscience*, 9, 266.

Berg, P. (1971). Protein synthesis: An epic on the cellular level. www.youtube.com/watch?v=u9dhO0iCLww (accessed March 2018).

Bermúdez, B., deLahunta, S., Hoogenboom, M., Ziegler, C., Bevilacqua, F., Fdili Alaoui, S., & Meneses Gutierrez, B. (2011). *The Double Skin/Double Mind Interactive Installation.* www.researchcatalogue.net/view/8247/8248/100/100 (accessed March 2018).

Bermúdez Pascual, B. (2013). (Capturing) intention: The life of an interdisciplinary research project. *International Journal of Performance Arts and Digital Media*, 9(1), 61–81.

Bläsing, B. E. (2015). Segmentation of dance movement: Effects of expertise, visual familiarity, motor experience and music. *Frontiers in Psychology*, 5, 01500.

Bläsing, B., Calvo-Merino, B., Cross, E. S., Jola, C., Honisch, J., & Stevens, C. J. (2012). Neurocognitive control in dance perception and performance. *Acta Psychologica*, 139(2), 300–308.

Bläsing, B., Tenenbaum, G., & Schack, T. (2009). The cognitive structure of movements in classical dance. *Psychology of Sport and Exercise*, 10(3), 350–360.

Block, B. & Kissell, J. L. (2001). The dance: Essence of embodiment. *Theoretical Medicine and Bioethics*, 22(1), 5–15.

Bloodlines Project: https://chimeranetwork.org/bloodlines/ (accessed March 2018).

Borgdorff, H. (2009). Artistic research within the fields of science. Conference presentation, *Close Encounters: Artists on Artistic Research in Dance*, University College of Dance, Stockholm.

Bremser, M. & Jowitt, D. (1999). *Fifty Contemporary Choreographers: A reference guide.* London: Routledge.

Bromham, L., Dinnage, R., & Hua, X. (2016). Interdisciplinary research has consistently lower funding success. *Nature*, 534, 684–686.

Brown, W. M., Cronk, L., Grochow, K., Jacobson, A., Liu, C. K., Popovic, Z., & Trivers, R. (2005). Dance reveals symmetry especially in young men. *Nature*, 438, 1148–1150.

Brown, S., Martinez, M., & Parsons, L. (2006). The neural basis of human dance. *Cerebral Cortex*, 16(8), 1157–1167.

Calvo-Merino, B., Ehrenberg, S., Leung, D., & Haggard, P. (2010). Experts see it all: Configural effects in action observation. *Psychological Research*, 74(4), 400–406.

Calvo-Merino, B., Glaser, D. E., Grèzes, J., Passingham, R. E., & Haggard, P. (2005). Action observation and acquired motor skills: An FMRI study with expert dancers. *Cerebral Cortex*, 15(8), 1243–1249.

Calvo-Merino, B., Grèzes, J., Glaser, D. E., Passingham, R. E., & Haggard, P. (2006). Seeing or doing? Influence of visual and motor familiarity in action observation. *Current Biology*, 16(19), 1905–1910.

Calvo-Merino, B., Jola, C., Glaser, D. E., & Haggard, P. (2008). Towards a sensorimotor aesthetics of performing art. *Consciousness and Cognition*, 17(3), 911–922.

Casile, A., Caggiano, V., & Ferrari, P. F. (2011). The mirror neuron system: A fresh view. *The Neuroscientist*, 17(5), 524–538.

Catmur, C. (2013). Sensorimotor learning and the ontogeny of the mirror neuron system. *Neuroscience Letters*, 540, 21–27.

Christensen, J. F. & Calvo-Merino, B. (2013). Dance as a subject for empirical aesthetics. *Psychology of Aesthetics, Creativity, and the Arts*, 7(1), 76–88.

Christensen, J. F. & Jola, C. (2015). Towards ecological validity in the research on cognitive and neural processes involved in dance appreciation. In: M. Nadal, J. P. Huston, L. Agnati, F. Mora, & C. J. Cela-Conde (Eds.), *Art, Aesthetics, and the Brain* (Chapter 12, pp. 223–253). Oxford: Oxford University Press.

Cross, E. S., Hamilton, A. F., & Grafton, S. T. (2006). Building a motor simulation de novo: Observation of dance by dancers. *Neuroimage*, 31(3), 1257–1267.

Cross, E. S., Liepelt, R., Hamilton, A. F., Parkinson, J., Ramsey, R., Stadler, W., & Prinz, W. G. (2012). Robotic movement preferentially engages the action observation network. *Human Brain Mapping*, 33(9), 2238–2254.

Cross, E. S. & Ticini, L. F. (2012). Neuroaesthetics and beyond: New horizons in applying the science of the brain to the art of dance. *Phenomenology and the Cognitive Sciences*, 11(1), 5–16.

Crotti, A. & Glass, C. K. (2015). The choreography of neuroinflammation in Huntington's Disease. *Trends in Immunology*, 36(6), 364–373.

Dale, J. A., Hyatt, J., & Hollerman, J. (2007). The neuroscience of dance and the dance of neuroscience. *The Journal of Aesthetic Education*, 41(3), 89–110.

Daly, A. (2002). *Critical Gestures: Writings on dance and culture*. Middletown, CT: Wesleyan University Press.

Daprati, E., Iosa, M., & Haggard, P. (2009). A dance to the music of time: Aesthetically-relevant changes in body posture in performing art. *PLOS ONE*, 4(3), e5023.

deLahunta, S. (2007/pub. 2014). (Capturing intention). Documentation, analysis and notation research based on the work of Emio Greco|PC. *International Journal of Performance Arts and Visual Media*, 4(1), 95–98.

deLahunta, S. & Bermúdez Pascual, B. (2013). Pre-choreographic elements: Scott deLahunta in conversation with Bertha Bermúdez. *International Journal of Performance Arts & Digital Media*, 9(1), 52–60.

deLahunta, S., Clarke, G., & Barnard, P. (2012). A conversation about choreographic thinking tools. *Journal of Dance and Somatic Practices*, 3(1–2), 243–259.

deLahunta, S. & Shaw, N. (2008). Choreographic resources agents, archives, scores and installations. *Performance Research*, 13(1), 131–133.

Dijk, J. v., Kerkhofs, R., Rooij, I. v., & Haselager, P. (2008). Can there be such a thing as embodied embedded cognitive neuroscience? *Theory and Psychology*, 18(3), 297.

Durning, J. & Waterhouse, E. (2013). 77 choreographic proposals: Documentation of the evolving mobilization of the term choreography. *International Journal of Performance Arts and Digital Media*, 9(1), 44–51.

Edwards, D. (2008). *Artscience: Creativity in the post-Google generation*. Cambridge, MA: Harvard University Press.

Elkins, E. (2011). *Why Art Cannot be Taught: A handbook for art students*. Champaign, IL: University of Illinois Press.

Forsythe, W. (2009). *Choreographic Objects*. Wexner Center for the Arts. http://synchronous objects.osu.edu/ (accessed March 2018).

Foster, S. L. (2008). Movement's contagion: The kinesthetic impact of performance. In: T. C. Davis (Ed.), *The Cambridge Companion to Performance Studies* (pp. 46–59). Cambridge: Cambridge University Press.

Gallagher, S. & Zahavi, D. (2008). *The Phenomenological Mind*. New York: Routledge.

Gallese, V., Gernsbacher, M. A., Heyes, C., Hickok, G., & Iacoboni, M. (2011). Mirror neuron forum. *Perspectives on Psychological Science*, 6(4), 369–407.

Gardner, H. E. (1985). *The Mind's New Science: A history of the cognitive revolution*. New York: Basic Books.

Gardner, T., Goulden, N., & Cross, E. S. (2015). Dynamic modulation of the action–observation network by movement familiarity. *Journal of Neuroscience*, 35(4), 1561–1572.

Gibbs, L. (2014). Arts–science collaboration, embodied research methods, and the politics of belonging: 'SiteWorks' and the Shoalhaven River, Australia. *Cultural Geographies*, 21(2), 207–227.

Golomer, E., Bouillette, A., Mertz, C., & Keller, J. (2008). Effect of mental imagery styles on shoulder and hip rotations during preparation of pirouettes. *Journal of Motor Behavior*, 40, 281–290.

Golomer, E. & Dupui, P. (2000). Spectral analysis of adult dancers' sways: Sex and interaction vision-proprioception. *International Journal of Neuroscience*, 105, 15–26.

Grosbras, M., Tan, H., & Pollick, F. (2012). Dance and emotion in posterior parietal cortex: A low-frequency rTMS study. *Brain Stimulation*, 5(2), 130–136.

Hagendoorn, I. G. (2010a). Dance, choreography and the brain. In: D. Melcher & F. Bacci (Eds.), *Art and the Senses* (pp. 499–514). Oxford: Oxford University Press.

Hagendoorn, I. G. (2010b). Dance, language and the brain. *International Journal of Art and Technology*, 3(2/3), 221–234.

Hamilton, A. (2013). Reflecting on the mirror neuron system in autism: A systematic review of current theories. *Developmental Cognitive Neuroscience*, 3, 91–105.

Hanna, J. L. (1983). *The Performer-Audience Connection: Emotion to metaphor in dance and society*. Austin, TX: University of Texas Press.

Hanna, J. L. (2002). Dance under the censorship watch. *The Journal of Arts Management, Law and Society*, 29(1), 305–317.

Herbec, A., Kauppi, J. P., Jola, C., Tohka, J., & Pollick, F. E. (2015). Differences in fMRI intersubject correlation while viewing unedited and edited videos of dance performance. *Cortex*, 71, 341–348.

Hoogenboom, M. (2007). Artistic research as an expanded kind of choreography using the example of Emio Greco|PC. In: S. Gehm, P. Husemann, & K. von Wilcke (Eds.), *Knowledge In Motion: Perspectives of artistic and scientific research in dance*. Bielefeld: TanzScripte Verlag.

Hurlburt, R. T. & Heavey, C. L. (2001). *Telling What We Know: Describing inner experience*. London: Elsevier Ltd.

Husemann, P. (2009). *Choreographie als kritische Praxis: Arbeitsweisen bei Xavier Le Roy und Thomas Lehmen* [*Choreography as Critical Practice: Working methods with Xavier Le Roy and Thomas Lehmen*]. Bielefeld, Germany: Transcript.

Imagining Autism: http://imaginingautism.org/(accessed March 2018).

In the Dancer's Mind: www.dancersmind.org.uk/ (accessed March 2018).

Jola, C. (2004). *Effekte der Medialität in der Konstruktion und in der Rekonstruktion*. Bern: ISSW.

Jola, C. (2006). Body and movement representation in science and dance. *Cinedans, Dance and New Media: New Ways of Creating and Documenting Dance*, July 2nd/3rd, Amsterdam.

Jola, C. (2013). Do you feel the same way too? In: G. Brandstetter, G. Egert, & S. Zubarik (Eds.), *Touching and To Be Touched: Kinesthesia and empathy in dance*. Berlin: DeGruyter.

Jola, C. (2016). The magic connection: Dancer–audience interaction. In: U. Eberlein (Ed.), *Zwischenleiblichkeit und Bewegtes Verstehen – Intercorporeity, movement and tacit knowledge* (pp. 269–287). Bielefeld: Transcript Verlag.

Jola, C., Abedian-Amiri, A., Kuppuswamy, A., Pollick, F., & Grosbas, M. -H. (2012). Motor simulation without motor expertise: Enhanced corticospinal excitability in visually experienced dance spectators. *PLOS ONE*, 7(3), e33343.

Jola, C. & Calmeiro, L. (2017). The dancing queen: Explanatory mechanisms of the 'feel-good-effect' in dance. In: S. Lycouris, V. Karkou, & S. Oliver (Eds.), *The Oxford Handbook for Dance and Wellbeing*. Oxford: Oxford University Press.

Jola, C., Davis, A., & Haggard, P. (2011). Proprioceptive integration and body representation: Insights into dancers' expertise. *Experimental Brain Research*, 213(2–3), 257–265.

Jola, C., Ehrenberg, S., & Reynolds, D. (2012). The experience of watching dance: Phenomenological–neuroscience duets. *Phenomenology and the Cognitive Sciences*, 11(1), 17–37.

Jola, C. & Grosbras, M. -H. (2013). In the here and now. Enhanced motor corticospinal excitability in novices when watching live compared to video recorded dance. *Cognitive Neuroscience*, 1–9.

Jola, C., Grosbras, M. -H., & Pollick, F. E. (2011). Arousal decrease in 'Sleeping Beauty': Audiences' neurophysiological correlates to watching a narrative dance performance of 2.5 hrs. *Dance Research Electronic*, 29(2), 378–403.

Jola, C. & Mast, F. W. (2005a). Dance images: Mental imagery processes in dance. In: J. Birringer & J. Fenger (Eds.), *Dance and Cognition* (Vol. 15, pp. 211–232). Münster: LIT Verlag.

Jola, C. & Mast, F. (2005b). Mental object rotation and egocentric body transformation: Two dissociable processes? *Spatial Cognition and Computation*, 5, 217–237.

Jola, C., McAleer, P., Grosbras, M. -H., Love, S. A., Morison, G., & Pollick, F. E. (2013). Uni- and multisensory brain areas are synchronised across spectators when watching unedited dance. *i-Perception*, 4, 265–284.

Jola, C., Pollick, F. E., & Calvo-Merino, B. (2014) 'Some like it hot': Spectators who score high on the personality trait openness enjoy the excitement of hearing dancers breathing without music. *Frontiers in Human Neuroscience,* 8, 718.

Jola, C. & Reason, M. (2016). Audiences' experience of proximity and co-presence in live dance performance. In: G. Sofia (Ed.), *Theatre and Cognitive Neuroscience*. New York: Bloomsbury Methuen Drama.

Karpati, F. J., Giacosa, C., Foster, N. E. V., Penhune, V. B., & Hyde, K. L. (2015). Dance and the brain: A review. *Annals of the New York Academy of Sciences,* 1337(1), 140–146.

Karpati, F. J., Giacosa, C., Foster, N. E., Penhune, V. B., & Hyde, K. L. (2017). Dance and music share gray matter structural correlates. *Brain Research,* 1657, 62–73.

Kattenstroth, J. C, Kalisch, T., Holt, S., Tegenthoff, M., & Dinse, H. R. (2013). Six months of dance intervention enhances postural, sensorimotor, and cognitive performance in elderly without affecting cardio-respiratory functions. *Frontiers in Aging Neuroscience,* 5, 5.

Kemp, M. (2011). Artists in the lab: Martin Kemp explores the nature of science–art collaborations after 15 years of major initiatives around the world. *Nature,* 477(7364), 278.

Keysers, C. & Fadiga, L. (2008). The mirror neuron system: New frontiers. *Social Neuroscience*, 3(3), 193–198.

Kirsch, L. P. & Cross, E. S. (2015). Additive routes to action learning: Layering experience shapes engagement of the action–observation network. *Cerebral Cortex*, 25, 4799–4811.

Kirsch, L. P., Dawson, K., & Cross, E. S. (2015). Dance experience sculpts aesthetic perception and related brain circuits. *Annals of the New York Academy of Sciences,* 1337, 130.

Kirsch, L. P., Drommelschmidt, K. A., & Cross, E. S. (2013). The impact of sensorimotor experience on affective evaluation of dance. *Frontiers in Human Neuroscience,* 7, 521.

Kirsch , L. P., Urgesi, C., & Cross, E. S. (2016). Shaping and reshaping the aesthetic brain: Emerging perspectives on the neurobiology of embodied aesthetics. *Neuroscience and Biobehavioral Reviews,* 62, 56–68.

Kiverstein, J. & Miller, M. (2015). The embodied brain: Towards a radical embodied cognitive neuroscience. *Frontiers in Human Neuroscience,* 9, 237.

Laland, K., Wilkins, C., & Clayton, N. (2016). The evolution of dance. *Current Biology,* 26(1), R5–9.

Loren, L. A. & Dietrich, E. (1997). Merleau-ponty, embodied cognition, and the problem of intentionality. *Cybernetics and Systems,* 28(5), 345–358.

Malina (2015). Fusion of ideas. *Dancing Times,* February, 89–93.

Maxwell, S. E., Lau, M. Y., & Howard, G. S. (2015). Is psychology suffering from a replication crisis? What does 'failure to replicate' really mean? *The American Psychologist,* 70(6), 487.

May, J., Calvo-Merino, B., deLahunta, S., McGregor, W., Cusack, R., Owen, A. M., Veldsman, M., Ramponi, C., & Barnard, P. (2011). Points in mental space: An interdisciplinary study of imagery in movement creation. *Dance Research,* 29(2), 404–432.

Molnár, Z., Higashi, S., & López-Bendito, G. (2003). Choreography of early thalamocortical development. *Cerebral Cortex,* 13(6), 661–669.

Munzert, J., Zentgraf, K., Stark, R., & Vaitl, D. (2008). Neural activation in cognitive motor processes: Comparing motor imagery and observation of gymnastic movements. *Experimental Brain Research,* 188, 437–444.

Niemann, C., Godde, B., & Voelcker-Rehage, C. (2016). Senior dance experience, cognitive performance, and brain volume in older women. *Neural Plasticity,* 9837321.

Noble, K., Glowinski, D., Murphy, H., Jola, C., McAleer, P., Darshane, N., Penfield K., Camurri, A., & Pollick, F. E. (2014). Event segmentation and biological motion perception in watching dance. *Art and Perception,* 2(1–2), 59–74.

Orgs, G. (2016). Synchronous movement cooperation and the performing arts. In: S. S. Obhi & E. S. Cross (Eds.), *Shared Representations: Sensorimotor foundations of social life* (pp. 627–654). Cambridge: Cambridge University Press.

Orgs, G., Dombrowski, J., Heil, M., & Jansen-Osmann, P. (2008). Expertise in dance modulates alpha/beta event-related desynchronization during action observation. *European Journal of Neuroscience,* 27(12), 3380–3384.

Orgs, G., Hagura, N., & Haggard, P. (2013). Learning to like it: Aesthetic perception of bodies, movements and choreographic structure. *Consciousness and Cognition,* 22(2), 603–612.

Palazzi, M. & Shaw, N. (2009). Synchronous objects for one flat thing, reproduced. *Proceedings of the Conference on Computer Graphics and Interactive Techniques.* 1, Article No. 2.

Pfeifer, R., Bongard, J., & Grand, S. (2007). *How the Body Shapes the Way We Think. A new view of intelligence.* Cambridge, MA: MIT Press.

Pilgramm, S., Lorey, B., Stark, R., Munzert, J., Vaitl, D., & Zentgraf, K. (2010). Differential activation of the lateral premotor cortex during action observation. *BMC Neuroscience,* 11(1), 89–89.

Ramsay, J. R. & Riddoch, M. J. (2001). Position-matching in the upper limb: Professional ballet dancers perform with outstanding accuracy. *Clinical Rehabilitation,* 15, 324–330.

Reason, M., Jola, C., Kay, R., Reynolds, D., Kauppi, J. P., Grosbras, M. H., Tohka, J., & Pollick, F. (2016). Spectators' aesthetic experience of sound and movement in dance performance: A transdisciplinary investigation. *Psychology of Aesthetics, Creativity, and the Arts,* 10(1), 42–55.

Reason, M. & Reynolds, D. (2010). Kinesthetic and related pleasures: Exploring audience responses to watching live dance. *Dance Research Journal,* 42(2), 49–75.

Rizzolatti, G., Cattaneo, L., Fabbri-Destro, M., & Rozzi, S. (2014). Cortical mechanisms underlying the organization of goal-directed actions and mirror neuron-based action understanding. *Physiological Reviews,* 94(2), 655–706.

Schachner, A. & Carey, S. (2013). Reasoning about 'irrational' actions: When intentional movements cannot be explained, the movements themselves are seen as the goal. *Cognition,* 129, 309–327.

Sevdalis, V. & Keller, P. E. (2011). Captured by motion: Dance, action understanding, and social cognition. *Brain and Cognition,* 77(2), 231–236.

Shared Creativity in Dance: www.cognovo.eu/projects/shared-creativity-in-dance.php (accessed March 2018).

Shaughnessy, N. (2013). *Affective Performance and Cognitive Science: Body, brain and being.* London: Bloomsbury.

Solano, M. B. (2016). Dance, somatics, and neuroscience. An interview with Glenna Batson about her book 'Body and Mind in Motion'. *Contact Quarterly,* Spring/Fall, 31–37.

Starkes, J. L., Helsen, W. F., & Jack, R. (2001). Expert performance in sport and dance. In: R. N. Singer, H. A. Hausenblas, & C. M. Janelle (Eds.), *Handbook of Sport Psychology* (pp. 174201). New York: Wiley.

Stevens, C. & McKechnie, S. (2005). Thinking in action: Thought made visible in contemporary dance. *Cognitive Processing,* 6(4), 243–252.

Stevens, C., Winskel, H., Howell, C., Vidal, L., Latimer, C., & Milne-Home, J. (2010). Perceiving dance schematic expectations guide experts' scanning of a contemporary dance film. *Journal of Dance Medicine and Science,* 14(1), 19–25.

Swoboda, V. (2013). Choreographer invites reflection; Avant-garde concept dance encourages viewers to think about what they're watching and the effect it has on them. *The Gazette.*

Synchronous movement cooperation and the performing arts: http://gtr.rcuk.ac.uk/projects?ref=ES/M000680/1 (accessed March 2018).

Vicary, S. A., Robbins, R. A., Calvo-Merino, B., & Stevens, C. J. (2014). Recognition of dance-like actions: Memory for static posture or dynamic movement? *Memory and Cognition,* 42(5), 755–767.

Walter, T. (1942). *Invitation to Dance.* New York: A. S. Barnes & Company.

Warburton, E. C., Wilson, M., Lynch, M., & Cuykendall, S. (2013). The cognitive benefits of movement reduction: Evidence from dance marking. *Psychological Science,* 24(9), 1732–1739.

Watching Dance: Kinesthetic Empathy: www.watchingdance.org/ (accessed March 2018).

Waterhouse, E., Watts, R., & Bläsing, B. (2014). Doing duo – A case study of entrainment in William Forsythe's choreography 'Duo'. *Frontiers in Human Neuroscience,* 8, 812.

Webster, S. (2005). Art and science collaborations in the United Kingdom. *Nature Reviews Immunology,* 5(12), 965–969.

Weisberg, D. S., Keil, F. C., Goodstein, J., Rawson, E., & Gray, J. R. (2008). The seductive allure of neuroscience explanations. *Journal of Cognitive Neuroscience,* 20(3), 470–477.

Weisberg, D. S., Taylor, C. V., & Hopkins, E. J. (2015). Deconstructing the seductive allure of neuroscience explanations. *Judgment and Decision Making,* 10(5), 429–441.

Wilson, M. (2002). Six views of embodied cognition. *Psychonomic Bulletin and Review,* 9(4), 625–636.

Winship, L. (2017). 'Let's turn the whole world around': Inside Siobhan Davies' dance laboratory. *The Guardian,* 12 Jan 2017. www.theguardian.com/stage/2017/jan/12/siobhan-davies-interview-dancer-science (accessed March 2018).

Zatorre, R., Evans, A., & Meyer, E. (1994). Neural mechanisms underlying melodic perception and memory for pitch. *Journal of Neuroscience*, 14(4), 1908–1919.

Zeki, S. & Lamb, M. (1994). The neurology of kinetic art. *Brain*, 117(3), 607–636.

Author index

Subject index

Locators in *italics* indicate figures or tables

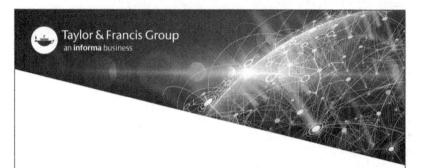